86340

THE
HUMAN
POLITY

THE HUMAN POLITY

A Comparative Introduction to Political Science

Brief Version

KAY LAWSON
San Francisco State University

Houghton Mifflin Company   Boston   New York

Sponsoring Editor: Melissa Mashburn
Associate Editor: Katherine Meisenheimer
Senior Project Editor: Kathryn Dinovo
Senior Manufacturing Coordinator: Marie Barnes
Marketing Manager: Sandra McGuire
Associate Marketing Manager: Beth Foohey

Cover design and photo research: Judy Arisman, Arisman Design
Cover image: Folio, Inc., Navy Memorial © 1993 Cameron Davidson

Glossary from Kay Lawson, *The Human Polity*, 4th ed. (Boston: Houghton Mifflin, 1997). Reprinted by permission.

Printed in the U.S.A.

Library of Congress Catalog Card Number: 98-72058

ISBN: 0-395-82453-2

123456789-QF-02 01 00 99 98

**For Marta and Ingrid
and all their junior editions**

CONTENTS

PART II
THE CONTEXT OF POLITICS   41

PART IV
THE WORK OF GOVERNMENT: LEGISLATIVE, EXECUTIVE, AND JUDICIAL FUNCTIONS   191

9   Making the Laws   192

PART V
ALTERNATIVE ARENAS OF GOVERNMENT   269

PREFACE

The Human Polity: A Comparative Introduction to Political Science, Brief Version, is an introduction both to an important field of study and to an important concept. The **human polity** is the world of interconnected and interdependent governments in which we live. It is a world that has refused to stand still, especially in the past ten years. New patterns have begun to emerge: the overwhelming triumph of capitalism, the shift to free elections, the continuation of limited but real and relentless warfare and terrorist activity, the rise of religious fundamentalism, the new and conflicting struggles to define the roles of women, the acceleration of the race between responsible environmentalism and planetary meltdown, and the growing difficulty of solving our problems within the nation state.

Who could possibly keep up? Yet it is the challenge of political science not only to keep up but to make sense, and *The Human Polity*, Brief Version, tries to do both. It is a book about politics and about the study of politics in a world that is increasingly and irreversibly interdependent. The human polity is a polity—a political community—to which we all belong merely by virtue of living together on the globe. At the same time that we proudly give our first loyalties to the separate nation states that lay claim to our citizenship, we also recognize that there are problems we can resolve only in unison with the citizens of other states. The study of politics has thus become the study of the web of life on our planet.

Why a Brief Version? The long edition of *The Human Polity* has known a considerable success and will continue to appear at regular intervals. But some instructors prefer to assign a briefer, paperback text for their Introduction to Political Science course, and this edition is intended to meet that need. Of course it hurts to cut beloved prose—and feelings are mixed at best to discover that what remains actually stands alone. Nonetheless, the author is proud to claim that for those who need a shorter work for pedagogical reasons of their own, this brief version will do the job capably and well.

Features of the Book

Writing Level and Style. The complexities of political science are an outgrowth of and an accompaniment to the increasingly complex scope of politics itself. Complexity is interesting and does not in itself make something difficult. We can respect the complexity of politics and at the same time write about it clearly, using a familiar vocabulary and explaining new terms in a context that makes their meaning immediately comprehensible and easy to remember. The style of *The Human Polity*, Brief Version, is one of informal but respectful dialogue between author and reader. Direct questions are occasionally posed in the text in order to stimulate the students' interest and to prompt them to apply their steadily increasing knowledge of political science to the more familiar experiences of their own lives. Students who take this opportunity to "talk back" to the author will find that as a consequence they are better prepared to enter into class discussions and to recall what they have read. Both normative and practical problems are raised throughout the book, in a manner intended not only to inform but also to encourage students to form their own opinions and make their own recommendations for change.

Thorough and Up-to-Date Coverage. *The Human Polity*, Brief Version, offers a full and comprehensive introduction to political science. It describes the nature of the discipline, explains the ways in which political scientists study politics, and offers introductory treatment of all the major topics we normally think of as constituting political science. Chapter 1 considers the meanings of interdependence, the nature of politics and polities, and the methods of political science. Succeeding chapters cover the language of politics, the most important political ideologies, the relationships between politics and economics and between politics and culture, the ways in which individuals can and do act in politics, political groups, political parties, executive leadership, the work of legislatures, executive bureaucracies, the judiciary and systems of law, local and provincial government, international relations, and the present era of post–cold war regime change. Special features include an important section noting the claims of feminism, ethnic nationalism, and religious fundamentalism to stand as separate ideologies and treating the first at length. New global issues are treated in the chapter on political economy (Chapter 4), and the questions of ethnicity and race are given special attention in the study of the reciprocal relationship between politics and culture (Chapter 5). Chapter 6 offers up-to-date coverage of how the individual act of voting is transformed into power differently by different electoral systems. The examination of the role of interest groups in politics covers a wide range of such organizations' activities (Chapter 7). Giving political parties a whole chapter of their own has been a source of satisfaction for an author who specializes in that subject; incorporating the love-hate relationship between parties and the media taught the expert to look at her own subject with new eyes; avoiding jargonistic specialist talk was a challenge we believe has been met (Chapter 8). Chapters 9 through 12 cover legislative, executive, and judicial behavior, clarifying with simple language and diagrams the differences among presidential, parliamentary, and quasi-presidential systems, stressing the positive as well as the negative roles of bureaucracy, and offering a comparison of different systems of law that should, the author believes, go a long way toward clearing up confusions often left standing in other texts. The differences among unitary, federal, and confederal systems, plus the roles assigned to different levels of government within a state, receive full and well-illustrated treatment in Chapter 13.

Finally, Chapter 14 examines changes initiated in the world in 1989, which have now reached the point where preliminary first assessments of the new regimes are possible; "Regime Change and the Human Polity" attempts to make those assessments. The chapter looks first at the criteria for establishing democracy and at expert opinion on the possibility and means of doing so. It then considers specific kinds of transitions that have been taking place: from communism to democracy and capitalism (Russia and Eastern and Central Europe); from communism toward capitalism (China); from noncommunist authoritarian rule to multi-party elections and the beginnings of democracy (Africa and Latin America). A third section looks at the widely varying impact such change has on certain categories of individuals, such as the newly rich, the newly poor, women, and those who live in stable democracies. The chapter concludes by looking at new evidence of the meaning of these changes for three kinds of international activities: international governance, international organization on behalf of specific interests, and international business. The findings are often surprising and dramatic, especially for those who are just beginning to realize how profoundly the human polity shapes the everyday life of every one of us.

Pedagogical Tools. *The Human Polity,* Brief Version, is characterized by several other features that strengthen direct and effective communication with its readers. Simple but telling examples are used throughout to highlight important points and clarify difficult concepts. Some of these are personal, drawing from the author's own experience or asking the students to reflect on their own, as a way of helping readers realize the relevance of topics and issues they might otherwise regard as remote or arcane. Almost all are recent; most students will recognize many of the cases cited from news reports. U.S. politics and government furnish many of the examples, but this text really *is* comparative, and the author has drawn illustrations from nearly every nation in the world. A particularly important feature in this respect are the **Regime Change** boxes, a unique feature of this volume. In combination with the final chapter devoted exclusively to the subject of regime change, these boxes, found throughout the text, give this edition a special timeliness and interest.

The Human Polity, Brief Version, is based as well on up-to-date scholarship in all the fields of political science. A text that will carry us from one millennium to the next cannot and does not draw its materials from a distant past. Careful perusal of the endnotes will make clear to students and instructors alike the solid scholarly foundations on which this text is built.

The *Instructor's Resource Manual with Test Items,* written by W. D. Kay of Northeastern University, provides a chapter outline, a chapter overview, questions for class discussion, and an annotated list of additional readings for each chapter. The test items include essay and multiple-choice questions for each chapter.

Acknowledgments

This book is itself the product of interdependence. I have leaned often and with profit on the work of student assistants, Paul Anderson and Dana Polk, who, in exchange for remuneration far from equal to their labors, helped me get the books I needed from libraries, find many of the examples, and work up several of the charts and tables. It is also a pleasure to thank the following reviewers, whose thoughtful comments and careful critiques have helped to guide the manuscript's development: Jose Z. Garcia, New Mexico State University; Susan Ann Kay, Miami University; Manwoo Lee, Millersville University; and Rolf H. W. Theen, Purdue University.

Also, as before, this edition owes a great deal to the support of family and friends, to some special members of which this edition is most happily dedicated.

Finally, for the short edition as I always have for the long, I willingly take responsibility for the book's faults but insist on my share of any praise for its merits. I hope the effort that I and others have given to making this edition a lively and interesting introduction to the ever-changing world of politics and political science will seem well worthwhile, especially to the students for whom *The Human Polity*, Brief Version, is *their* introduction to political science.

PART

I THINKING ABOUT POLITICS

1 Politics and the Human Polity

Today the world of nations is more interdependent than ever. Increasingly, our lives and welfare depend on developments beyond our nation's borders, however well secured those borders may be and however strong the social and economic systems within those borders. The need to preserve and replenish the limited resources of our planet while meeting the massive energy demands of advanced civilization and the need to develop and expand this civilization while protecting it from the destructive havoc our own technology has made possible are needs we can meet only collectively and cooperatively. We can no longer comfortably assume that "we" means "we Americans" or "we Swiss" or "we Japanese" when such matters are to be resolved. More and more often, "we" means "we humans," and "our" problems, resources, and efforts are those of the species, not of any single **nation-state**. We live in the human polity.

THE MEANING OF THE HUMAN POLITY

What is the human polity? **Polity** is a word with several meanings. It can mean a state or any society that has an organized government. More generally, it refers to a "body politic"—that is, any group of persons who have some form of political relationship with one another. The *human polity* is a polity in the second sense. It includes all the people presently living on the planet who have become so interdependent that they now constitute a body politic.

However, the *human polity* is made up of separate polities in the first sense of the word, too—individual nation-states. It is to these states that most people pledge their loyalty. For this reason, the capacity of human beings to interact effectively across national boundaries depends very much on what goes on inside those boundaries. If the citizens of individual polities are able to address their internal problems efficiently, equitably, and cooperatively, then they will be able to address the problems that extend into the international arena. On the other hand, citizens of individual polities that suffer from severe internal conflict and dissent, inequitable distribution of inadequate **national resources**, inappropriate or outmoded political institutions, and/or exploitative intervention by other polities in their own affairs must inevitably find it difficult to function effectively in the world at large.

Unfortunately, there is no nation in the world that does not suffer from one or more of these problems, a fact that influences the nature of the human polity in which we all must live. To understand that larger polity, we must therefore learn to recognize and understand these problems as they manifest themselves in our own nation, in other nations, and in international relations. Once we have a better understanding of the politics and government of individual nation-states, we will be better able to deal with the complexities produced by the increasing global interdependence of those separate polities.

It may seem obvious that in any enterprise, knowledge of the parts (individual nation-states and their political components) is essential to an understanding of the whole (the human polity) and that the whole will inevitably be greater than the mere sum of all the parts. However, it is not necessarily obvious that increasing interdependence produces complexities. Let us take a closer look at that association.

The Challenge of Interdependence

The word *complexities* was chosen carefully. Although interdependence will increasingly bind all states together and make their individual security, especially their economic fortunes, dependent on one another, this increased interdependence does not necessarily make our problems more *difficult*.[1] In fact, the more interdependent we become, the more we recognize our shared interests and our need to work together to meet those interests. Still, the very conditions that make it imperative for us to cooperate—and thus make it easier to do so—tend to make that work considerably more complex.

Today, economic change tends to be global in scope. Changing interest rates, growth rates, and rates of unemployment and inflation in one nation mean related changes in many other nations as well. If the international market goes into a decline (as it did beginning with the oil crisis of 1973), almost every nation is affected. If the stock market of a major nation suffers a sudden drop (as it did in the United States in 1987 and in Japan in 1992 and 1997), all other major markets are likely to respond, recognizing that the affected nation may now buy fewer exports, invest less abroad, and possibly be less competitive in the international market as smaller manufacturers are squeezed out by more conservative banking practices. If the economic system of a superpower ceases to function with at least minimal success (as was the case in the former Soviet Union in 1989), a chain reaction of change can result, extending far beyond its borders, as other nations consider the prospects for their own markets and political stability and react accordingly. The imminent failure of a trading partner can provoke the stronger partner to take drastic steps to prop up an economy other than its own. When failing investor confidence sent the currency of Mexico into a free fall in early 1995, the Clinton administration and the U.S. Congress were quick to take remedial action, firmly in agreement that "if Mexico's economic growth slows or stops because of this crisis, the impact on trade, on immigration and the whole strategy of spreading free trade in the region could be enormous."[2]

In the past, it might have been possible for stronger nations to retreat to isolationist policies when the economies of other nations were in danger, and even today such ideas have their appeal. But stronger nations need the income they receive from exports and from overseas investment. They also need conditions for peaceful trade, a state of affairs not likely to be fostered by **protectionism** or **nationalism**: "If goods cannot cross borders, solidiers will" goes the cliché, and Renato Ruggiero of the World Trade Organization argues further, "Protectionism is a road that leads to economic nationalism [which] can easily transform itself into political nationalism."[3] Leonard Silk carries the argument to its logical conclusion in our increasingly interdependent world: "Protectionism and an aggressive nationalism . . . as the world has learned over and over, endanger both peace and prosperity."[4]

The complexities produced by global interdependence are particularly apparent in the species' most fundamental quest: the maintenance of our planet as an environment fit for human habitation. In this domain, we have been slow to recognize not only that solutions must depend on international cooperation but even that we have a problem, and one of the most serious dimensions. As early as 1962, Rachel Carson was attracting attention with her book *Silent Spring*, a study of the damage done by the indiscriminate use of pesticides, and her work was preceded and followed by many others.[5] More and more authors have attempted to call our attention to the pressures of our ever increasing global population, the blindly selfish use of agricultural and industrial methods that destroy and/or pollute as they produce, the decline of our natural resource base, and our steadfast insistence on pursuing the objects of individual and national greed—sometimes through the use of weapons that do even more damage to the earth than to our enemies. All these factors place our collective home in greater danger than any natural disaster is ever likely to do.[6]

The message has been loud and clear for nearly forty years, and often the solutions that must be adopted are as unambiguous as the problems they address. But these problems cannot be solved by single individuals, or even by single nations. Motivated individuals can recycle and avoid environmentally destructive behavior, and nations can pass laws and establish agencies, but finally a worldwide effort of staggering dimensions is required. It is not merely that the task of saving the planet is complex and expensive; the task also poses extremely difficult social and political problems on an international scale.

There are many examples of interdependence. Some forms are negative. Military expenditures may grow to unreasonable proportions of national budgets in a world tangled in a web of defensive pacts: Iraq spent 27.4 percent of its gross national product on military expenditures in 1990, and in that year just prior to the outbreak of the Gulf War every other Middle Eastern nation also spent well above the global average of 3.8 percent (Israel spent 13%, Jordan 12.2%, Oman 17.9%, Qatar 12.5%, Saudi Arabia 14%, Syria 13.5%, and Yemen 14.9%).[7] Or home industries may suffer when economic treaties give too favored a status to foreign competitors. In other cases, one nation may accrue benefits while the other realizes only costs; the interdependence relationship is asymmetrical.

At other times, the effect of interdependence may be strongly positive, as when two or more nations recognize their mutual need for a period of peaceful coexistence in order to restore economies damaged by war. The present relatively good relations between France and Germany grew out of such a recognition after World War II, and today the French remain particularly aware that German markets and German military security are crucial to France's own prosperity and safety.[8]

In any case, it is important, as Robert Keohane and Joseph Nye remind us, not to succumb to "interdependence rhetoric" while recognizing that nearly every problem we attempt to solve, and nearly every action we endeavor to promote, forces us to consider, sooner or later, the effects our plans will have on those beyond our borders—and the effects their responses will have on us and other peoples.[9]

Still, there are only too many signs of our globally inadequate response to the challenges posed by the vast and amazing transformation in the nature of the world we must live in. Continued and often genocidal warfare, brutal acts of terrorism, growing unemployment, poverty, and homelessness in the world at large along with a seemingly uncontrollable international drug trade are only some of the sad signs of our inability, so far, to take back positive control of our collective destinies. Yet if we can, however slowly and painfully, learn to accept the complexity of the world we now live in, and the consequent necessity of moving more carefully and compassionately to pursue the goals we cannot help sharing across the planet, our chances for success are great. We have the technical capacity to acquire the information we need to put all the resources of our planet and our human intelligence to work for our collective good.

Will we ever decide to do exactly that? What choice will we humans make? Will we cast aside our responsibilities as citizens in the human polity, forget the quest for answers as soon as we see that they will not be easily or selfishly found, and allow those we cannot hold accountable to squander our goods and destroy our future? Or will we organize our resources—natural and intellectual—and establish democratic, equitable, and efficient control of our shared life on this planet?

The Task at Hand

You will not find the answers to these questions in this book. What you will find is an introduction to a field of study, political science, that is hard at work on the puzzles these questions pose. *The Human Polity* introduces you to all of political science and invites you to pay particular attention to the way these questions of interdependence arise in the study of politics. To accomplish this task, in Part I we begin by looking at the scope of political science itself. We consider the means political scientists have developed (and are constantly improving) to organize the study of questions like those we have been talking about, the conceptual language they employ to clarify the intricacies of these matters, and the variety of ideological perspectives they and others use to evaluate the world of politics.

With these tools in hand, political scientists have begun to find some answers to the questions that intrigue us all and that must be answered if we are to understand the nature of the human polity and its prospects for the future. For example, they know something about the impact of social relationships and economic resources on the human condition and on the political choices that citizens make in endeavoring to improve that condition. They know how to identify popular opinions on an issue, how individual opinions sometimes coalesce into "public opinion," and how citizens around the world participate (or do not participate) in their nations' politics and governments, either individually or via political organizations. Political scientists have investigated the constitutional structures and decision-making processes of nearly every existent government and can speak with some authority on questions of political leadership, the legislative functions of government, the bureaucratic organization of different states, and the judicial process. Political scientists have also studied arenas of government other than the nation-state, from local government bodies to international organizations to those unofficial agencies—such as multinational corporations and religious institutions—that sometimes take a powerful yet unacknowledged part in the work of governing nations.

Studying human interaction is not like studying the physical laws of the universe. There are no fixed principles we can use to predict with certainty how human beings will interact in the future. We can, however, identify some of the more common kinds of change in human relationships over time and consider what these changes may mean for the human polity. And we can remember at all times that our problems are seldom merely national in scope. The interdependence of nations is profound, yet at the same time there are national and natural forces at work that shape our lives regardless of the policies of other nations. The human polity cannot be understood only in terms of international interdependence; neither can it be understood without recognizing the impact of such interdependence, an effort we make throughout this book. We turn now to the first of our tasks, an exploration of the scope of politics in the human polity.

THE SCOPE OF POLITICAL SCIENCE

Political science is the study of **politics**. This means the work of political science is to seek the answers to a number of important questions: What attitudes and values produce political conflict and dissent? What political organizations are active in the struggle to achieve political consensus? What is the nature of the socioeconomic relationships inside a polity? How adequate are resources to meet needs, how equitably are resources distributed, and how are material interests pursued, protected, or changed by the course of public policy? What are the constitutional structures and the decision-making procedures of each nation, and how well suited are they to that nation's needs? What internal structures and procedures exist for the debate and resolution of problems with other nations? What assistance is available from international agencies and the international community at large?

Political science does not have all the answers to these questions, but it does have some, and, what is more important, it has the means of finding others. Becoming a political scientist means joining a community of people who work on just these sorts of questions. Like politics itself, the work of political science has developed over the centuries, expanding and subdividing. Scholars, critics, playwrights, correspondents, and poets have been observing and commenting on political processes since pen was first put to paper (or stylus to tablet). Confucius wrote on moral and ethical issues relevant to the concept of authority as early as 500 B.C.E. In 450 B.C.E., Herodotus' history of the Persian Wars included his reflections on the issue of tyranny versus the rule of law, and Aristophanes wrote *Lysistrata*, an antiwar play, in 412 B.C.E. Over the years the focus of political studies has changed and expanded. The subfields of political science have multiplied accordingly. To our original study of political philosophy (now more commonly termed *political theory*) we have added, one by one, constitutional law, public administration, international relations, U.S. government, comparative government (by which we really mean the study of foreign governments), political behavior (the study of political attitudes as well as political acts), political economy, political organizations, urban politics, and public policy. In addition, some of us devote most of our time to studying and developing the methodology of political science, while others are interested in such newer, less well-established areas of study as *biopolitics* (the study of how the physical characteristics and conditions of political actors may sometimes influence their behavior).

The Puzzles of Political Science

How do political scientists do their work? They often begin with very ordinary activities: They read what other people have to say, they follow current events, they note what appear to them to be certain interesting tendencies, they wonder why such things are happening, and they wonder what will happen next. What makes a political scientist different, however, is the capacity and the will to make systematic inquiries into a political puzzle. The political scientist does not simply say, "Hmm, I see by the paper that our president has vowed to save the American worker from the competition of cheap foreign imports while at the same time protecting the principle of free trade. That's a good trick," and turn the page. The political scientist tries to solve the puzzle such a statement presents.

But what is that puzzle? When we stop to think about it, this statement, like almost every statement about politics, is replete with puzzles. The president of the United States promises to save American workers while encouraging the freedom of international trade that threatens the livelihood of many of them. What do you think is puzzling about that promise? Take a moment and write your answer out. Does it seem to you that what you just wrote is the only possible answer? Perhaps it does, but in fact, we all differ in how we perceive political reality, and thus in how we formulate the puzzles it poses. Just consider some of the possibilities:

1. What puzzles me is what endangered workers think about this announcement. Did this president win the steelworkers' vote? Is he likely to do so again?
2. What puzzles me is how the *president* can do anything to save jobs. Isn't it the work of the legislature to make the laws and of the president to carry them out?
3. What puzzles me is why the president suddenly gave this nod to the protectionists. He has always been strongly committed to free trade. Is it because an election is coming up, or has he decided the effects of foreign competition are so harsh they require a serious change of direction?
4. What puzzles me is the perennial conflict between policies that help, in the short term, to solve a national problem and long-term policies that seem necessary if we are ever going to have a human polity that is economically stable and at least minimally responsive to the needs of human beings everywhere. Must we always sacrifice the needy of another nation to care for the needy at home?
5. What puzzles me is how the president can act as if all the trade treaties we have made with various nations can simply be set aside at will. Are our agreements no longer worth the paper they are written on?

6. What puzzles me is what the impact of protectionism—if that is the policy we really adopt—is going to be on those nations whose economies depend on cheap exports to the United States. Will our policies destabilize those economies and, as a consequence, those polities? Will there be other effects in international relations stemming from these changes?

As you can see, how we formulate our puzzles makes a big difference in the questions we ask and in the work we need to do to find answers to them. Just as not all political scientists study the same subfield, so not all of them puzzle about political phenomena in the same way. Some kinds of questions interest you, other kinds interest me, and across the room our good friend Bob is probably thinking about this same problem in some entirely different way—or simply doesn't care at all.

How we formulate the problems we wish to study as political scientists also has some relationship to the subfields that interest us. Wondering about how workers will react at the polls or about whether or not policy statements are governed by upcoming elections are questions about political behavior as well as about U.S. government. Those interested in constitutional law might worry about presidential interference in the legislative domain, and so might political scientists whose studies are concentrated in U.S. government or public administration. The philosophical tone of the fourth puzzle suggests the work of political theorists, but political economists might want to claim this puzzle as their own, since it stresses the relationship between politics and economics, whereas those interested in comparative politics will appreciate the focus here and in puzzle 6 on the internal affairs of other nations. Arguing for the validity of international treaties suggests an interest in international affairs, as does considering the impact of the president's decision on the welfare of foreign states.

Six Approaches to the Study of Political Puzzles
The way we puzzle over political phenomena does more than reveal which subfields of political science are likely to interest us most. It is also strongly related to our method of inquiry and the approach we take in our quest for an answer. There are six main approaches to the study of politics: (1) behavioral, (2) structural-functional, (3) phenomenological, (4) philosophical, (5) documentary, and (6) predictive. Each of the preceding six puzzles is related to one of these approaches.

Studying Political Behavior. "What puzzles me is what endangered workers think about this announcement." The **behavioral approach** to politics means focusing on how individuals act politically and seeking explanations for that behavior within those individuals. Behavioralists are not especially interested in what the rules say or what philosophers recommend about political action. They want to know what human beings really do when they act politically—that is, when they discuss politics, vote, contact government officials, demonstrate, riot, or otherwise act out their political convictions.

Once political scientists have what seems to them to be reliable evidence about the facts of political behavior, they want to know what motivated that behavior. What does the actor feel, believe, or think about politics that caused him or her to act in that particular way? Sometimes the behavioralist carries the inquiry another step: What factors seem to be associated with having those particular feelings, beliefs, and opinions? Does growing up in a certain kind of home or having a certain kind of job influence what kind of a political actor a person will be?

How can this kind of information be gathered? A key method for the behaviorialist is survey research—that is, research that studies a large number of individuals, finding out, by asking them, about their political behavior (voting, joining groups, writing letters, and so on). Such research permits the acquisition of a great many answers, often in simple, uniform format (*yes, no, often, one, two . . . five*), and these answers may in turn be subjected to complex statistical analysis, permitting the researcher to draw far-reaching conclusions about political behavior and its causes with considerable confidence. In the United States we know, for example, not only the characteristics most commonly associated with voting but also what other kinds of political participation voters engage in, how much more likely they are to do so than nonvoters, and what difference various kinds of voter registration arrangements are likely to make in voter turnout.[10] Such knowledge does not always tell us what to do next—we have not yet been able to increase the number of people who vote in the United States—but it does give us an important part of the factual base we need.

The behavioral approach is appropriate when the puzzle at hand requires and permits the accumulation of information about human behavior and its motives. It helps if those data can be gathered in discrete but uniform bits, permitting statistical analysis. The study of the personality of a single political actor, however, may be as important—and is every bit as "behavioral"—as the study of thousands of voters or hundreds of political elites.

Studying Political Structures and Functions. "Isn't it the work of the legislature to make the laws and of the president to carry them out?" When political scientists adopt the **structural-functional approach,** they focus on the important political roles established in a society, what functions they perform, and how the carrying out of these roles influences the quality of life.

Structural-functionalism is an approach that was first developed by anthropologists looking for ways to free themselves from Western biases when studying non-Western cultures. It soon became clear to such scholars that different structures might well perform different functions in different societies. For example, religious institutions may have the function of conducting seasonal ceremonies to ensure that planting and harvesting are done at the appropriate times of the year as well as the functions of setting codes of interpersonal behavior and guiding believers to presumed eternal happiness. Even where familiar political structures seem to be missing, closer observation may reveal that very familiar functions are still being performed, although through other structures. For exam-

Political behavior takes many forms. Here Indonesian students demonstrate against their president and his policies by burning him in effigy, May 8, 1998, in Djakarta, Indonesia.

(Kees/Sygma)

ple, there may be nothing that calls itself a political party, but when the members of the club Mr. X belongs to are busily asking everyone to vote for him, while those in the club Ms. Y belongs to are equally active on her behalf, then at least one of the key functions of parties—campaigning on behalf of chosen candidates—is not neglected.

The structural-functional approach helps us focus on what is really happening. It tells us to look at structures objectively: What are their role occupants really doing? It reminds us that certain functions are probably being performed even when persons with positions inside the structures normally responsible for them are not doing the job: Someone is creating political issues, someone is choosing the leaders, someone is making rules for society, someone is carrying them out, someone is deciding disputes arising under those rules. Who is doing what, in what office or role, and with what effect?

Structural-functionalists are sometimes accused of finding functions for every structure that exists and thereby implicitly defending that structure, no matter how unfortunate its effects. Where others may study the Spanish Inquisition as an example of religious intolerance, for example, the functionalist may consider it an interesting illustration of how religious bodies can take over the government functions of making and carrying out the laws and settling disputes. But this does not mean the functionalist *approves* of the takeover. Understanding how particular structures perform essential functions is obviously important, regardless of our opinion of their worth. Furthermore, if in fact we strongly disapprove of what is being done by persons within a particular structure, knowing what they offer to those who support them (i.e., what functions they fulfill) is essential before we offer our recommendations for replacing the structure within which they work. Practicing structural-functionalists may have a bias (or may not), but the method itself seems reasonably neutral.

A further testimony to the usefulness of this mode of analysis is the rapid growth of a "new" subfield in political science, known as the "new institutionalism." As we see in Chapter 2, *institutions* are *structures*. In political science, as in botany, a rose by any other name sometimes does smell sweeter, whatever William Shakespeare had to say on the subject.[11]

Studying Political Phenomena. "What puzzles me is why the president suddenly gave this nod to the protectionists. He has always been strongly committed to free trade." One criticism often leveled at the two approaches we have considered so far is that they are not useful for considering political change. Behavioralists rely on opinion polls that may be useless two days after they are taken. How many Soviet citizens do you suppose felt exactly the same about the likelihood of their nation's making a peaceful change to a capitalistic market system before, during, and after the attempted **coup d'état** by old-guard communists in 1991? The structural-functionalist determination that a structure does or does not perform a particular function may be equally shortsighted. The role of the Guinean Confédération Générale du Travail, an early trade union in what later became the West African nation of Guinea, changed with dramatic speed when that union staged the first successful strike by black workers in West Africa. Shortly thereafter, the trade union became the nation's leading political party.[12] In such cases, goes the critique, what is missing is any allowance for change. An approach to politics that does not find a way to take into account the inevitability of change can never get more than a fleeting hold on the slippery facts of political reality.

The **phenomenological approach** to the study of politics does not suffer from the same problem. It begins with an interest in change. The question this approach asks first and foremost is What are the causes of a significant change in a political system? Specifically, what are the events (the *phenomena*) that led up to that change, and which of these were significant in producing that change?

As the preceding discussion suggests, the political scientist gives a broad interpretation to what constitutes a political phenomenon. For the political scientist, a **political phenomenon** is any event that affects the right to allocate scarce resources. It may be one brief happening, or it may be the general consequence or outcome of a series of interrelated political acts. Nearly everyone would agree that the American Revolution was a political phenomenon, but it might take a political scientist to see the development of commercial wealth in the United States early in the nineteenth century as a political phenomenon, one that forced significant changes in the authoritative allocation of resources as the people who acquired such wealth successfully insisted on their right to share political power and as the right to vote ceased to depend exclusively on the ownership of land.

Note that in the effort to find the roots of major change, the student of phenomena inevitably asks and answers numerous questions that could properly be considered the work of the behavioralist and the structural-functionalist. What sets this approach apart is its commitment to the study of structures, functions, behavior, and events *over time.*

Studying Political Ideas. "Must we always sacrifice the needy of another nation to care for the needy at home?" The **philosophical approach** to the study of politics focuses on the meanings of political life. Like the behavioralist approach, this mode of study is closely associated with a single subfield of political science, in this case *political theory* (so called even though theory is in fact used in every subfield of the discipline). Typically, the political theorist is interested in general questions relevant to politics. What are the limits on the exercise of political power, if any? What are the various meanings of *representation* in the political arena? Can the apparent conflict between economically sound and humanely caring public policy ever be resolved?

All such questions have specific applications. When we argue about whether any conditions exist under which investigative agencies like the FBI (Federal Bureau of Investigation) should be allowed to tap private telephones, we are arguing about the limits that should be imposed on political power. If we are angered when one of our senators votes his or her conscience even though that vote is contrary to known popular opinion in our state, we are expressing an opinion about the meaning we prefer to see given the concept of representation in the political arena. The controversy over whether or not the U.S. public debt can be reduced while maintaining programs for social welfare reflects the eternal conflict between good budget management and social responsibility in the making of public policy.

The political philosopher seldom makes more than passing reference, however, to specific problems illustrative of the more general question under consideration. The emphasis in this approach to the study of politics is on examining the work of other philosophers who have grappled in a useful—or at least an interesting—way with the topic at hand and then endeavoring to deduce one's own logical conclusions. Sometimes this form of study involves simply allowing the comments of accepted classical authors, carefully selected, to make the desired point. In other cases, political scientists using this approach make their own arguments, backed up by authoritative citations. Sometimes the theorist's chief object is to offer a new interpretation of a classic text. In other cases, the object is to draw together the comments of several political philosophers on a particular matter of interest to the political scientist.

Because they place so much emphasis on political ideas—their own and others'—political philosophers are often criticized for being too *normative* in their approach to politics and insufficiently *empirical,* that is, for worrying too much about what should be and too little about what is. But, in fact, all political scientists have values that guide the work they do. The political philosopher differs in placing greater emphasis on general ideas and values and in keeping alive the arguments for and against their application.

Studying Political Documents. "What puzzles me is how the president can act as if all the trade treaties we have made with various nations can simply be set aside at will." The art and practice of reading **political documents**, from constitutions to campaign speeches, is one of the oldest forms of political science—and currently one of the least appreciated. Political scientists have learned the hard way that documents cannot always be trusted as guides to political practice. Constitutional and statutory law, treaties, party statutes and platforms, leaders' speeches and memoirs, records of legislative proceedings, authorized biographies, judicial decisions, and newspaper accounts of political happenings are among the forms of the written word that political scientists have discovered they must approach with caution. They offer rich lodes of information about politicians' intent and officeholders' official commitments, but often only fragmentary evidence of motivation and practice, and they are sometimes replete with self-serving distortions of the truth.

Even a constitution, the "highest law of the land," is not always to be trusted as an infallible guide to reality. No constitution did a better job, on paper, of protecting democratic principles than did that of the Union of Soviet Socialist Republics (USSR), yet nothing in that constitution could effectively block Joseph Stalin from transforming the Soviet government into an instrument of personal tyranny. Similarly, Adolf Hitler came to power under the terms of the well-respected constitution of the Weimar Republic of Germany.[13] Democratic nations have also shown surprising gaps between constitutional theory and political practice. Charles de Gaulle refused to take power in France in 1958 until he was assured that he would have the right to rewrite that nation's constitution, yet only four years later he blithely put through a major constitutional change (direct election of the president) by popular referendum, in bold contravention of his own prescribed method of constitutional amendment.

Nevertheless, studying political documents remains an important and useful mode of inquiry in political science. As long as such pronouncements are not openly repudiated or revised, any violation of their provisions invites attention and protest. Political scientists who explicate the meaning of such materials may well make the fact of such violation clear for the first time and provide a means of holding officials accountable to their word—and to their words. Or they may simply make clear how ambiguous certain key clauses in important documents may be, such as the wording of the idea of maintaining the separation of church and state, contained in the First Amendment to the U.S. Constitution.[14] The fact is that political truth is difficult to come by, and we need every useful method we can devise to track it down.

Studying the Political Future. "What puzzles me is what the impact of protectionism—if that is the policy we really adopt—is going to be on those nations whose economies depend on cheap exports to the United States." In a sense,

Documents as key instruments of our shared political life. Here representatives of both sides of the abortion debate argue for and against the *Roe v. Wade* decision long after it was issued.

(UPI/Corbis-Bettmann)

every political scientist studies the future, and all the approaches thus far discussed can be applied to the study of the future. Our interest in politics is sharply honed by our desire to be prepared for what might be coming next. But some political scientists take the responsibility to make well-founded **predictions** about the feared or hoped-for events of the future more seriously than do others.

Efforts to predict the future must necessarily be based on our knowledge of the past. We cannot predict the future from the present—not if we use that term literally. How much does any of us know about what is happening right now? We need time to acquire information, organize it, assimilate it, and make sense of it—and by then the present will be the past. However, the time-honored certitude that "the past is prologue" has been shaken by the course of events in the twentieth century. Too often and too obviously the past has proved an untrustworthy guide. Periodic angry denunciation of the North Atlantic Treaty Organization (NATO) and its members by members of the Warsaw Pact of the eastern bloc did little to prepare us for the day in 1992 when many of the latter would seek to join the former, having dissolved their own alliance the year before.

I used to teach the politics of South Africa in one of my courses but gave it up, too disheartened by what seemed the ever-tightening hold of the white supremacists on that nation's destiny. Yes, I knew something about Nelson Mandela, a brave leader in an island jail, but little did I dream that someday you would, too, and that you would learn about him not in a college course but on the front page of your newspaper. Our species' capacity for rapid change that shatters old patterns of political relationships forever—a capacity that seems to have grown only stronger as our century draws to its close—has been a major stimulus to the effort to find ways to use information about the past more systematically to predict the future. One such way is by building **models**.

What is a model? Scratch fifty political scientists and you will probably find fifty different definitions. Let me try to offer a fifty-first here, one that encompasses most of what is said in the other fifty. To begin with, a model is an imitation of something that is, or that is thought to be, or that might someday be. It is an *ideal* in the Platonic sense—that is, a representation of the essence of the subject, not the best possible version. Thus, a model is also a simplification. It does not tell the whole truth about a subject, nor does it purport to do so.

Models can be used in all the approaches of politics that we have looked at so far but are particularly useful in efforts to study the future. Models, as any child with glue-covered fingers and leftover extra parts can tell you, can be material objects. The models of political scientists, however, almost never are. They are abstract—verbal, mathematical, or diagrammatic descriptions or imitations of reality. For example, political scientists have formulated verbal models of political development, trying to help us understand how the relationship between political and economic factors will affect a nation's ability to develop and to modernize. Some development models suggest that modernization requires the centralization of political power, others stress the need for a division of labor (leading to a division of political power), and still others argue that development will never take place until the poor nations of the world free themselves from dependency on richer nations whose only goal is to continue to exploit them.[15]

Statistical models are used to predict electoral outcomes, among other things. Suppose you had wanted to know what the chances of the Liberal Democratic Party of Russia, led by hard-liner nationalist Vladimir V. Zhirinovsky, were likely to be in the parliamentary elections of 1993. In fact, the Zhirinovsky party took over 24 percent of the vote in that election, more than any other single party, a result that First Deputy Minister Yegor T. Gaider termed "a big and unpleasant surprise." The controversial leader of this party, often labeled a fascist by his opponents (but see Chapter 3 or the Glossary for a better definition of fascism), campaigned on a platform of law and order and the restoration of Russia's imperial legacy. He said he wanted to "stop the outflow of assistance from Russia, stop the conversion of the military industry and deal a crushing blow to crime."[16] These issues were obviously important to a large minority of Russian voters, and the postelection comments of the government were rueful: "We saw the threat posed by the radical extremists too late, and we didn't reorient the focus of our campaign quickly," said Gaider, whose party, Russia's Choice, had first been favored to win but in fact took 10 percent less of the vote than the Liberal Democratic Party did.[17]

The election surprised Gaider, most Russians, and most of the rest of the world, but it probably would not have surprised political scientists who knew how to use statistical models. Before the election they would have gathered as much information as possible about public opinion on the issues of the day, the loyalty of voters to particular parties (unlikely to be strong when most of the parties were new), and the personal popularity of the candidates. They would have fed all this information into a computer and, using formulas drawn from probability theory, would have produced a statistical model, a **simulation** of the actual election. If their work had been well done, they would have known that the issues of fighting crime and restoring lost prestige would have a strong appeal in postcommunist Russia, stronger than the platform of any of the parties favoring continuation of economic and governmental reforms.

Rational choice theory is a kind of modeling that is both verbal and mathematical. It uses the model of the game to predict the political future. Any game has players who play to win, rules, and information. Rational choice theorists use this model and imagine politicians as players; international treaties, laws, and electoral systems as rules; known political conditions as information; and desired political outcomes as what the players are trying to win. Using this model, they attempt to deduce the decisions the players will make to move rationally toward their goals.[18]

Yet another kind of modeling, one that is both verbal and diagrammatic, is found in **political systems analysis**, a form of analysis suitable for the study of whole nations.[19] Studying whole nations as political systems means treating them as structures with interdependent parts and exploring the relationships among those parts. Figure 1.1 offers an example of the kind of diagram this form of analysis uses. To understand the diagram and this way of studying politics, let us work our way through it, beginning with ourselves—that is, with "members of a polity." We citizens do not come into the political system untouched by life—we have all been shaped by our "nonpolitical environments" as well as by the dominant "political culture and patterns of **political socialization**." Now follow the arrows on the diagram, moving left and upward. "**Feedback**" means that once we take on the identity of "members of a polity," we inevitably find some way of letting those in positions of authority know what we think of their performance. We may do this simply by keeping quiet, thereby letting the government know that its work is at least being tolerated, if only for the time being. Or we may pro-

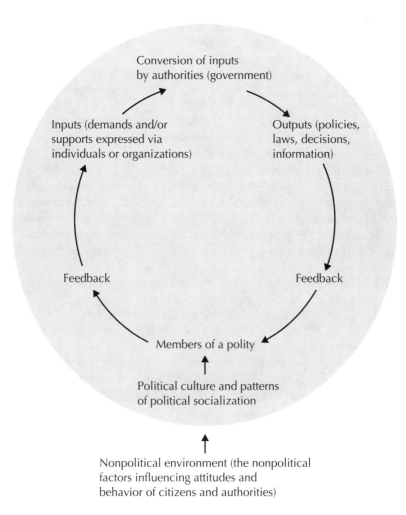

FIGURE 1.1   The Nation as Political System

vide more substantive "**inputs**," expressing our "support" (for example, by voting to reelect the same men and women to office again and again or by paying our taxes without protest) or making "demands" (for example, by forming new pressure groups or parties or by using those that exist to carry our wishes for different policies into the arenas of power). Those who receive these inputs, the "authorities," convert them into "**outputs**" by making and enforcing policies, laws, and decisions or simply by passing on information. Much of this output becomes a kind of "feedback" to the citizens, who are expected to obey the laws, suffer punishments for criminal offenses, accept the rewards good government brings, and so forth. The ways we experience the impact of government in our daily lives enter into our consciousness, become part of our citizen selves, and help shape what we have to say to that government and how we choose to say it. The systems loop is complete; the spiraling history of the **political system** continues on its way.

Some critics have argued that the systems model overemphasizes the interdependence of the parts of any given political system and fails to distinguish among parts that are more or less important in ensuring the successful functioning of the whole system. Others point out that it underestimates the interdependence of different political systems and of their citizens: Where does something like the loss of jobs caused by the competition of government-subsidized firms in other nations fit in the political system diagram? And still others object to the language of systems analysis, arguing that words like *input, output,* and *feedback* are scarcely suitable for conveying the rich spectrum of shared social life that makes up today's world of nations.

How good are the various approaches to the study of political science? Do they really work to solve political puzzles? That depends on what you mean by work. If you mean, "Are political scientists able to figure out what is really going on behind the superficial appearance of political phenomena?" the answer is, "Yes, quite often." But if you mean, "Can they come up with lasting solutions to the puzzles of politics?" the answer is almost certainly, "No." As we have already had occasion to point out, political life is both complex and constantly changing. One plus one is likely to remain two for all eternity, but the factors causing political phenomena to take the form they do may well disappear and be replaced by others—or they may not. What is most likely to happen as a result of a political scientist's work on a puzzle is that the puzzle will become a little less puzzling—at least for a while.

Normative versus Empirical Political Puzzles
One further distinction needs to be drawn about political puzzles: the difference between those that are normative and those that are empirical. A *normative* puzzle is a puzzle about values. Facts will be pertinent, of course, but the final solution of the puzzle is one that depends on what standards, or **norms**, an individual, a group, or a social system decides to apply to the facts uncovered. When we find instances of political corruption, we seldom think it is enough merely to describe the mechanics by which bribes exchanged hands. The study of the political

causes of warfare, terrorism, poverty, or famine cannot fail to evoke our compassion for those who suffer and our hope that revealing the facts will somehow produce positive change. Political scientists cannot and do not work in a normative void.

Nevertheless, at various times political scientists have been tempted to rule the consideration of normative puzzles out of order. In the throes of the "behavioral revolution" of the 1960s, many political scientists were persuaded that the more scientific their discipline could be made, the less concern anyone who worked in it would have with matters of moral choice. The question of the proper role of normative considerations, if any, in the work of the political scientist is still an open one, but most political scientists now recognize that in political science, as in all the sciences, the very decision that a puzzle is interesting and worthwhile is itself a normative one—as is the contention that "should" should not be part of political science! Furthermore, almost every article and book in the field begins with an effort, explicit or implicit, to persuade the reader that the subject matters, and most end by noting the implications the findings have for one or more widely cherished values (such as popular representation, freedom, or peace on earth). When David Geller offers a study of the "impact of political system structure on probability patterns of internal disorder" that employs some of the discipline's most difficult and sophisticated modes of statistical analysis, he nevertheless makes it very clear that what interests him are the "forms and patterns of political conflict" and, in particular, whether "violence breeds violence."[20] Geller never tells us he favors the reduction of violence, but we feel pretty confident that he does, and that his choice of topic is at least in part related to what he considers to be an important normative quest.

In any case, there is now a widespread conviction that the political scientist "should" confront and acknowledge his or her own normative biases and then pursue the work at hand as objectively as possible. I may have a strong bias against government interference in personal freedom and also a strong bias in favor of my own country. Unless I confront those biases very clearly, it may be difficult if not impossible for me to recognize infringements on personal freedom in my own country with the same ease that I ferret them out in other nations.

Thus, the normative component of the puzzles of political science requires special attention and consciousness. It is not going to disappear. Politics itself is largely concerned with the establishment and implementation of values and the distribution of resources, and those who care enough to study politics are not likely to be individuals coldly unmoved by questions of right and wrong. All we can do—and all we "should" do, to my way of thinking—is acknowledge the values that inevitably underlie our work and prevent them, if we can, from distorting our perception of the facts.

The puzzles of politics are large and formidable, and, given the constancy of change, it is true we may never find absolute solutions for any of them. But the recognition of that complexity is itself an encouraging sign of progress. Political scientists no longer simply label nations as *totalitarian*, *democratic*, and *developing*, as if such labels in themselves tell us exactly what amount of individual liberty, political participation, bureaucratic centralization, or industrialization of production we might confidently expect to find. We know that simply tacking on labels does not do the job. We have been working hard to improve our methods of inquiry and to acquire a body of significant and readily applicable knowledge. Much of this book is devoted to summarizing the knowledge political scientists have acquired. Our work is not done—but if it were, what would be the fun of studying how to do it?

SUMMARY AND CONCLUSION

The human polity is the world of politics. In a time of increasing international interdependence, we have all become members of a global body politic as well as citizens of individual nation-states. This means that the only way we will be able to cope with the problems of today's world is to study not only our own nation's politics but those of other nations as well, and the relationships among nations. This increased interdependence does not necessarily make our problems harder to solve, since it can have the effect of making cooperative work with other nations an easier task, but it does increase their complexity. Still, if we learn to accept that complexity and move carefully as we pursue the goals we cannot help sharing, our chances of being able to put all the resources of our planet to work for our collective benefit are good. Whether or not we will do so remains to be seen. We may well be at the most significant crossroads our species has ever faced.

The scope of political science is vast, and the puzzles of political science are all interrelated. Political scientists need one another's work, and that work is divided into subfields. Political theory, constitutional law, public administration, U.S. government, and comparative government are some of the oldest. More recent additions include political behavior, international relations, methodology, political economy, political organizations, and biopolitics. These may or may not endure; political science changes and evolves.

Men and women constantly make observations about what interests and perplexes them about politics. Political scientists treat these observations as puzzles and set to work to understand them. To do so, they use various approaches, singly or in combination: behavioralism, structural-functionalism, phenomenology, the study of ideas, the study of documents, and prediction. Whatever the approach, the political scientist inevitably confronts normative questions, questions that are related to our values. This cannot be avoided. Politics itself is concerned with the establishment and implementation of values, and those who care enough to study politics are likely to be people who care deeply about questions of right and wrong. We should, however, make an effort to acknowledge our values and to prevent them from distorting our perception of the facts.

In this chapter we have only begun the introduction to political science that is the task this book has set for itself. A key aspect of that task is to explain the terms and concepts political scientists use to describe the phenomena of politics, and this is the work we turn to in Chapter 2, "The Language of Politics."

Selected Readings

Cohen, Mitchell, and Nicole Fermon, eds. *Princeton Readings in Political Thought.* Princeton: Princeton University Press, 1996. A survey of writings on Western political thought that have influenced current society and politics.

Crotty, William, ed. *Political Science: Looking to the Future: The Theory and Practice of Political Science.* Vol. 1. Evanston, Ill.: Northwestern University Press, 1992. A book of essays that offers a useful overview of political science theories and methods.

Edelman, Murray J. *Constructing the Political Spectacle.* Chicago: University of Chicago Press, 1988. An examination of political psychology, symbolism in politics, and sociolinguistics.

Farr, James, John S. Dryzek, and Stephen T. Leonard, eds. *Political Science in History: Research, Programs and Political Traditions.* Cambridge: Cambridge University Press, 1995. Essays by political scientists on the history of the field of political science.

Johnson, Janet Buttolph. *Political Science Research Methods.* Washington, D.C.: Congressional Quarterly Press, 1986. An examination of political science research techniques ranging from formulation of the questions posed to statistical analysis and observation. Uses case studies.

Lasswell, Harold D. *The Analysis of Political Behavior: An Empirical Approach.* New York: Oxford University Press, 1947. One of the early explanations of behavioralism, by a leading practitioner.

Ordeshook, Peter C. *Models of Strategic Choice in Politics.* Ann Arbor: University of Michigan Press, 1989. A collection of articles on the application of mathematical models to political science.

Parsons, Wayne. *Public Policy: An Introduction to the Theory and Practice of Policy Analysis.* Gloucestershire, England: Edward Elgar, 1995. A detailed study of the theory and practice of public policy that provides a good introduction to the role of government.

Purvis, Hoyt. *Interdependence: An Introduction to International Affairs.* Chicago: Harcourt Brace Jovanovich, 1992. Uses established principles and theories of international relations to study emerging interdependence in contemporary world politics. Analyzes environmental questions, population trends, and advances in communications and technology.

Ross, Marc Howard. *The Management of Conflict: Interpretations and Interests in Comparative Perspective.* New Haven: Yale University Press, 1993. A comparative study of political conflicts and solutions worldwide.

Tansey, Stephen D. *Politics: The Basics.* London: Routledge, 1995. A historical survey of politics that is a useful resource for those new to the field or seeking a review.

Wilentz, Sean, ed. *Rites of Power.* Philadelphia: University of Pennsylvania Press, 1985. A collection of ten essays on symbolism and politics throughout history.

Notes

1. John Spanier, *Games Nations Play,* 6th ed. (Washington, D.C.: Congressional Quarterly Press, 1987), p. 651.
2. *New York Times,* 13 Jan. 1995, A1, and 10 Mar. 1995, D1.

3. Renato Ruggiero, "Agenda for Trade," *Financial Times*, 5 Oct. 1994, 22.

4. Leonard Silk, "Dangers of Slow Growth," *Foreign Affairs* 72, no. 1 (1992): 167–82.

5. Rachel Carson, *Silent Spring* (Boston: Houghton Mifflin, 1962).

6. For U.S. Vice President Albert Gore, "the consequences of unrestrained exploitation" of the earth are now "every bit as unthinkable as the consequences of unrestrained nuclear war." *Earth in the Balance: Ecology and the Human Spirit* (Boston: Houghton Mifflin, 1992), p. 31. See also Richard A. Falk, *This Endangered Planet: Prospects and Proposals for Human Survival* (New York: Vintage, 1971), pp. 1–92.

7. Ruth Leger Sivart, *World Military and Social Expenditures* (Washington, D.C.: World Priorities, 1993), p. 44.

8. *Christian Science Monitor*, 22 Jan. 1988, 10.

9. Robert O. Keohane and Joseph S. Nye, *Power and Interdependence: World Politics in Transition* (Boston: Little, Brown, 1977). See also Robert O. Keohane, *After Hegemony: Cooperation and Discord in the World Political Economy* (Princeton: Princeton University Press, 1984).

10. Michael M. Gant and Norman R. Luttbeg, *American Electoral Behavior: 1952–1988* (Itasca, Ill.: Peacock, 1991), and Steven J. Rosenstone and John Mark Hansen, *Mobilization, Participation and Democracy in America* (New York: Macmillan, 1993).

11. William Shakespeare, *Romeo and Juliet*, act 2, scene 2, lines 43–44.

12. Claude Rivière, *Guinea: The Mobilization of a People*, trans. Virginia Thompson and Richard Adloff (Ithaca, N.Y.: Cornell University Press, 1977).

13. On the Soviet constitution, see Robert LeFevre, *Constitutional Government in Soviet Russia: The Constitution of the USSR* (New York: Exposition Press, 1962). On that of the Weimar Republic, see Herbert Kraus, *The Crisis of German Democracy: A Study of the Spirit of the Constitution of Weimar* (Princeton: Princeton University Press, 1932).

14. See, for example, Robert S. Alley, *School Prayer: The Court, the Congress, and the First Amendment* (Amherst, N.Y.: Prometheus, 1994).

15. Samuel H. Beer, *Modern Political Development* (Boston: Little, Brown, 1966), p. 25; Immanuel Wallerstein, *The Modern World System*, vols. 1 and 2 (New York: Academic Press, 1980).

16. Celestine Bohlen, "The Russian Vote: Nationalists Move Far Out in Front in Russian Voting," *New York Times*, 14 Dec. 1993, 1.

17. Ibid.

18. For further discussion of game theory as it relates to international politics, see Duncan Snidal, "The Game Theory of International Politics," *World Politics* 38, no. 1 (Oct. 1985): 25–57; and R. Harrison Wagner, "The Theory of Games and the Balance of Power," *World Politics* 38, no. 4 (July 1986): 546–76.

19. The concept of the political system has been most fully developed by David Easton in *A Framework for Political Analysis* (Englewood Cliffs, N.J.: Prentice Hall, 1965). See also his *An Analysis of Political Structure* (New York: Routledge, 1990). For another, more imaginative, use, see Karl W. Deutsch, *The Nerves of Government* (New York: Free Press, 1966).

20. David S. Geller, "The Impact of Political System Structure on Probability Patterns of Internal Disorder," *American Journal of Political Science* 31, no. 2 (May 1987): 217–33.

2 The Language of Politics

When an aspect of our experience interests us, we begin to develop language for talking about it. The words we choose are not important in themselves. We might decide to call the people who decide disputes "munchkins" or "sweethearts" instead of "judges." What is essential is that a name, once we settle on it, always refer to the same aspect of our experience. The *concept* is important—in this case, the idea that some people have the job of making authoritative decisions in disputes between other people.

Some names, as in the preceding example, refer to concepts or phenomena that we have little or no trouble recognizing. We can see them and touch them. We can confirm their existence *ad lapidum*—that is, in the same way we can confirm the existence of a stone, by looking at it, touching it, picking it up, or giving it a kick. (Most of these are not seriously recommended when verifying the existence of judges.) Other concepts are more difficult or even impossible to confirm through single sensory perceptions. We develop an awareness of what seems to us an important component of the nature of reality, and we pick what seems like a good name for it. That way we can at least talk about it and describe it more carefully. We may discover that we were wrong. The divine right of kings to rule, the unseen hand of the free market, and the biological inferiority of women and of nonwhite races are all examples of concepts that have been developed, explored, found inadequate, and abandoned by most social scientists.

The study of politics is rich with language about concepts. Some political scientists argue persuasively that our discipline is still too young for us to have achieved full agreement on the concepts we use and the language we employ. However, we do agree on the meanings of many important terms and are unanimously persuaded that these terms refer to phenomena that really do exist.[1] Such terms can be divided for convenience into three categories: those that name kinds of structures, those that name relationships of control, and those that name certain qualities of daily life that are subject to political determination. We cannot review all the accepted terms, but we will consider some of the more important examples in each category.

CONCEPTS THAT NAME STRUCTURES

As used in the social sciences, the word **structure** itself refers to a concept. It denotes a set of patterned role relationships. Any time human beings interact by adopting specific roles and carrying out those roles in a specific way, they have created a structure. Three structures that particularly interest political scientists are organizations, institutions, and states.

Organizations

An **organization** is a body of persons working together in a structured way to achieve a common purpose. In the case of a political organization, that purpose is political. Interest groups, political parties, candidates' campaign organizations, revolutionary movements, and even terrorist groups are examples of political organizations. Political organizations may be long lived or short lived, large or small, important or unimportant. Such seemingly nonpolitical organizations as flower clubs, hobby associations, and poetry reading groups may find themselves temporarily politicized under certain circumstances. If the park in which the city's finest chrysanthemums are grown is threatened by the extension of the freeway, the members of the flower club may find themselves devoting much of their time to lobbying the state legislature and engaging in various tactics to enlist public opinion on their side. Under these circumstances, the club will have become, for the time being, a political organization.

Institutions

When a structure becomes an institution, its activities are widely viewed as helping to meet one or more of the basic needs of a society. An **institution** is a structure with established, important functions to perform, well-specified roles for carrying out those functions; and a clear set of rules for governing the relationships between the people who occupy those roles. Organizations may be institutions, but not all are—and not all institutions are organizations. The members of an organization may have a common purpose, but they may not be viewed by society as having an important function; the people working through an institution may have a common and important function to perform, but they may not have a common purpose. A single political party is an organization; political parties, collectively, may or may not have the status of institutions in a given polity. If they are routinely expected to carry out such important functions as recruiting political leaders in a particular way, political parties in that system have achieved the status of institution.

Any given institution may be wholly or partly political, or absolutely nonpolitical. Courts, legislatures, civil services, and political parties are examples of wholly political institutions. Most institutions are at least partly political; when the occasion arises, they will engage as institutions in the political process. Many of the world's corporations, trade unions, and educational and religious institutions routinely commit a portion of their resources and attention to attempts to influence political decisions.

Institutions are important to political scientists because most significant political action takes place within and between institutions. This action is performed by individuals playing the roles assigned by their institutions, usually in accordance with the rules and established modes of procedure of those institutions. This is true whether we are speaking of the king of Norway or a crime syndicate's hit man. Role players *can* act contrary to the stated purposes and precepts of their institutions and can even do so with the full consent of their superiors. Political scientists have thus learned not to take written rules too literally.

It is also wrong to imagine all institutions as fixed, rigid, ossified structures. Effective institutions are the ones that can adapt successfully to changing conditions. The U.S. Supreme Court and the Catholic church are examples of institutions that maintain power by making some effective adaptations to changing conditions. The communist parties of eastern Europe that came tumbling down soon after the Berlin Wall are examples of institutions that did not. When the Argentine military junta that ruled from 1975 to 1983 refused to respond to popular demand for democratization and undertook instead to suppress opposition by torture and murder, to engage in an ill-fated venture to take the Falkland Islands back from Great Britain, and to pursue economic policies that produced an inflation rate of over 600 percent, it demonstrated that it was an institution incapable of adjusting effectively to change.[2] What about the British monarchy? Is this an institution that is failing, given recent scandal and disasters plus the growing public awareness not only of these deficiencies but also of the high cost to them of maintaining an institution the citizens of so many other nations find, at best, amusingly archaic?

States

A **state** is a structure that has the legal right to make rules that are binding over a given population within a given territory. As such, it has geographic as well as political characteristics. A state is a political institution, but it differs from other political institutions in having **sovereignty**—that is, it has the power to make decisions that cannot be overruled by any other body. This definition may seem reasonable and clear enough, but in practice the term *state* is often very ambiguous. There is no better example of this ambiguity than the practice of referring to the constituent units of the federal system of government in the United States as *states*. These units were never *sovereign states*—although some of them nearly met the conditions of that definition in the few years between the Declaration of Independence and the adoption of the present Constitution.

Other problems with the concept emerge when we consider states with constitutions that specifically allow for the contingency of ceding some of the nation's decision-making power to a supernational body. The constitutions of the African states of Ghana and Guinea had such clauses when those states first achieved independence, because it was hoped that a larger African state would be formed in the near future. The Organization of African Unity was formed in 1963, but it is not a state and does not require its member states to cede any measure of their sovereignty as a condition for joining.[3] On the other hand, the European Community has evolved to the point where it now routinely expects its interdependent member states to obey its collective decisions in matters reaching far beyond simple economic pacts. Most of the member states' constitutions do not allow for this infringement on the sovereignty of the state, but their silence on the matter does not make the change any less real. The French, who are perhaps slightly more likely than other peoples to insist on a rational match between what they say and what they do, added an appropriate sovereignty-ceding amendment to their constitution before voting to ratify the European Community's Treaty of Maastricht in 1992.[4]

Finally, certain geographical entities are states only by legal definition and international courtesy. Lesotho, Monaco, and Panama are "states" that remained under the nearly absolute power of a neighboring or surrounding state long after achieving legal independence. What is the true status of the ex-Soviet republics of Eurasia: Armenia, Azerbaijan, Belarus, Georgia, Kazakhstan, Kyrgyzstan, Moldova, Tajikistan, Turkmenistan, the Ukraine, and Uzbekistan?[5] Do the Baltic states of Estonia, Latvia, and Lithuania have the resources to practice the absolute independence they so boldly claimed when the Soviet Union collapsed?

Nevertheless, whatever answer we give these difficult questions and however remote political practice may sometimes appear to be from theory, the study of international relations and of the interdependence of the various units that make up the human polity seems impossible without recourse to the concept of the state.

CONCEPTUALIZING RELATIONSHIPS OF CONTROL

Engaging in politics means engaging in efforts to control the acts of others. Many of the key concepts of political science have to do with relationships of control. Here we briefly consider four: power, influence, authority, and legitimacy.

Power

We are usually ready to endorse such glib comments as "Power is the very heart of politics." In fact, however, the concept of **power** is one of the most difficult to define. Robert Dahl has pointed out three common fallacies in the analysis of power. The "lump-of-power" fallacy is the mistaken assumption that power comes in lump sums and cannot be shared, so all one needs to ask is Who's in charge? "Confounding power with resources" is what we do when we take literally such aphorisms as "Money is power." Money may be a resource on which power rests, but the two are different entities. Finally, "confounding power with rewards and deprivations" happens if we look beyond the powerful act to its ultimate consequences for the people it has been exercised for or against. One consequence of a law calling for lower defense expenditures may mean fewer jobs in California, but "reducing the number of jobs" is *not* power.[6]

What, then, *is* power? Dahl suggests that power means getting others to comply "by creating the prospect of severe sanctions for noncompliance."[7] He quotes Harold Lasswell and Abraham Kaplan to the same effect. "It is the threat of sanctions which differentiates power from influence in general. Power is a special case of the exercise of influence: it is the process of affecting policies of others with the help of (actual or threatened) severe deprivations for nonconformity with the policies intended."[8] When Adolf Hitler forced significant changes in the foreign policy of the British prime minister Neville Chamberlain by making clear the devastation he was prepared to wreak, that was power. When President Franklin Roosevelt persuaded the U.S. Supreme Court to stop declaring New Deal legislation unconstitutional, by threatening to induce Congress to increase the number of justices so he could "pack" the Court with fellow liberals, that was power.

Thus defined, power involves two parties and two steps. In the first step, party A threatens unpleasant consequences if party B acts or does not act thus and so. In the second step, party B acts as party A wishes *because* party A has made the specified threat. It is a relationship of control. Sometimes the power relationship is interestingly reciprocal. The 1995 decisions of the British to withdraw troops from Northern Ireland and of the Irish Republican Army to end its acts of

"At least we always know who's in charge around here."

guerrilla warfare were clearly both made in partial response to the continued "deprivations" the other had threatened and imposed.

Dahl's formulation seems to place chief emphasis on the *threat* of sanctions; although Lasswell and Kaplan mention *actual* deprivations, Dahl himself does not. In today's world, however, power is all too frequently achieved only when threats have been carried out. Iraq withdrew from Kuwait in 1991 only after the Gulf War had taken some 100,000 Iraqi lives. Both the British Army and the Irish Republican Army carried out many murderous threats against one another before making mutual concessions to the other's power. And most commentators on the war in the Balkans believe that a major reason it became such a long, drawn-out, and bloody affair was that so often the threats made by the United States, by the North Atlantic Treaty Organization, by the European Community, and by the United Nations either were not carried out or were carried out with such minor damages that neither Serbs nor Bosnians, Christians nor Muslims found the sanctions sufficiently compelling. Not every leader or nation yields to even the most believable threats; if in doubt, consider the fierce resistance so long waged by the fighters for Chechyen independence inside the boundaries of contemporary Russia. Nor does agreement reached after threats of violence have been carried out always endure, as the cases of Ireland and the Middle East have made clear.[9]

Influence

Whether exercised by threat or use of force, power is a limited method, one that cannot be used effectively in all relationships. Political scientists have lately been giving more attention to a broader relationship of control: **influence**. Again following Dahl, we can say that influence includes all cases when one party's desires affect the behavior of another party. As just noted, power is a form of influence. But influence can take place without the threat of sanctions or use of force, as well as without the promise of personal rewards. The neoconservative economists whose arguments lent scholarly credence to the policies of Britain's former prime minister Margaret Thatcher exercised influence in that government, as did their counterparts during the presidency of Ronald Reagan in the United States. The articulate witness who persuades a committee of the U.S. Congress to support (or not support) a proposed bill authorizing increased arms exports to a Latin American dictatorship about to be tumbled from power by revolutionary insurrection is exercising influence. The Islamic religious leaders known as marabouts who convince the president of the West African state of Senegal that they can increase his popularity by supporting him, and who promise to do so as long as he does not depart from the moderate policies of his predecessor, are men of influence.

Where does influence come from? Why do some people have the form of influence we call power? As we can deduce from the preceding examples, influence over political decisions is not confined to public officials. This is true even of power. Organized groups of voters can make threats (such as refusing to help with campaign costs) that have the effect of changing policy; revolutionary or terrorist movements can succeed in changing the allocation of resources by their threats of continued violence.

Differences in capacity to influence public policy can be traced to a wide range of factors. More money, more information, more friends, more skill in the art of persuasion, more weapons, better organization, a better job, better means of communication, and stronger motivation are all attributes that—depending on other circumstances—can give one person more influence over public policy than others who are less well endowed. One important resource for the exercise of influence is *not* on this list, however, and that is the occupancy of public office. Public office is, after all, the proper home of political decisions. If one occupies a public office, one is authorized to make certain political decisions. One has authority.

Authority

Authority is the right to exercise the power and influence of a given position that comes from having been placed in that position according to regular, known, and widely accepted procedures. We sometimes speak of "the authorities" as if they were remote figures, self-created, hopelessly beyond our reach. It is a misuse of language, however, to confuse those who usurp political power by means of force or trickery with those who have obtained such power by accepted means. In a democratic system, accepted means are normally either elections or appointments by elected officials. Citizens in such a system who are not content with the performance of "the authorities" have means of redress that go considerably beyond angry expostulation about remote figures of power. If enough of them agree, they can throw the rascals out.

The means of acquiring authority vary greatly. An Indian president must be elected by an electoral college consisting of the elected members of the Indian Parliament and the state legislatures, by means of a complicated system of weighted voting.[10] A Japanese prime minister must win the approval of the leaders of all factions of the party that wins the most seats in the Diet, Japan's legislative body.[11] An Australian aboriginal headman comes to his office through traditional paths of kinship.[12] A French judge must have studied for and passed a competitive exam; only those who do best will receive appointments from the Ministry of Justice.[13]

A sign that significant change is taking place in any country is a shift in the rules for authorizing access to political power. The declaration of American revolutionaries that British agents had no authority to collect taxes from subjects who were not represented in British decision-making processes initiated a set of changes leading to the formation of a new nation. Some older inhabitants of the African continent have witnessed an amazing series of changes in the procedures for authorizing leadership. The precondition for attaining the right to rule in many parts of Africa has shifted over the past century from (1) place in the kinship lineage to (2) position as representative of foreign conquerors to (3) good behavior as "native administrator" (the title given African chiefs willing to serve as agents of colonial rule) to (4) "reasonableness" and "representativeness" (when leadership shifted to Africans who represented key groups that were willing to make the transition to independence on colonial terms) to (5) number of votes (in the early days of independence) to (6) having the backing of armed strength (as the first military coups took place and/or personal dictatorships were established), and back again to (7) number of votes (when the military returned power to civilian hands or other leaders, keen to reduce corruption and improve the nation's eligibility for foreign aid, forced the dictators out of office, and reestablished democratic elections).[14]

Legitimacy
Legitimacy means having the approval of others. It is the condition of being regarded as correctly placed in a particular role and as carrying out the functions of that role correctly (whether or not one is actually doing so). **Political legitimacy** means having widespread approval for the way one exercises political power. Under normal circumstances, authority gives legitimacy to power; it is possible, however, to have authority but lack legitimacy. If a president is seen as failing to take adequate steps to resolve an economic crisis, such as a wildly fluctuating financial market or a seemingly unending recession, he or she may lose legitimacy without losing authority. The authority to rule and the power to rule legitimately may rest in different hands. If a king is insane, a grateful people may permit the

cardinal to rule and grant his orders legitimacy. In some circumstances, no duly constituted authority may be able to take charge when leadership is required. Isolated survivors of catastrophes accept as legitimate the orders of someone whose directions make sense and save lives; they will worry later about who should be "authorized" to take charge of the little polity they may be forced to create.

Standards of legitimacy do not always change with standards for achieving authority. When communist political systems were established in the nations of eastern Europe, the new rulers placed strong emphasis on single-party rule, centralized at the top. As long as they remained in power, gaining a position of authority was possible only by working through that single party and receiving its approval for one's candidacy, which would then be uncontested in the pro forma election that followed. The new rulers also worked hard to change their nations' standards of legitimacy, stressing the importance of reducing ethnic rivalries and eliminating organized religion (which had often played a powerful role in the earlier political systems). To all appearances, their efforts were successful, or largely so. Yet as soon as the communist systems began to crumble and fall, both ethnic identity and religious guidance resumed their former function as legitimizing agencies. In postcommunist states, the various peoples who originally formed these polities are now once again granting legitimacy on the basis of answers to the age-old questions: Is this leader one of ours? Does he or she come from the same ethnic group and have the same religious faith? In the former Yugoslavia, the answers to these questions have assumed such overriding importance that hundreds of thousands of lives have been lost when the answer seemed "wrong" and the questioners have had the armed might to insist on *their* standards of legitimacy.[15]

In any case, the distinction between legitimacy and authority is an important one to keep in mind. When the exhortation "Question authority!" is widely uttered and widely followed, existing authorities are in danger of losing their legitimacy. When the people authorized to rule lose legitimacy, the chances are good that an attempt will be made to replace them with others; if a change in the basis of authority is required to replace the people who have authority, that change may well be made. On such foundations do revolutions rise.

POLITICAL CONCEPTS REGARDING THE QUALITY OF LIFE

Politics is a fascinating subject in and of itself, but the reason most of us care enough about politics to study it is both more personal and more global. We are well aware that the quality of the life we lead together is strongly influenced by the quality of our politics. We rely heavily on political processes to organize our interactions with one another. We know we need one another to live and prosper, but we do not always find that aspect of the human condition entirely satisfactory. Three questions in particular are likely to concern us here: How different are we, or should we be, from one another? How free from control by one another are we, or should we be? How peaceful, stable, and orderly can we make our interactions with one another?

Puzzling over these questions has given rise to the concepts of equality, freedom, and order. Although these terms refer to qualities of daily life that, in practice, are inextricably meshed, I will endeavor here to treat them one by one. (My purpose is simply to explore what aspect of reality each of these words denotes. The ways different forms of government endeavor to cope with the problems they pose is considered in Chapter 3.)

Equality

Contemporary political systems nearly all give at least lip service to some version of the happy thought that all men are created equal. Some even go so far as to include women in this blessing. Rational observers may protest that there are obvious differences, from birth, in the physical and intellectual abilities of human beings. However, most of us are willing to grant that there are important ways in which we all *are* created equal, if we focus not on our abilities but our needs. All

Slums and high-rise housing in Caracas, Venezuela. Such inequities in status and prosperity are met throughout the world.

(Peter Menzel/Stock Boston)

of us need shelter, food, sleep, safety, various forms of social responsiveness (love, sex, affection, kindness, respect), and interesting activity. We may even agree that this fundamental **equality** in neediness is more important in determining the role of government than innate or acquired differences in abilities.[16]

Political equality means an equal right to participate in the political process and to be treated fairly by it. When Oliver Cromwell's momentarily victorious troops sat around the campfire on the fields of Putney during the English Civil War debating the order of the future society they intended to establish, one eloquent soul argued for political equality (as opposed to basing the right to vote on the possession of property) on the grounds that government affects everyone. "Verily," he said, "I do believe that the poorest he that is in England hath a life to live as the richest he."[17] In the seventeenth century such a notion was nothing short of radical, and in the twentieth century its implications are still not accepted everywhere. The right to vote and to hold office is hemmed in with numerous restrictions, and equal treatment under the law is routinely denied women, children, aliens, and racial and religious minorities in various parts of the world.

Social equality is the right to be treated as a social equal, at least with respect to one's basic characteristics and needs. When governments attempt to outlaw discrimination in housing, jobs, and education on the basis of race, religion, or sex, they are asserting that such differences do not make some persons more socially worthy than others. Constitutional provisions that forbid governments to grant titles of nobility, laws that establish egalitarian standards of salutation ("citizen," "comrade"), and judicial rulings that limit the right of private associations to grant or deny membership privileges are all motivated by the belief that government has a role to play in ensuring that if we cannot all be truly equal socially, our differences of rank will nevertheless not be permitted to extend to painful extremes.

Are governments properly concerned with fostering **economic equality**—that is, with ensuring that every citizen has approximately the same amount of material goods? That controversial question is often sidestepped by arguing that government is responsible only to provide equality of opportunity in the economic domain—that the goal of economic equality is sufficiently served when government sees to it that opportunities to get the necessary training and education are equal and that there are enough jobs for everyone. After that, goes the argument, natural and acquired inequalities in ability should be allowed to have whatever effect they may in producing unequal economic rewards. Others argue that such an approach will never eliminate the suffering of the poor and that governments must assume a greater role by carrying out rigorous tax, land redistribution, or other policies designed to limit the growth of private fortunes.

Freedom

It is impossible to determine what government's role should be in ensuring any form of equality without confronting the concept of **freedom**. Any political measures taken to make us more equal are likely to make us both more and less free: more free to pursue some measure of happiness, less free to disregard the welfare of others while pursuing our happiness. But what is freedom? The Old English word *freo*, from which the word *freedom* comes, meant "not in bondage, noble, glad, illustrious." Even today the word carries a connotation of pride, of a sense of personal accomplishment in the fact of not being in bondage. Thus *freedom* means something more than *liberty*, which suggests simply the absence of constraint. In practice, however, the two terms are often used interchangeably.

There is general agreement today that it is the responsibility of all governments to keep their citizens free, in the sense of "out of bondage." At the same time, most people would agree that there are times when governments must limit individual liberty. The question is Where shall the line be drawn? No one has argued more eloquently for maximizing individual freedom than John Stuart Mill, whose nineteenth-century essay *On Liberty* provides the classic defense of liberty as the guarantor of human progress. Only when men and women are free to explore and propound any idea they wish can there be a hope of discovering truth, said Mill, for only in the struggle against error can truth emerge. He went so far as to regret the "universal recognition" of any particular truth, because there is no better "aid to the intelligent and living apprehension of a truth [than] is afforded by the necessity of explaining it to, or defending it against, opponents."[18] Mill was also keenly aware of the threat posed to liberty by what seemed to him to be an excessive concern with political equality. If all are given an equal vote, politicians will simply comply with the will of the majority, however uninformed or misguided that will might be. There "ceases to be any social support for nonconformity."[19] According to Mill, "Eccentricity has always abounded when and where strength of character has abounded; and the amount of eccentricity in a society has generally been proportional to the amount of genius, mental vigor, and moral courage which it contained. That so few now dare to be eccentric, marks the chief danger of the time."[20]

Like equality, freedom comes in various forms. Political freedom means the freedom to dissent without fear of punishment. Social freedom means the freedom to behave as one wishes. Economic freedom means the freedom to acquire and dispose of one's personal wealth without hindrance. None of these freedoms is absolute in any land, but the extent to which each is protected varies enormously from nation to nation and from time to time. It is an unending debate, one that often pits one kind of freedom against another, and different nations arrive at different resolutions. Governments in underdeveloped nations are sometimes so determined to maintain political stability that they use brutal means to stifle the free expression of ideas while encouraging a shift to greater economic freedom at the same time in order to stimulate the livelier competitiveness essential for joining a capitalistic global economy. In a series of military governments, contemporary Nigeria allowed crop prices to be determined by the market (abolishing price-fixing commodity boards), reduced the number of commodities requiring import licenses from seventy-four to sixteen, deregulated the banking system and foreign exchange market, and set up a privatization committee to sell off state-owned enterprises. But it also banned all political parties and any political assembly, severely restricted freedom of the press, and did nothing at all about the fact that women do not receive equal pay for equal work, are often denied commercial credit, and receive less than one-third the education given to men. Some European polities, on the other hand, prefer limiting economic freedoms to ensure that the gap between rich and poor does not become too great, while taking freedom of expression, even for the most "dangerous" opinions, absolutely for granted.[21] How would you characterize your own nation in this regard?

Order

The problem of balancing government's responsibility to aid the needy with its responsibility to protect individual freedom is compounded by our need for order and stability. As we saw in Chapter 1, our life as a social, interacting species requires us to organize our relationships with one another, to create **order** out of chaos, and to develop some ability to predict what will happen next. Order is essential, yet it is often difficult to establish without sacrificing other desired conditions.

Consider, for example, the fact that one way order is achieved is through the division of labor; certain persons are authorized to perform certain functions. Inevitably, some functions prove more essential than others to the collective good, and it is likely that those functions will come to be better rewarded than others, which means the loss of whatever socioeconomic equality may have existed. A hierarchy of jobs evolves, including the job (usually at or near the top) of making decisions binding throughout the society—that is, the job of political leadership. Creating this job inevitably means creating institutions of government, which, aside from their more positive functions, provide the means by which those leaders, if left unchecked and so inclined, can suppress their subjects' most cherished personal freedoms. The quest for order seems inevitably to impede the quests for equality and freedom.

As should be apparent by now, the ten concepts we have examined are strongly interconnected, and it is often difficult to discuss one without entering into a discussion of the others. These ten are, of course, only a fraction of the total number of concepts with which political scientists routinely deal. Here I have provided the beginning of an initiation into the language of political science. Throughout the rest of this book, other terms and concepts are introduced as they are needed. But as you can see, the language of political science is not difficult. Most of the terms are already familiar to you, and others are explained as we go along. When in doubt, consult the Glossary at the end of the book.

SUMMARY AND CONCLUSION

Political scientists commonly use three kinds of concepts in their work: those that name kinds of structures, those that name relationships of control, and those that name certain qualities of daily life that are subject to political determination.

Concepts that name structures include organizations, institutions, and states. An organization is a body of persons working together in a structured way to achieve a specific purpose. An institution is a structure with established functions to perform, roles for carrying out those functions, and rules for how to do so. A state is a structure that has the legal right to make rules that are binding over a given population within a given territory.

Concepts that name relationships of control include power, influence, authority, and legitimacy. Power is a relationship in which control is achieved by threatening and sometimes carrying out severe sanctions for noncompliance with the power holders' wishes. Influence is a broader form of control: It includes the exercise of power but it also includes persuasion without the threat of sanctions or the use of force; it includes all cases when one party's desires affect the behavior of another party. Authority is the right to exercise the power and influence of a given position that comes from having been placed in that position according to accepted procedures. Legitimacy is the condition of being regarded as correctly placed in a particular role and as carrying out the functions of that role correctly.

Political concepts regarding the quality of life include equality, freedom, and order. Political equality means an equal right to participate in the political process and to be treated fairly by it. Political freedom means the freedom to dissent without fear of punishment. Political order is the organization of our relationships with one another within a polity. The efforts made to achieve equality, freedom, and order often conflict with one another.

Selected Readings

Beetham, David. *The Legitimation of Power.* Atlantic Highlands, N.J.: Humanities Press International, 1991. An introductory discussion of the concept of legitimacy in contemporary politics.

Bourdieu, Pierre. *Language and Symbolic Power.* Cambridge: Harvard University Press, 1991. A collection of the writings of a noted French sociologist on politics, language, and discourse.

Connolly, William E. *The Terms of Political Discourse.* Princeton: Princeton University Press, 1993. A study of political concepts such as freedom and interests.

Freeden, Michael. *Rights.* Minneapolis: University of Minnesota Press, 1995. An examination of the evolution of the concept of rights in relation to politics.

Green, David. *The Language of Politics in America: Shaping Political Consciousness from McKinley to Reagan.* Ithaca, N.Y.: Cornell University Press, 1992. A historical study of the effects of political language on U.S. politics.

Laski, Harold J. *A Grammar of Politics.* London: Allen and Unwin, 1925. A classic study, dated but still informative, on the meaning and use of political terms.

Safire, William. *Safire's New Political Dictionary: The Definitive Guide to the New Language of Politics.* New York: Random House, 1993. A guide to the meaning and use of political words.

Shafritz, Jay M., Phil William, and Ronald S. Calinger. *The Dictionary of Twentieth Century World Politics.* New York: Holt, 1993. A useful reference for information on modern political terminology.

Sowell, Thomas. *A Conflict of Visions.* New York: William Morrow, 1987. A discussion of how concepts such as freedom and equality are viewed differently depending on whether one has a constrained vision (in which case one sees these rights in terms of *process*) or an unconstrained vision (in which case one looks for *results*).

Notes

1. In 1981, however, Ralph Goldman, Philip G. Schoner, and DeVere E. Pentony developed *The Political Science Concept Inventory* (Oxford: Clio, 1981), which lists 21,927 terms used in political science, of which 1,075 are considered terms that "undergraduate majors in political science should know well." Most of these 1,075 terms will be used in this book. Many (e.g., "Industrial Revolution," "American Bill of Rights," "veto") will already be familiar to most readers. For a more recent work on the concepts of our discipline, see Andrew Heywood, *Political Ideas and Concepts: An Introduction* (New York: St. Martin's, 1992).
2. When failure continues, the institution almost always falls: the members of the Argentine junta disbanded in December 1983. *New York Times*, 11 Dec. 1983, 1.
3. Jan Woronoff, *Organizing African Unity* (Metuchen, N.J.: Scarecrow Press, 1970).
4. William Drozdiak, "French Parliament Votes Europe Changes," *Washington Post*, 24 June 1992, p. 23.
5. Gregory W. Gleason and Susan J. Buck, "Decolonization in the Former Soviet Borderlands: Politics in Search of Principles," *PS: Political Science and Politics* (Sept. 1993): 522–25.
6. Robert A. Dahl, *Modern Political Analysis*, 4th ed. (Englewood Cliffs, N.J.: Prentice Hall, 1984), pp. 20–22.
7. Ibid., p. 41.
8. Harold Lasswell and Abraham Kaplan, *Power and Society: A Framework for Political Inquiry* (New Haven: Yale University Press, 1950), p. 76, quoted in Dahl, *Analysis*, p. 47, n. 5.
9. For the argument regarding the Balkans, see *Wall Street Journal*, 28 July 1995, A1, A4. For the return to violence in Ireland, see *New York Times*, 9 Mar. 1996, 3.
10. Weighted voting means giving more votes to certain groups or official bodies than to others. On the Indian political system, see Zoya Hasan, S. N. Jha, and Rasheeduddin Khan, *The State, Political Processes and Identity: Reflections on Modern India* (New Delhi: Sage, 1989).
11. Percy R. Luney Jr. and Kazuyuki Takahashi, *Japanese Constitutional Law* (Tokyo: University of Tokyo Press, 1993).
12. M. J. Meggitt, "Indigenous Forms of Government among the Australian Aborigines," *Tot De Tall-, Land-en Volkenkunde* 6, no. 120 (1964): 163–80.
13. Mary L. Volcansek and Jacqueline Lucienne Lafon, *Judicial Selection: The Cross-Evolution of French and Amerian Practices* (New York: Greenwood Press, 1988), p. 110.
14. The European conquest of some African peoples was completed as late as 1911. See Robert I. Rotberg, *A Political History of Tropical Africa* (New York: Harcourt, Brace and World, 1965), p. 258. For an interesting fictionalized view of the relationship between authority and legitimacy, see Chinua Achebe, *A Man of the People* (Garden City, N.Y.: Anchor Books, 1967).
15. Robin Alison Remington examines the role played by rising nationalisms in contemporary Bosnia in "Bosnia: The Tangled Web," *Current History* 92, no. 577 (Nov. 1993): 364–69.

16. Abraham A. Maslow identifies a "hierarchy of needs" in *Motivation and Personality* (New York: Harper and Row, 1954), pp. 35–58.
17. C. H. Firth, ed., *The Clarke Papers: Selections from Papers of William Clarke*, vol. 1 (Westminster, England: Nicholos and Sons, 1891), p. 301.
18. John Stuart Mill, *On Liberty* (New York: Appleton-Century-Crofts, 1947), p. 43.
19. Ibid., p. 74.
20. Ibid., p. 67.
21. "Nigeria: Anybody Seen a Giant?" in "Nigeria Survey," *The Economist* (21 Aug. 1993): 6–7; and Adrian Karatnycky, *Freedom in the World: The Annual Survey of Political Rights and Civil Liberties* (New York: Freedom House, 1994), pp. 434–37.

3 Political Ideologies

Sometimes the political questions we ask ourselves are explicit and specific. What is our government's role in providing free education? What domestic as well as foreign policy goals were served when the United States undertook to put the Jean Aristide government back in power in Haiti in 1994? How did the victory of Jacques Chirac in the 1995 French presidential election affect the power relationships between parliament and the presidency in the French system of government? Sometimes, however, we find ourselves thinking about politics in much broader terms, asking much more fundamental and far-reaching questions. Why has our political system taken the form it has? What would be the ideal political system? Would the ideal system be ideal for all peoples or just for us? How could an ideal system be established?

When we try to find answers to these more fundamental questions, we are involved in an age-old quest, the search for a system of political beliefs. If we are concerned enough to do a little research, we will find a few well-formulated ideologies from which to choose, such as conservatism, liberalism, and socialism. If we are looking for something radically different from the status quo, we may explore the tenets of some of the more extreme ideologies, such as fascism or a branch of religious fundamentalism. Or perhaps the insights of contemporary feminism will seem to cover more of the problems we must deal with today—or the passions of ethnic nationalism will strike us as more relevant than any more comprehensive world view. Some of us will shop around, picking up an idea that makes sense here, another that seems exciting there, and gradually piece together a more or less coherent but still very personal view of political reality and possibilities. Not all of us will become *ideologues*.

WHAT IS AN IDEOLOGY?

Ideology is a word with almost as many definitions as there are people using the term. Most scholars would agree that an ideology attempts to offer answers to at least the first two questions just cited: Why have our political systems taken the form they have, and what would be the ideal political system? Beyond this, there is little consensus. Some scholars argue that an ideology must be "accepted as fact or truth by some group," but others believe individuals can have personal ideologies, unshared and unadvertised.[1] Some think an ideology always claims "a monopoly of truth" and thus seeks to "explain everything and in so doing [will] refuse to tolerate rival views or opposing theories," whereas others believe most ideologies leave room for some opposition and point out that in fact a key component of liberalism is its insistence on the importance of the open competition of points of view.[2] Some think an ideology must be revolutionary to merit the name: "The ideologue is a revolutionary, dedicated to the overthrow of the existing system and concerned above all with the means by which this can be accomplished."[3] Others suggest that it is possible for an ideology to be simply a defense of the status quo (in which case its doctrine presumably suggests that the answers to the first and second questions are one and the same and that the other questions are without interest).

A little empirical work suggests that in each of these various controversies "others" are right. Individuals do develop personal, idiosyncratic ideologies; listen to any talk show for an hour or so if you are in doubt. Most ideologies are not entirely closed systems of thought, nor do their supporters claim they are—the very multiplicity of meanings we give to the words *conservative*, *liberal*, and *socialist* testifies to how far from closed these three dominant ideologies have been.

Similarly, not all ideologies preach revolution. Once a socialist system has been established, socialist ideologues can become strong defenders of the status quo—and of course the chief object of conservatism can be to make sure that nothing changes. (On the other hand, even conservatives can be change oriented when the present system appears unsatisfactory to them and their goal is to establish a more orderly political system.)

Saying that an ideology can be personal or shared with a group, open or closed, and revolutionary or defensive is all well and good, but it does not give us our own working definition; it simply tells us what to leave out of that definition. Let us approach the problem more assertively: an **ideology** is a comprehensive set of beliefs and attitudes about social and economic institutions and processes. It offers a critique of the existing system and a view of the ideal system. Where these differ, it suggests the means for moving from the existing to the ideal. It also presents a theory of human nature and, thereby, of human potentiality and of the need for particular modes of social control.

These various characteristics of all ideologies become clearer as we discuss specific examples. But before we proceed, note the word that is missing from the preceding paragraph: *political*. All ideologies that merit the name deal extensively with political questions; all ideologies are, in some sense, political ideologies. But not all ideologies are predominantly political ideologies. Because they are comprehensive systems of beliefs and attitudes, they usually have as much to say about economic and social relationships as they do about matters purely political—or even more. When we talk about *political ideologies*, we usually mean that we are stressing the political aspects of ideologies. In the discussion that follows we look at the political tenets of five systems of belief. We consider some economic and social factors taken up in each of these, but keep in mind that our focus is political and that the range of each ideology considered is far wider than the focus of this discussion permits us to show.

The most important ideas incorporated in the systems of belief that we examine are ideas that were conceived long ago. Most of them have been on the philosophic agenda ever since men and women first began to consider whether the system under which they lived was necessarily the best of all possible systems. On the other hand, political *ideologies* as we know them today did not fully emerge until relatively recent times. The major economic and social upheavals of the past three hundred years have both forced and enabled more of us to take the questions of ideology seriously and to seek new hope in the promise these systems of thought hold for creating a better world.

The ideologies that have evolved thus far in the course of human affairs have not all shown equal concern for the question that provides the theme of this book, global interdependence, and the conflict among their followers has often been a major cause of global conflict. Nevertheless, most of them have something to say about what the relationship between polities should be. Indeed, their approaches to this problem reveal some of the most intriguing and significant differences among them, as I try to make clear in what follows.

Conservatism

Conservatism is well named. The conservative believes first and foremost in conserving what exists, in the idea that "the accumulated wisdom and experience of the countless generations gone is more likely to be right than the passing fashion of the moment."[4] Thus, conservatives have a certain bias in favor of the existing political system. If change is needed, it should be approached very cautiously: "Man's hopes are high, but his vision is short. Efforts to remedy existing evils usually result in even greater ones."[5]

The conservative view of human nature is not entirely positive and is definitely nonegalitarian. Conservatives believe that some people contribute more than others to society and should therefore be more honored by society.[6] One such honor is the right to positions of political authority. If ordinary people are given the power to rule themselves, they are likely to be intolerant of anyone who does not fit the common mold and to sacrifice the protection of minority rights in order to ensure majority rule.[7] Personal liberty is the individual right conservatives hold most dear, but this does not mean that everyone must be left to pursue his or her own interests with no restraint: "The result will be self-indulgence, anarchy, and a turn toward totalitarianism."[8] It makes sense to use the power of government to support traditional moral standards, because "genuinely ordered freedom is the only sort of liberty worth having: freedom made possible by order within the soul and order within the state."[9] But the individual must not, in "the mindless assertion of appetite," depend on the state for security; to do so is to abdicate to the power of the state, to become part of a mass society, and to risk falling prey to tyranny. Self-determination means, on the contrary, "achieving the appropriate fit between personal character and the society's institutional requirements."[10]

Conservatives are divided on the question of international interdependence. Respect for the past and for established institutions, combined with the belief that each nation is an organic whole in which everyone has a place and function, leads naturally to a strong sense of patriotism, if not outright nationalism.[11] Some conservatives do tend to see other nations as threatening the values, confidence, or security of their own land and are likely to place greater trust in military might and action than in seemingly endless diplomatic negotiation.

At the same time, however, conservatives do not entirely deny the fact of interdependence. The staunch defense of imperialist ventures that European conservatives have advanced has traditionally been based on their assertion of the responsibility of the more advanced nations to bring the blessings of civilization to those less fortunate. This view emphasizes the dependence of others rather than interdependence, but most contemporary conservatives are willing to go a step further. The need to defend one's own system against external enemies makes it desirable to have external friends. It is important to give aid and comfort to allies, to keep them as allies, and to prevent them from becoming the friends of one's enemies.

Conservatives are sometimes viewed by others as unbending and incapable of compromise, but on many matters they show themselves to be far less dogmatic than supporters of other ideologies. They do not, for example, specify particular institutional forms of government as necessarily better than others, nor do they believe that those who rule must follow a consistent program of domestic and foreign policy. For the conservative, it is far more important that the basic principles of conservatism (order, continuity, loyalty, protection of individual freedoms, piety, and nationalism) be maintained and that those who rule exercise practical wisdom in ensuring that they are. In that sense, conservatives are among the most pragmatic of political thinkers. Andrew Heywood goes so far as to say

BOX 3.1   HOW THE WORD *LIBERAL* CAME TO HAVE OPPOSITE MEANINGS IN THE UNITED STATES AND EUROPE

Classical liberalism says government must "help" the unfortunate and yet must also "protect freedom."

Some early liberals placed the emphasis on freedom, especially the freedom of the market and gave less attention to helping the poor. Contemporary European liberals have followed this tradition.

Other early liberals placed the emphasis on helping and saw protecting freedom more as a matter of protecting individual liberties of speech and association. Contemporary American liberals have followed this tradition.

Contemporary Americans who place great emphasis on the freedom of the market think of themselves as conservatives. Because they disagree with contemporary Americans who call themselves liberals, they never think of themselves as liberals at all. Nevertheless, Europeans call this kind of conservative a liberal. And Americans call the European kind of liberal a conservative.

Now is that perfectly clear?

Source: Kay Lawson, *The Human Polity,* 4th ed. (Boston: Houghton Mifflin, 1997). Reprinted by permission.

that "conservatism is the most intellectually modest of political ideologies. . . . [It] has prospered because it has been unwilling to be tied down to a fixed system of ideas."[12]

Liberalism

The chief difference between conservatism and **liberalism** is the view each takes of human nature. Where the conservative is at best cautiously hopeful that the ordinary person will, in a well-ordered state, manifest the admirable characteristics of loyalty, patriotism, and piety, the liberal takes a much more egalitarian view. The liberal believes that human beings—all human beings—are capable of reason and rational action but that they are often caught in difficult situations in real life. People are not born equal, but everyone has the capacity to live a satisfactory and productive life if given the chance. An essential role of government is to ensure that all citizens have the opportunity to develop their skills and abilities, whatever they may be.[13] This view of human nature virtually guarantees that the liberal will be optimistic about the possibility of improving a particular political system and will expect the ordinary citizen to play an important role in bringing about such an improvement. The liberal is seldom a revolutionary, however, and never imagines that progress is inevitable. Given the positive attributes of human nature, it is worthwhile to try, but the outcome is uncertain.

Furthermore, progress cannot and should not be forced on an unwilling populace. The responsibility of people in power is to make it possible for all men and women to exercise reason, work for a better life, and make their own important choices. The liberal hopes that their choices will be wise, but individual liberty includes the right to make choices that work against one's own interests.

Liberalism, as may begin to be clear, is a difficult and sometimes ambiguous creed. It suggests that government should intervene to "help" but never to "curb freedom." In practice, it is often difficult to accomplish one without the other. Liberalism says that ordinary men and women are entitled to satisfactory lives but that individual liberties, including the right to prosper from one's efforts, should not be curtailed. This same ambivalence is apparent in the liberal approach to the question of interdependence, both among individuals and among nations. People and polities are interdependent and must show a humane concern for one another, but at the same time the individual person or state has the right to pursue individual interests. When these goals conflict, liberals (like conservatives) are content to look for pragmatic solutions according to the circumstances rather than to spell out one specific way to establish the ideal social system.

Socialism

For socialists, the most important characteristic of human nature is each individual's natural sociability. Socialists believe that human beings readily engage in co-operative social activity when given a chance. Unfortunately, some individuals have selfishly established structures of control that make it impossible for this natural cooperative instinct to flourish. These structures have become progressively more oppressive, causing ever greater human suffering. The ideology of **socialism** evolved out of concern for the suffering caused by human exploitation of other humans.

Socialists have traditionally been critical of existing social systems, certain that better systems could be established and determined that an important characteristic of any new system would be the limitation, if not complete abolition, of private property. The possibility of acquiring unlimited private property, argues the socialist, has stimulated the greed that causes some people to exploit others and at the same time causes the people who are exploited to endure their lot, hoping thus to obtain a better share of the world's goods. The only solution is to enlarge the public domain dramatically, establishing a community in which the land, the factories, and perhaps all the means of production are owned by the state. The state itself should be controlled by the workers, who should use their new power to guarantee a job and a fair share of the national largesse to every citizen. Above all, human want and suffering must not be allowed to continue.

The world has seen many varieties of **socialism**. The early socialists argued for the abolition of private property or simply acted out that belief by establishing communal ownership of land and other goods. Utopian socialists argued that human beings should and could work together for their common good in small communities. Marxist socialists follow the teachings of Karl Marx and believe that human history is moving inexorably through five stages of economic organization—communalism, slavery, feudalism, capitalism, and communism—each characterized by a different dominant mode of production and a different form

Socialism. Lionel Jospin, leader of the French Socialist Party, with supporters during his campaign for the presidency. Democratic socialists believe that if the working class is given a voice in government, socialist goals can be attained without revolution.

(Harley/Bordas/Sipa Press)

of class struggle over ownership of the means of production. The final stage will be communism, in which control over the means of production will be restored to the workers, probably by means of a violent revolution. Soviet communists added to the ideas of Marx the teachings of Vladimir Lenin: that a communist revolution is possible even in a state that has been only partially industrialized, that only the emergence of imperialism has been able to extend the stage of capitalism, that the communist revolution is always the work of a small "vanguard" party of dedicated and informed revolutionaries, and that such a revolution leads at first only to a socialist system, in which the apparatus of the state will still be necessary, and only later to true communism. Later amendments to the doctrines of Soviet communism can be seen, from the vantage of hindsight, as the quest for philosophical arguments on behalf of political reforms whose ultimate result was to bring the experiment with the Soviet form of socialism to an end in most of the states in which it had been practiced. Other forms of socialism, as far apart as Chinese communism and democratic socialism, continue to attract adherents.

Does socialism have new meanings today? A 1989 conference of American professors attempted to formulate an answer. Socialism means, they said, that there will be "(1) no exploitation of man by man, (2) a comprehensive guarantee of social-economic rights, (3) concern for equality, (4) collective ownership, and (5) communal participation in the disposal of resources."[14] More recent developments have led some to argue that ideological demands for a fully socialist system are now out of the question—"There is no alternative to mixed economies, with ever-changing relations between public and private sectors, and with social minimums and safety nets," says Arno Mayer. Along these lines, John Roemer recommends a new form of mixed economy, one he calls "market socialism" in which money will be divided into two forms: "commodity money" to be used for ordinary consumer goods and "share money" that would be distributed equally and used only for buying ownership rights in firms.[15]

In any case, the socialist dream is far from dead, and as the dust of do-it-yourself democratization and marketization raised in the revolutions of 1989 slowly settles we are likely to see more and more systematic efforts to bring this ideology into keeping with contemporary reality.

Fascism

Conservatism, liberalism, and socialism are all concerned with the problem of how a political system can best serve the needs of the citizens who compose it. They may all become distorted in practice into apologies for systems of exploitation, but all at least give lip service to the idea that what matters most is the lot of the citizen. Not so fascism. **Fascism** is predicated on the belief that what matters most is the nation itself. This ideology begins with the argument that citizens can prosper only when the nation prospers, but it carries this argument so far that the fate of the citizens becomes secondary to that of the nation they live in. Fascism is nationalism carried to the extreme.

Like conservatives, fascists think that some human beings are naturally better than others, but for fascists being better is not a matter of social class or circumstance but of race and nationality: If one person is better than others, it is because that person belongs to the "right" race or is a citizen of the "right" nation. There are, however, two qualities shared by all humankind. In the first place, all human beings are motivated by their emotions, not by their reason. According to the French historian Ernest Renan (1823–92), later quoted approvingly by Benito Mussolini: "To expect reason directly from the people and through the people is a chimera."[16] Second, everyone is struggling to survive. The quest for self-preservation motivates us all. For the fascist, this fundamental human condition does not suggest the need for cooperative arrangements, acknowledging our interdependence and seeking the fairest possible distribution of the world's goods. On the contrary, the fascist agrees with Adolf Hitler that in such a world, "if men wish to live, then they are forced to kill others. . . . On earth and in the universe force alone is decisive. Whatever goal man has reached is due to his originality plus his brutality. . . . Struggle is the father of all things in this world."[17]

Given these characteristics of humanity, the greatest good that could be achieved would be for superior people to put themselves in the service of an organization that would permit them to engage in this perpetual struggle on the best possible terms. Such an organization is the fascist state, engaged in perpetual warfare. If the present system is such a state, there is no higher destiny than to commit oneself to its service. If it is not, the individual's task is to help bring that state into being. In serving their nation, fascists serve themselves, because only thus are they able to protect themselves from others, and only thus can they hope to impose their own dominion in a world where everyone is engaged in a ruthless battle to take the largest possible share of life's rewards, regardless of the needs of others.

The fascist state is characterized by absolute discipline ("No dogma! Discipline suffices" was Mussolini's slogan in the early days), by a ruling party, and above all by submission to the leader. Glorification of the leader is carried to the ultimate extreme: "Mussolini is always right" was one of the ten points in the Italian Fascists' Decalogue, and under Hitler the German National Socialist Party (the Nazis) stated that "the authority of the Führer is complete and all-embracing; it unites in itself all the means of political direction, it extends into all fields of national life, it embraces the entire people, which is bound to the Führer in loyalty and obedience."[18] In such a system all human interactions, including economic exchange, come under the sway of the state and the leader. Industry is nationalized or heavily regulated, not to benefit the workers but to benefit the nation (hence the German term *national socialism*). One Italian fascist wrote that "there cannot be any single economic interests which are above the general economic interests of the State." All industry is to be organized into "corporations"— guilds composed of employers and employees who work in the same branch of industry. "Through these corporations the State may at any time that it deems fit, or that the need requires, intervene within the economic life of the individual to let the supreme interests of the nation have precedence over his private, particular interests, even to the point where his work, his savings, his whole fortune may need to be pledged, and if absolutely necessary, sacrificed."[19]

IS FEMINISM A NEW IDEOLOGY?

Conservatism, liberalism, socialism, and fascism are all commonly accepted as ideologies. They meet the terms we set out at the beginning of this chapter: An ideology is a comprehensive set of beliefs and attitudes about social and economic institutions and processes. It offers a critique of the existing system and a view of the ideal system. Where these differ, it suggests the means for moving from the existing to the ideal. It also presents a theory of human nature, and, thereby, of human potentiality and of the need for particular modes of social control.

Today, however, political thought is moving in new directions—or moving with surprising passion in directions that are very, very old. Feminism, ethnic nationalism, and religious fundamentalism are three ways of thinking about politics that have achieved remarkable importance in the past few decades, often making our more conventional approaches seem out of date, perhaps irrelevant. To what extent are these new *isms* true ideologies? To what extent are they simply effective ways for groups to assert threatened or never realized identities?[20] The only way to find out is to put them to the test, examining the beliefs and attitudes of each and determining whether they do in fact constitute "a comprehensive set

Algerian women wave prodemocracy banners and demonstrate against the Muslim fundamentalists seeking to keep all women in traditional roles. New ideologies may come into serious conflict with older forms of thought, stimulating demands for social and political change.

(AP/Wide World Photos)

of beliefs and attitudes about social and economic institutions and processes." Of course, we know to begin with that whether or not they are full ideologies, each of these ways of thinking about politics has assumed enormous importance in recent years. For that reason alone, we need to know more about them all. Here, we examine only the first. Is feminism a new ideology?

To begin with, we may say that all feminists believe that women are at least the equals of men, that they deserve equal inclusion in society, and that they have been denied that status for centuries of human history.[21] This belief is, of course, profoundly political, if not in itself fully ideological. In fact, early feminists were not seeking to create a new ideology; they wanted to modify those that did exist, especially liberalism and Marxist socialism, in ways that would make them inclusive of women. Those who worked in the liberal tradition typically stressed the need for women as well as men to gain greater individual rights and equality of opportunity. One of the earliest liberal feminist tracts was *A Vindication of the Rights of Women* by Mary Wollstonecraft, published in 1779; another was Harriet Taylor's *The Enfranchisement of Women*, on which her husband, John Stuart Mill, based his own *The Subjection of Women* (which, of course, things being as they were, became far better known).[22] In this century, Betty Friedan (*The Feminine Mystique*, 1963) and Alice S. Rossi ("Sentiment and Intellect," 1970) have been among those also identified as liberal revisionists.[23]

Others have approached the problem of the oppression of women from the perspective of Marxist socialism. In theory at least, Marxism also gave some attention to the oppression of women from the very beginning: Friedrich Engels, Karl Marx's collaborator explained in 1884 how in a class society women were oppressed in the home just as the proletariat (presumably male) was outside the home, both by the ruling bourgeoisie.[24] More contemporary Marxist feminists include Claudia von Werlhof, interested in all workers who are either unpaid (mostly women) or earning only subsistence wages (men and women, mostly in the Third World), and Maria Mies, who has studied the impact of capitalist roles and technologies on poor rural women in India.[25]

If all feminists could be identified as revisionist liberals or Marxists, we could stop right here and say, sorry, this may be very important, but it is not a distinct ideology. But feminism has gone far beyond such revisionism. Often incorporating liberal and/or Marxist insights, contemporary feminists have placed more and more emphasis on themes all their own, particularly the idea of the *patriarchal* social system. The oppression of women by men precedes all other forms of oppression, they argue. "It is the hardest form of oppression to eradicate" and "causes the most suffering to its victims."[26] When we come to understand the oppression of women we will, suggests Shulamith Firestone in *The Dialectic of Sex*, be able to understand racism, classism, and all other forms of oppression.[27] Thus, for example, Suzanne Pharr explains the oppression of gay men and lesbian women in feminist terms; she argues that by denying lesbians and gay men the fundamental civil rights that heterosexual women are allowed, heterosexual men ensure that most women will accept and depend on the patriarchal family structure.[28]

Other feminists have combined Marxist and patriarchal modes of interpretation, noting, for example, how patriarchy has for so long given men control of women's property or pointing out how control over women's labor enhances men's control of all productive resources.[29]

Also not normally found in the more conventional ideologies (although not unknown in contemporary socialist thought) is the deconstructionist approach of some feminists. As early as 1952, when she published *The Second Sex* in Paris, Simone de Beauvoir saw the importance of challenging not only current definitions of women and women's roles but also the very idea of the concept "woman"— "Are there women?" de Beauvoir asked.[30] Contemporary feminist poststructuralists are convinced that only by challenging (deconstructing) all established categories (structures) of social identity, including race, class, and gender, can we hope to break free of the confines of patriarchal language and practice.[31]

Insistence on the impossibility of separating oppression based on race and class from that based on gender is another poststructuralist feminist theme. Those who hope to understand and eradicate any form of oppression, feminists say, must pay attention to the structural factors that intersect to create sex, class, and race inequality.[32]

As the foregoing summary suggests, contemporary feminism has moved well beyond mere amendment of earlier modes of thought. Its critique of all existing political systems as profoundly patriarchal, its goal of species-wide egalitarianism, and its insistence on the interconnectedness of all forms of oppression summon up its own view of an ideal world.

Feminism also suggests how to effect change. Although most feminists seem to agree that the contemporary state is profoundly suspect, they emphasize that it is important nevertheless to change the policies of existing political systems. Joyce Gelb has examined how feminists in Britain, the United States, and Sweden have worked within their respective "political opportunity structures" to struggle for labor force equality, higher welfare benefits, better child care, and other specific policies relevant to women's condition.[33] Mary Hawkesworth has looked at feminist studies of substantive policy domains, commenting on the shift "from the critique of bias in existing programs to the formulation of proposals for alternative, equitable policies" in the areas of "health, housing, welfare, education, employment, equal protection, occupational safety, defense, foreign policy, development, abortion, reproductive rights, reproductive technology, rape prevention, sexual harassment, domestic violence, criminal justice, divorce, privacy, and pornography."[34]

Although many feminists thus seek specific short-range ameliorative reforms, all appear to agree that in the long run a more basic change must be made. For women and other oppressed persons to achieve equality, nothing less than a revolution is required. But it is a revolution of understanding, of consciousness, of meaning. Those who share these problems and these views must meet, discuss, write, and talk to others. International gatherings are particularly important, so that no one will forget the many forms that patriarchy and related kinds of oppression take across the globe. For most feminists, the concept of interdependence takes a negative form at the level of the state, as patriarchically dominated systems interact to maintain oppression, but a positive form at the level of the individual, as women meet from across the globe in forums such as the periodic United Nations conferences on women, to share their histories and their insights and to move toward fundamental and global transformations in the way the human polity thinks about oppression.

Feminism thus clearly meets the criteria we have laid out to define what constitutes an ideology.

THE LANGUAGE OF IDEOLOGY

The political questions we term *ideological* are, as we have seen, of the most serious import to humanity. What are human beings really like? What kind of social organization do we have the natural ability and talent to set up and make work? Why have we established our present social systems? What would the ideal social system look like? These questions matter deeply, and when we figure out answers that seem correct and satisfactory, many of us find it difficult to accept the fact that not everyone else agrees with us. This discovery may lead us, if we are not careful, to seek to persuade by oversimplifying, and by labeling all systems of thought pernicious and false except the one we endorse—in short, by making irresponsible use of the language of ideology.[35] This all too common human failing causes others among us to turn away in disgust, making the very word *ideological* a pejorative term nearly synonymous with *fanatical*, and thereby depriving ourselves of the opportunity to consider matters of the most serious significance to our shared lives on this planet.

Is there any way to stop the human tendency either to preach intolerantly or to treat all such questions as socially "off limits"? Probably not. But we can make an effort in that direction by resolving to use the language of ideology with care and restraint, giving the key terms of ideological discourse their correct meaning and no other. It will help to keep in mind that terms such as *conservative, liberal, socialist, fascist,* and *feminist* are all words with specific and often complex meanings, not just buzzwords suitable for the quick labeling of friends and foes. Before concluding, let us undertake a brief examination of five other terms that are often misused in ideological debate: *left, right, authoritarian, totalitarian,* and *democratic.*

Politically, *left* and *right* are comparative terms, used to locate ideological perspectives in relation to each other. Generally, **left** is used for ideologies that take a positive view of human nature and demonstrate a conviction that change and progress are necessary and possible to improve the human condition and that governments have an important role to play in bringing this about. **Right** usually means a somewhat more pessimistic view of human nature and a conviction that it is more important to use the powers of government to maintain tradition and order than to attempt to create a more equal society. It should be fairly obvious that liberalism and socialism and most forms of feminism are on the left, with socialism moving farther to the left as we talk about the more extreme versions, and that conservatism and fascism are on the right, with fascism on the far right. Figure 3.1 suggests how these spatial designations can be used to compare the five ideologies we have discussed in these pages.

There is nothing wrong with this exercise, provided we do not give it more or less meaning than it has. Placing conservatism and fascism on the same side should not cause us to use the terms interchangeably, and the same is true for liberalism, socialism, and feminism. It is also important to remember that this spatial arrangement refers only to certain characteristics of the ideologies *as ideologies,* not to the practices of political control adopted by people who assume power in the names of those ideologies. Some have argued, for example, that communism and fascism have much more in common than calling one *far left* and the other *far right* suggests. What these people are referring to, however, is not the content of the two ideologies but rather the authoritarian practices of rulers who call themselves communists or fascists. To lump the two together ignores the extremely different principles of leadership in the two ideologies—not to mention all the other significant differences.

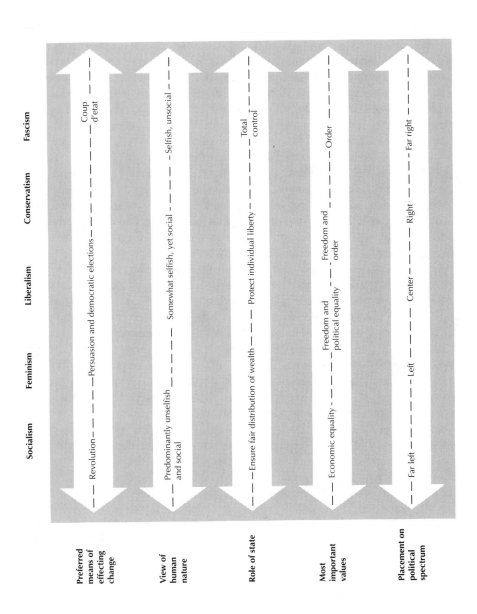

FIGURE 3.1   Key Characteristics of Major Political Ideologies

Authoritarian and *totalitarian* are two other often misused terms. Neither refers to a belief system or to an ideology. Both refer to political systems in which political power is concentrated in the hands of a few. An **authoritarian system** is one in which the power of the authorities is virtually unlimited, although this power is not always exercised in all domains. A **totalitarian system** is one in which the authorities not only have unlimited power but also attempt to exercise it over all domains of life. It is authoritarianism carried to the ultimate extreme. You will often find, however, that the words are used—incorrectly—to distinguish between capitalist systems ruled by an authoritarian elite (called *authoritarian*) and socialist systems ruled by an authoritarian elite (called *totalitarian*). Both kinds of systems are in fact authoritarian, just as there are both capitalist and socialist democratic systems. Furthermore, capitalist authoritarian systems are not necessarily less concerned about controlling every aspect of their citizens' lives than are socialist authoritarian systems. The control exercised by an Adolf Hitler or a Benito Mussolini was every bit as totalitarian as that of a Joseph Stalin or a Mao Zedong, and in underdeveloped nations that have fallen under dictatorial rule neither the socialist nor the capitalist tyrant is likely to find it physically possible to extend the power of government to every corner of the land.

In this text I use the term *authoritarian* to refer to all states that are elite controlled and drop the word *totalitarian* altogether. When it becomes necessary to distinguish between economic systems, I add such economic terms as *capitalist, socialist,* and *mixed economy* (see Chapter 4). This leaves us with the semantic problem that *socialism* is both an ideology and an economic system, but that conflation cannot be avoided. As we have seen in this chapter, the very essence of the ideology of socialism is the demand that a specific economic system be established. This leaves one question that must surely be puzzling many readers: Why isn't democracy one of the ideologies discussed in this chapter? The answer is that democracy, like authoritarianism and nationalism, is not a political ideology. It is a description of the relationship between citizens and their leaders. The conditions of personal freedom, free elections, and political equality are strongly associated with democracy and help make it possible, but the literal meaning of **democracy** is simply rule by the people. Such rule may be direct or, as is much more likely in today's crowded world, it may be effected through representatives elected by the people. But unless the citizens—and not just a few, but the people, a term that includes all adults not seriously disqualified by criminal behavior or mental incapacity—have the right and the means to exercise some form of genuine control over the government, democracy cannot be said to exist.

SUMMARY AND CONCLUSION

An ideology is a comprehensive system of beliefs and attitudes about social and economic institutions and processes. It is an attempt to explain how an existing political system has come into being and to describe the ideal political system. It may be either strictly personal or shared with a group, open or closed, and revolutionary or defensive. An ideology offers a theory of human nature and thereby of human potentiality and of the need for particular modes of social control. Five major ideologies are conservatism, liberalism, socialism, fascism, and feminism.

Conservatives believe in conserving what exists. They have a nonegalitarian view of human nature, believing that some people are born into a "natural aristocracy" and that those people can best protect the individual liberty of all. Personal liberty is extremely important to conservatives, which helps explain why they often wish to see the power of government reduced. On the other hand, they frequently propose that government power be used to ensure that traditional moral standards are maintained. Conservatives have traditionally believed that it is the responsibility of the more advanced nations to bring the blessings of civilization to those less fortunate and that it is necessary to maintain good relations with allies as a means of protecting one's own system against external enemies. Although conservatives are sometimes viewed by others as incapable of compromise, they take a pragmatic approach to many questions, provided that the end result will further the basic principles of conservatism (order, continuity, loyalty, protection of individual freedoms, piety, and nationalism).

Liberals believe that all human beings are capable of reason and rational action and should be helped by their governments to fulfill their potential. However, although governments should be ready to help, they must never force such assistance on unwilling citizens—it is also an important liberal value to maintain personal freedom. As much as liberals would like to create a more egalitarian society, they are unwilling to invade individual rights to do so. Thus, they hold two beliefs that are in practice extremely difficult to reconcile. Liberals commonly believe in some form of social contract—that is, in the idea that human beings consent to be ruled by others, but only on condition that individual rights and liberties be maintained. If the terms of this contract are not met, the consent to be ruled may be withdrawn. Liberals believe, however, that political change should be made by peaceful, not revolutionary, means.

Socialists believe that human beings are naturally sociable and cooperative and that only the establishment of nonsocialist governments and exploitative work arrangements has interfered with these natural instincts. They believe that the solution is to limit or even abolish outright the institution of private property—which, they say, should be owned by a state that is in turn controlled by the workers. The word *socialism* covers a wide range of beliefs, from moderate **democratic socialism** to hard-line Maoist **communism**. Despite their agreement on the need to eliminate suffering by limiting private property, socialists disagree sharply on such matters as whether revolutionary methods will be required to set up the ideal system; whether a socialist revolution will necessarily be worldwide; what conditions make revolution possible; how extensive the limitations on private property should be; how large the ideal socialist community should be; and what roles, if any, government and the state should play.

Fascism begins by arguing that the citizen can prosper only when the nation prospers and ends up placing the fate of the nation above that of its people. Like conservatives, fascists think that some human beings are naturally better than others, but for them being better means belonging to the "right" race or nationality. They think human beings are motivated by their emotions, not by their reason, and by the struggle for survival. Because this is so, citizens should accept the rule of the fascist state, which will permit them to engage in that struggle on the best possible terms. Under fascism, all human interactions—including economic exchange—are necessarily subject to the absolute discipline of the state and its leader.

Feminism is a relatively new ideology that began when women sought to modify liberalism and/or Marxist socialism to fit their needs and found it necessary to move on to formulate the concept of patriarchy and adapt the tools of poststructural deconstructionism. Feminists have a positive view of human nature and argue for the right of all to share equally in the creation of our collective destiny, but they have a highly negative view of the state. They seek to move toward the ideal society by achieving a better understanding of the causes of all oppression, including that based on class and race as well as gender; they believe that all forms of oppression are interconnected. While working for this understanding, often internationally, they also work for policy reform on questions of relevance and concern to women.

In developing our personal systems of belief, we must not oversimplify or label every other ideology except the one we endorse false and pernicious. Being ideological is not the same thing as being fanatical, although ideologues do sometimes carry their convictions to that extreme and fanatics may believe they find confirmation in an organized system of thought. We frequently misuse such terms as *left, right, authoritarian, totalitarian,* and *democratic* as well as the terms that name the ideologues we have studied. *Left* means taking a positive view of human nature and believing that change and progress are necessary and possible to improve the human condition. *Right* means taking a somewhat more pessimistic view of human nature and placing greater emphasis on the importance of maintaining order and continuity. Many variations are possible, however, within this simplistic dichotomy.

Authoritarian and *totalitarian* refer to political systems in which political power is concentrated in the hands of a few, the difference being that in a totalitarian system more effort is made to exercise that power in all domains of human existence. *Democracy,* like *authoritarianism,* is not a political ideology but rather a description of the relationship between citizens and their leaders. The conditions of personal freedom, free elections, and political equality are strongly associated with democracy and help make it possible, but the literal meaning of *democracy* is simply rule by the people.

We now have a shared language for speaking and writing about politics. We can turn next to the context of politics—that is, the economic and social settings in which politics must take place and the ways they affect the nature of politics. Many of the ideas we have touched on so far assume new life when we consider the ways social and economic relationships really do shape our political lives together.

Selected Readings

Daniels, Robert V., ed. *A Documentary History of Communism and the World: From Revolution to Collapse.* Hanover, N.H.: University Press of New England, 1994. A comprehensive study of communism worldwide, including the failure of communism in the Soviet Union.

Girvin, Brian. *The Right in the Twentieth Century: Conservatism and Democracy.* London: Pinter, 1994. An in-depth and historical overview of right-wing political movements worldwide.

Grey, John. *Liberalism.* Milton Keynes: Open University Press, 1986. Historical background and current significance of economic and political liberalism.

Heywood, Andrew. *Political Ideologies: An Introduction.* New York: St. Martin's, 1992. An overview of a wide range of current political ideologies.

Honderich, Ted. *Conservatism.* Boulder, Colo.: Westview Press, 1991. An introduction to conservative theory and opinion.

Kymlicka, Will. *Contemporary Political Philosophy: An Introduction.* Oxford: Clarendon Press, 1990. An examination of the major schools of modern political thought.

Rawls, John. *Political Liberalism.* New York: Columbia University Press, 1993. A collection of Rawls's lectures that provides an extensive study of liberalism.

Rejai, Mostafa. *Political Ideologies: A Comparative Approach.* Armonk, N.Y.: Sharpe, 1995. A framework for the comparative study of the major political ideologies.

Tong, Rosemarie. *Feminist Thought: A Comprehensive Introduction.* Boulder, Colo.: Westview Press, 1989. A balanced overview and useful source for those seeking to learn more about feminist theory.

Notes

1. Lyman Tower Sargent, *Contemporary Political Ideologies,* 5th ed. (Homewood, Ill.: Dorsey, 1961), p. 3.
2. Andrew Heywood, *Political Ideologies: An Introduction* (New York: St. Martin's, 1992), pp. 7–8.
3. David E. Ingersoll, *Communism, Fascism and Democracy* (Columbus, Ohio: Charles E. Merrill, 1971), p. 8.
4. F. J. C. Hearnshaw, *Conservatism in England* (London: Macmillan, 1933), p. 22.
5. Samuel P. Huntington, "Conservatism as an Ideology," *American Political Science Review* 51, no. 2 (June 1957): 456.
6. Sargent, *Contemporary Political Ideologies,* p. 67.
7. Alexander J. Groth, *Major Ideologies* (New York: John Wiley, 1971), p. 88.
8. Kenneth R. Hoover, *Ideology and Political Life,* 2nd ed. (Monterey, Calif.: Brooks/Cole, 1994), p. 41.
9. Russell Kirk, cited in Sargent, *Contemporary Political Ideologies,* p. 67.
10. Hoover, *Ideology and Political Life,* p. 41.
11. Ibid., p. 40.
12. Heywood, *Political Ideologies,* p. 56.
13. Ibid., pp. 21–22.
14. "Soviet Economic Reform: Socialism and Property," report of the Thirtieth Strategy for Peace, U.S. Foreign Policy Conference, Stanley Foundation, Muscatine, Iowa, 19–21 Oct. 1989.

15. Arno Mayer, "Past and Prologue," *The Nation* (16 Sept. 1991): 290; and John E. Roemer, "A Future for Socialism," *Politics and Society* 22, no. 4 (Dec. 1994): 451–78. Under Roemer's scheme everyone would be given an equal share of coupons on reaching the age of majority, and on a person's death all shares and unspent coupons would revert to the state for redistribution. The market would otherwise function freely, but there would be a far more egalitarian distribution of property than under unrestrained capitalism.

16. See Benito Mussolini, *The Doctrine of Fascism* (1932), excerpted in Carl Cohen, ed., *Communism, Fascism and Democracy* (New York: Random House, 1962), p. 358.

17. Quoted in Cohen, *Communism, Fascism and Democracy*, pp. 409–10.

18. From Mussolini, *Doctrine of Fascism*, excerpted in Cohen, *Communism, Fascism and Democracy*, pp. 349–64, and from Ernst R. Huber, *Constitutional Law of the Greater German Reich* (1939), excerpted in James A. Gould and Willis H. Truitt, *Political Ideologies* (New York: Macmillan, 1973), pp. 123–26.

19. See Mario Palmieri, *The Philosophy of Fascism* (1936), excerpted in Cohen, *Communism, Fascism and Democracy*, pp. 369–90.

20. See Valentine M. Moghadam, *Identity Politics and Women: Cultural Reassertions and Feminisms in International Perspective* (Boulder, Colo.: Westview Press, 1994), for a variety of approaches to this possibility.

21. Jane C. Ollenburger and Helen Moore, *A Sociology of Women* (Englewood Cliffs, N.J.: Prentice Hall, 1992), p. 16. The following discussion draws heavily on Ollenburger and Moore, who note their own indebtedness to Alison M. Jagger and Paula S. Rothenberg, *Feminist Frameworks* (New York: McGraw-Hill, 1984), for their explanation of the different forms of feminist theory.

22. J. M. Todd, ed., *A Wollstonecraft Anthology* (Bloomington, Ind.: Indiana University Press, 1977); John Stuart Mill and Harriet Taylor Mill, *The Enfranchisement of Women and The Subjection of Women* (London: Virago, 1983).

23. Betty Friedan, *The Feminine Mystique* (New York: Norton, 1963); and Alice Rossi, ed., *Essays on Sex Equality by John Stuart Mill and Harriet Taylor Mill* (Chicago: University of Chicago Press, 1970).

24. Friedrich Engels, *The Origin of Family, Private Property and the State* (1884; reprint, New York: International Publishers, 1972).

25. Claudia von Werlhof, "Women's Work: The Blind Spot in the Critique of Political Economy," in *Women: The Last Colony*, ed. Maria Mies, Veronika Bennholdt-Thomsen, and Claudia von Werlhof (London: Zed Books, 1988), pp. 13–26, and Maria Mies, "Capitalist Development and Subsistence Production: Rural Women in India," in Mies, Bennholdt-Thomsen, and Werlhof, *Women*, pp. 27–50.

26. Jagger and Rothenberg, *Feminist Frameworks*, p. 86.

27. Shulamith Firestone, *The Dialectic of Sex: The Case for Feminist Revolution* (New York: Quill, 1993).

28. Suzanne Pharr, *Homophobia: A Weapon of Sexism* (Inverness, Calif.: Chardon Press, 1988); Andrea Dworkin, *Women Hating* (New York: Dutton, 1974), *Pornography: Men Possessing Women* (New York: Putnam, 1979); and Charlotte Bunch and S. Pollack, *Learning One Way: Essays in Feminist Education* (Trumansburg, N.Y.: Crossing Press, 1983). Dworkin, Bunch, and Pollack believe heterosexual women are too closely linked to their oppressors to be able to confront them. See also Roberta Hamilton, *The Liberation of Women: A Study of Patriarchy and Capitalism* (Winchester, Mass.: Allen and Unwin, 1977).

29. Juliet Mitchell, *Woman's Estate* (New York: Pantheon, 1971), and *Psychoanalysis and Feminism* (New York: Pantheon, 1974); Heidi Hartmann, *Women and Revolution: The Unhappy Marriage of Marxism and Feminism* (London: Pluto Press, 1981).

30. Simone de Beauvoir, *The Second Sex* (New York: Knopf, 1952). De Beauvoir might well ask: She did far better than her fellow student (and lover), Jean Paul Sartre, when the two of them took an important philosophy exam, but their professors decided nevertheless to award the highest prize (and thereby significant financial aid for further study) to "the man."

31. S. Bordo, "Feminism, Postmodernism and Gender Skepticism," in *Feminism/Postmodernism*, ed. L. J. Nicholson (New York: Routledge, 1990), and R. Tong, *Feminist Thought: A Comprehensive Introduction* (Boulder, Colo.: Westview Press, 1989).

32. M. B. Zinn, "Family, Feminism and Race in American Society," *Gender and Society* 4 (1990): 68–83; and Ollenburger and Moore, *Sociology of Women*, pp. 26–27.

33. Joyce Gelb, *Feminism and Politics* (Berkeley and Los Angeles: University of California Press, 1989).

34. Mary Hawkesworth, "Policy Studies within a Feminist Frame," *Policy Sciences* 27, nos. 2–3 (1994): 99, 114–15. The entire issue of *Policy Sciences* is devoted to "Feminism and Public Policy," under the guest editorship of Hawkesworth. Other political scientists who have brought a feminist perspective to policy studies in recent years (dates following their names refer to years of publication of key works) include Ellen Boneparth and Emily Stoper (1988); Margaret Conway, David Ahern, and Gertrude Steuernagel (1994); Janet Flammang (1985); Jo Freeman (1989); Joyce Gelb and Marian Lief Palley (1987); Joni Lovenduski (1986); Barbara Nelson (1984); Sue Tolleson Rinehart (1992); Anne Schneider and Helen Ingram (1993); and Dorothy McBride Stetson (1991).

35. A particularly pronounced example today is the unfortunate proclivity of some in the Western world to assume that all followers of Islam are fundamentalists and that all Muslim fundamentalists believe in the use of the tactics of terrorism. This is untrue, unfair, and a sad example of how the language of ideology can be abused.

4 Political Economy

What was a central theme in the 1996 U.S. presidential election? Why are some Russians less than enthusiastic about the recent changes in their political system? Why did the Iranian government begin making conciliatory statements to the West condemning all terrorist activities? Why did Fidel Castro visit François Mitterrand in 1995, just at the end of the latter's tenure as president of France? What is the underlying subject matter of most of the bills that come before the Canadian National Assembly? What was one of the central motives for white South Africans to accept black majority rule at last?

These important yet seemingly unrelated questions all have the same answer: the state of the national economy. Economic values are primary in politics and have always been so. The need for government (and thus the introduction of politics) arose in the first place because human beings were developing more complex economic relationships and required a more orderly means of regulating their affairs. Try to think of a war that has been waged in which economic nationalism did not play a part. Indeed, try to think of any important political question that does not turn, at least in part, on economic considerations.

Trying to understand political processes without knowing about the economic interests that often guide them would be like trying to figure out the rules of a game of chess just by watching the players. You might eventually figure it out, but you would certainly waste a lot of time. Politics is a phenomenon that flows from the entire network of human relationships, and we cannot proceed without some direct attention to one of the most fundamental of those relationships, the quest for material well-being.

The theme of this chapter is **political economy**—that is, the relationship between economic conditions and the political choices we make.[1] We begin with a brief examination of some specific economic factors that shape our political choices: the size of a nation, the natural resources available to it, and its level of economic development. Then we consider the more common modes of political response to economic imperatives—that is, the ways different political systems, based on different ideologies, have addressed the problems of providing material welfare by institutionalizing different economic systems: capitalism, mixed economy, and socialism. We conclude by exploring the way the growing interdependence of the human polity has raised many of the issues of political economy to the global level, making these problems simultaneously more difficult and more urgent to resolve. In this final section we focus in particular on the problems posed to the world at large by the environmental crisis, by increasingly interdependent international trade, and by the indebtedness of underdeveloped nations.

Although the emphasis in this chapter is on the interrelationship between economic factors and politics, this should not be seen as suggesting that all political life is guided by material considerations. In previous chapters we have already considered the power of political thought in guiding political developments, and in succeeding chapters we examine how cultural and social factors and individual initiatives can also help to determine the course of political action. Economic motives do guide political choice, but they are only one force among many. Furthermore, as we note here and elsewhere, the pattern of cause and effect is always reciprocal. Our quest for material wealth influences our politics; our politics help determine the distribution of material wealth.

This chapter moves us briskly, perhaps even brusquely, into the present, a good place for political scientists to be. It carries us into considerations of how the present is changing and what the future may bring.

ECONOMIC FACTORS THAT COMMONLY INFLUENCE POLITICS

A nation's size, its supply of natural resources, and its level of economic development are three characteristics that help shape its internal politics as well as its political and economic relations with other nations.

The Size of a Nation

The size of a nation can be measured either as its territorial extent or as the number of citizens inhabiting its territory. Both these measures are influenced by geography as well as economics. Geographic conditions help determine how large a polity will be as well as how many people will seek their living within its boundaries. Climate, natural resources, and the likelihood of natural disasters (such as earthquakes, hurricanes, or floods) determine the suitability of any terrain for habitation. Such natural barriers as mountain ranges or bodies of water help to determine which people live and work together and which are considered "foreigners," with whom intercourse is infrequent and limited.

Once size is established, it inevitably becomes an economic factor. As such, size often has a profound impact on the course of political life. The territorial extent of a nation limits the number of people who can be fed and sheltered, given that society's particular level of development. If the resources within the polity's physical domain are inadequate to its population's needs, then the economic struggle for scarce resources may lead to political strife as well. Whether such economic and political strife is internal or directed outward often depends on another factor related to size, *jurisdictional integration*—that is, the extent to which all the units composing a state are legally integrated with one another. José M. Gonzalez-Eiras points out that the economic modernization and imperialistic ventures of Japan followed the Meiji Restoration of 1867–68, when that small nation's three hundred separate feudal domains were finally integrated and the entire nation turned toward foreign conquest as the way to secure the resources it lacked at home.[2]

The causal relationship between the economic consequences of size and the course of politics works both ways: the size of the system affects a nation's politics, and a nation's politics affects the size of the system. Political factors change territorial extent. Wars shift boundaries outward or inward, governments finance voyages of discovery and conquest, and legislatures grant free land to those who push into the wilderness and statehood or other formal recognition to distant territories. Political decisions also influence the number of citizens a state will have. Deciding to go to war can lead to enormous loss of life, offering government family allowances after such wars can lead to population growth, and pursuing governmental sterilization or contraceptive programs in nations where the supply of food is inadequate can reduce growth or even cause population to decline.

Despite the polite fiction of international law, which holds all sovereign states to be equal, small states *are* different from large states. When the Baltic states of Lithuania, Estonia, and Latvia first began to clamor for independence from the

FIGURE 4.1 The Baltic States

Source: Kay Lawson, *The Human Polity,* 4th ed. (Boston: Houghton Mifflin, 1997). Reprinted by permission.

Soviet Union in 1991, even those most sympathetic to their concerns had to wonder how such tiny states could possibly expect to survive in the modern world (see Figure 4.1). However, not all small states are weak: consider the size of Denmark—or Japan!

Natural Resources

One of the reasons small states are often at a disadvantage is inadequate natural resources. There is, of course, no direct relationship between size and natural wealth. Most nations' boundaries were established long before a full inventory of their resources could be taken. Furthermore, what constitutes a "resource" is constantly changing. Yesterday's frustratingly hard earth may have concealed today's uranium mine; today's thorny patch of scrub brush may turn out to be tomorrow's cure for cancer.

As new discoveries of hitherto hidden wealth are made, political forces shift and respond. The twentieth-century politics of oil offers us numerous examples. The oil-producing nations that have made common cause in **OPEC** (the Organization of Petroleum Exporting Countries) have done so for political as well as economic gain. Iraq invaded Kuwait in 1990 in order to take possession of oil deposits that would help restore its economy after a disastrous decade of war with Iran, and it would be foolish to imagine that the willingness of the United States and its allies to come to the rescue of Kuwait in 1991 was not owing in large part to the need to keep that tiny kingdom's oil flowing in the right directions (and the profits therefrom into the right pockets).

The question of the importance of natural resources to the economics and politics of a nation is not always unambiguous, however. The polities of Hong Kong and Singapore are only two examples of small polities, poor in natural resources, that nevertheless became strong exporters of manufactured goods. Their ability to attract foreign investment permitting the import of others' raw materials and goods allowed them a degree of development that has had little to do with what can be found above or below their own soil.[3] Furthermore, even abundant natural resources mean little so long as they remain entirely natural. If they are dramatic or beautiful to see, they may constitute important tourist attractions. They may even contribute to the psychic well-being of a citizenry and thus indirectly to its productivity. But in most cases, resources, whether natural or imported, must be changed in some way if they are to bring economic rewards. Making those changes is the first step in economic *development*.

The Level of Wealth Achieved

Economic development means acquiring the ability to transform natural resources (the nation's own or those imported from other nations as raw materials) into various more valuable processed goods, to provide valuable services, and to market those goods and services domestically and internationally in order to improve the material well-being of the nation's own people.

As this definition makes clear, the motivation spurring economic development is the desire to improve material well-being. (It need not be *greed*, which normally refers to a desire to get as much as possible of a desired entity without regard for the needs of others.) If natural resources can be processed in a way that makes them more useful or attractive, they are likely to bring greater profits, thus permitting the purchase of more goods from others. This economic fact of life spurs the **division of labor**, as we learn to process raw materials in different ways, and stimulates **technological development**, as we seek—and find—more interesting and more profitable ways to change the rocks, trees, water, and sunshine of our natural habitat into useful goods and services. As work becomes more specialized and products more varied, a nation's ability to meet its own needs and assume a competitive stance in the world market is likely to improve, which usually leads in turn to a significant increase in national wealth. Table 4.1 illustrates this point: the more workers employed in professional and technological occupations, the

TABLE 4.1   Technological Development and National Wealth

Country	Gross National Product per Capita (1991)	Professional and Technical Workers as a percentage of the Economically Active Population (1993)
Japan	27,300	11.5
Denmark	24,230	24.3[a]
United States	22,550	16.5
Canada	20,840	17.3
Kuwait	19,510	16.8
United Kingdom	17,400	11.5[a]
Mexico	3,051	9.5
Venezuela	2,609	11.9
South Africa	2,573	7.2
Chile	2,215	8.2
Syria	1,909	13.0
Philippines	694	5.7
Indonesia	577	3.4
Pakistan	369	4.5
India	303	2.9

[a]1991 figures (1993 figures not available).
Sources: GNP data from U.S. Bureau of the Census, *The Statistical Abstract of the United States: 1994*, 114th ed. (Washington, D.C.: U.S. Bureau of the Census, 1994), p. 862. Professional and Technical Workers data from *International Marketing Data and Statistics 1995*, 19th ed. (London: Euromonitor, 1995), pp. 283–85; and *1993 Yearbook of Labour Statistics,* 52nd ed. (Geneva: International Labour Office, 1993), pp. 482–516.

greater a nation's overall wealth, as measured by gross national product (GNP) per capita. The relationship is far from perfect, but it goes in the expected direction.

Once national wealth is achieved, those who achieve individual wealth in that prosperous nation are more likely to receive respectful attention when they offer advice on political affairs; the followers of billionaire Ross Perot in the United States constitute only one recent example of this common phenomenon. Of course, in all nations the wealthy are likely to have the means to influence the direction of politics behind the scenes (a practice we explore further in Chapter 8), but it is safer to exercise that influence openly as well when those less fortunate have quasi-realistic hopes of enlarging their own portion of a good-sized national pie.

Furthermore, as international entities, wealthier nations are more influential in world politics than poor nations, often use that political strength to further their

Technological interdependence stimulates economic development and political change. Here a Japanese technician aids his Malaysian counterparts in a joint economic venture.

(Charlie Cole/Sipa Press)

economic dominance, and may do so in ways that make it difficult for smaller and poorer nations to achieve the diversified labor force so clearly related to economic development (a tendency we discuss further later in this chapter).

POLITICAL DETERMINATION OF ECONOMIC SYSTEMS

Politics and economics are mutually causative. Economic conditions produce political responses, but political conditions also produce economic responses.

How do political decisions determine economic conditions? Stop for a moment and consider some of the powers the ordinary government has to shape a nation's economy. Even a few moments' reflection will give you a formidable list:

- The power to tax
- The power to spend revenue, including the power to subsidize particular sectors of the economy (by agricultural price supports, for example, or tax exemptions for religious institutions, or grants of support for the arts)
- The power to regulate the conduct of business (laws governing nationalized industry, for example, or the development of private business, or the formation of trade unions)
- The power to issue and regulate currency
- The power to determine interest rates

- The power to make economic pacts with other nations
- The power to declare war and to make peace
- The power to levy fines
- The power to control the entry into and exit from the national territory of people and goods (including laborers, entrepreneurs, products, and currency)
- The power to make comprehensive long-range plans incorporating any of these specific powers

Each of these powers is an important means of shaping the direction of an economy and the distribution of its wealth. Consider, for example, the probable significance of the different allocations for defense, education, health, and social security and welfare made by the nations included in Table 4.2.

The decisions each nation makes about exercising political control over its economic life will depend in large part on the nature of the economic system to which it is committed: capitalism, socialism, or some form of mixed economy. It can be argued, however, that the choice of economic system—and of whether to keep or change the existing system—is itself a political decision, often based on a political ideology.

TABLE 4.2   Selected Nations' Spending Priorities per Capital Expenditures (in Percentages)

Nation	Defense	Education	Health	Social Security and Welfare
Australia	8.6	7.0	12.7	31.2
El Salvador	16.0	12.8	7.3	4.7
Israel	22.1	11.1	4.4	31.3
Kenya	9.2	20.1	5.4	3.4
Korea	22.1	16.2	1.2	12.5
Namibia	6.5	22.2	9.7	14.8
Nepal	5.9	10.9	4.7	6.8
Netherlands	4.6	10.8	13.9	40.9
Pakistan	27.9	1.6	1.0	3.4
Paraguay	13.3	12.7	4.3	14.8
Sweden	5.5	9.3	0.8	56.2
Thailand	17.2	21.1	8.1	6.7
Turkey	11.3	20.0	3.5	3.9
United States	20.6	1.8	16.0	31.1

Source: *Government Finance Statistics Yearbook,* vol. 15 (New York: International Monetary Fund, 1991), pp. 58–61; and *World Development Report 1994: Infrastructure for Development* (New York: World Bank, 1994), pp. 180–81.

Capitalism

Do political systems govern the choice of economic systems? Govern is perhaps too strong a word, but they certainly play a major part in sustaining specific choices and in aiding transitions from one economic system to another. Consider the role of politics in the transition from feudalism to capitalism that took place in Europe in the sixteenth and seventeenth centuries.

Under feudalism the quantity and kind of economic production was determined by the contracting parties: serfs, lords, and—where he had the power to make his will prevail—the king as the representative of the emerging national interest. The growth of centralized monarchies eventually caused the breakup of the feudal empires within the emerging nation-states. This collapse of the feudal system meant that goods could now be exchanged in a wider and freer market. The quest for yet broader markets and for expanded resources motivated another political development—the decision to finance foreign exploration and conquest. The spoils of imperialism made some goods cheaper to produce and more desirable than ever before. In response to increased demand, as well as to their new opportunity to conduct their enterprises free of feudal domination, the producers of such goods began plowing some of their profits back into their businesses in order to expand their productive capacity. This behavior—free entrepreneurs putting profits back into capital expenditures—is the essence of **capitalism**.[4]

Thus, political developments—the rise of the nation-state and the conquest of foreign territories—spurred the shift to a new economic system, capitalism. By the middle of the seventeenth century, the interaction between economic and political forces to make that system work was considerably more conscious and deliberate. It was then that the stronger nation-states adopted **mercantilism** as the surest means of maintaining the wealth and power of the state. The mercantilist theory of the relationship between the public and private spheres urges that the state use its powers openly to provide the best possible conditions for private entrepreneurs to carry on their business, thereby identifying the interest of the state with that of private business. Uniform monetary systems and legal codes were the positive achievements of mercantilism; permitting the often inhuman exploitation of laborers at home and abroad was the other side of the coin.[5]

The main point, of course, was that there should be plenty of coins, whichever side one looked at. And the mercantilist nations did prosper, so much so that the steady accumulation of capital provided the base for the eighteenth-century Industrial Revolution. As profits grew and the exploitation of labor worsened, however, the arguments in favor of having a supportive yet interfering partner—the state—began to seem less compelling to those who were developing great wealth. A new rationale was needed, one that would set business free to pursue the untrammeled growth that was to characterize the evolution of capitalism in the nineteenth century.

The answer was found by consulting and amending liberal political thought (see Chapter 3). "Let them do as they will," argued British theorist Adam Smith, asserting that if economic decisions were left to the free play of self-regulating market forces, the best of all possible systems for production and distribution of the world's goods would be found.[6] A **laissez-faire** economy is one in which government stays out of the world of business as much as possible. Laissez-faire economists believe that all government needs to do is ensure sound money (as when it backs the currency with gold deposits), balance its own budget (because allowing a budget deficit represents an unfair incursion of government into the private economy), encourage free trade, and keep welfare expenditures to an absolute minimum.

By the beginning of the twentieth century, and especially after World War I, the world had changed. International markets were shrinking, colonized peoples were beginning the long trek to independence, and trade barriers were multiplying as individual nations sought to cushion their separate economies against the spreading Great Depression. The hope that capitalism would automatically provide plenty for all began to fade, and the people whose rewards had so far been limited to this hope began to lose their patience.

Alternatives to Capitalism: Socialism and the Mixed Economy

In its purest form, socialism carries the natural connection between the political and economic spheres to its logical conclusion. It calls for the absolute merger of the two. In the ideal socialist system, the state would control all the means of production and would itself be controlled by the workers. With absolute control, the state would in theory be able to establish and carry out long-range comprehensive plans of economic development. The socialist economy is a **planned economy.** Furthermore, knowing that the state acted only in their own best interests, and that in working for the state they were working for themselves, the workers in the ideal socialist state would no longer be alienated from their jobs. They would therefore produce as well and as much as they possibly could. Either each would "give according to his or her ability and receive according to his or her need,"[7] or all would be paid equally regardless of the quality or usefulness of their work.

Efforts to put some form of socialist economic system into operation were undertaken in nearly every part of the world once the failings of unrestrained capitalism became apparent. Furthermore, even where the socialist prescriptions were consistently rejected, some form of a **mixed economy**—that is, an economy based on a mixture of public and private ownership of the means of production and on considerable public regulation of the private sector—was likely to be adopted. Soon there was no nation in the world in which every productive enterprise was in private hands, in which no effort was made by the state to consult workers' representatives in making economic policy, and in which the government never undertook to regulate prices or wages.

Why, once the inadequacies of unrestrained capitalism became clear, did some states choose socialism while other states were content simply to introduce certain socialistic practices into a capitalist system? No single definitive answer is possible, but once again it is important to consider the power of political decisions to guide our economic destinies. As a rough generalization, we can say that wherever political leaders were willing, for whatever mixture of self-serving and humanitarian motives, to permit the relatively free development of democratic political processes during the heyday of capitalism—by extending suffrage to ordinary men and women and by permitting the formation of competitive political parties—there it was possible to work out modifications of the capitalist system without abrupt political and economic change. By the end of the nineteenth century, and in many instances long before, the United States, Britain, and most of the nations of western Europe (Germany, Spain, and Italy are important exceptions) had completely accepted the idea of popular sovereignty. Full rights of citizenship were extended to one group after another, often after determined resistance but never in open repudiation of the basic principles of democracy. These nations developed and maintained mostly capitalistic economic systems.

On the other hand, in nations like the Soviet Union, many of the eastern European nations, and China as well as in the young African states and older Latin American political systems dominated by northern imperialist powers, the increasing concentration of economic power in the early capitalist period was accompanied by authoritarian leadership, either indigenous or imposed from without, that rigorously rejected all demands that political power be shared. In such political systems it was much more likely that political and economic revolution would take place, resulting, when successful, in the establishment of a socialist regime.

However, even as the more moderate aspects of socialism were being adopted in predominantly capitalist systems, and new more or less fully socialist experiments were being attempted in Central American and African states, the world's political-economic pendulum was starting its swing back in the opposite direction. Almost all of the states that had opted for the socialist solution in its purest form began to find it politically convenient to restore some characteristics of the much maligned capitalist system, producing their own form of mixed economy. Significant advantages in wages and other material rewards were given to those with the greatest political power, new forms of social rank were allowed to evolve, and private enterprises began to flourish here and there, with or without the overt approval of the state.

But this was not all. As we have seen in the amazing changes of the past few years, this time the pendulum seemed to swing its way right out of the clock: The Soviet form of socialism has fallen apart, and the entire former eastern bloc has begun the shift to a capitalist economy. The continued existence of communist regimes in China and Cuba and of strong (and sometimes ruling) social democratic parties in much of western Europe means that socialism is far from dead, but for now the capitalist system is clearly ascendant.

GLOBAL ISSUES OF POLITICAL ECONOMY

The interaction of political and economic factors is one of the most striking characteristics not only of individual polities but also of the human polity as a whole. The economic problems we encounter more and more frequently require at least some international political solutions, and political developments around the globe are more and more likely to have international economic repercussions. We are becoming increasingly dependent on one another's resources and levels of productivity—and consequently on the search for international agreements that will keep these economic factors in some kind of mutually satisfactory balance. In an era of environmental crisis, interdependent international trade, and outdated government economic policies, the human polity must somehow learn to manage its household.

Environmental Crisis: Resources and Population

In the past two decades, we have been forced to recognize that the energy sources the more fortunate nations have grown accustomed to using lavishly to meet their needs are limited and that the date of their exhaustibility is closer than we once imagined. Early in 1981, reporter Leonard Silk put the problem for Americans in stark and simple terms: "This nation, long self-sufficient in energy and indeed a leading exporter of oil, woke with a shock in the mid-1970s to discover that its way of life—and the stability and growth of its economy—were dependent on millions of barrels of oil a day from the politically shaky Middle East and other Third World countries."[8]

The political results of this recognition have been profound, as the world's citizens have argued over whether the proper response is to cut back consumption—and if so, whose consumption—or to work harder to find alternative sources—and if so, what alternatives. This second choice has meant increased politicization of the issues of using nuclear reactors, strip mining for coal, and a host of other environmental concerns.

How serious *is* the problem? At current consumption levels we have enough petroleum for about 26 more years, enough natural gas for 47 years, and enough bituminous coal for about 170 years. Copper ores will be exhausted in about 80 years, meaning that copper must then be extracted from common rocks, a far more expensive process. The cheaper sources of gold, silver, tin, and lead will have been exhausted somewhat earlier.[9] Although commercial energy consumption appears to be leveling off somewhat, the overall trend continues upward.

Thus, the resource crunch is a matter of serious concern. Even if we are granted a few years of oil "glut," as the profit-hungry oil-producing nations put more oil on the market than necessary to meet demand, we know that the long-term picture is one of steady decline.

Our need for the energy to run our machines is related to another, earlier change in our energy resource base—the shift away from animal and human labor to machines. The consequent surplus of such beasts of burden as horses, donkeys, and water buffalo was fairly easily dealt with, but clearly we have a harder time thinking of *ourselves* as merely surplus labor.

Indeed, even as fewer and fewer persons are needed to run our machines, the world's population has been steadily growing, because we are finding ways to reduce infant mortality rates, combat disease, and extend the lives of the elderly. As

TABLE 4.3   Selected Rates of Population Growth

Nation	Population in 1990 (in thousands)	Growth Rate in 1990–2000 (in percentage)	Estimated Population in 2000 (in thousands)
Nigeria	86,551	3.2	118,620
Iraq	18,425	2.9	24,731
Kenya	24,229	2.9	32,479
Nicaragua	3,617	2.7	4,759
Mongolia	2,186	2.6	2,826
Ecuador	9,806	2.0	11,945
Venezuela	18,776	2.1	23,196
India	852,656	1.8	1,018,105
Albania	3,249	1.1	3,610
China	1,136,626	1.0	1,260,154
United States	249,924	1.0	275,327
Poland	38,112	0.4	39,531
France	56,720	0.5	59,354
Japan	123,540	0.3	127,554

Source: U.S. Bureau of the Census, *The Statistical Abstract of the United States: 1994*, 114th ed. (Washington, D.C.: U.S. Bureau of the Census, 1994), pp. 850–52.

Table 4.3 makes clear, however, the population pattern is varied. Not all nations are moving in the same direction at the same pace. The world's population is increasing, but in some nations the number of citizens is either on the decline or growing so slowly as to be a serious cause of concern to those who fear that a smaller population will in fact prove inadequate for meeting the nation's needs. All of the nations of western and eastern Europe except Albania either are growing at rates of less than 1 percent per year or are in fact registering a net decline for some years (net losses have occurred in recent years in Austria, Germany, Switzerland, and the United Kingdom; they are predicted in the near future for Denmark, Hungary, Luxembourg, and Sweden as well). The United States and Japan have been able to reduce their population growth rates, and other nations formerly plagued by runaway population growth have begun to get the problem under control.

The problem is severe in Asia and very mixed. In newly industrialized South Korea the birth rate has dropped below the "fertility replacement level"—that is, fewer than two children born per woman—whereas in India fertility has leveled off at about four children per woman. There has been a sharp decline in Bangladesh from its earlier rate of seven children per woman, but the rate is still high: nearly five per woman.[10] In China, officials hope that the present population of over 1 billion (1,130,065,000 as of 1991) will never increase to more than 1.2 billion and will in fact drop to less than 700 million by the year 2080; some of the most stringent birth control policies in the world (theoretically limiting each family to a single child) have brought that nation down to below the replacement level sooner than expected.[11] Overall, Asian families add some 57 million people to the world's population every year.[12] And neither Latin America nor Africa is expected to reach replacement level fertility rates until the middle of the twenty-first century.[13]

Thus, it is in the poorest and most underdeveloped nations of the world—those least able to provide decent livelihoods for their citizens now living—that the rates of population growth remain worrisomely high and are getting higher. A growing population means higher rates of unemployment, a greater demand for social services, and, above all, more mouths to feed. The last problem causes the most severe human suffering. Despite a decrease in the absolute number of undernourished people in the world, our problems in this domain are far from resolved, particularly in Africa. The number of chronically undernourished on that continent increased from about 101 million in 1969–71 to 168 million in 1988–90.[14] And although the world's food distribution system has improved, political factors can still prevent relief from reaching those for whom it is intended. In 1991, southern Somalia suffered a prolonged drought and severe famine conditions at the same time that rival clans were fighting bitterly for political power. When international relief agencies attempted to respond, "an estimated 80 percent of food shipments were looted by armed groups affiliated with various clans."[15]

Even without such added impediments, meeting the global food demand is likely to become still more difficult in the future; by the year 2050, that demand is expected by some to be three times greater than today. Furthermore, the production growth rate for food is declining, and in 1991 there was actually a net decline for the first time in eight years. Again, the problem is most severe in Africa, where food production rates have fallen more sharply than in the world at large and do not keep up with population growth.[16]

Interdependent International Trade

The environmental crisis can be said to be natural, economic, and political, in that order. Natural causes (human greed as well as resource decline) create the crisis, which in turn causes economic problems, which lend themselves, with greater or lesser ease, to political solutions. We turn now to a global issue that is economic, political, and *psychological*—and in which these three forces are impossible to order either chronologically or in relative importance, so intimately are they intertwined. That issue is international trade.

The Great Depression of 1929 set off a severe economic crisis that reverberated throughout the world. Those reverberations continued even after the worst effects of the depression had been overcome, as nation after nation maintained policies of economic nationalism and isolationism. Each nation sought to curb imports and strengthen exports, acting with only its own immediate benefits in

(Plantu/Cartoonists & Writers Syndicate)

mind. However, the spread of protectionist policies inevitably has the negative effect of increasing costs of production within societies (as other industries pay higher than world market prices for protected manufactured goods they need for their own production) and can seriously reduce productive efficiency as well.[17] This kind of response to the Great Depression may have had short-term benefits, but it also helped create the conditions of competition and hostility that played a key role in the outbreak of World War II.

In an effort to prevent the recurrence of such a response to domestic economic problems, the major Western nations created three important international institutions: the World Bank and the International Monetary Fund (IMF) in the Bretton Woods agreement of 1944 and the General Agreement on Tariffs and Trade (GATT) in 1947. All of these institutions have assumed new importance and new functions in recent years; to give a necessarily brief explanation of these developments, we begin with the last, GATT.

The purpose of GATT is to promote international trade that is as free as possible from protectionist limitations. This goal has been interpreted as meaning, in essence, mutual reduction of tariffs and equal treatment by each nation of all other nations in matters of trade (in accordance with the *most favored nation principle*, which means that no nation will be treated any less well than the nation with whom the most favorable conditions of trade are arranged).[18] As a result, tariffs have been significantly reduced across the globe, and, partly because of these reductions, world exports increased from $94 billion in 1955 to nearly $2 trillion in 1982, while the global GNP grew from $1.1 trillion to $11.4 trillion. As of 1996, there were 131 signatories. The latest set of agreements, known as the Uruguay Round, bring trade in agricultural and textile products into "regular GATT discipline" and establish the World Trade Organization (WTO), giving the GATT signatories a far more elaborate institutional structure (a secretariat, a director general, a staff) than it had in its first fifty years of existence.[19]

A key characteristic of GATT is its insistence on arriving at decisions by consensus among the participants in any set of agreements. Their relative strength naturally influences the outcome of those agreements, but within GATT itself there are no procedures for coercing consent. The World Bank and the IMF have not, however, proved so restrained. Decision-making power within these structures is not based on national sovereignty (one nation, one vote) but on level of participation; wealthy nations that contribute more have more power. And their influence determines which of the poorer nations will receive IMF funds for which projects.

To understand the new powers of the world's wealthiest nations via the World Bank and the IMF, we need to take a closer look at what has been happening to the world's poorest nations. The first thing to say is simple enough: They have been getting poorer. Overall expansion in world trade does not bring equal benefits to all nations, and poorer nations are not well placed to prosper from the world trade conditions fostered by GATT. The most favored nation principle makes it impossible to protect the less developed nations from the competition of more affluent nations, and their standing in the international economic arena has fallen rather than improved. Even among the more developed nations, the prosperity of some has come at the expense of others.

Partly in response to the conditions created by GATT, transnational corporations flourished in the postwar years, no longer so impeded by isolationist policies, and began moving their assets from country to country, taking advantage of changing interest rates, currency fluctuations, and other marginal shifts in financial conditions that can mean production advantages that are anything but marginal. The rise of transnational corporations included multinational—or transnational—banks (TNBs). During the 1970s, loans made by such banks came to account for nearly 70 percent of all international finance, and the rate of return was impressive (Citibank, for example, earned 20% of its profits in the late 1970s from loans to a single nation, Brazil[20]).

The 1980s were, however, a time of reckoning. Many of the debtor nations, especially in Latin America, were unable to make their payments on these loans and defaulted. Defaults in Mexico (1982), Brazil (1983), Venezuela (1983), and Peru (1985) were serious enough to produce a massive international debt crisis. By the end of 1990, Western commercial banks were owed $350 billion by debtor countries in the developing world.[21] The response of the TNBs was to reduce and refinance foreign debts, providing lower interest rates and longer-term loans, in exchange for which the debtor nations have improved opportunities and conditions for foreign investments.[22] Such bargaining, aided by the IMF and

World Bank policies discussed below, normally permits the delinquent nations to avoid default and even resume growth, but it also places yet more of the profits from such growth in foreign hands. According to one assessment, "Households in Latin America were poorer in 1990 than they were in 1980, in Subsaharan Africa [poorer than in] 1960. . . . Education and health budgets have been slashed in some debtor countries, further threatening the process of development that the loans were intended to support."[23] India, Russia, and most of the nations of eastern Europe are now major debtors as well. The problem of debt may be under a control of sorts, but it is far from resolved.

As the poverty of the poorest nations has increased rather than decreased in the 1980s and 1990s, the IMF and the World Bank moved in to offer their solution: Loans from these institutions for development projects would henceforth be made only after serious internal "structural adjustments" were made in the would-be borrower's internal economy. These "adjustments" normally are of a type to open up that economy to further foreign control. To show they are worthy of the funds, such states must now usually privatize a significant portion of the public sector, stop subsidizing inadequately profitable businesses, liberalize trade agreements with other nations, and pursue export development projects rather than focus on domestic consumption.[24] Such agreements will not only merit IMF funding but will also give foreign investors new incentives to move their businesses (and their jobs) abroad. The economies will prosper.

Or will they? Since the World Bank initiated these new lending practices in the early 1980s, the Third World's debt burden has risen from $785 billion to $1.5 trillion.[25] The IMF loans *have* helped bail out Western commercial banks; between 1984 and 1990 $178 billion flowed from the Third World to commercial banks through loan repayments.[26] And the World Bank is not losing money, as Herman Daly and John B. Cobb, Jr., explain:

> The fact is that the World Bank will almost always be repaid, even if the project or policy it finances produces only losses. This is because the Bank lends to sovereign governments that have the power to tax and print money. They cannot print foreign exchange, but they can buy it by printing more of their own money and accepting the consequences of inflation and devaluation—or they can tax their people honestly, rather than by inflation. In either case they can pay back the World Bank, and nearly always will do so rather than default and lose their credit rating. . . . Repayment flows on past loans are now so large that there is a "negative net flow" of funds to the nations in the southern hemisphere from the Bank [that is, the Bank is receiving more than it is giving out].[27]

Furthermore, there is a growing body of evidence that the development projects financed by the World Bank seldom work out as planned. At the end of a soberly empirical assessment of efforts made under structural adjustment programs in Ghana, Uganda, Tanzania, Kenya, Mozambique, and Zambia, Peter Gibbon, Kjell J. Havnevik, and Kenneth Hermele conclude, "While there have been significant problems encountered in the implementation of adjustment programs, insofar as they have been implemented, the accompanying trends are not encouraging. Where it has occurred, growth has been generally low and/or temporary. In those few cases where it has been higher or more sustained, the results seem to have little to do with adjustment. . . . A moratorium is probably merited, in which other options are explored."[28]

Finally, the massive shifting of assets from nation to nation, both for investment and for production purposes, is producing further shifts in the value of currencies on the world market and in interest rates, leading in turn to new decisions regarding where liquid assets might best be put to work. This new and potentially extreme volatility of the world's money markets is all but beyond political control and definitely beyond unilateral political control; no single nation can legislate stability under such conditions.

What, then, is the answer? On one hand, it appears that political action to ensure mutually acceptable international agreements providing a measure of stability is becoming ever more essential. On the other hand, how can we find a way to make such agreements work for the world's poorer peoples—and to keep the richer and more powerful nations from taking control of the process and seeking to make it work in ways that simply improve their own advantage?[29]

Inflation, Lowered Growth, and Unemployment in Developed Economies

In addition, the problems resulting from environmental crisis; from the indeterminacy, complexity, and volatility of international trade; and from the disappointing results of intervention by international financial institutions are compounded by the efforts made *within* developed economies to maintain advanced standards of living despite declining rates of growth. The desire to keep profits and wages at levels that can be sustained only by continued growth has produced widespread **inflation**, or rise in price levels, in the world's more developed economies. The difficulty of selling goods to consumers with fewer jobs makes access to the world market all the more important, but goods that are too costly at home are even more overpriced for the world market, where other nations, paying their workers lower wages and/or relying heavily on automation to save on labor costs, are able to offer their goods at lower prices. And the poorly paid or underemployed workers of those nations are unable to serve as eager consumers of expensive foreign goods.

Lowered demand leads to still lower growth, to layoffs and the spread of unemployment, and to business failures. Efforts to curb inflation by setting higher interest rates and making money harder to attain may slow the rate of price increases, but they also put another brake on growth in many sectors of the economy, and they do not make the goods produced by the nations that attempt this solution significantly more competitive on the world market.

The governments of the world's industrialized nations have attempted to solve the problems posed by slowed growth, inflated prices, and unemployment with a range of solutions matching the range of their political and economic systems. Conservative capitalist systems such as the United States and Great Britain have experimented with raising and lowering interest rates, counting on the "supply side" of the free enterprise system to produce the necessary adjustments. Nations

BOX 4.1   BEHIND THE BANK

The World Bank, made up of 176 member countries, is controlled by those that contribute the most money. The largest contributors are the United States (17.9%), Japan (7.43%), Germany (5.74%), France and Britain (5.5% apiece). Each of these nations appoints its own "executive director," who has the responsibility of determining World Bank policies and approving loans. The remaining 171 countries must share 19 executive director positions. Traditionally, the Bank's president is nominated by the U.S. president and is a U.S. citizen. . . .

The Bank is primarily comprised of three lending agencies: the International Bank for Reconstruction and Development (IBRD), the International Development Association (IDA), and the International Finance Corporation (IFC).

The IBRD lends money to the governments of Third World countries. In 1993, the IBRD approved $16.9 billion in loans to 45 countries. Most IBRD funds come from bond sales, guaranteed by creditor governments.

Unlike the IBRD, the IDA lends money at below-market rates to the poorest countries. IDA loans are directed at infrastructure, such as roads, irrigation, agriculture and energy projects. In 1992, IDA loans totalled $6.5 billion. 100% of IDA funds comes from taxpayers' money.

The IFC lends money directly to the private sector to encourage the growth of private enterprise, and has no government guarantees. Although the IFC occasionally takes out loans from the Bank, the bulk of its funding comes from capital subscriptions (tax dollars) from member countries.

The World Bank and the International Monetary Fund are "sister" institutions; membership in the IMF is a prerequisite for membership in the Bank. The IMF was established to oversee currency exchange rates, and it offers short-term loans which require countries to follow its economic plan, known as structural adjustment. The same five countries that control the World Bank also control the IMF, between them accounting for 40% of voting power.

—*Shea Cunningham*, Dollars and Sense

Source: Shea Cunningham, *Dollars and Sense* 195 (Sept.–Oct. 1994): 12. Reprinted by permission of *Dollars and Sense*, One Summer Street, Somerville, MA 02143.

with more mixed economies, such as France, the Scandinavian nations, and most of southern Europe, try to stretch world-battered currencies sufficiently to make traditional welfare state responses to the problem, buying up major private businesses, pouring government funds into job-creating projects, and (sometimes) increasing the taxes of the wealthy. In the more authoritarian capitalist systems of Asia and Latin America, the response to slowed growth is more likely to be a severe austerity program at home combined with improved conditions for investments from abroad. In 1995, Argentinean leaders demanded of their citizens that they accept wage cuts, pay higher taxes, reduce the consumption of imported goods, work harder, and even buy "patriotic" government bonds—and at the same time offered foreign companies sufficient inducements to maintain their investments.[30] And the world's few remaining communist systems, which have typically sought to keep everyone employed regardless of records of productivity, find themselves either adopting ever more ruthless labor policies or moving in the opposite direction and adopting their own brand of mixed economy. The Chinese now claim to have a "socialist market economy"—whether or not that is a good name for it, laid-off "lifetime employees" are now discovering for themselves some of the more negative effects of free enterprise (see Box 4.2).

Although each of these approaches has brought about some change, particularly in the reduction of inflation, growth rates in many nations have remained unimpressive and unemployment figures stubbornly unresponsive. Ours is not an era in which simple remedies can be easily deduced from any single ideological approach. The satisfaction of seeing whole nations suddenly commit themselves to "our way" must necessarily be accompanied by sober thoughts of how to make "our way" work. Political scientists who know how to confront the complexity of

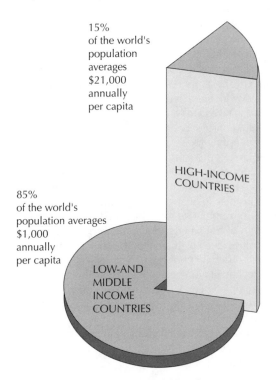

15% of the world's population averages $21,000 annually per capita

HIGH-INCOME COUNTRIES

85% of the world's population averages $1,000 annually per capita

LOW-AND MIDDLE INCOME COUNTRIES

Percentage of World Population

FIGURE 4.2   Average Annual per Capita Earnings

Source: Ian Worpol/Scientific American, 1993. Reprinted by permission.

BOX 4.2   REGIME CHANGE

The "Iron Rice Bowl" Comes Up Empty in China

Wang Xiujun is 38 years old, a mother of one tireless nine-year-old boy, and jobless. A former technician at Shanghai's China Record Factory, she was laid off during the summer of 1992. Her voice quakes with frustration from countless months of not finding new employment. "This is unfair," she insists. "I was supposed to be a lifetime employee."

She recalls when there were as many as 1,600 workers at the China Record Factory. Today, management wants to maintain a staff of 400 to 500. There are only two executives remaining in Wang's workshop.

"These managers are arrogant," she complains. "They're . . . sitting in their Mercedes-Benzes, and they don't care whether the workers . . . have jobs or not."

For Wang, and hundreds of thousands like her, the "iron rice bowl" has cracked apart in China's economic reform and enterprise restructuring. According to the Ministry of Labor, urban unemployment stands at 2.6 percent, or 4 million of the total urban work force. Although this number is low by Western standards, it conceals a statistical time bomb. At least 10 million of China's 74 million state-enterprise workers are now considered surplus.

The mammoth Wuhan Iron and Steel Corp. is in the midst of shedding two-thirds of its employees, or 80,000 people. China's textile industry, which as of 1993 employed 7.5 million workers, is planning to "switch" 4 million employees to other sectors within the next three years. Meanwhile, the central government is cutting its own bloated work force by 25 percent, or 8.5 million employees.

The problem is how to take care of them. The socialist state enterprise has functioned as a social-welfare institution. It is the sole provider of housing, medical care, and retirement pensions for more than half of the urban labor force. "As things stand now, we can't let these insolvent factories just close down," one trade-union official says. In Shanghai, workers at insolvent state enterprises are being encouraged to retire early and find other work to supplement a reduced income.

Unemployment subsidies in Shanghai vary widely depending on the factory involved, but they seldom amount to more than 210 yuan ($24) a month, and are usually much lower. In a city where per-capita monthly income averages 324 yuan ($37), the difficulties faced by the unemployed are apparent to anyone who has tried to manage a household budget.

While those with technical training and manual skills have an easier time finding new or part-time employment, workers who are middle-aged and lack education must hit the streets and try their luck at parking bicycles, selling papers, or peddling fruit and clothing.

"I'm good at repairing houses," one laid-off machine operator says. "So I have been working for friends rather steadily. But others from my factory are out on the street selling eggs and spices."

—T. S. Rosseau, "Eastern Express"

Source: T. S. Rosseau, "Eastern Express" from *World Press Review* (July 1994): 12. Reprinted by permission of "Eastern Express," Hong Kong and *World Press Review* magazine, New York.

the relationships between economic and political developments have an important role to play in this vital task.

SUMMARY AND CONCLUSION

In this chapter we have explored the relationship between politics and economics. Any economy is a system of producing, distributing, and consuming wealth. Whatever system is in operation strongly influences the course of politics—and political decisions, in turn, help shape the economic system.

Some of the specific economic factors that shape a nation's political choices are its size, available natural resources, and level of economic development. A nation's size can be measured by either its territorial extent or the number of its citizens, but in either case small states function very differently from large states. Those differences include economic considerations, which influence political relationships. The nature and extent of a nation's natural resources also help shape its political decisions. Economic development means developing the ability to process and market raw materials in order to improve the material well-being of the nation's own people. The relationship between politics and economic development is complex and variable. Economic forces do shape politics, and profoundly, but they do not do so in isolation from one another or from other social forces.

Different political systems have led to the institutionalization of different economic systems: capitalism, socialism, and mixed economies. Capitalism is a system in which entrepreneurs are free to plow their profits back into capital expenditures. Unbridled capitalism can lead to such inequalities of wealth that a demand will arise for either socialism or some form of a mixed economy. Under socialism, the state controls all the means of production and is itself supposedly controlled by the workers. Nearly every nation in the world, however, has a mixed economy, an economy based on a mixture of public and private ownership of the means of production and on considerable public regulation of the private sector.

The growing interdependence of the human polity has raised many of the issues of political economy to the global level, making these problems simultaneously more complex and more urgent to resolve. Particularly urgent are our shared problems of declining energy resources and increasing population—with population growth often most pronounced in nations that are already unable to meet the pressing needs of their people. Shortsighted government policies sometimes only deepen our economic dilemmas as we struggle separately and often ineffectually to cope with problems produced by interdependent international trade, widespread unemployment, unimpressive rates of growth, and the economic costs of a period of massive global political and economic change on a scale unseen since World War II.

In sum, the relationship between politics and economics is as close today as it was in our earliest efforts to establish a civilized life in common with our neighbors. In fact, our ever more elaborate political structures and our continued material development make that relationship constantly more complex—especially when we realize that for many purposes "our neighbors" are the nearly 6 billion people now living on the planet.[31]

Despite the immensity of the challenge, there is nevertheless reason to hope that we are finding new ways to address the present crisis in the world economy. Gone are the days of instant and dogmatic declarations of simplistic cures. When the needs are as urgent as they are at the present time, and when no nation, including our own, is exempt from the effects of global transformation, it is clearly time to extend our widest sympathies and to put our surest knowledge to work in the quest for solutions that reach far beyond the borders of a single state.

Selected Readings

Caporaso, James A., and David P. Levine. *Theories of Political Economy.* Cambridge: Cambridge University Press, 1992. A useful framework for understanding the relationship between politics and economics.

Fardoust, Shahrokh, and Ashok Dhareshwar. *A Long-Term Outlook for the World Economy: Issues and Projections for the 1990s.* Washington, D.C.: World Bank, 1990. A comprehensive look at major indicators of growth and decline in the world economy.

Galbraith, John Kenneth. *A Journey through Economic Time: A Firsthand View.* Boston: Houghton Mifflin, 1994. A consideration of the effects of war, revolutions, ideologies, and government policies on the major economic and social events after World War I.

Krueger, Anne O. *Political Economy of Policy Reform in Developing Countries.* Cambridge: MIT Press, 1993. A clear explanation of the interaction between economic and political variables in economic development.

Reich, Robert B. *The Work of Nations: Preparing Ourselves for Twenty-first Century Capitalism.* New York: Knopf, 1991. A call to U.S. citizens to learn to think of the economy in global terms, and to develop "a positive economic nationalism."

Singer, Hans Wolfgang, and Sumit Roy. *Economic Progress and Prospects in the Third World: Lessons of Development Experience since 1945.* Gloucester, England: Edward Elgar, 1993. A balanced explanation of the economics of developing nations, providing a detailed historical analysis and case studies in Nigeria and India.

Spero, Joan Edelman. *The Politics of International Economic Relations.* New York: St. Martin's, 1990. A useful introduction to economic relations between the industrialized nations and between rich and poor nations, including a discussion of the economics and politics of money, trade, and foreign investment from 1945 to 1990.

Widner, Jennifer A., ed. *Economic Change and Political Liberalization in Sub-Saharan Africa.* Baltimore: Johns Hopkins University Press, 1994. A discussion of the economic crisis in Africa in the 1980s, analyzing the effects of structural adjustment and economic reform programs.

Notes

1. For a good brief discussion of the various and shifting meanings of the term *political economy*, see Eileen R. Meehan, "Rethinking Political Economy: Change and Continuity," *Journal of Communication* 43, no. 4 (Autumn 1993): 105–9.

2. José M. Gonzalez-Eiras, "International Trade and Economic Nationalism," in *Economic Development and Social Change: United States–Latin American Relations in the 1990s*, ed. Antonio Jorge (New Brunswick, N.J.: Transaction, 1992), p. 3.

3. Gonzalez-Eiras, "International Trade and Economic Nationalism," p. 3.

4. The birth of capitalism is said to have occurred when sixteenth-century textile manufacturers in England began using profits to expand (rather than just to maintain) productive capacity. For a study of this era of development, see Immanuel M. Wallerstein, *The Modern World System: Capitalist Agriculture and the Origins of the European World Era in the Sixteenth Century* (New York: Academic Press, 1976).

5. Douglas A. Irwin, *Mercantilism as a Strategic Trade Policy* (Washington, D.C.: Federal Reserve System, 1990); and Immanuel M. Wallerstein, *The Modern World System II: Mercantilism and the Consolidation of the European World-Economy, 1600-1750* (New York: Academic Press, 1980).

6. Adam Smith, *Inquiry into the Nature and Causes of the Wealth of Nations* (New York: Modern Library, 1937).

7. Lenin's formula was "from each according to his ability—to each according to his needs." V. I. Lenin, *State and Revolution* (New York: International Publishers, 1932).

8. Leonard Silk, "A Growing Interdependence," *New York Times*, 8 Feb. 1981, sec. 12, p. 1.

9. International Institute for Environment and Development and the World Resources Institute, *World Resources 1987* (New York: Basic Books, 1987), p. 299.

10. World Resources Institute, *World Resources 1994–95* (New York: Oxford University Press, 1994), p. 30.

11. *The World Almanac and Book of Facts 1991* (New York: Pharos Books, 1990), p. 479; and James C. F. Wang, *Contemporary Chinese Politics: An Introduction* (Englewood Cliffs, N.J.: Prentice Hall, 1992).

12. Lester R. Brown, *State of the World 1995* (New York: Norton, 1995), pp. 3–20.

13. World Resources Institute, *World Resources 1994–95*, p. 30.

14. Food and Agriculture Organization of the United Nations (FAO), *The State of Food and Agriculture 1992* (Rome: FAO, 1992), pp. 16–20.

15. Helen Chapin Metz, ed., *Somalia: A Country Study* (Washington, D.C.: Library of Congress, Federal Research Division, 1993), p. 154.

16. World Resources Institute, *World Resources 1994–95*, pp. 107–8. See also Lester R. Brown, "Reassessing the Earth's Population," *Society* (May–June 1995): 7–10.

17. Gonzalez-Eiras, "International Trade and Economic Nationalism," pp. 9–10.

18. David H. Blake and Robert S. Walters, *The Politics of Global Economic Relations*, 2nd ed. (Englewood Cliffs, N.J.: Prentice Hall, 1983), p. 12.

19. John H. Jackson, "The World Trade Organization, Dispute Settlement, and Codes of Conduct," in *The New GATT: Implications for the United States*, ed. Susan M. Collins and Barry P. Bosworth (Washington, D.C.: Brookings Institution, 1994), pp. 63–83.

20. Stuart Corbridge, ed., *World Economy* (New York: Oxford University Press, 1993), p. 27.

21. Ibid., p. 28.

22. See, for example, Kenneth N. Giepin, "Brazil in an Accord with Large Banks on Cutting Its Debt," *New York Times*, 16 Apr. 1994, A1.

23. Corbridge, *World Economy*, p. 29.

24. Herman E. Daly and John B. Cobb, Jr., *For the Common Good* (Boston: Beacon Press, 1994), p. 440.

25. Walden Bello and Shea Cunningham, "Reign of Error: The World Bank's Wrongs," *Dollars and Sense* 195 (Sept.–Oct. 1994): 11.

26. Ibid.

27. Daly and Cobb, *For the Common Good*, p. 440.

28. Peter Gibbon, Kjell J. Havnevik, and Kenneth Hermele, *A Blighted Harvest: The World Bank and African Agriculture in the 1980s* (Trenton, N.J.: Africa World Press, 1993), pp. 128–29.

29. Daly and Cobb argue in *For the Common Good* that the task is so difficult the real answer is simply to return to national control of indigenous economies.

30. Matt Moffett and Jonathan Friedland, "Taking a Huge Risk, Argentina Intentionally Deflates Its Economy," *Wall Street Journal*, 21 Mar. 1995, A1, A17.

31. *The Statistical Abstract of the United States: 1994*, 114th ed. (Washington, D.C.: U.S. Bureau of the Census, 1994), p. 850, gives the world population as 5,643,290,000 persons as of 1994 and projects that it will be 6,165,079,000 as of the year 2000. The global rate of population growth is now 1.5 percent per year; there is an average of 112 persons per square mile on the planet's land mass.

5 Politics and Culture

Are you a patriotic citizen? Do you get a lump in your throat when you see your country's flag waving in the breeze? Or do you feel rather cynical about what seems to you to be nothing more than nationalistic nonsense? Do you have stronger feelings of affiliation with a particular ethnic group than you do with the nation-state in which you live? Would you like to see the United Nations become a stronger body—or a weaker one? Do you think it might make sense to decriminalize the sale and use of drugs? What is your stand on the issue of abortion? How do you feel about welfare policies? Do you support the candidates of a particular political party? Which of the ideologies discussed in Chapter 3 made the most sense to you?

The point of all these questions is not to persuade you that you have political attitudes and opinions, but to get you ready for another question: Where did you get them? Why do you have these views about politics? And here's still another question: So what? Your beliefs may be important to you (let's hope they are), but does it make any difference to your political system that you hold the views you do? What about your counterparts in other political systems? Do the views of the Russian or Thai college students on matters of political significance have any impact on their nations' politics?

Perhaps your first instinct is to answer these questions more or less like this:

1. I have the opinions I have because I have given these matters rational thought and have made intelligent decisions.
2. My opinions matter when I vote, because I live in a modern democracy. Most of the time, however, no one besides my mother and my dog pays very much attention to what I think (and neither of them is really all that interested either).
3. The political opinions of an ordinary citizen who lives in a nation that is not a modern democracy do not matter to anyone.

If these are your answers, then this chapter should give you grounds for rethinking them. First, the good news: Your political opinions (and those of your counterparts in other nations, whatever the nature of their political system) probably matter a great deal more than you think, especially if they are expressed by means other than merely voting. Then the not-so-good news: You may have worked out fine, logical reasons for holding the opinions you do, but chances are you got them in the first place because you were influenced by other forces in your life.

The subject of this chapter is the social and cultural context within which we make our political decisions and the effect these have on politics. Here we explore how different societies, and different groups within societies, develop and disseminate the values that shape political opinions, structures, and policy decisions. Our interest now is in **cultural values**—that is, values shared by a group of people in a given culture. (**Culture** is a word that has many meanings, as a quick trip to the dictionary will remind you; here I am using it to mean the ideas and customs shared by a given people in a given period of time.) Some cultural values are widely shared throughout a polity; others are shared less widely, by specific groups within that polity, or sometimes more widely, by groups whose boundaries are larger than those of specific states. In this chapter, we consider first how cultural values are important at the level of the nation-state and then consider their nature and impact at the subnational (or supranational) level. We emphasize the cultural values of ethnicity, race, and religion, but we also give attention to the values that groups share on the basis of shared class, language, gender, age, or region of residence.

THE POLITICAL CULTURE OF THE NATION-STATE

Almost every polity has something that political scientists call a **political culture**—that is, a widely shared set of "cognitions, perceptions, evaluations, attitudes, and behavioral predispositions" that permit the members of that polity to "order and interpret political institutions and processes, and their own relationships with such institutions and processes."[1] Of course, the values that compose a culture may and normally do change over time. A recent study of U.S. values finds, for example, that while acceptance of different ethnic groups and diverse lifestyles has increased in recent years—as has concern for the environment—the importance attached to obligations to others, to work for its own sake, and to following the conventions of the larger society has steadily declined.[2] But there are also continuities in the U.S. value system: Walter S. Jones points out that U.S. citizens continue to be much more concerned about how to protect political and religious liberty than about the capacity of a political system to ensure economic well-being and economic justice.[3]

The political cultures of other nations have also been analyzed and reanalyzed over time. In one study, German citizens were found to have a "detached, practical and almost cynical attitude toward politics," while Mexicans were said to reject bureaucratic authority as "corrupt and arbitrary," and the Italian political culture was described as one of "unrelieved political alienation and . . . social isolation and distrust."[4] These comments are all drawn from *The Civic Culture*, a large-scale comparative study of the political cultures of five nation-states—the United States, Great Britain, Germany, Mexico, and Italy—made in the early 1960s. In this important study, authors Gabriel Almond and Sidney Verba set forth the ideal of a **civic culture**, one in which citizens combine a commitment to moderate political participation with a belief in the legitimacy of officialdom and a mild tendency toward **parochialism**—that is, toward withdrawing into the private sphere. Such an orientation, they argued, serves the citizen and the polity by "keeping politics, as it were, in its place" and ensuring the "balance between governmental power and governmental responsiveness" necessary to maintain a stable democracy.[5]

The question of an *ideal* political culture is, of course, a normative one. As Mattei Dogan and Dominique Pelassy, among others, have pointed out, it is important to remember that sometimes negative evaluations of a system arise from historical and political fact rather than from dysfunctional cultural attitudes.[6] Furthermore, when belief in the duty and value of political participation is low, especially among the less-advantaged groups in a society, the surface calm of the civic culture can be both deceptive and short lived. Great Britain was described by Almond and Verba as a "deferential civic culture" in 1963 but since that time has become subject to sporadic rioting by members of groups that were politically passive before.[7] Such groups have now felt the impact of recent reductions in public spending on social welfare, health, and education, as the British government has initiated an austerity program a more contemporary author describes as an outright "attack upon social citizenship rights."[8]

Dramatic changes have also taken place in the German political culture since *The Civic Culture* was published. In 1963, Almond and Verba found that only 7 percent of their German sample cited "governmental and political institutions" as "the things about this country that [they] were most proud of." A follow-up study done in 1978, after the memory of the institutions that nation had established during the Nazi regime had had fifteen more years to fade, found 31 percent of West Germans ready to give this answer to the same question.[9] Then came German reunification in 1990, posing immense new problems of national identity. According to Anne-Marie Le Gloannec, unification meant recovering "both the East German past and the past common to both states. . . . Unification entails the coupling, however uneven, of two ideological visions, two political and cultural projects, two different kinds of legitimacy and logic."[10] It is disappointing but perhaps not surprising that the evolving political culture of the new Germany includes such dangerous trends as increased hostility to the nation's large Turkish and Romish (gypsy) populations and renewed emphasis on bonds of German kinship.

Italian political culture has also changed significantly since the 1960s. In assessing Italian political culture a key question has been the changing role of the family. In a book published about the same time as the Almond and Verba study, Edward Banfield argued that Italians always put the family and its interests first, regardless of the impact on community or national interests, an interpretation that seemed to explain why Almond and Verba found them so politically alienated and distrustful.[11] In recent decades, however, the role of the family has greatly changed in Italy. Women have acquired more education, the birth rate has fallen, a feminist movement has emerged, and families often need more than one income to make ends meet, so that more and more women have moved into the workforce. At the same time, it has become more difficult for young adults to earn enough to live on their own. Staying at home unwillingly, they tend, says Donald Sassoon, to "challenge the very institution of the family, to develop an anti-familial ideology." Sassoon sees Italian youth as anti-authoritarian, often highly politicized, and having a strong sense of solidarity with their own age group, even across national borders.[12] Italian lack of respect for their own political system can no longer be explained as merely the by-product of an unusually strong sense of respect for the family, nor are the most alienated always simply uninformed and disinterested.

Nevertheless, family values remain important in the study of national political cultures, as research unrelated to *The Civic Culture* has shown. According to Lucian Pye, the high value the citizens of Myanmar (Burma) place on obedience to parents is the basis for their apparent readiness to accept authoritarian leadership. To yield to the wishes of the parents is to act in an exemplary fashion. At a very early stage in life, the children in Myanmar are taught to be completely submissive before any form of authority and to expect that a passive and yielding attitude will be most likely to please those with power.[13] Pye has also stressed the importance of conformity in Chinese political culture: "The imperative of conformity fosters a make-believe world of politics, where . . . the emotional importance attached to maintaining 'face' produces a style of human relationships in which feigned compliancy is often the norm."[14] Note that Pye is not claiming that the Chinese always obey, but only that they usually pretend to be doing so: "Conformity and rebellion are the breath of Chinese politics," says Pye.[15]

Sometimes the most important value in a nation's political culture is simply pride in shared nationhood, or *nationalism*. This value is particularly likely to be stressed in the early years of a new nation or when a nation has been through a particularly harrowing period in its history. When France suffered humiliating defeats, both in World War II and in the loss of empire, the insistence by general and then-president Charles de Gaulle that French grandeur could yet make its mark in the world brought him strong support—especially as France struggled to keep from being overwhelmed by U.S. wealth and power in the immediate post-war years—and a marked revival of French nationalistic spirit.

Of course, the task of creating a new sense of national unity is often complicated by the presence of groups whose tendency is to give their first loyalty to their own members. National leaders must find a way to balance the demands of such groups against the need for national solidarity. Precisely because a value is an opinion to which the holder attaches importance, acting without regard to values widely held in a society is one way to ensure a very brief tenure in office.

However, a wide repertoire of responses is available to those in authority, ranging from outright oppression to nationalistic exhortation to careful and pragmatic efforts to accommodate diversity without allowing it to tear the nation apart. Charles Tilly has suggested that when groups become sufficiently powerful to threaten the established leadership, more effort will be devoted to suppressing the group than to meeting its demands.[16] At such times, national leaders may engage in overt acts of repression, making it clear that to hold the contested value is to risk the wrath of the state and political punishment, as in China in June 1989 when then-premier Li Peng ordered the troops to clear Tiananmen Square of student protesters seeking a democratic political system, killing and injuring hundreds, and later arresting thousands more.[17]

When leaders are more concerned about the survival of the nation-state than about staying in power, they may rely more on exhortation than on repression. When the new state of Zimbabwe was created after years of colonial domination by the British, the Ndebele and Shona peoples no longer had a common oppressor to hold them together, and tribal conflict reemerged. In an effort to bring it to a halt, Joshua Nkomo, leader of the minority Ndebele, told the people of his tribe, "We are one people. You have got to accept that principle. We are one nation. There is no question of swallowing one another. Pick yourselves up, pull up your socks, and say we shall be one."[18]

But the most effective ways for nation-states to develop a shared sense of nationhood when significant differences exist within the polity is to find ways to accommodate those differences—ways that do not undermine the state. It may be possible to reach compromise positions on conflicting values, neither fully pleasing nor fully outraging any single set of sensibilities, as in an Irish decision to delay a referendum on permitting divorce while passing legislation to protect the property rights of persons divorced elsewhere.[19] Sometimes the nation-state seeks to ensure the trust and loyalty of diverse groups by enshrining such compromises in the nation's constitution. In multilingual India, for example, the constitution explicitly recognizes fourteen languages in addition to the principal one, Hindi (although in fact about 1,650 languages and dialects are spoken in that nation).[20] Federal systems, in which the constituent units (states, departments, provinces) have independent power over certain matters (as discussed in Chapter 12), permit different geographical regions to maintain different social norms on the matters under their jurisdiction. (Exactly which norms are protected in such systems is not always crystal clear: Canadians have recently battled over whether or not legislation forbidding businesses in the province of Quebec to use any language other than French on their outdoor signs really comes under the protection of that nation's federal constitution.)[21]

Other important constitutional accommodations of conflicting values are clauses that ensure the protection of individual rights and liberties. The Bill of Rights in the U.S. Constitution, the French Declaration of the Rights of Man, the Indian Bill of Fundamental Rights, and the Venezuelan Bill of Rights are all examples of the ways polities attempt to ensure in their constitutions that citizens will be able to live according to their personal values as long as they do not interfere with the rights of others. Such clauses are usually addressed to individual values, but when they refer to matters of religion or language, or to the right of equal treatment under the laws regardless of gender, race, or ethnicity, then they are obviously of major significance for particular organized groups as well.

THE POLITICAL CULTURE OF SUBNATIONAL AND SUPRANATIONAL GROUPS

In the previous section, our focus has been on the shared culture of a nation-state and the different ways such polities may seek to repress, limit, and/or accommodate subnational cultural differences that threaten national unity. It is time now to look more directly at the nature and significance of subnational and supranational group cultures. What is the basis for their formation? Such a question, of course, has no single answer. Individuals within a polity may feel separated from their compatriots—and closer to the citizens of other states—because of such personal characteristics as ethnicity (or race), religious affiliation, class identity (see Box 5.1), gender, age, language, or regional origins. This sense of difference may be present when the polity is first formed, in which case it may constitute one of the chief hurdles to the original establishment of the nation. Or it may develop during the lifetime of the polity, as wars shift national boundaries, as patterns of immigration and emigration change the mix of humanity contained within those boundaries, as the gap between rich and poor grows or declines, as values change regarding gender roles, or as the proportion and health of the aged change. The significance of group values for the political system can be better understood by looking briefly at two of the key variables—ethnicity and religion—in turn, and then considering two contemporary examples of the impact these forces have had in national and international politics.

BOX 5.1   CLASS

In most social systems, differences in level of income, level of education, and kind of occupation tend to cluster together and to produce, sometimes in combination with differences in the way we talk and dress and the kind of material goods we acquire, a **class** identity.[22]

Class identity can be a powerful force urging citizens to adopt distinctive political attitudes and beliefs. This is especially likely to be the case when two other conditions are met: First, the members of a class are conscious of that membership, and second, class membership is "bonded" with one or more other group identities.[23] To cite an example of the latter condition, trade unions have often been formed by people who have a sense of common destiny owing to shared social class, as well as by those seeking to improve conditions of employment. Class identity thus becomes bonded with union identity, and the possibility of acting on behalf of the two identities simultaneously gives added power to the members' political action. The Polish trade union Solidarnosc was formed by members of the Polish working *class* who were then able to use their years of experience working to defend the always embattled organization to engage in a political struggle of yet greater significance: helping to bring about the downfall of communism in their nation by forming a *party* and successfully campaigning to make their own leader, Lech Walesa, president of the new republic.[24]

Of course, the politicization of class interests is not always a working-class phenomenon. The social and business contacts of the more affluent with one another can also stimulate a sense of shared class, shared values, and shared responsibility to protect those values through political activism. Traditional middle-class occupational groups that feel threatened as much by changing social mores as by automation and advanced technology sometimes seek political expression in new political movements, and rising class consciousness among peasant populations has played a key role in the growth of organized and sometimes successful rebel movements.[25]

Source: Kay Lawson, *The Human Polity,* 4th ed. (Boston: Houghton Mifflin, 1997). Reprinted by permission.

Ethnicity and Race

Determining whether a given person belongs to a racial or an **ethnic group** or not is a highly subjective issue. This is particularly true of ethnic subdivisions within the same race. As Robert J. Thompson and Joseph R. Rudolph Jr. have pointed out, "Ultimately, membership in an ethnic group is largely a matter of ascription. One belongs because one perceives oneself as a member of a group or because others so perceive one."[26]

Those who accept membership in a particular group, be it out of passionate conviction or passive acceptance, tend to share more than a single belief or value, and the values they share may well assume political significance. As Danuta Mostwin reminds us, "Ethnic ties are among the strongest human feelings. They

Politics and cultures collide. African and Arab immigrants, once welcome to carry out jobs not wanted by others but now blamed for high rates of unemployment, demonstrate near the Eiffel Tower to protest the French government's determination to send home all those whose papers or work permits have expired. (The photos carried by the demonstrators show fellow immigrants on hunger strikes.)

(Reuters/Jacky Naegelen/Archive Photos)

are the core of a person's self, the cornerstone of . . . identity."[27] The views of the group on such easily politicized issues as the content of schooling, employment services, welfare aid, the standards for promoting individuals to positions of responsibility, and procedures for adjudicating disputes, may well run counter to the views of the larger society on the same kinds of issues. The consequences of such conflict can run the gamut from constant negotiation to open oppression to civil war.

The conditions of ethnic and racial distinctiveness, rivalry, struggle against oppression, and full or partial assimilation into the national ethos are not new, nor are they found with any greater frequency in one part of the world than in any other. It is useful to remember that the Chinese absorption of the Mongol and Tibetan peoples, the struggle of immigrants from former colonies for equal treatment in Great Britain, the determination of the Jewish people in Israel to build a state of their own, the rivalry between the Luo and Kikuyu groups in

BOX 5.2   RACE AND ETHNICITY IN THE UNITED STATES

What racial or ethnic group do you belong to? U.S. citizens often refuse to play that game and proudly assert, "I am an American and that's that." Others are hard pressed to give an answer: "Well, my mother's mother was Welsh, and her father was a mixture of English, French, and Norwegian. My father's mother was half Cherokee, one-fourth African American and one-fourth Scottish, and his father was part German, part Dutch, and part Indonesian. So you tell me: What ethnic group do I belong to?" But even in so large and heterogeneous a nation as the United States, there are many for whom racial or ethnic identity is a matter of great importance and whose values and attitudes are shaped by this primary reference group.

FIGURE 5.1   U.S. Population Percentages by Race, 1810–2050

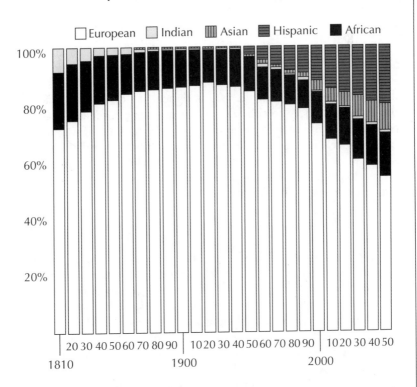

Source: Antonio McDaniel, "The Dynamic Racial Composition of the United States," in *An American Dilemma Revisited: Race Relations in a Changing World,* ed. Obie Clayton, Jr. Copyright © 1996 Russell Sage Foundation, New York. Reprinted by permission.

Kenya, the battle of African Americans in the United States for equality in the land their ancestors were brought to by force, and the treatment of indigenous populations throughout the Americas—different as they may be in other respects—are all manifestations of the conflict between group and national political cultures and the quest for a political resolution of that conflict, be it peaceful and accommodative or harsh and oppressive.

Yet the net result of such struggles is not always negative. The very process of politicizing group values and bringing them into a wider arena can serve as an important means of integrating the group into a larger world, blurring the distinctions between the political cultures of group and nation or group and world community. This process can also serve to revitalize and strengthen the wider political culture, as everyone (or almost everyone) learns to incorporate some of the values of the newly assimilated group—perhaps adopting hitherto unfamiliar techniques for solving problems, perhaps gaining respect for a wider range of lifestyles and social values.

Religion

Many of the comments made about group distinctiveness based on ethnicity apply with equal force to groups based on religion. Indeed, ethnic and religious characteristics are often bonded, in the sense that the group identity is based on both, and the line between the two is difficult to distinguish. Catholicism is nearly as important as French ancestry in providing Canada's largest minority population with its sense of group identity. Judaism is a religion, but Jews share an ethnic as well as a religious heritage and constitute important minority populations in numerous countries. Significant Armenian-Christian populations exist in the predominantly Arab-Muslim nations of Iraq and Syria. The second largest ethnic group in the predominantly Malay-Muslim nation of Malaysia is Chinese Buddhist.

There are, however, societies that encompass separate group cultures based exclusively on religious differences. Muslim, Jewish, Buddhist, and Christian communities persist in cultures where the dominant religion is a different one and where the members of the religious minority are similar to the dominant populations in all other respects. In some cases, the religious distinction even arises within the same denomination, as separatist sects develop among those who belong to the dominant religious group but practice their religion "with a difference." Members of both the Sunni and Shiite Islamic sects are Muslim, but the incompatibility between these two groups is severe; it played a major role in provoking war between Iraq and Iran and periodically produces armed clashes within nations like Pakistan in which both sects are found.[28]

In other cases, the distinction is not between religions or sects but simply between dramatically different interpretations of the same religion and the significance of its rulings for political affairs. Almost every Algerian is Muslim, but those who believe that the Qu'ran gives women full civil, social, and political rights and those who believe it says that women should remain invisible and in the home are presently in violent conflict. Over 30,000 persons have been killed over that issue in the past few years, including many women whose sole offense was to appear in public in Western clothes or wearing makeup.[29]

Religious values are, almost by definition, nonnegotiable, and the stakes are high. If I believe I will achieve eternal life and happiness by following a certain religious code, I will not be persuaded easily to give it up in the interests of such temporary comforts as peace on earth. Furthermore, the more my religious beliefs are challenged by the dominant culture, the more likely I am to be persuaded that I am being tested. Do I really believe? Then I will endure any hardship rather than sacrifice one tenet of the faith I have chosen. The members of a minority religious group, scorned or perhaps actively oppressed by members of the dominant group, must either break away or develop a strong enough attachment to their religious values to be able to endure the insults and injuries that come their way. It is for these reasons that religious fanaticism is more common in minor sects. Of course, the fanaticism itself makes the group less and less acceptable to the dominant groups in the society. If the boundary between the religious sphere and the political sphere cannot be established and maintained, the result may well be a spiral of increased fanaticism on one hand and increased public condemnation on the other. (See Box 5.3.)

IMPACT OF CULTURAL DIVISIVENESS ON THE NATION-STATE

The divisions created in societies by ethnicity and race, or by religion, are among the deepest we know. They can, of course, be a source not only of diversity but also of important contributions to the strength and creativity of a polity. Furthermore, different peoples living harmoniously together in a single nation-state already know what it means to live in the human polity and are in that sense inevitably better equipped than more homogeneous peoples to function effectively internationally.

In recent years, however, many groups that formerly lived together in relative contentment (or resignation) within the same nation-state have become determined to break apart or establish new rules for living together. The end of the Cold War has meant the end of polarized conflict between blocs of nations, each unified by a common goal of resisting the territorial and ideological encroachment of the other. Peoples whose struggle to maintain separate identities seemed long ago to have been forever submerged in this global battle have reemerged with seemingly undiminished needs to assert themselves and their nationhood. This has been particularly true of peoples whose cultural identity rests heavily on ethnicity or race. The breakup of former Yugoslavia and of former Czechoslovakia as well as the efforts of the Baltic states and of the Chechyns to establish independence from Russia are obvious examples of how the fall of the Soviet Union has permitted this kind of nationalism to reappear.

Not all ethnic intergroup struggles are clearly related to the end of the Cold War, however. The genocidal attacks of the warring peoples of Rwanda upon one another, the renewed insistence of some Canadians of French descent on the

BOX 5.3   REGIME CHANGE

Political Change and Culture: The Case of Afghan Women

The Taleban of Afghanistan, a fundamentalist Islamic group, had taken over more than two-thirds of that nation by 1997. Under the leadership of Mullah Mohammed Omar, the Taleban began to apply stricter rules regarding the conduct of women than any other Islamic state. Women are not allowed to work in any domain except medicine, where regulations governing what they may do must be carefully followed. Since many men died in the civil war that lasted nearly twenty years, women who cannot work often have no way to feed their families, and the government provides no family benefits. Foreign aid agencies must get the permission of the state to hire or to assist destitute women. Girls' schools have been closed. Women are banned from visiting male hospital patients in wards that contain nonfamily members. They are prohibited from wearing shoes that make noise as they walk. Disobeying these and similar laws brings severe punishment: flogging, stoning, imprisonment.

The Taleban takeover was not made possible because of the popularity of such policies, but neither was it due simply to military prowess. By 1994 the Afghans had become desperately eager to be rid of the previous rulers, religious mujahidin who, after taking part in the battle against Russian conquest, were now plundering and killing their own people. When Mullah Omar, then an obscure former guerrilla commander, led a small band of followers in a counterattack against the mujahidin, he became a local hero. His swift rise to power was aided by Pakistan, hoping to strengthen its economic and political alliance with the Muslim states of central Asia, and by Saudi Arabia, another state pursuing a very conservative form of Islam. Although none of the member nations of the United Nations recognized the Taleban government, neither did they intervene on behalf of the Afghan women. The United States's own close ties with Pakistan and the Taleban's promise (so far unkept) to halt the poppy growing and opium producing that have made Afghanistan the world's largest single-nation source of opium have all contributed to keep the United States from taking a strong line against the oppression of women under the new leadership. The Talebans, who are Sunni Muslims, also win U.S. favor by being deeply hostile toward Iran, the ruling majority of which belongs to the rival Shiite sect of Islam.

Sources: Elvira Cordileone, "No Help for Women in Afghanistan," *Toronto Star,* 12 Aug. 1997, E1; and John F. Burns and Steve LeVine, "For Afghans, Taleban's Rise to Power Was Deliverance from Tyranny," *International Herald Tribune,* 2 Jan. 1997, 2.

need for a separate state, and the complete transformation of legal and social relationships between white and black South Africans are examples of ethnic struggles that are affected only indirectly, if at all, by the fall of the Soviet Union. Their genesis is in more ancient battles: those of imperialist conquest and the resultant imposition of common nationhood on peoples who would have rather kept apart.

As merely mentioning these examples reminds us, the determination of different ethnic groups to redefine their legal and social relationships with other groups may be amply well motivated. They may also sometimes be peacefully pursued. Why do they sometimes lead to bloodshed and even civil war and sometimes not? Looking more closely at two very different cases, that of the former Yugoslavia and that of Canada, may help us find the answer to that question.

The background of the ethnic disputes in the territory of the former nation of Yugoslavia and in the present nation of Canada have a certain number of points in common. In both cases, national boundaries were determined by conquest and subsequent warfare, ultimately bringing together, not terribly long ago, people of different religions and different languages as well as different ethnic backgrounds. In both cases, the smoldering coals of old resentments have been periodically fanned by leaders seeking political gain, and these resentments have been deeply felt by many members of the general populace. Yet the struggle in Canada, while certainly intense and as yet unresolved, has for many years been waged within the confines of the democratic process, whereas in Yugoslavia it provoked open warfare and even attempted genocide.

To understand the differences, we must go beyond these superficial similarities and back in time—much farther back in the Yugoslav case than in that of Canada. The early nations of Croatia and Serbia were two groups of Slav settlers in the Balkans. During the Middle Ages each practiced different forms of Christianity, the Croatians becoming Roman Catholics within the Austro-Hungarian empire (beginning with the Treaty of Zagreb in 1102) and the Serbs following the tenets of Eastern Orthodoxy. The spread of the Ottoman empire in the fourteenth century meant the conversion of many in both groups to Islam. This third religion proved particularly strong in Bosnia-Herzegovina, a land in which both Croatians and Serbs had settled and over which both ruled at different times. Some historians believe there is no separate Bosnian identity, pointing out that Bosnia had never been an independent state and that even "among Bosnian Muslims themselves . . . there are those who would argue that all Bosnian Muslims are simply Croats or Serbs who converted to Islam."[30] However, religious identity appears to be ascendant for Muslims, whereas ethnic identity as Serb or Croatian is at least as important as religion for the self-identification of the Christian populations. Language is also a factor. Although all these peoples speak the same language, they use different scripts (Latin and Cyrillic) for writing it, and there are multiple dialects.[31] (See Figure 5.2.)

The first Yugoslav state bringing these peoples and others together was founded in 1918. In little more than a decade the more numerous Serbs imposed their rule over Croatia in the person of King Aleksander Karadjordjevic, who dissolved parliament and established a personal dictatorship. An underground Croatian resistance movement, Ustashe, led by Ante Pavelic, was formed, and in 1934 the king was assassinated. As World War II began, the Yugoslav state was dissolved by Hitler, who gave the Croatian fascist movement, led by Pavelic, a free hand in the slaughter of somewhere between 350,000 and 750,000 Serbs, Jews, Roms (gypsies), and dissident Croatians. To the extent they could, Serbs

Nationalism is often at its strongest and most irrational when formerly united peoples decide to form separate polities. Here Serbians (above) and Croatians (opposite page) each raise their national flags in fervent demonstrations for separate nationhood, whatever the cost to their peoples and the land once known as Yugoslavia.

(Above: AP/Wide World Photos; opposite: L. Delahaye/Sipa Press)

retaliated in their own resistance movement, the Yugoslav Army of the Fatherland (often referred to as the Chetniks) combining the pursuit of vengeance against the Croatians with the battle against the Nazis. When Yugoslavia was recreated after the war, its communist leader, Marshal Josip Broz Tito (and his successors after his death in 1980), sought to overcome this history, in part by suppressing it, in part by trying to substitute the ideals of communist egalitarianism for ethnoreligious competition, and in part by loosening ties with the Soviets and reforming the tenets of communist ideology to suit Yugoslav realities. But these efforts proved inadequate, especially as there continued to be different levels of economic development throughout the nation.

The fall of communism brought the Yugoslavs the opportunity to complete a process of separation from the Soviet bloc that was thus already well begun. Even more important, it brought them the chance to break away from each other, once and for all. Croatia and the more northern republic of Slovenia declared independence in July 1991. Each had maintained relatively cohesive religious, ethnic,

and geographic identities, and these declarations were accepted by most of the international community. The Christian Serbs, however, were settled extensively throughout most of Yugoslavia and were determined to keep what remained of the nation intact, as well as to fight for the autonomy of Christian Serbian communities within the newly independent states. Muslim peoples, heavily concentrated in Bosnia but living throughout the region, were caught in the middle, whatever their lines of Slavic descent.

The difficulties of untangling this web have been tragically compounded by the readiness of demagogic leaders on both sides to stir up old memories that seemingly had begun to fade away and to speak as if those guilty of crimes long past were in fact all the currently living members of the enemy group.[32] In addition, international forces such as the European Community, NATO, and the United Nations, as well as the world's strongest single power, the United States, all proved unable to work out timely, consistent, and realistic plans to avert the civil war that broke out in 1991.[33] It can be hoped that more recent diplomatic efforts to establish ceasefires, to redraw the map of Bosnia, and to create some form of confederal arrangement (see Chapter 12) will succeed, but whether or not the peace they bring will endure is inevitably more dubious. This latest siege of genocidal slaughter and rape adds another not-to-be-forgotten chapter to a

FIGURE 5.2   The Present Boundaries of the Former Yugoslavia

long history of conflict.[34] It is a history only too easy for leaders to summon up whenever they believe it can be made to serve their own political ambition—and do not care how many additional lives are squandered to that end.

The conflict between the English-speaking and French-speaking populations in Canada is very, very different. First, the history of both peoples in this part of the world goes back less than 500 years, and large-scale settlement began only at the beginning of the seventeenth century. Second, both groups considered themselves colonists for the nations from which they had migrated, rather than independent peoples and states. Third, one group, the French settlers, came under the control of the other after only about 150 years of separate settlement and after only one relatively brief war; the so-called French and Indian wars ended with French defeat in 1759, and in 1763 the French ceded the colony to Britain.[35] A brief rebellion in 1837 was rapidly suppressed. Fourth, in combination, the

British and French settlers soon outnumbered and outfought the indigenous residents of what later became the provinces of Quebec and Ontario, particularly the Iroquois and the Algonquins.

Fifth, from the beginning the nation of Canada, established in 1867 when the British granted nearly complete independence to their own compatriots, has been dominated by one contingent, the English-speaking citizens. Although relatively small indigenous Indian and Inuit populations combined with relatively large-scale immigration from other nations in Europe, Southeast Asia, and Latin America have meant that by the end of the twentieth century nearly half of all Canadians are of neither French nor British origin, the politics and government were nevertheless originally formed by and for those of English descent.[36] Newcomers have arrived as individuals, and although some have settled in ethnic enclaves (e.g., the Ukrainians and the Dutch), they have accepted Canadian structures as they found them and most have learned to speak English.

Sixth, despite this continued dominance of the English-speaking population, those of French descent have always had a special status as the largest and most cohesive ethnoreligious group, concentrated in a single region and present from the beginning of modern Canadian history. Canada thus has two official languages, English and French, and the province of Quebec, 80 percent French speaking, has numerous other special dispensations.

A seventh and final crucial difference between the Yugoslav and Canadian cases is that other nations have never attempted to play out their own struggles by waging warfare on Canadian soil (as did Hungary, Turkey, Germany, and the Soviet Union, in the case of Yugoslavia). Although the French have given their North American cousins strong moral support, they have never promised serious military aid for a battle for independence.

In combination, these factors have meant that Catholic French Canadians have really had no choice but to pursue their ends by peaceful means, and English-speaking Canadians have had no need to engage in violence to protect their ascendant position. The divisions between these two peoples are, compared to those between Croatians and Serbs in the former Yugoslavia, tidy and relatively peaceful. The absence of a history of repeated warfare between British and French-speaking Canadians means there are no memories of recent bloodshed and pillage by the other side that ambitious politicians can exploit to motivate new wars and build new careers. (The Indian and Inuit peoples who remain may have such histories, but they lack the power to form additional contingents in the current battle.)

But make no mistake. The struggle between French- and English-speaking Canadians is serious, ongoing, and very real. Today's French Canadians do not take their religion or their ethnicity less seriously than the embattled peoples of the former Yugoslavia, and they have an extremely strong commitment to maintaining a different language from the majority population. They have often believed this heritage to be threatened by the policies of the national government. But they have been compelled by circumstance, not weakened by faintheartedness, to wage their battle politically and constitutionally. This battle has not led them back to war, but it could yet lead them forward to secession. It provides ample fuel for occasional flareups of demagogic leadership.

The case of Quebec and the French Canadians is an interesting one that illustrates many other points we make later in this book. We return to them, and explain the current sources of their discontent as well as English-speaking Canadians' response, more fully later on. But for now, this example, contrasted with the Yugoslav case, does help us understand some of the reasons why ethno-religious struggle sometimes leads to bloodshed and sometimes does not. It should help us as well to stifle the impulse to call for simple solutions, insisting that if one set of peoples can find peaceful ways to conduct their battles with one another, others "should" be able to do the same. History has worked for peace in eastern Canada but for recurrent slaughter in southern Europe. The conditions present in the Yugoslav case cannot be transformed overnight. People raised in battle and the memories of battle cannot be expected suddenly to value peace over revenge and order over victory. An immense task of political resocialization lies before those who seek an end to religious-ethnic strife in this and similarly affected polities.

SUMMARY AND CONCLUSION

The culture that we live in powerfully shapes the political values we hold dear. When political values are bonded with cultural values, they have an added strength; we do not take lightly the efforts of any individuals or institutions to prevent us from living our lives according to those values. For this reason, our leaders, our institutions, and other nations interested in maintaining successful relations with us must give such values careful consideration and response or risk the loss of legitimacy, political alienation, social unrest, and possibly even revolution or war. The formation of cultural values and their significance for the political process are summarized graphically in Figure 5.3.

Conflicting cultural values can trouble international relations in time of peace as well as in time of war. In some cases, problems develop because the parties involved do not even recognize that they are operating on different normative assumptions. In most African systems, great emphasis is placed on one's responsibility to take care of other members of one's extended family, if one is in a position to do so. In most European systems, great emphasis is placed on hiring the most qualified candidate for any job, regardless of that person's family ties. When African and European management teams attempt to work together on a development project, misunderstandings and recriminations over hiring practices are highly likely if both sides have not understood and resolved this fundamental difference in cultural values.

As the nations of the world grow more interdependent, will our cultural values grow more similar? Probably. After all, socialization can take place across national boundaries as well as across the living room table or the village well. The process is complex, as a simple personal example may serve to illustrate. When I

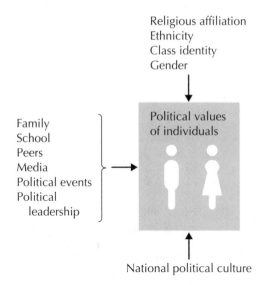

Religious affiliation
Ethnicity
Class identity
Gender

Family
School
Peers
Media
Political events
Political
    leadership

Political values
of individuals

National political culture

FIGURE 5.3   The Cultural Formation of Political Values

am invited to a home in West Africa, I am unlikely to be offered kola nuts—but when my host passes the bowl to his other guests, he is now likely to be aware that I may find the omission disturbing and to take the trouble to explain to me that it is not the tradition to include women in this practice. I myself, aware of the many courtesies that have been extended to me, may be able to put my Western feminist instincts on hold, yet I feel compelled to make a point of including his wife in the political discussion we are having, whether she is interested or not. What is happening in such a case? Several persons whose cultural values are not the same are interacting. Although we disagree, we listen to each other and we are unavoidably socializing each other. It is unlikely that no change is taking place.

Then again, how desirable is it that the same values be shared throughout the whole human polity? Might one of the values we come to share be respect for each other's differences? Or might some values be called *requisite* values for humanity? Perhaps there really are values that must be universally held if there is to be any hope at all of harmonious resolution of the problems we confront—and share—in the human polity.

Selected Readings

Aaron, Henry J., Thomas E. Mann, and Timothy Taylor, eds. *Values and Public Policy.* Washington, D.C.: Brookings Institution, 1994. Essays discussing how values are formed and can mediate the effects of public policies.

Almond, Gabriel, and Sidney Verba. *The Civic Culture.* Boston: Little, Brown, 1963. The classic study of political culture, focusing on political attitudes and democracy in Italy, Mexico, the United Kingdom, and West Germany. See also their edited volume, *The Civic Culture Revisited.* Newbury Park, Calif.: Sage, 1989.

Carment, David. "The Ethnic Dimension in World Politics: Theory, Policy and Early Warning." *Third World Quarterly* 15, no. 4 (1994). An excellent summary of the different ways ethnic conflict may be studied, stressing the importance of developing ways to recognize "early warnings" of the imminent outbreak of such struggles.

Coyle, Dennis J., and Richard J. Ellis. *Politics, Policy and Culture.* Boulder, Colo.: Westview Press, 1994. A text that argues that politics, policies, and preferences cannot be understood without a consideration of culture.

Farah, Tawfic E., ed. *Pan-Arabism and Arab Nationalism.* Boulder, Colo.: Westview Press, 1987. A series of articles on various aspects of Arab nationalism, including survey research studies, history and development of the movement, religious connections, current attitudes toward the movement, and its impact on the Arab/Israeli conflict.

Gellner, Ernest. *Culture, Identity, and Politics.* Cambridge: Cambridge University Press, 1987. An examination of the relationships among the state, civil society, and culture in the context of political concepts such as nationalism and egalitarianism.

Hermann, Margaret G., ed. *Political Psychology.* San Francisco: Jossey-Bass, 1986. A reader on various psychological aspects of politics, including environmental beliefs, values, and areas of study such as the psychology of terrorism and the psychology of protest movements.

Ryan, Michael. *Politics and Culture.* Basingstoke, England: Macmillan, 1989. An application of new modes of study derived from critical theory and poststructuralism as well as more traditional Marxist and psychoanalytic approaches to questions of the relationship between culture and politics.

Notes

1. This definition of political culture is taken from Ann L. Craig and Wayne A. Cornelius, "Political Culture in Mexico: Continuities and Revisionist Interpretations," in *The Civic Culture Revisited*, ed. Gabriel Almond and Sidney Verba (Boston: Little, Brown, 1980), p. 340. Reprinted by permission of the author.

2. Henry J. Aaron, Thomas E. Mann, and Timothy Taylor, eds., *Values and Public Policy* (Washington, D.C.: Brookings Institution, 1994), p. 5.

3. Walter S. Jones, *The Logic of International Relations*, 7th ed. (New York: HarperCollins, 1991), p. 53.

4. Gabriel Almond and Sidney Verba, *The Civic Culture* (Boston: Little, Brown, 1963), pp. 308–11.

5. Ibid., pp. 338–40.

6. Mattei Dogan and Dominique Pelassy, *How to Compare Nations* (Chatham, N.J.: Chatham House, 1990), p. 74.

7. Almond and Verba, *Civic Culture*, p. 315.

8. Desmond S. King, *The New Right, Politics, Markets and Citizenship* (Chicago: Dorsey, 1987), pp. 121, 198; *New York Times*, 6 May 1985, 3, and 4 June 1985, 1.

9. David B. Conradt, "Changing German Political Culture," in Almond and Verba, *Civic Culture Revisited*, p. 230.

10. Anne-Marie Le Gloannec, "On German Identity," *Daedalus* 124, no. 2 (Winter 1994): 133–34.

11. Edward Banfield, *The Moral Basis of a Backward Society* (New York: Free Press, 1967).

12. Donald Sassoon, *Contemporary Italy: Politics, Economy and Society since 1945* (Essex, England: Longman, 1986), pp. 102–3, 114–16.
13. Lucian W. Pye, *Politics, Personality and Nation Building* (New Haven: Yale University Press, 1962), pp. 183–84.
14. Lucian W. Pye, *The Mandarin and the Cadre: China's Political Cultures* (Ann Arbor: University of Michigan Press, 1988), p. 31.
15. Ibid.
16. Charles Tilly, *From Mobilization to Revolution* (Reading, Mass.: Addison-Wesley, 1978), p. 122.
17. *Los Angeles Times*, 9 June 1989, I1–I16; 13 June 1989, I8; 14 June 1989, I1, I7.
18. *Washington Post*, 17 Feb. 1988, A14.
19. *New York Times*, 8 Jan. 1995, 4.
20. *World Encyclopedia of the Nations: Asia and Oceania* (New York: Worldmark Press, 1988), p. 92.
21. Barry Came, "A Grievance Upheld," *Maclean's* 106, no. 18 (3 May 1993): 26.
22. Standard works on the problem of class include Karl Marx, "Manifesto of the Communist Party," in *The Marx-Engels Reader*, ed. Robert C. Tucker (New York: Norton, 1978), pp. 469–500; "The Class Struggles in France," in ibid., pp. 586–93; "The Eighteenth Brumaire of Louis Napoleon," in ibid., pp. 594–617; Max Weber, "Class, Status, Party," in *From Max Weber: Essays in Politics*, ed. H. H. Gerth and C. Wright Mills (New York: Oxford University Press, 1946), pp. 180–95; and Thomas Humphrey Marshall, *Class, Citizenship and Social Development: Essays* (Garden City, N.Y.: Doubleday, 1964). For a contemporary summary and analysis, see Berch Berberoglu, *Class Structure and Social Transformation* (Westport, Conn.: Praeger, 1994).
23. On the question of class consciousness, see Clem Brooks, "Class Consciousness and Politics in Comparative Perspective," *Social Science Research* 23 (June 1994): 167–95.
24. Lawrence Goodwyn, *Breaking the Barrier: The Rise of Solidarity in Poland* (New York: Oxford University Press, 1991), pp. ix, xxvi–xxvii. Goodwyn argues that the shared experiences of the activist members of Solidarnosc (Solidarity) were more important in bringing success than all the "documents of written exhortation—leaflets, public demands, organizing appeals, and the like" that others produced in their support (xxvii).
25. For an interesting study of peasant revolts, see Eric Wolf, *Peasant Wars of the Twentieth Century* (New York: Harper and Row, 1968). A recent example of a political party formed by both farm and working-class interests in an effort to protect cherished values and defy "technocratic decrees" is the Hunt-Fish-Nature-Tradition Party of France, whose members are as resistant to modern environmentalist values as they are to the automation of the traditional agricultural and artisan labor they represent. *L'Express*, 5 Mar. 1992, 60–62.
26. Robert J. Thompson and Joseph R. Rudolph Jr., "Ethnic Politics and Public Policy," in *Ethnicity, Politics and Development*, ed. Dennis L. Thompson and Dov Ronen (Boulder, Colo.: Rienner, 1986), p. 32.
27. Danuta Mostwin, "Ethnic Identity and the Polish Immigrant in America," *Migration World* 16, nos. 4–5 (June 1988): 25–31.
28. Akbar S. Ahmed, *Living Islam: From Samarkand to Stornoway* (New York: Facts on File, 1994), pp. 49–51.

29. Nora Boustany, "Targets of Opportunity," *Washington Post National Weekly Edition* (13–19 Mar. 1995): 17; "If Islamists Rule Algeria," *The Economist* (25 Feb. 1995): 98. See also Karima Bennoune, "Algerian Women Confront Fundamentalism," *Monthly Review* 46 (Sept. 1994): 26–39.

30. Robin Alison Remington, "Bosnia: The Tangled Web," *Current History* 92, no. 577 (Nov. 1993): 364–69. I have drawn extensively from this useful article; the quotation comes from p. 366.

31. Ian D. Armour, "Nationalism vs. Yugoslavism," *History Today* 42 (Oct. 1992): 11–13.

32. Svetlana Slapsak, "Trains, Times Lost Forever," *The Nation* (31 May 1993): 740.

33. *Wall Street Journal*, 28 July 1995, A1–A4. For a discussion of the belief held by many Muslims that international reluctance to interfere effectively came from the fact that the West "does not want a viable Muslim nation in Europe," see Akbar S. Ahmed, "Ethnic Cleansing: A Metaphor for Our Time?" *Ethnic and Racial Studies* 18, no. 1 (Jan. 1995): 18.

34. The use of rape as a weapon of ethnic warfare, particularly against societies where illegitimate sexual acts dishonor entire families, is explained in Ahmed, "Ethnic Cleansing," pp. 19–20.

35. The French and Indian wars were actually a struggle between the British and the French for control of that part of North America which later became the Canadian provinces of Quebec and Ontario; the struggle began as the two European peoples sided with different Indian tribes engaged in battle—hence the name.

36. The word *Indian* is the official term used in Canada, although *Native American* would, of course, apply there as well as in the United States.

III ACTING IN POLITICS

6 The Individual in Politics

Powerful forces shape our political life: institutions, ideologies, social pressures, and economic conditions. Even those of us who live in democratic systems often tend to assume that we have no way, as individuals, to influence the course of politics. We vote because we think we should, not because we believe our single vote can possibly change very much. If we want to bring about serious change, we usually try to do so in the company of others who agree with us; we join a group, a political party, or a social movement. We may try to prepare ourselves for a kind of employment that we hope will bring benefits to others, but usually we plan to do that work within an organization. We like to read about great men and women who have made a difference by following their dreams, but we imagine such exploits are unique, and perhaps no longer possible.

However, even in today's densely populated and increasingly complex world, the individual retains the capacity for meaningful political action. A Chinese student standing strong and firm against the advancement of a tank containing soldiers ordered to crush the demonstration he and his fellows have organized may attract the world's amazed respect and sympathy and thereby give courage to those who are determined to carry on the battle for democracy. A Latin American journalist may persist in telling the world of her government's repressive acts, even after she herself is imprisoned and tortured, and thus force changes in that nation's way of dealing with political dissent. An African-American social worker who never misses a meeting of his city's board of supervisors or an opportunity to speak on behalf of those he serves may influence the decisions of that body more than even he can tell.[1]

Individual political acts may be positive or negative—a dedicated artist may find the means to make the public newly aware of an endangered civil liberty, or a raving maniac may shoot and kill a president—but the point is the same: individuals can make meaningful changes in the course of human history.

Sometimes the individual's act is meaningful only because other individuals are performing the same act simultaneously. Even then, however, if there is no organized cooperation, it is still individual political behavior that is influential. Individual voters, acting in unwitting concert, can change the composition of parliaments and the content of national policy. Individual citizens, each responding to specific internal promptings as well as to the exhortations of others, can form a jury that issues a verdict so patently unfair that riots break out, costing many lives and millions of dollars of damage. Individual persons, acting alone, sometimes *can* change the world.

Furthermore, even when individual actors are not interested in change, their political behavior can still be significant. The same kinds of personal action that we use to try to bring about change (voting, protesting, testifying) can be used with equal effectiveness to prevent change. The reelection of an incumbent president, a deluge of telegrams protesting a government's announced intention to send troops abroad, or the passionate testimony of a series of unacquainted and unorganized witnesses against a proposed new law or the appointment of a high official are all individual acts that can shape our collective destinies by preventing change rather than bringing it about.

Finally, even when individual political actions have no significant impact on the polity at large, they may still be very meaningful to the individual actor. Your grouchy grandfather may decide (as mine did) to send his Social Security check back to the government, muttering, "I've decided I don't believe in it." A Croatian tour director in Dubrovinik may decide, after the Serbs have leveled his apartment building, the hotel where he works, and a portion of the ancient city whose wonders provided him his livelihood, that the best thing to do is move his family and his skills to Italy. Or a soldier in the army of the Ivory Coast may opt

Maggie Kuhn, founder of the Gray Panthers. The individual can make a difference in politics, sometimes by organizing others.

(UPI/Corbis-Bettmann)

not to reenlist, because he is unhappy with the way the army is used for domestic chores (road building, peacekeeping), even though his fellows are all persuaded that the relatively good pay makes a second tour of duty attractive. In all these cases, individuals have made and acted on choices that are at least partly political but that are also atypical and attract very little attention. Such choices are unlikely to have any noticeable impact on the political system, but they can be very significant for the individual actors who make them. There are, then, at least three good reasons to study the individual political behavior of ordinary citizens: (1) It can change the course of government, (2) it can prevent the course of government from changing, and (3) it can have a profound significance in the lives of individual actors.

In this chapter we emphasize the most common act of individual political behavior, the vote, but we begin by giving some attention as well to a form of political behavior that is both individual and collective: the part each of us plays in forming that mysterious entity known as "public opinion." We also consider, briefly, the wide range of political acts we can and do perform besides voting or telling pollsters what we think. (See Box 6.1.)

PUBLIC OPINION

An opinion is a conviction that a certain thing is probably true, often combined with an evaluation. Political opinions are the most common motive force behind our political behavior and do not come to us out of the blue. We acquire some of them as we grow up and some in adulthood. We gather them from a wide range of socializing agents: family, school, peers, political leaders, the media, and the impact of political events on our own lives. And collectively we each contribute to the creation of **public opinion.**

We hear a great deal about public opinion these days. Is there any such thing? If so, what is it and what role does it play? In fact, when we speak of public opinion, we are usually referring to nothing more substantial than a more or less informed guess about the collective nature of a body of individual, more or less informed guesses. But this does not mean that there is no such thing or that it is insignificant. On the contrary, public opinion—or at least what is taken, rightly or wrongly, to be public opinion—is one of the most powerful forces at work in any polity. Let us try to push our way a little bit farther into this rather large conundrum.

The concept of public opinion is as old as the art of political inquiry. Aristotle, Plato, Niccolò Machiavelli, Jean Jacques Rousseau, Thomas Hobbes, and Karl Marx all debated the proper relationship between the ruler's will and that of the general public—seldom if ever doubting that the latter might be conceived of as a singular entity. Yet when we give the subject a moment's thought, we realize that public opinion can be only the sum of private opinions and, further, that in any polity, on any issue, private opinions will surely be found, on examination, to be varied and conflicting, held with different degrees of intensity by persons with very different degrees of access to political decision-making processes. Can we, then, really ever justify speaking of *public opinion?*

We can, but only if we keep the nature of the public in each case clearly in mind. For some observers the public means those citizens who really do take an active interest in politics and who take steps to make that interest known and felt. When the public is thus defined, the content of public opinion is usually determined impressionistically: the observer has witnessed a lively debate in the village square, listened to her concerned and influential friends at social and business events, followed the drift of letters and editorials in the newspapers, and—more and more likely—paid attention to talk show opinion on the subject at hand. This kind of public normally constitutes a very small percentage of the total population. For example, although 42 percent of the U.S. public listens regularly to a talk show where public issues are discussed, only about 4 percent has

BOX 6.1   REGIME CHANGE

An Individual Makes a Difference: Nelson Mandela

Nelson Mandela was born into the Xhosa Tribe in the Transkei, on land reserved for black South Africans under the long reign of white supremacy. His father died when Mandela was twelve, and he became the ward of his cousin, who was the paramount chief of the region. His political career began early; at Fort Hare University he was suspended for political activism. By 1941 he was a lawyer in Johannesburg, where he founded the Youth League of the African National Congress. As the white supremacist state escalated its repression of the African National Congress (ANC), Mandela helped organize its illegal guerrilla army. When brought to trial (the Rivonia Trial) after seventeen months of eluding the police and working underground, his eloquence as lead defendant among a group of ANC leaders accused of plotting acts of sabotage against the state brought him international attention: "Mandela turned the defendant's stand into an orator's stage. He never denied the charges; he simply spent hours explaining why he felt that justice compelled him to carry out such acts." He and his seven codefendants were sentenced to life imprisonment.

Mandela was 44 when he went to prison and 71 when he was freed. During much of that time he was forced to do menial labor, but he also studied, read, learned Afrikaans, and managed to lead his fellow prisoners, "the cream of South Africa's anti-apartheid movement," in "a kind of running seminar in liberation strategy." The prison where he was incarcerated on Robben Island became known by some as "Mandela U."

He also learned how to form coalitions with friendly forces (representatives of other liberation movements who became his fellow inmates) and how to negotiate with the enemy (the guards and warders first, the leaders of the white South African government second). When the government offered to free him if he would renounce armed struggle, or accept a form of house arrest, he said no, and he kept saying no until the authorities agreed to legalize the liberation movement, free all political prisoners, and allow all exiles to return.

When Mandela emerged from prison in 1990, regime change had only begun. He had to transform the ANC "from an underground, exiled, imprisoned organization into a government-in-waiting. . . . He had to engender a culture of trust in a society that had spent more than four decades codifying its racial fears and hates into a grotesque body of law. He had to teach blacks not to wallow in bitterness, and whites not to fear retribution." He had to supervise the writing of the new South African constitution, and bring about true majority rule.

No one claims that Mandela did all this alone or even that it was accomplished without enormous cost: over 15,000 persons were killed in factional fights (black versus white but also black versus black) in the first four years after his release. But no one doubts that the great leap forward made by South Africa at the end of the twentieth century was in fact very largely owing to the courage, intelligence, and indomitable will of a single individual.

Source: Paul Taylor, "Father of His Country." © 1994, The Washington Post. Reprinted with permission.

had the experience of speaking on the air.[2] Such "public opinion" may be very influential, but it may or may not be representative of the people who have not bothered to speak out.[3]

But for other commentators, the term *public opinion* indicates a very different public. For them, the public means a representative sample of the entire population, including those who have no opinion or who simply create one in a hurry in response to a pollster's inquiry. **Public opinion polls** are studies of the opinions of this public. Very rarely is any effort made to determine the intensity with which the opinion is held or the effort any individual might have made (beyond voting) to convey that opinion to those who have the political power to act on it. On the other hand, such statistical reporting usually makes much clearer the fact that public opinion is divided and conflicting; we are told exactly what percentages of the population think what.

Between these two extremes, all manner of variations in defining, determining, and reporting public opinion can be found. Statistical **polls** may or may not break down the collective data over time, by income or occupational categories, or into various other subcategories. Impressionistic opinion sampling may or may not include "person in the street" interviews. Writers may refer to both kinds of data in their analyses of what the public wants. Serious distortions can be introduced just in the way the question is asked: "When did you first start hating President Clin-

(ROB ROGERS reprinted by permission of United Feature Syndicate, Inc.)

ton?" Questions that interest the writer may be posed; questions that interest the respondent may never get asked. Journalists may try to find the answers to questions that require serious research and about which ordinary citizens have little or no information, just by taking a poll. (When we stop to think about it, we know perfectly well that asking a random sample of the population whether or not Bosnia should be a separate state, welfare recipients cheat, or O. J. Simpson was guilty of murder is a very poor way to seek the truth or decide what policy should be.)[4]

In any case, popular readiness to answer such inquisitive surveys varies from community to community, from nation to nation, and from time to time. Scots prefer to keep their opinions to themselves, and if pressed may find it amusing to mislead the self-important scholars who come their way. U.S. citizens used to feel offended if they had not been consulted, and when asked would try to answer as honestly as they could, but have lately been less forthcoming: the Gallup Organization reports that only 60 percent of those contacted will now cooperate, whereas the figure used to be 80 percent.[5] And, of course, questions that make sense in one polity may make none at all in another. Daniel Lerner long ago discovered a classic case when he began an interview by asking a Turkish peasant what he would do if he were president: "'Me,' exclaimed the astonished man, 'How can I . . . I cannot . . . a poor villager . . . master of the whole world.'"[6]

Given all these difficulties in determining what public opinion really is and in using polls intelligently, why do we bother? In the first place, the system of representative democracy as presently practiced does not provide any systematic means for keeping those in power informed between elections of the will of those who have elected them. Political parties, pressure groups, and other political movements normally provide selective and limited input to elected representatives, who need to know public opinion at least in order to plan future campaign strategy, if not for the more noble goal of showing some respect for that opinion while in office. Parties and groups themselves need to know the public's views on the leaders and issues they support. Challengers to officeholders wonder if their alternative views or programs will find a receptive audience.

Public opinion polling is also proving to be extremely important as a tool for monitoring the impact on people's lives of the global shift away from communist rule to free market economies. Seeing this massive transformation as nothing more than the long-overdue introduction of democracy and personal freedom is clearly simplistic, and polls have helped the outside world understand the confusion and disillusionment of those who welcome their new liberty but not the sometimes desperate hardship that accompanies it. It may be disappointing to learn that five years after the revolution, 71 percent of Hungarians said they were either worse off or no better off today than in the communist era and that in Russia, 27 percent believe the takeover by Boris Yeltsin was "a tragic event with ruinous consequences for the country and its people," whereas, at the other extreme, only 7 percent say the coup was "a victory of the democratic revolution"— but it is important to have this kind of sobering evidence of how difficult it is to make such a massive change.[7]

In sum, however flawed our present definition of public opinion—and however unsophisticated our mode of discerning and evaluating its content—the human polity and the nation-states that compose it have many reasons for taking the aggregate of individuals' opinions seriously and using available means to discover its content.

MODES OF INDIVIDUAL PARTICIPATION

Individuals engage in politics more directly than just by giving answers to inquiring reporters and pollsters who are looking for that mythical beast, public opinion. They vote, they write letters or go to see those persons who have or appear to have political power, they donate money to groups working for causes they believe in, they demonstrate, they join community organizations or political movements. Sometimes a single issue can provoke every form of response; the debate over the 1991 nomination to the U.S. Supreme Court of a man accused by a respectable law professor of sexual harassment led to a wave of telegrams and letters addressed to U.S. senators, a march on the Senate, the formation of angry coalitions, and an apparent increased determination on the part of many women to use the vote in order to elect more members of their own sex to positions of power.[8]

Sometimes persons who disagree with each other on many other issues will find themselves making common cause and using common means to seek a particular political response. Thus, advocates of free speech, "sex-positive" feminists, and persons openly engaged in producing pornographic materials have all sought to defend pornography, whereas feminists who believe pornography inflicts harm on individuals have been joined by those Christian fundamentalists who attack all forms of what they call sexual "deviance," including homosexuality.[9] Such spontaneous coalitions of concerned individuals may bring together persons who would rather not be seen in each other's company—but can nevertheless have a powerful effect in stimulating new legislation or working to prevent its enactment.

Not all individual political activity is peaceful and law abiding. Some political activists are ready to engage in civil disobedience, breaking the law on behalf of causes they believe in. Such acts of defiance may be relatively limited in means and scope, as when U.S. political activists deliberately violated U.S. immigration laws and helped illegal aliens fleeing political repression in Central America find sanctuary in U.S. churches, or far more drastic and far reaching, as when the citizens of Poland, Hungary, Czechoslovakia, Bulgaria, Romania, and the former nation of East Germany carried disobedience to the point of revolutionary action and brought their repressive governments down. Civil disobedience does not always work, of course, and can bring yet greater repression; the demonstrations in favor of democracy in Tiananmen Square in the People's Republic of China in 1989 brought brutal repression to many of those known to have taken part.[10]

A useful way of categorizing individual political participation has been provided by Lester Milbrath and M. L. Goel. Using data collected by themselves and others, they propose seven common *modes of participation:*

1. *Apathetic Inactives*: engage in no participatory activity, not even voting.
2. *Passive Supporters*: vote regularly, attend patriotic parades, pay all taxes, "love my country."
3. *Contact Specialists*: contact local, state, and national officials on particular problems.
4. *Communicators*: keep informed about politics, engage in political discussions, write letters to newspaper editors, send support or protest messages to political leaders.
5. *Party and Campaign Workers*: work for party or candidate, persuade others how to vote, attend meetings, give money to party or candidate, join and support a political party, serve as party candidate.
6. *Community Activists*: work with others on local problems, form a group to work on local problems, maintain active membership in community organizations, contact officials on social issues.
7. *Protesters*: join in public street demonstrations, protest vigorously if government does something morally wrong, attend protest meetings, refuse to obey unjust laws.[11]

As Milbrath and Goel stress, it is possible to belong to one mode and still perform some of the activities of participants in other modes.[12] One belongs to a mode by virtue of one's most common style of political behavior. Dominant modes vary from nation to nation. Aside from voting, citizens in the United States and Great Britain are most likely to sign petitions (and so are the Germans and the French, but in lesser numbers—the French are also noteworthy for their readiness to take part in political demonstrations), the Dutch are most likely to contact a local official about a personal problem, Nigerians and Indians are most likely to take part in local community organizations, Austrians favor joining parties or other political organizations or attending political rallies, and the Japanese are more likely to attend a political rally than to take part in any other nonvoting political behavior.[13]

PARTICIPATION BY VOTING IN ELECTIONS

The most common act of individual participation in politics is to vote. It seems a simple act: Just register, then walk in on election day and mark your choice. But it is not that simple at all. To understand participation by voting, we must look at voter turnout, of course, but also at the great variety of electoral systems throughout the human polity. Achieving effective participation by voting depends not only on whether or not citizens vote but also on the nature of the institution that makes voting possible.

Voter Turnout
One of the most puzzling—and, for some, one of the most distressing—facts about voting is how very few citizens take part in this easiest form of political behavior in the United States. Voter turnout in the United States is low by any

Voter registration in Spanish Harlem in New York City. Despite recent improvements, U.S. laws still make registration more difficult than in other major democracies.

(Lisa Quinones/Black Star)

standards and certainly low comparatively; in modern democracies, only the Swiss, who are called to the polls more frequently, have a worse record for average turnout (see Table 6.1). Voter turnout in presidential elections in the United States has decreased steadily in recent years, with the exception of 1992, when the first candidacy of independent Ross Perot helped produce a temporary 4 percent boost in the figures.[14] Voting in nonpresidential elections is marked by even lower turnout; in the 1994 congressional elections, only 36 percent of those eligible voted, and the rate in municipal elections has at times fallen even lower.[15]

TABLE 6.1   Average Turnout in Twenty Democracies 1980–1989

Country	Percentage Voting	Country	Percentage Voting
Belgium	94	Israel	79
Austria	92	Greece	78
Australia	90	Finland	74
New Zealand	89	United Kingdom	74
Sweden	88	Ireland	73
West Germany	87	Canada	72
(pre-reunification)		France	70
Denmark	86	Japan	68
Italy	84	United States[a]	53
Netherlands	84	Switzerland	49
Norway	83		

[a]U.S. turnout is lower when legislative elections are held in "off" years—that is, years when presidential and legislative elections are not being held simultaneously.
Source: Adapted from Ruy A. Teixeira, "Make Voting Easy, More Interesting," *Insight into the News* 10 (7 Feb. 1994): 28. Data are from national legislative elections, except in the United States, where they are from presidential elections.

What explains this phenomenon? Not only is the answer hard to determine but also the question is one that has caused considerable dispute among political scientists. For some authors, social demographics tell us all we need to know. Having little education, being young, having a low income or being unemployed, belonging to a minority racial group, and living in the south are all demographic factors that have been associated with nonvoting in the United States. For others, psychological factors such as "civic attitudes" or political opinions such as "views of the parties" are more important.

But other authors reject the social-psychological approach altogether, arguing that political institutions and electoral law play a more important role. For Frances Fox Piven and Richard A. Cloward, the fact that in other nations social factors are not "so dramatically associated with high rates of nonvoting as they are in the United States" means we must look elsewhere.[16] They note that although Australia, Belgium, and Italy legally require citizens to vote, inflicting minor penalties on those who do not, the significantly higher voting rates of almost all the other industrial democracies cannot be thus explained. For them, the chief institutional culprits are U.S. registration laws, which they describe as "Byzantine compared with those that prevail in other democracies." They note that "the United States is the only major democracy where government assumes no responsibility for helping citizens cope with voter registration procedures" and argue that this explains why, on the average, 40 percent of U.S. citizens eligible to register and vote are not registered—and so cannot vote. And indeed, when we look at voting rates of *registered* voters, we find the United States tied with the Netherlands and Germany for seventh place, rather than next to last (see Table 6.2).[17]

Passage of the so-called motor-voter bill in 1993, a law that requires states to permit registration when one applies for or renews a driver's license, to permit registration by mail, and to make forms available at certain public assistance agencies, would seem to be a good step in the right direction, although voter turnout has continued to decline.[18] And not everyone is convinced that the problem can be solved simply with better registration procedures. Raymond Wolfinger and Steven Rosenstone have shown that even if all voters were allowed to register right up to election day, registration offices were kept open during regular working hours and in the evening or on Saturday, and absent civilians were permitted to register by mail (in ten states, only military absentee registration is permitted), U.S. turnout rates could be expected to increase by less than 10 percent.[19] Of course, 10 percent is, in fact, a rather good improvement, and significantly missing from this list of possible reforms is the idea of having the government itself take the responsibility to register voters (keeping track of all residents and sending them the necessary papers), as is done in Switzerland, Italy, Germany, Austria, France, Sweden, Great Britain, Belgium, and Canada.[20] Nor do Wolfinger and Rosenstone consider the possible impact of holding elections on weekends, as in Germany and France. Paying closer attention to the experience of other democracies and combining psychological attitudes, registration laws, and other institutional factors, including the party system, G. Bingham Powell Jr. argues that the first (attitudes) actually give the United States a 5 percent advantage over other nations, whereas the second gives a 14 percent disadvantage and the last a 13 percent disadvantage.[21]

More recent analyses of the problem of low voter turnout in the United States suggest yet another cause: campaign targeting. We discuss this technique more fully in Chapter 8, but its impact on turnout must be considered here. According to Marshall Ganz, the guiding principle of modern campaign management is "the allocation of each dollar to achieve maximum possible effect in the current election. . . . Precious campaign dollars should be invested in persuading more likely voters."[22] Targeting campaign resources means, says Ganz, ignoring those who have not voted and also those who have voted only occasionally. Furthermore, it makes sense to focus only on those whose electoral or personal histories suggest the possibility of a "swing" vote: Why bother with those who are always loyal to the same party? Taking all these factors into consideration, the "targeted" population for a modern campaign will be as little as 22 to 27 percent of the total potential electorate. Ganz adds that "these uncontacted voters are far more likely to be of lower socioeconomic status than those who are contacted. They never hear from a campaign and thus will likely stay at home on election day or vote the way they always have. The assumption that past voting behavior is predictive of future behavior becomes a self-fulfilling prophecy."[23]

TABLE 6.2   Voter Registration and Turnout for the 1996 U.S. Presidential Elections, State by State

State	1996 VAP[a]	1996 REG	%REG of VAP	TURNOUT	%T/O OF VAP
Alabama	3,220,000	2,470,766	76.73%	1,534,349	47.65%
Alaska	425,000	414,815	97.60%	241,620	56.85%
Arizona	3,145,000	2,244,672	71.37%	1,404,405	44.66%
Arkansas	1,873,000	1,369,459	73.12%	884,262	47.21%
California	22,826,000	15,662,075	68.62%	10,019,484	43.90%
Colorado	2,862,000	2,346,253	81.98%	1,510,704	52.78%
Connecticut	2,479,000	1,881,323	75.89%	1,392,614	56.18%
Delaware	548,000	421,710	76.95%	270,810	49.42%
District of Columbia	422,000	361,419	85.64%	185,726	44.01%
Florida	11,043,000	8,077,877	73.15%	5,300,927	48.00%
Georgia	5,418,000	3,811,284	70.34%	2,298,899	42.43%
Hawaii	890,000	544,916	61.23%	360,120	40.46%
Idaho	858,000	700,430	81.64%	489,481	57.05%
Illinois	8,754,000	6,663,301	76.12%	4,311,391	49.25%
Indiana	4,374,000	3,488,088	79.75%	2,135,431	48.82%
Iowa	2,138,000	1,776,433	83.09%	1,234,075	57.72%
Kansas	1,897,007	1,436,418	75.72%	1,063,452	56.06%
Kentucky	2,928,000	2,396,086	81.83%	1,387,999	47.40%
Louisiana	3,131,000	2,559,352	81.74%	1,783,959	56.98%
Maine	945,000	1,001,292	105.96%	679,499	71.90%
Maryland	3,820,000	2,587,978	67.75%	1,780,870	46.62%
Massachusetts	4,649,000	3,459,193	74.41%	2,556,459	54.99%
Michigan	7,072,000	6,677,079	94.42%	3,848,844	54.42%
Minnesota	3,422,000	3,067,802	89.65%	2,192,640	64.07%
Mississippi	1,967,000	1,715,913	87.24%	893,857	45.44%
Missouri	3,995,000	3,342,849	83.68%	2,158,065	54.02%
Montana	656,000	590,751	90.05%	407,083	62.06%
Nebraska	1,211,000	1,015,056	83.82%	677,415	55.94%
Nevada	1,212,000	778,092	64.20%	464,279	38.31%
New Hampshire	871,000	754,771	86.66%	499,053	57.30%
New Jersey	6,034,000	4,320,866	71.61%	3,075,860	50.98%
New Mexico	1,224,000	851,479	69.57%	556,074	45.43%
New York	13,564,000	10,162,156	74.92%	6,439,129	47.47%
North Carolina	5,519,000	4,318,008	78.24%	2,515,807	45.58%

TABLE 6.2   *Continued*

State	1996 VAP[a]	1996 REG	%REG of VAP	TURNOUT	%T/O OF VAP
North Dakota	476,000	N/A	N/A	266,411	55.97%
Ohio	8,347,000	6,879,687	82.42%	4,534,434	54.32%
Oklahoma	2,426,000	1,979,017	81.58%	1,206,713	49.74%
Oregon	2,411,000	1,962,115	81.38%	1,377,760	57.14%
Pennsylvania	9,197,000	6,805,612	74.00%	4,506,118	49.00%
Rhode Island	751,000	602,692	80.25%	390,247	51.96%
South Carolina	2,771,000	1,814,777	65.49%	1,151,689	41.56%
South Dakota	535,000	459,971	85.98%	323,826	60.53%
Tennessee	4,035,000	2,849,910	70.63%	1,894,015	46.94%
Texas	13,597,000	10,540,678	77.52%	5,611,644	41.27%
Utah	1,333,000	1,050,452	78.80%	665,629	49.93%
Vermont	445,000	385,328	86.59%	258,449	58.08%
Virginia	5,083,000	3,322,135	65.36%	2,416,642	47.54%
Washington	4,115,000	3,078,128	74.80%	2,253,837	54.77%
West Virginia	1,417,000	970,745	68.51%	636,459	44.92%
Wisconsin	3,824,000	N/A	N/A	2,196,169	57.43%
Wyoming	356,000	240,711	67.62%	211,571	59.43%
UNITED STATES	196,511,000	146,211,960	74.40%	96,456,345	49.08%

[a]VAP, voting age population.
Source: Federal Elections Commission, "1996 Presidential Election Results," *Journal of Election Administration,* 18 (1997): 7.

The Electoral System

So far we have been stressing what makes individuals *want* to vote, which is a be-havioral question. But it is also important to consider the institution that makes voting *possible*, which is a structural question (see Chapter 1). This institution is the *electoral system*, a structure that seldom receives the attention it deserves. We know that elections can be burdened with more issues than a legislative session, bring about judgments more far reaching than those of a court, attract more at-tention to qualities of leadership than a presidency, and sometimes stir up battle spirit as fiercely as any army. But we tend to act as if their existence and their characteristics were all preordained, immutable. We tend to forget that every election is the product of an electoral system and, further, that any electoral sys-tem is itself the entirely changeable product of fallible human beings, often guided at least in part by the desire to serve their own political fortunes.

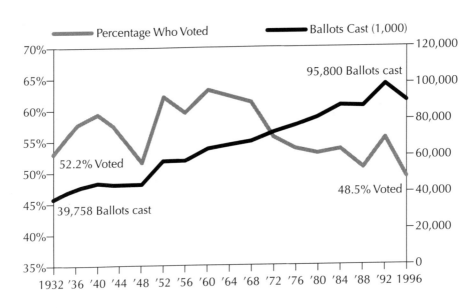

FIGURE 6.1 U.S. Voter Turnout 1932–96
Except for the 1924 election, the first contest following the introduction of women's suffrage, the 1996 election is believed to have had the lowest turnout rate since mass popular voting was first introduced in the 1830s (but because statistics are not available for
earlier elections one cannot be certain).

Source: Adapted from *The Public Perspective,* December/January 1997, p. 5. © The Roper Center
for Public Opinion Research, University of Connecticut. Reprinted with permission.

What is an **electoral system**? The term is sometimes used simply to indicate
how many offices are to be contested and how votes are to be cast and counted,
but we use it here in its broader sense to include all the rules and regulations governing the vote.

Every nation has some form of electoral system, but the opportunities for
meaningful participation on the part of the would-be voter vary enormously according to the kind of system in effect. In a single-party dictatorship, elections
may be held merely for ceremonial purposes, with no competition allowed. Or
competition may be allowed within the party, as several candidates, all expressing their loyalty to the ruling party, are permitted to compete for a particular
constituency's legislative seat.

It is not unusual for a nation to have two electoral systems—one dictated by
law that calls for fair elections at specified times with full competition and a second, determined by tradition and the actual distribution of political power, that
allows for infrequent and irregular balloting, rigged in advance. The military
coup makes a mockery of any electoral system, even one rigged to keep a single
party in power, although some have argued that when coup follows upon coup,

as has been the case in several African and Latin American nations, *that* is the electoral system.[24]

Furthermore, even where the electoral system is fair and scrupulously carried out, great variations are possible. There are, for example, important differences, worth taking a moment to understand, between the two ways the vote is translated into legislative seats in most Western democracies: the use of single-member districts or the adoption of a system of proportional representation.

Single-Member District System. The system most commonly used in the United States for state and congressional offices is the single-member district system. Under this system, the voters in each electoral district (also called a **constituency**) choose one person to fill a specific post, be it state legislator or representative to Congress. Whoever gets the most votes is elected. Several variations are possible. First, election may be by simple *plurality* (which means that whoever has the most votes wins, even if that number is less than 50 percent of the total). This system is used in Canada, India, Pakistan, and Great Britain as well; using a racing metaphor, the British call it *first past the post* (or FPTP). It also produces the greatest discrepancies between the vote and the actual allocation of seats. In Great Britain the Alliance Party won one-fourth of the total votes cast in legislative elections in 1983, but gained only twenty-three seats in the House of Commons, less than one-twenty-fifth of the total.[25]

To avoid the drawbacks of the plurality system, some nations with single-member districts require the winner to have a majority. This may mean scheduling a runoff election if no candidate wins over 50 percent of the vote on the first ballot. In French legislative elections, any candidate with more than 12.5 percent of the vote may take part in the runoff, held two weeks later; in the race for the French presidency, only the top two candidates will be present at the second ballot. This system encourages minor parties to participate—one can never be certain which candidates will make it into the runoff—and thus provides individual voters with a wide choice, but at the same time it ensures strong support (usually an absolute majority) for the winner of the run-off.

A third variation designed to maximize the chances of majoritarian support while maintaining single-member districts is the *alternative vote* system, used in Australia for its lower house. In this system each voter *ranks* the candidates. When the votes are counted, if no candidate has a majority of first-choice rankings, then the candidate who is ranked first the least often is eliminated, and the votes of voters who preferred this candidate are assigned to the persons they ranked second. If this doesn't produce a majority for one candidate, the process is repeated; eventually, of course, the process of elimination means that one candidate *will* have a majority. Again, individual voters benefit by having a wide choice to begin with and by knowing that their votes (including, if need be, their second and third choices) have been thoroughly taken into consideration. Collectively, everyone benefits by knowing that the most preferred candidate has been selected. He or she may in fact be "everyone's second choice" but can never be a widely hated figure who has won only a slim plurality.

Proportional Representation. Proportional representation (often referred to by its initials as PR) requires multimember districts. Each district chooses several representatives, and each political party offers the voters a list of its candidates for those posts. In some nations, such as Belgium, the voter can vary the order of the candidates on the list; in others, as in Switzerland, the voters have multiple votes that they may spread around as they wish among the lists. In the simplest and most usual version, however, each voter casts one vote for one party list and the parties are then awarded seats according to the proportion of the vote they received. If a party gets 40 percent of the vote, the top 40 percent of its list is elected. But of course real life is seldom that tidy, and in practice it is necessary to have some kind of formula for determining how to assign the seats. The two most common formulas used are the *largest remainder* and the *highest average* systems (see Box 6.2). Whatever formula is used, the goal is to assign seats proportionately to the vote. Minor parties with very few votes may thus get a seat or two in the legislature and do not necessarily feel encouraged to drop out or to combine with other small parties just because they are not doing well. Although this gives voters the maximum amount of choice and ensures a parliament that is not only closely keyed to the actual vote but also much more fully representative of all points of view, it can also have the effect of making it difficult to form majorities behind a government program. In the Netherlands, for example, where a party needs only .67 percent of the total vote to gain a seat in the 150-member parliament, it sometimes takes up to six months to organize a government after an election.[26] To avoid this effect, other nations using proportional representation normally require a party to obtain at least 5 percent of the vote in order to be entitled to representation. Establishing such a threshhold has helped the new political systems in eastern Europe reduce the number of parties actually taking seats in their new parliaments, despite the amazing proliferation of parties in the first years of their transition to democracy: Eighty parties competed in the 1992 Czechoslovakian elections; that same year, there were 131 parties in Poland.[27]

It is possible to use both systems in the same polity. The Germans, for example, elect 664 deputies to their legislature, the Bundestag, by a dual procedure: Half are elected in direct balloting in their respective constituencies, while the other half are selected proportionally from party lists of candidates in each of the *Länder* (states). Similarly, the Spanish senate is elected by simple plurality but its lower house by the highest average version of proportional representation. Italy, long known for its most elaborately "fair" system of proportional representation, has recently switched to a system that is 75 percent plurality, 25 percent proportional representation.[28]

The range of choice is indeed wide and confusing, and there are no simple decision-making rules for nations wondering which method will work best.[29] Although some political scientists have customarily argued that proportional representation tends to produce fragmented and unstable government, they almost always cite the case of postwar Italy, where numerous other factors contributed to produce those conditions (and where a single party, the Christian

BOX 6.2   HOW PROPORTIONAL REPRESENTATION WORKS: THE "LARGEST-REMAINDER" AND "HIGHEST-AVERAGE" SYSTEMS

The largest-remainder system, common in Latin America, works like this: Say in a five-seat district 100 votes are cast: Blue 38, Red 32, White 17, Green 13. Each 20 votes ($100 \div 5$) get one seat. Any seats left go to whoever has the most votes remaining. Result: Blue ($20 + 18$) gets two; Red ($20 + 12$) one; White ($0 + 17$) one; Green ($0 + 13$) one. Hardly proportional. And see how small parties are favoured. Had White and Green merged, the joint "Lime" party's 30 votes would have earned only one seat.

Bigger districts are fairer. Say there are ten seats. Blue gets four; Red three; White two; Green one. And if White and Green had merged, "Lime" would still get three. Fair enough? In either case, "swings and roundabouts" even out the national result—but still with a bias to small parties.

The highest-average formula widely used in Europe allocates seats, one by one, to whichever party thereby shows the highest votes-per-seat. To do this, divide the party votes by 1, 2, 3 and so on, then pick out the highest five (or ten or whatever) figures from the resultant matrix, below. The winning figures are shown in **bold** for a five-seat district (the seat-number is indicated by a superscript figure), plus five more in *italics* for a ten-seat one:

	Blue	Red	White	Green
$\div$ by 1	**38**^{1}	**32**^{2}	**17**^{4}	*13*
$\div$ by 2	**19**^{3}	**16**^{5}	*8.5*	*6.5*
$\div$ by 3	*12.7*	*10.7*	*5.7*	4.3
$\div$ by 4	9.5	8	4.2	3.2
Seats won:				
Five-seat	two	two	one	none
Ten-seat	four	three	two	one

Small parties suffer: were there only three seats, Blue would get two, Red one, White and Green none (where "Lime" would have got one). With eleven, even Red would get a fourth seat, Green still only one. But larger districts are usually fairer than small. The divisors can be varied: Scandinavian countries divide by 1.4, 3, 5 and 7, which aids medium-sized parties.

Democrats, nevertheless stayed in power until 1994!), and do not look at the stable and effective coalition governments other nations, such as those in Scandinavia, have managed to produce using the same system. Similarly, single-member districts do not always close out minor parties altogether, although they do have a strong tendency to do so. Arguments that proportional representation works better for minority populations are shaky, unless such minorities form parties of their own, in which case they almost certainly limit their appeal. Expecting proportional representation to increase the number of women in office is also dubious. Although the parties can easily place women candidates on their lists, putting them at or near the top is less likely, says Karen Beckwith, unless other conditions are present such as "an active, visible feminist movement, and a climate of improved or improving status for women."[30]

Initiative and Referendum

So far we have been talking about ways the institution of an electoral system can offer citizens an opportunity to participate in the choice of representatives to lawmaking bodies. But elections can be devoted to other offices and to matters other than the choice of representatives. A polity's electoral system may include provisions for the **initiative**, enabling citizens to vote directly on specific proposals for new legislation. The only requirement is that a certain number of citizens (usually at least a specified percentage of the population that voted in the previous election) sign a petition within a specified number of days (frequently ninety days) proposing that a question be put on the ballot for everyone to vote on.

Somewhat more common is the **referendum**, a provision enabling a group of citizens, following procedures similar to those for an initiative, to "refer" a piece of legislation passed by the government to the voting public. Only if a majority approves does the legislation actually become binding. Some issues must automatically be made subject to such a procedure; state laws, for example, often require that school bonds be placed on a referendum ballot.

Another version of the referendum is found in systems that allow the executive branch of the government, under certain conditions, to rule by referendum—that is, to take a new proposal directly to the people. This kind of referendum is permitted in the French constitution and was a favorite device of former president Charles de Gaulle, who frequently staked his political life on a referendum vote, telling the French to vote for his proposal or accept the consequences—his own resignation. The inevitable result was that he won every single referendum vote except the last one he tried.[31]

It is often taken for granted that electoral systems allowing initiatives and referenda provide for more participation than those that do not, and there are many who urge the adoption of a national initiative system in the United States. The matter is not quite as simple as it looks, however. It is no easy job to gather large numbers of signatures for a petition in a short period of time, and some observers have suggested that well-financed groups have an even greater advantage when this system of lawmaking is used than when laws are made by ordinary legislative processes. Such groups are far better able to hire the workers needed to gather the necessary number of signatures and to bombard the general public with the political advertising likely to persuade them to vote "correctly" than are less wealthy groups. It is also pointed out that debating complex issues in the public arena, without the benefit of careful deliberation by experienced representatives, makes the initiative and the referendum prime targets for demagogic politicking—that is, for appeals based on emotional sloganeering rather than on full and rational discussions of the issues.[32]

Other Electoral Opportunities to Participate

Other opportunities to participate by voting may include **recall elections**, held when a sufficient number of voters petition for a special election to vote on removing an official (usually an elected official) from office. The grounds for demanding a recall vary from genuine *malfeasance*—that is, acting contrary to law or failing to carry out the terms of office—to simple public discontent with the policies or style of the offending incumbent.[33] Other, more constructive options for participation include the election of such executive officers as attorney general and controller; the election of judicial officers, such as lower court judges in many states of the United States; and the political party primary election.

The **party primary** is a special form of election indeed, almost unique to the United States. (Belgium has a roughly comparable system, and in some nations with runoff elections the first election is referred to—not really correctly—as the primary election.) Although U.S. party primaries—elections to choose the nominees who will appear on the *general* election ballot—are set up and monitored by state governments, many of them are *closed*, which means that only the voters who have registered as supporters of the party are allowed to vote. This makes sense, because the supporters are not voting for a government official but simply for a candidate to run as the nominee of a private organization, the political party. On the other hand, the right to choose nominees for office has such far-reaching effects for all citizens that many states have adopted the institution of the *open* primary as a way to encourage greater individual participation in the political process. Still other states have continued to allow the party to control its own nominations (by internal party elections known as *caucuses*). This too makes sense: Why should persons who have taken no part in party affairs be allowed to tell the party which person it should run for office? As we see in Chapter 8 it can also be argued that adoption of the primary, far from strengthening democracy, has served so to weaken political parties as agencies of linkage between the citizen and the state that the net effect of this unique institution is actually antidemocratic.

SUMMARY AND CONCLUSION

The concept of "public opinion" is old, yet still defined differently by different persons, and under some circumstances the public opinion poll does not always measure what it claims to. Individuals adopt different modes of participation, depending on the opportunities open to them but also upon their own interests and propensities.

The mystery of low voter turnout in the United States is not such a mystery—not when we compare what other nations with higher turnout have done to facilitate and encourage voting. Achieving effective participation by voting also depends on the nature of the electoral system adopted. The two main types are the single-member district and proportional representation, but many variations are possible.

Although our emphasis throughout has been on conditions that enhance or obstruct participation, it is important that before quitting our subject we note that there is a whole other side to this coin, and that is the role individuals are *constrained* to play, whether or not they choose to participate. The laws governments make, with or without their citizens' consent, require a great deal of obedient responsiveness. Like it or not, we are all caught up in the world of politics in one way or another. We pay our taxes, obey traffic regulations, fulfill military obligations, conform to safety regulations, and otherwise comply with the rules imposed on us—or suffer the consequences, when our failure to do so is noted and the laws are fairly enforced. This other side of the individual's role in politics, the "subject" role, receives more attention in Chapters 9 through 12, when we consider the national and local institutions that make the rules we are expected to obey. Our emphasis here has been on the part we as individuals can play in influencing the rules those institutions make. We turn now to the natural sequel to that topic—the part we can play as members of political organizations.

Selected Readings

Asher, Herb. *Polling and the Public: What Every Citizen Should Know.* 3rd ed. Washington, D.C.: CQ Press, 1995. A balanced and thorough explanation of survey research and polling.

Craig, Stephen C. *The Malevolent Leaders: Popular Discontent in America.* Boulder, Colo.: Westview Press, 1993. An examination of the rise and causes of political discontent in the United States since the 1960s.

Dalton, Russell J. *Citizen Politics.* 2nd ed. Chatham, N.J.: Chatham House, 1996. A comparison of citizen participation, value orientations, and elections in the United States, Great Britain, West Germany, and France.

Dionne, E. J. Jr. *Why Americans Hate Politics.* New York: Simon and Schuster, 1991. A text that argues that political apathy has increased because the choices offered by conservatives and liberals do not address the values and concerns of a majority of U.S. citizens.

Ginsberg, Benjamin, and Alan Stone, eds. *Do Elections Matter?* Armonk, N.Y.: Sharpe, 1996. Questions the connection between the election choices of voters and policy decisions of politicians once they are elected.

Lijphart, Arend. *Electoral Systems and Party Systems: A Study of Twenty-seven Democracies.* Oxford: Oxford University Press, 1994. A comprehensive study of electoral systems, including how they influence election results and legislative representation.

Lipset, Seymour M., and Stein Rokkan, eds. *Party Systems and Voter Alignments: Cross-National Perspectives.* New York: Free Press, 1967. An early and still often cited effort to compare voting behavior across nations.

Peterson, Steven A. *Political Behavior: Patterns in Everyday Life.* Newbury Park, Calif.: Sage, 1990. Argues that researchers need to focus more on how ordinary voters interpret their own political behavior and how their interpretations of what is political differ from those of the specialists.

Piven, Frances Fox, and Richard A. Cloward. *Why Americans Don't Vote.* New York: Pantheon, 1988. A persuasive argument that the underlying cause of low voter turnout is that U.S. politics is primarily oriented toward the interests of economic elites, seriously compounded by difficult requirements for voter registration.

Notes

1. For some interesting examples of "dedicated community activists," see Janny Scott, "The Ultimate Volunteers," *New York Times,* 4 Sept. 1994, 1QU.
2. Times Mirror Center for the People and the Press, *The Vocal Minority in American Politics* (Washington, D.C.: Los Angeles Times, 1993), cited in Sidney Verba, "The 1993 James Madison Award Lecture: The Voice of the People," *P.S.: Political Science and Politics* 26, no. 4 (Dec. 1993): 679.
3. The early studies of public opinion did not go beyond the articulate few. See, for example, Walter Lippman's *Public Opinion* (New York: Harcourt, Brace, 1922). V. O. Key had a similar entity in mind when he spoke of the "political stratum" in *Politics, Parties and Pressure Groups,* 5th ed. (New York: Crowell, 1965).
4. For other reasons poll data may be misleading, see "All Polls Are Not Created Equal," *U.S. News and World Report,* 28 Sept. 1992, 24–25; and chap. 3, "The Anatomy of a Public Opinion Poll," *High-Tech Campaigns: Computer Technology in Political Communication,* by Gary W. Selnow (Westport, Conn.: Praeger, 1994), pp. 27–43. On the other hand, in chap. 4, pp. 45–66, "Technical Advances in Polling," Selnow shows how technology has revolutionized polling in recent years, improving its precision.
5. Daniel Schorr, "Washington Notebook," *New Leader* 75 (4 May 1992): 3.
6. Daniel Lerner, *The Passing of Traditional Society: Modernizing the Middle East* (Glencoe, Ill.: Free Press, 1958).
7. Robin Knight and Victoria Pope, "Back to the Future," *U.S News and World Report* (23 May 1994): 40–43; and Lee Hockstader, "Three Years Later, Russians Revising View of Coup Plotters," *Washington Post,* 21 Aug. 1994, A34.
8. *New York Times,* 9 Oct. 1991, A1, and 13 Oct. 1991, 34.
9. David Futrelle, "The Politics of Porn," *In These Times* (7 Mar. 1994): 14–17.
10. *New York Times,* 4 June 1989, 11, 120, A2.
11. Lester W. Milbrath and M. L. Goel, *Political Participation,* 2nd ed. (Chicago: Rand McNally, 1977), pp. 18–19.
12. For example, most of those in modes 4 through 7 are also regular voters, and protesters may also be active in modes 4 through 6. One is assigned a mode by the distinctiveness of the package of activities in which one engages. Ibid., p. 20.
13. For these and other relevant data, see Sidney Verba and Norman H. Nie, "Political Participation," in *Handbook of Political Science,* vol. 4, ed. Fred I. Greenstein and Nelson W. Polsby (Reading, Mass.: Addison-Wesley, 1975), pp. 24–25; Dennis Kavanagh, *Political Science and Political Behavior* (London: Allen and Unwin, 1983), pp. 181–84; and Russell J. Dalton, *Citizen Politics in Western Democracies* (Chatham, N.J.: Chatham House, 1988), pp. 47, 65.
14. According to Curtis Gans, director of the Committee for the Study of the American Electorate, nonmajor party voting increased by one-third in 1992, as compared to 1988, and most of that vote went to Ross Perot (interview of Gans, 9 Nov. 1992).

15. For a summary of recent trends in voter turnout in the United States and their effect on the parties, see Paul Allen Beck and Frank J. Sorauf, *Party Politics in America*, 7th ed. (Boston: HarperCollins, 1992), pp. 212–25. For the 1994 results, see U.S. Bureau of the Census, *The Statistical Abstract of the United States:1995* (Washington, D.C.: U.S. Department of the Census, 1995), p. 291.

16. Frances Fox Piven and Richard A. Cloward, *Why Americans Don't Vote* (New York: Pantheon, 1987), p. 15.

17. Ibid., pp. 17–19.

18. *World Almanac and Book of Facts* (New York: Funk and Wagnalls, 1995), p. 71.

19. Raymond Wolfinger and Steven Rosenstone, *Who Votes?* (New Haven: Yale University Press, 1980), p. 73. See also Steven J. Rosenstone and Raymond E. Wolfinger, "The Effect of Registration Laws on Voter Turnout," in *Controversies in Voting Behavior*, 2nd ed., ed. Richard Niemi and Herbert Weisberg (Washington, D.C.: Congressional Quarterly Press, 1984), pp. 66–67.

20. Dalton, *Citizen Politics in Western Democracies*, p. 39. See also William J. Keefe, *Parties, Politics and Public Policy in America*, 7th ed. (Washington, D.C.: Congressional Quarterly Press, 1994), p. 193.

21. G. Bingham Powell Jr., "American Voter Turnout in Comparative Perspective," *American Political Science Review* 80, no. 1 (Mar. 1986): 17–41.

22. Marshall Ganz, "Voters in the Crosshairs: Elections and Voter Turnout," *American Prospect* (Winter 1994): 4–10.

23. Ibid., p. 8. Ganz notes, "With both campaigns . . . using this kind of reasoning, it is not so surprising that, despite the city's troubles, less than 25 percent of the Los Angeles electorate turned out to vote" in the mayoral election under discussion.

24. Walter Dean Burnham, "Parties and Political Modernization," in *Political Parties and the Modern State*, ed. Richard L. McCormick (New Brunswick, N.J.: Rutgers University Press, 1984), p. 123.

25. "Electoral Reform," *The Economist* 327 (1 May 1993): 19.

26. Kavanagh, *Political Science and Political Behavior*, p. 79.

27. *International Herald Tribune*, 5 June 1992, 7.

28. Martin Jacques, "The Godmother: Italy's Meltdown—and Ours: Crisis of Government Credibility," *New Republic* (20 Sept. 1993): 23–27.

29. For recent studies of the variety of electoral systems possible, see Arend Lijphart, *Electoral Systems and Party Systems: A Study of Twenty-seven Democracies 1945–1990* (Oxford: Oxford University Press, 1994); and Joseph F. Zimmerman, "Alternative Voting Systems for Representative Democracy," *P.S.: Political Science and Politics* 27, no. 4 (Dec. 1994): 674–77.

30. Karen Beckwith, "Comparative Research and Electoral Systems: Lessons from France and Italy," *Women in Politics* 12, no. 1 (1992): 7.

31. Henry W. Ehrmann and Martin Schain, *Politics in France*, 5th ed. (New York: HarperCollins, 1992), pp. 213–19.

32. For a good discussion of the advantages and disadvantages of instituting a national initiative and referendum, see Thomas E. Cronin, *Direct Democracy: The Politics of Initiative, Referendum and Recall* (Cambridge: Harvard University Press, 1989), pp. 157–95. See also Bruno S. Frey, "Direct Democracy: Politico-Economic Lessons from Swiss Experience," *American Economic Review* 84, no. 2 (1994): 338–41.

33. See Peter McCormick, "The Recall of Elected Members," *Canadian Parliamentary Review* (Summer 1994): 11–13, for an argument in defense of this institution and a recommendation that it be adopted in Canada.

7 Organizing for Politics: Interest Groups

Jogging contentedly around the familiar track, a middle-aged runner is startled to see a fellow jogger arrive with a poster: "Save Our Track. Sign the Petition." After completing her twenty laps, she trots over to see what is going on. The track is on the grounds of a school for the deaf and blind that is being sold to the local university. The school for the disabled has always allowed the public to use the track; the university refuses to make any such promises. Fearful of being excluded, the alarmed joggers meet at the home of one of their number, choose a name (East Bay Community Track and Field Association), elect a president and a recording secretary, gather dues, distribute leaflets, write letters to city council members and state legislators, and arrange for a meeting in the mayor's office with representatives of the university. The smiling university attorney now assures them there will be "no problem." Continued public access to the track will be permitted. Three days later they have this promise in writing.

In this example of organizing for politics, the joggers form an interest group spontaneously as a way to use political means to meet nonpolitical needs.[1] This is a common beginning for interest groups but not the only way to organize for political purposes. Let's look at another example.

Labor costs are seriously reducing profits, the chairman of a rapidly expanding Japanese electronics firm reports to his governing board. It is his view that government unemployment benefits are unrealistically generous, stimulating workers to hold out for higher wages. After heated discussion, the board resolves to attack the matter through the Unemployment Policy Committee of the Nikkeiren (Japanese Federation of Employers' Associations), to which the company has belonged since its formation in 1948. If the government expects to continue to receive the backing of Japanese business, declares the chairman, it must take steps to reward that loyal support. No one on the board appears to disagree.[2]

In this case, what is happening? A nonpolitical group (a business corporation) is itself a member of a political group (the employers' federation). When the members of the nonpolitical group decide to take political action, they may do so through the exterior group, drawing on the larger group's expertise and numerical strength to pressure the government for change. Their success in doing so will depend on their ability to persuade the other members in the federation that this is an appropriate path to pursue. Sometimes, however, belonging to an existing political group is not a satisfactory way to organize for one's own political purposes. Consider the next example.

Fascinated by politics and determined to devote his life to the struggle for his people's freedom, a student newly arrived in London from an African colony under British dominion soon assumes a leadership role in the activities of the West African Students' Union in London. His work in organizing international conferences brings him to the attention of the leaders of the United Gold Coast Convention (UGCC), the strongest political party in his native land, and he responds to their request to come home and take the post of general secretary. Soon, however, he finds himself in disaccord with the other leaders of the party, who move too slowly and too cautiously for his taste. Quietly, he helps a friend form a Youth Study Group, which brings together young men and women eager to wage a more active struggle against colonialism. When this organization becomes strong enough, he aids in its transformation to the Convention People's Party, breaks with the UGCC, and leads the new party to electoral victory—and the Gold Coast to independence as the new nation of Ghana.[3]

This third example is the true story of the early political career of Kwame Nkrumah, the former president of Ghana. So far we have looked at three ways individuals use political groups to accomplish their ends: They may form a group spontaneously, they may belong to a nonpolitical group that in turn belongs to a political group, or they may work within one political group to develop the strength to form another group more suitable to their purposes. But we have not yet considered the way most of us work through political organizations—that is, we simply join the one that suits us best, stay with it, and gradually come to accept its goals as our own. Those goals may vary from the most ordinary to the most extreme. Our next and final example falls into the extreme category.

The young Colombian university graduate, angry at her inability to find employment appropriate to her level of education despite apparent national prosperity and dismayed by large-scale corruption involving drug trafficking and criminal violence, joins others similarly situated to complain and argue over the causes of the nation's plight. She is gradually persuaded that the nation's turning point came on May 19, 1970, when General Gustavo Royas, a conservative reformist who had been in power in the early 1950s, was denied reelection (by voter fraud, her new friends insist). The only answer now, they say, is political revolution, and the only way to achieve that revolution is by violent means, such as those employed by M-19, a terrorist group named for the day of infamy. They decide to join, and in June 1985 they are among the M-19 members who take over the country's Palace of Justice, in which Colombia's Supreme Court is housed. The military fights back, and in the battle half of the Supreme Court justices and all of the M-19 participants are killed, including the angry young woman. In the aftermath, a few minor political reforms are enacted, but the problems of criminal dominance of the nation's politics are not resolved.[4]

The forms that political organizations take vary as greatly as the routes individuals follow to join them. The spontaneous, short-lived interest group, the permanent lobby, the political party, and the guerrilla movement mentioned in these examples only begin to suggest the range of political organizations found throughout the world. In fact, since a **political organization** is "any organization that is not itself a government agency but whose main purpose is to affect the operation of government," the subject is too vast to be covered in a single chapter.[5] Our solution is to discuss interest groups in this chapter and political parties in Chapter 8 and not to discuss violent revolutionary groups at all, beyond making clear what is distinctive about that form of organization.

All three types of groups are, of course, political organizations, and the differences among them are not always easy to identify. But there are distinctions. An **interest group** is an organization that seeks to affect the operation of government by using peaceful means to persuade key persons in government to act in accordance with the group's **interests**. The first two cases discussed in the opening pages of this chapter are examples of interest groups. A **violent revolutionary group** is an organization that seeks to achieve change in government policy—or to change the government altogether—by violent means; the fourth case tells of such a group. A **political party** is an organization that nominates and campaigns on behalf of candidates seeking office in an existent government through popular election; the third case describes the beginning of a new political party.

Although at any given moment in its life, a political organization is usually easily identified as an interest group, a political party, or a violent revolutionary organization, that same organization might well have begun as a different type and may yet change again. Interest groups may become violent revolutionary groups when they despair of achieving their objectives by peaceful means; revolutionary groups, once successful or partially so, may change themselves into political parties; political parties may be forced underground by government repression and become violent revolutionary groups—or may lose so many elections at such great expense that they abandon the quest for office and become ordinary interest groups, exerting peaceful pressure on those who do win control of the government. Many other permutations are possible. Normally, it is the leaders of political organizations who choose the form (and when to change it), basing their choice on their values, their skills, their experience, and what they believe most likely to work for pursuit of the group's particular goals in its particular circumstances. Rank-and-file members—or potential members—may or may not be consulted.

As noted, this chapter is devoted to the study of interest groups. We consider the benefits they offer to those who join them, the nature of their organizational apparatus, the goals toward which they are directed, and the tactics they employ. We also devote an entire section to an important problem posed by some interest groups today: their growing ability to substitute themselves for constitutional government.

BENEFITS TO JOINERS OF INTEREST GROUPS

Individuals must be motivated to combine with others before group action can be effective in influencing government. No one joins a group without seeking some kind of reward. Robert Salisbury has suggested that individuals join groups seeking one of three kinds of benefits: material, solidary, or purposive.[6]

Material benefits are goods and services made available to group members. Salisbury points out that members may join a group to improve their supply of these benefits either directly or indirectly. A group exercising political pressure to keep access to a jogging track is pursuing a material benefit directly. But a group trying to change government unemployment benefits so that businesses may employ workers at lower wages and thus retain greater profits for owners is pursuing such a reward indirectly.

Others join groups less for what they can get materially than for the good feelings they get from joining. For some, these "good feelings" are **solidary benefits.** Joining the group gives these people a sense of belonging, a chance to socialize with others, or improved social status. Some of the men and women at the Gray Panthers annual picnic may be there just to help raise funds for the lobbying efforts of this activist senior citizen group, but for most the opportunity to have a good time in congenial surroundings with others who share their interests may be the primary motive for attendance. And the chance to go to the picnic may well have brought them into the Gray Panthers in the first place.

Some groups offer their members another kind of "good feeling" reward: **pur-**

"You go on home without me, Irene. I'm going to join this man's cult."

posive benefits. Working on behalf of a value or cause they believe in can give some members so much satisfaction that they need seek no personal rewards. Groups fighting for such causes as human rights (the International League for the Rights of Man), environmental safeguards (Friends of the Earth), and consumer protection (the British Public Interest Research Centre) are likely to attract members in search of this kind of reward.

The categories are far from discrete. Individuals may join a group for a combination of motives, and groups may offer a combination of rewards. Suppose, for example, that one summer evening you are sitting at home watching the local news on television, after spending a hard, boring day at a temporary job as a word processor—a job you have taken just to earn some money for school expenses. Suddenly you see some familiar faces on the television screen. It is your good friend Angela and her boyfriend Jerry. Then suddenly Jerry is being knocked down by some very tough-looking characters, and Angela is being roughly shoved away. You sit up straight, pay close attention, and learn that your friends were peacefully marching in front of city hall for a cause they believe in— one that you yourself happen to think is worthwhile and important. The people who assaulted them do not agree and, furthermore, seem to have little or no re-spect for other people's rights of free expression. Before you know it, you are on the phone to Angela and Jerry, offering your support. The next night you attend a meeting of their group, and for the rest of the summer you are one of its most ardent members, joining in all its activities. You scarcely mind that boring job anymore, you have so much to think about. Your coworkers are impressed when they see you being interviewed on television during the group's next major demonstration. The group itself likes your work so much that it offers you a paid staff position for the following summer. What were your rewards? Were they ma-terial, solidary, or purposive?

Rewards also vary with intensity of membership. Many groups consist of a handful of activists, backed up by lists of supporters—who are merely all the people who have ever sent in a membership form, with or without a check at-tached. Active participation by the great majority of the members of interest groups is rare. Some groups deliberately limit the number of active members, ei-ther because they prefer a cohesive core to a larger and more heterogeneous group beset by factionalism or because by making membership a privilege and an honor they increase the readiness of those who belong to be generous in dona-tions of time and money.[7] Presumably, those who take an active part in highly selective groups receive very significant solidary benefits, whereas those whose participation is limited to sending a check are more likely to be seeking and gain-ing only material or purposive rewards.

Finally, it is entirely possible for individuals to reap some of the rewards of in-terest group membership *without being a member.* **Collective benefits** are benefits that go to all the members of a polity whether they helped work for them or not. As a result, groups may find it difficult to recruit members even though the ben-efits their work eventually produces may be highly desirable to many. This is what is known as the *free rider* problem; the nonparticipants take a free ride on the hard work of a few. It is often the most difficult problem for a group that is de-termined to attract a mass membership.[8]

HOW ORGANIZED IS THE INTEREST GROUP?

Interest groups vary not only in the kind of benefits they offer to their members but also in the degree to which there is a formal organization devoted to politi-cal action. Drawing on the work of others and observing groups in action today, we can identify seven levels of interest group organization.

Amorphous groups are groupings of individuals who share an interest and act on its behalf in a way that indirectly affects government policy, even though they do not see themselves as taking any action that may be called political.[9] **Sponta-neous groups** are groups of unorganized individuals who act together politically and deliberately but in unconventional and often violent fashion.[10] Student demonstrations in France, race riots in Great Britain, and wildcat strikes in the United States all fit into this category, as long as they begin without the participation of any formal organization. Only slightly more organized are the nonassociational groups, which make occasional representations to government officials on behalf of unorganized—or loosely organized—individuals who share a particular demographic characteristic. Mexican Americans who testify in favor of bilingual education but do not organize an ongoing group around that issue or around their own ethnic identity provide an example of this level of group activity.

At a fourth level of organizational complexity are institutional groups. These are subgroups *within* such institutions as churches, business corporations, and armies. They take special responsibility for the institution's political interests by such tactics as lobbying individual government officials, testifying at hearings, and placing advertisements to arouse public support. When public agencies, officially part of the government, assume the guise of interest group, lobbying another part of government (the legislature or the chief executive), they may be seen as a particular kind of institutional group.

Fifth are associational groups, those fully organized groups that are formed specifically to represent the interests—political or other—of their members. These are the groups we most commonly think of when we speak of interest groups. Trade unions, business federations, professional associations, neighborhood associations, political action committees (PACs), and ethnic associations all fit here. Most of this chapter is devoted to their activities.

Sixth are *ad hoc coalitions*. An ad hoc coalition is a temporary organization created to allow several political organizations (which may be any combination of interest groups, parties, or other political organizations) to pool their resources in a joint effort in which all are temporarily interested. When various women's groups, such as the National Organization for Women, the National Council of Jewish Women, the League of Women Voters, and the General Federation of Women's Clubs, engage in *collective lobbying* on behalf of specific issues and then disband to pursue their more distinctive interests, they are creating ad hoc coalitions.[11] Antiwar sentiment may also produce ad hoc coalitions, as when the National Campaign for Peace in the Middle East, the Coalition for Democratic Values, the Coalition to Stop U.S. Intervention in the Middle East, and several Catholic and Protestant peace groups all united in an effort to rally public opinion against the Gulf War.[12] Such organizations are possible among enemies as well as among friends; this form of organization is purposive, pragmatic, and usually temporary.

Social movements may be called a seventh form of interest group, although they are in reality a kind of organization that is very difficult to classify. Such groups are interested in the reform of entire polities, normally on behalf of its least privileged members. If they employ—as many do—violent means, then they fall into the category of violent revolutionary groups; the Shining Path of Peru is an example. If they work primarily—as many do—via political parties, then they fall into that category; a principal example are the Green movements in many western European nations. But if they avoid the use of violence and enter partisan politics only intermittently and tangentially, then even though they may grow to dimensions that threaten to break its bounds, they still fit better in our present category, the interest group. Social movements are often inspired by religious thought—the Christian Right in the United States, liberation theologists in Latin America—but not always, as we see in the examples of nonpartisan ecologist movements, the feminist movement at its height in the 1970s, the Polish trade union movement Solidarity, and the U.S. civil rights movement.[13]

THE GOALS OF INTEREST GROUPS

Interest groups may also be distinguished according to the purposes for which they work. Some work only on behalf of the immediate interests of their members, others on behalf of causes that their members believe will benefit all (or a significant portion of) humankind. Some work for a single purpose, others for a wide range of causes that seem to them to fit under a common rubric.

Special Interest Groups and Public Interest Groups

The most common goal of interest groups is to serve the "special interests" of their members. In almost every nation of the world, **special interest groups** that focus exclusively on the interests of business, labor, or agriculture are among the best organized and most powerful of all. The Colombian National Association of Manufacturers (ANDI), the American Federation of Labor-Congress of Industrial Organizations (AFL-CIO), and the German Farmers League (Deutscher Bauernverband) all work for interests that are found worldwide and that tend to make strong representations to government wherever the most minimal freedom of assembly is protected. Other types of special interest groups, such as teachers (the Quebec Teachers Federation), students (the Akhil Bharatiya Vidyarthi Parishad, which is India's largest student organization), and oppressed minorities (the Original Cherokee Community Organization), are also found around the globe, whereas some groups, such as the Anti-Vivisection League or the Ku Klux Klan, are more truly "special."

In their efforts to influence government, special interests often struggle against one another. The Pacific Coast Federation of Fishermen's Association, a group representing West Coast commercial fishermen, believed the livelihood of its members depended on maintaining the terms of the 1973 Endangered Species Act. However, the National Endangered Species Reform Coalition, an ad hoc coalition of 185 U.S. groups and companies, including major timber, mining, ranching, and utility interests, believed that same piece of legislation was seriously jeopardizing its ability to meet *its* economic needs. In 1995, both groups were actively lobbying Congress, one to maintain and the other to remove major provisions of that act.[14]

Other groups organize for causes they claim are in the public's interest, not their own. The Sierra Club, the Consumer Federation of America, and Ralph Nader's Public Interest Research Group are U.S. examples of groups that claim the identity of **public interest group**.[15]

Claiming such a status is clearly a good way to discourage opposition, but the question of when a group's goals are truly in the public interest is not always simple to resolve. The nineteenth-century British Union for the Abolition of Vivisection clearly worked for its members' special feelings about animal welfare and against research many others considered essential for human welfare. Contemporary animal protection leagues have also been accused of neglecting basic human needs—for example, the economic well-being of Inuit (Eskimo) families engaged in whaling—in their concern to protect other species. (Perhaps you have seen the bumper strip showing a picture of a concerned whale pleading, "Save the Humans.") Such cases require careful study and, finally, a normative choice to determine where the public interest truly lies.

Nor is it always certain that claiming that larger identity will improve a group's political effectiveness. The large and powerful American Association of Retired Persons sometimes remains quiet on major issues so as not to offend its diverse membership; when it does take action, it often aligns itself with congressional Democrats. In both cases, it risks the loss of partisan members who lean to the right and who have in response recently formed such frankly conservative and usually pro-Republican groups as the Seniors Coalition, the 60/Plus Association, and the United Seniors Association.[16]

Single-Issue Groups and Multiple-Issue Groups

Another distinction to be made between groups is the number of goals a group works toward. Some groups focus on single issues; others attack a broad range of political problems that they believe are linked to their members' interests. Large business federations, such as Italy's Confindistria or India's Chambers of Commerce and Industry; labor organizations, such as the Nigerian Trade Unions Congress or the U.S. AFL-CIO; and some public interest groups, including Common Cause and the League of Women Voters, regularly undertake a program for government action that covers a wide range of topics. (Common Cause began in 1970 with a wide-ranging list of issue areas, including antiwar action, government reform, urban concerns, welfare, and the environment, but soon learned it would be more effective with a more limited agenda. Since then it has emphasized the reform of political procedures and institutions.)

Other groups, such as People for the Ethical Treatment of Animals (PETA) or the National Rifle Association (NRA), confine themselves to a single issue. Multiple-issue groups are sometimes accused of having too broad an agenda, but single-issue groups are often criticized for taking too little interest in the larger concerns of government, supporting or attacking government officials strictly according to the actions they take in their one area of concern. The conservative NRA has carried its battle against gun regulation to the point of targeting a Republican congressman whose only competition was a Socialist independent but who had dared to announce his support for a ban on assault weapons.[17] Another criticism of single-issue groups is that their members become so passionate about the single cause that they forget the importance of bringing various interests together in a wide-ranging program for social change, with the result that those who might be political allies—be they on the left, right, or center—and thus helpful to one another, become competitors for public attention and resources, hurting each other's causes and accomplishing less for their own than cooperative tactics would permit.

THE TACTICS OF INTEREST GROUPS

How *do* interest groups work to achieve their goals? To answer that question, we need to consider both **pressure methods**, the means groups use to exert pressure on government, and **pressure points**, the levels and branches of government that groups seek to influence.

Pressure Methods

The means of influencing government that is most often associated with interest groups is **lobbying**. In practice, however, groups have a large arsenal of methods at their command, and lobbying itself can take many forms. Waylaying the public official in the lobby of his or her workplace is still a lively art, and making personal offerings ranging from simple lunches to lavish gifts to outright bribes, another time-honored way of doing this kind of business, has by no means vanished from the globe.

The campaign contribution, whether made legally or illegally, is often a means of gaining access that smacks of bribery. Carol Greenwald quotes one former Pennsylvania politician's very personal explanation of how it works: "I believe in a division of labor. . . . You send us to Congress, we pass laws . . . under which you make money . . . and out of your profits you further contribute to our campaign funds to send us back again to pass more laws to enable you to make more money."[18]

When successful candidates owe their election in significant part to financial assistance during the campaign, they usually know that they are in debt and that such debts must be repaid with appropriate policy decisions or appointments. They themselves will normally deny that such is the case (former senator Boies Penrose, quoted above, is an exception), but the contributors themselves are often more forthcoming. Thus, when asked whether he thought the $1.3 million worth of financial support his savings and loan firm had provided for various Democratic political campaigns had influenced the recipients to take up his cause, Charles H. Keating Jr. answered candidly, "I want to say in the most forceful way I can: I certainly hope so."[19] Such contributions tend to flow to those already in power ($324,000 of Keating's contributions went to five incumbent Democratic senators), and when power changes hands, so does the flow of money. In the first half of 1995, after the Republican sweep of both houses of the U.S. Congress, the beleaguered tobacco industry gave over $1.5 million to the newly powerful party and only $154,950 to national Democratic committees.[20]

Under campaign finance law in the United States, any group wishing to contribute money or services to a candidate must create a political action committee, and that committee must note detailed disclosure of expenditures both directly to candidates and independently on their behalf. PACs may not contribute more than $5,000 directly to any candidate, but there is no limit on independent expenditures—that is, on the amount of money that a PAC may spend directly on campaigning for a candidate. Furthermore, there is no limit on the amount that may be given to party committees (note the tobacco industry's contributions above), and although such monies are supposed to be spent for "party-building" purposes, the Federal Election Commission and the courts have been very liberal in their interpretation of what kind of activities may be covered by that term. The Federal Election Commission requires elaborate reports of all receipts and disbursements by a candidate but requires only the most simple accounting of itemized independent expenditures (see Box 7.1.).

Independent expenditures have steadily risen in recent elections, accounting for an ever higher percentage of total expenditures. However, not every PAC was happy with the new freedom to make direct expenditures on behalf of favored candidates: "It's a lot more difficult than handing out a $5,000 check," said one PAC director. "It's expensive to get into. We spend a lot of money on polling. We do a lot of research. And if it's not handled correctly, it can cause a rift in your membership."[21] On the other hand, independent spending is often now viewed as the only way to be seen as a "serious player." According to the director of the Auto Dealers and Drivers for Free Trade PAC, which spent approximately $1.5 million independently in 1988, the message is clear: "Auto dealers will back their friends no matter how much trouble they are in."[22]

In recent years, yet another means for funneling private money into political campaigns has emerged: the creation of tax-exempt foundations affiliated with elected officials or candidates for office. The most dubious version is the voter registration group or foundation. Such an association may accept unlimited sums without having to meet the Federal Election Commission's disclosure requirements—and the contributions are tax deductible. But such "nonpartisan" registration groups often focus their efforts on signing up only those persons likely to vote their way. Contributing to such groups was one way savings and loan officer Charles H. Keating Jr. was able to contribute more than $1 million to the campaigns (or "causes") of several U.S. senators who attempted to save his failing company.

However, when the government official who has received PAC funding wishes to cooperate, be it out of innocent agreement or dishonest avarice, he or she will be more likely to be able to persuade colleagues if a majority of the general public is on the same side as the donor. When they have the means, interest groups therefore do not confine themselves to contributions. The health and insurance industries that were opposed to the plans for health care reform by the Clinton administration were estimated to have spent over $40 million in campaign contributions but also another $60 million in advertising, public relations, and lobbying in their efforts to defeat that plan.[23]

Effective lobbying today usually means spending a great deal of time preparing the arguments and documentation that will help the cooperative official get the necessary agreement of other officials. Successful lobbyists seek to become such trusted sources of high-quality credible information that they create a dependency. Such dependency can be carried very far. In 1995, attorneys from a

BOX 7.1   RUNNING FOR CONGRESS—AND KEEPING THE BOOKS

Here are two pages from the Federal Elections Commission (FEC) form to be filled out by a candidate for the United States Congress (the "Summary Page" and the "Detailed Summary Page"), with illustrative entries. The FEC tells the candidate where to find information about what is required for each entry, for example, "Reporting Forms," page 26; "When to Report," page 25; "Who Reports," page 24; "Where to File Reports," page 24; "When to Itemize Receipts," page 27; "Types of Contributions," page 5; "Loans," pages 5, 13, 29 and 50–53; "How to Itemize Disbursements" and "When to Itemize Disbursements," page 29; "Contribution Refunds," pages 30 and 49; "Contributions to Other Candidates," pages 29 and 49.

SUMMARIZING CAMPAIGN FINANCE ACTIVITY

REPORT OF RECEIPTS AND DISBURSEMENTS
For An Authorized Committee
(Summary Page)

USE FEC MAILING LABEL OR TYPE OR PRINT

1. NAME OF COMMITTEE (in full)

SAM JONES FOR CONGRESS

ADDRESS (number and street) ☐ Check if different than previously reported.

319 MAIN STREET

2. FEC IDENTIFICATION NUMBER

000015551

CITY, STATE and ZIP CODE   STATE /DISTRICT

CITY, STATE ZIP   ST/01   ☐ YES   ☒ NO

4. TYPE OF REPORT

☐ April 15 Quarterly Report

☐ July 15 Quarterly Report

☐ October 15 Quarterly Report

☐ January 31 Year End Report

☐ July 31 Mid-Year Report (Non-election Year Only)

☒ Twelfth day report preceding __Primary__ (Type of Election)

☒ election on __9/13/94__ in the State of __(STATE)__

☐ Thirtieth day report following the General Election on

_____ in the State of _____

☐ Termination Report

This report contains activity for   ☒ Primary Election   ☐ General Election   ☐ Special Election   ☐ Runoff Election

SUMMARY

	COLUMN A This Period	COLUMN B Calendar Year-to-Date
5. Covering Period __7-1-94__ through __8-24-94__		
6. Net Contributions (other than loans)		
(a) Total Contributions (other than loans) (from Line 11(e))..........	$20,802.67	$37,475.95
(b) Total Contribution Refunds (from Line 20(d)).........................	$250.00	$640.93
(c) Net Contributions (other than loans) (subtract Line 6(b) from 6(a) ..	$20,551.67	$36,835.02
7. Net Operating Expenditures		
(a) Total Operating Expenditures (from Line 17).........................	$15,124.07	$27,785.67
(b) Total Offsets to Operating Expenditures (from Line 14)..............	$489.73	$724.15
(c) Net Operating Expenditures (subtract Line 7(b) from 7(a))...........	$14,634.34	$27,061.52
8. Cash on Hand at Close of Reporting Period (from Line 27).............	$23,230.48	
9. Debts and Obligations Owed TO the Committee (Itemize all on Schedule C and/or Schedule D)...................	0	
10. Debts and Obligations Owed BY the Committee (Itemize all on Schedule C and/or Schedule D)...................	$14,432.39	

For further information contact: Federal Election Commission 999 E. Street, NW Washington, DC 20463 Toll Free 800-424-9530 Local 202-219-3420

I certify that I have examined this Report and to the best of my knowledge and belief it is true, correct and complete.

Type or Print Name of Treasurer

Joseph Dougherty

Signature of Treasurer

Date
8/31/94

NOTE: Submission of false, erroneous, or incomplete information may subject the person signing this Report to the penalties of 2 U.S.C.. §437g.

FEC FORM 3
(revised 4/87)

DETAILED SUMMARY PAGE
of Receipts and Disbursements
(Page 2, FEC FORM 3)

Name or Committee (In full)	Report Covering the Period:	
Sam Jones For Congress	From: 7-1-94 To: 8-2-94	

I. RECEIPTS	COLUMN A Total This Period	COLUMN B Calendar Year-to-Date	
11. CONTRIBUTIONS (other than loans) FROM:			
(a) Individuals/Persons Other Than Political Committees			
(i) Itemized (use Schedule A)	$2,900.00		11(a)(i)
(ii) Unitemized	$6,701.67		11(a)(ii)
(iii) Total contributions from individuals	$9,601.67	$22,496.12	11(a)(iii)
(b) Political Party Committees	$2,000.00	$3,000.00	11(b)
(c) Other Political Committees (such as PACs)	$8,000.00	$10,000.00	11(c)
(d) The Candidate	$2,000.00	$1,979.83	11(d)
(e) TOTAL CONTRIBUTIONS (other than loans)(add 11(a) (iii), (b), (c) and (d)).	$20,801.67	$37,475.95	11(e)
12. TRANSFERS FROM OTHER AUTHORIZED COMMITTEES	0	0	12
13. LOANS:			
(a) Made or Guaranteed by the Candidate	$3,000.00	$3,000.00	13(a)
(b) All Other Loans	$3,000.00	$13,000.00	13(b)
(c) TOTAL LOANS (add 13(a) and (b)	$6,000.00	$16,000.00	13(c)
14. OFFSETS TO OPERATING EXPENDITURES (Refunds, Rebates, etc.)	$489.73	$724.15	14
15. OTHER RECEIPTS (Dividends, Interest, etc.)	$204.64	$969.35	15
16. TOTAL RECEIPTS (add 11(e), 12, 13(c), 14 and 15)	$27,496.04	$55,169.45	16

II. DISBURSEMENTS

	COLUMN A	COLUMN B	
17. OPERATING EXPENDITURES	$15,124.07	$27,785.67	17
18. TRANSFERS TO OTHER AUTHORIZED COMMITTEES	0	0	18
19. LOAN REPAYMENTS:			
(a) Made or Guaranteed by the Candidate	$317.64	$317.64	19(a)
(b) Of All Other Loans	$882.80	$2,378.37	19(b)
(c) TOTAL LOAN REPAYMENTS (add 19(a) and (b)	$1,200.44	$2,696.01	19(c)
20. REFUNDS OF CONTRIBUTIONS TO:			
(a) Individuals/Persons Other Than Political Committees	$250.00	$640.93	20(a)
(b) Political Party Committees	0	0	20(b)
(c) Other Political Committees (such as PACs)	0	0	20(c)
(d) TOTAL CONTRIBUTION REFUNDS (add 20(a), (b) and (c))	$250.00	$640.93	20(d)
21. OTHER DISBURSEMENTS	$350.00	$350.00	21
22. TOTAL DISBURSEMENTS (add 17, 18, 19(c), 20(d) and 21)	$16,924.51	$31,472.61	22

III. CASH SUMMARY

23. CASH ON HAND AT BEGINNING OF REPORTING PERIOD	$ 12,942.81	23
24. TOTAL RECEIPTS THIS PERIOD (Line 16)	$ 27,496.04	24
25. SUBTOTAL (add Line 23 and Line 24)	$ 40,438.85	25
26. TOTAL DISBURSEMENTS THIS PERIOD (from Line 22)	$ 16,924.51	26
27. CASH ON HAND AT CLOSE OF THE REPORTING PERIOD (subtract Line 26 from 25)	$ 23,514.34	27

law firm representing numerous electric utilities were given the job (normally that of the appropriate congressional staff) of explaining to the Senate Judiciary Committee the latest version of a bill that would give such industries important new powers to challenge government regulations. It was unusual to see, commented one observer, "congressional staff members so openly and publicly embrace . . . legislative outsiders with extensive interests in the outcome."[24]

An old form of lobbying, writing letters, has taken a new form in the United States, as groups with the money to do so may now hire lobbying firms to generate what appears to be "grass roots lobbying." Thus in 1992 the Coalition to End Abusive Securities Suits hired the Wexler Group, a Washington lobbying firm, to ask companies and associations first to join the coalition and then to ask their members and employees to write to Congress, using packets of sample letters and computer disks supplied by the firm. Other such firms have used mass mailings of preprinted post cards and have even used phone banks to call potential supporters, transferring the calls to congressional offices when consent is secured.[25]

Interest groups with limited funds are particularly likely to employ means other than making financial contributions and lobbying to bring home their arguments. They hold demonstrations, organize boycotts, wage strikes, advertise, write books, stage various events to attract the attention of the news media, and use whatever means they can to call public and official attention to their cause. Student movements, from the Free Speech Movement of the 1960s in the United States to the Brazilian Youth Corps of Popular Action to the French students protesting educational reforms proposed by a right-wing government in early 1992, have moved into the streets with alacrity on behalf of a wide range of causes. Environmentalists have staged many kinds of theatrical events, from sailing into nuclear test zones to burying automobiles, in their efforts to arouse public interest and concern. Members of the AIDS Coalition to Unleash Power (ACT UP), who are middle-class professionals, have used "their clean-cut looks and natty attire [to] gain entry to the halls of government, finance and religion . . . halt the proceedings by shouting, playing dead, or handcuffing themselves to a fixture [in order] to force people to confront the AIDS crisis, and help get drugs for those dying of the affliction."[26]

Pressure Points

The choice of means is often closely linked to the second tactical question, the choice of whom or what to pressure. Interest groups seek to bring influence to bear on those capable of making a difference. In the U.S. presidential system, the separation of the legislative and executive branches and the increasing power of the executive, combined with the declining importance of political parties, means that groups must develop numerous points of access to be effective in promoting government actions they desire or in blocking actions they deplore. The successful group stays on good terms with the bureaucrats and congressional aides who draft legislation relevant to its interests, with the members of Congress who vote on it, with the members of the executive branch who counsel the pres-

An interest group at work in the global polity. Here German members of Greenpeace have locked themselves in a cage outside the French embassy in Bonn to protest France's renewal of nuclear testing in the Pacific. The banner in the background reads: "You can stop our ships, but not our resistance."

(Reuters/Ulli Michel/Archive Photos)

ident on such matters, and with the bureaucrats who see to the actual implementation of the policies adopted.[27]

In a parliamentary system, on the other hand, access to individual deputies and to members of the executive branch is very often through the political parties that play such strong roles in this form of government. In Great Britain, the close ties between the business interests of Great Britain and the Conservative Party, and between the labor unions and the Labour Party, mean that each kind of group has a vested interest in seeing the party it trusts take power. The business interests of Germany and the Christian Democratic Party have also always been close, as have business and the Rally for the Republic (the party whose leader, Jacques Chirac, was elected president in 1995) in France. French groups have also linked themselves to the strength of the presidency under the Fifth Republic by working with the Social and Economic Council, which includes in its membership more than 200 delegates from trade unions, agricultural associations, business organizations, and professional groups.[28]

In a highly centralized state such as France, bureaucratic ministries exercise great power and will also be the direct focus of industry efforts to influence policy.[29] In Japan, it is important for business to maintain good relations with the Japanese Ministry of International Trade and Industry (MITI), although the powers of that agency often prove limited in practice. Unrestrained by antitrust laws, Japanese firms are permitted to unite in massive holding companies, known as *zaibatsu* and typically consisting of a conglomeration of banks, insurance companies, and manufacturing concerns.[30] Such major business interests are able to offer strong incentives to high government officials and party leaders, incentives that may take the form of direct bribes or, more commonly, the practice of *amakudari*, which means "descent from heaven" and refers to the fact that bureaucrats from the ministry often take comfortable positions with these firms when they leave the government. Thus, their power has often proved more than a match for any efforts the MITI might make to direct their destinies. In 1991, it was revealed that several *zaibatsu* brokerage houses were closely linked to known gangsters and had compensated 187 of their larger clients for stock market losses and furthermore that the MITI had known of the practice a full two years before the scandal broke but had done nothing whatsoever about it.

HOW WELL DO INTEREST GROUPS DO THEIR WORK?

What role do interest groups play in strengthening individual polities? Political scientists, like the general public, seem to be of two minds on this subject. Some have argued that all politics consists of the struggle among groups and the best system is the one that best protects the rights of free association and intergroup bargaining. Groups serve the interests of individuals far better than individuals are capable of serving themselves, say these political scientists, and those who find no suitable group should form one for themselves. Groups that are able to influence governments deserve to do so; they have shown the strength of their cause on the battleground of politics.[31] This theory of the relationship between groups and government is called **pluralism**.

Other political scientists, however, have been far less optimistic and find the tenets of pluralism to be naive and unrealistic. Known as *elite theorists*, they trace their intellectual roots to the work of the late sociologist C. Wright Mills, whose book *The Power Elite* charged that effective control of power in the United States was in the hands of the wealthy and other powerful groups in society. Elite theorists point out the difficulties many underrepresented groups face in attempting to organize, given lack of time, energy, or political freedom (or all three), as well as the particular advantages the better-organized groups may have had in achieving that status.[32] Government oppression may be sustained by the more powerful segments of public opinion; in states where women, racial minorities, or immigrant workers are openly denied equal rights with other citizens, the control of the dominant groups over the shaping of public opinion can sometimes lead even the oppressed to believe their treatment is inevitable and just.

On the other hand, interest groups that seek support for "acceptable" causes may find that almost any tactics they use to gain their ends are tolerated, if not officially approved. Vigilante groups, whether composed of cowboys lynching horse rustlers in the Old West of the United States, armed guerrillas executing drug dealers in Medellín, Colombia, or revolutionary crusaders meting out summary justice to discredited leaders in postcommunist Romania, are an example of groups using illegal means to accomplish socially approved ends.[33] Even when the ends accomplished are not acceptable to a broader public, illegal means may be tolerated and even abetted by agencies officially responsible for their elimination. Under the ultraconservative leadership of J. Edgar Hoover, the U.S. Federal Bureau of Investigation not only failed to curb the known illegal activities of the Ku Klux Klan but even helped the Klan organize forty-one chapters in North Carolina.[34]

Finally, say some antipluralists, even people who are able to achieve significant roles in effective and well-established pressure groups are not necessarily adequately represented in the political process. After all, citizenship means a concern for national policy and practice that extends beyond the range of one's liveliest personal interests. Short-term personal interests may indeed be best served by joining specific groups, but for the broader concerns and responsibilities of true citizenship, a broader, more all-encompassing form of political organization, such as a social movement or a political party, is required. (See Box 7.2.)

A SPECIAL PROBLEM OF INTEREST GROUP BEHAVIOR: EXTRACONSTITUTIONALISM

Let us introduce the problem of extraconstitutional behavior by interest groups with an example or two, starting with one from Southeast Asia. When General Sukarno and his supporters ousted the Dutch in Indonesia after World War II, they had so much financial aid from Indonesian business interests that the new regime was considered to be "mortgaged" from the start. To this day the business community remains, according to Ulf Sundhausen, "relatively small and comparatively rich in a sea of poverty."[35]

Here's another example, from another continent, and about another interest. In Colombia, the Catholic church is one of the largest landowners and 90 percent of Colombians are Catholic. This makes the church a powerful force and ensures that its views on matters political are given close attention. The church has almost exclusive control of education, is a strong voice in determining social welfare policies, and has periodically influenced the government to engage in severe persecution of the minority Protestant population. There are reform-minded progressives within the Colombian Catholic hierarchy, but whether conservatives or progressives are dominant, the fact remains that state policy in such matters is determined by clerical rather than secular leadership.[36]

Finally, an international illustration: The agreement made among Sweden, the United States, and Liberia for the creation of the Liberian American Swedish Minerals Company (LAMCO) geared the marketing of Liberia's high-grade iron

BOX 7.2   REGIME CHANGE

Organizing to Protect Human Rights in the New Latin America

Authoritarian regimes have given way to ostensibly democratic regimes in most of the nations of Latin America, yet serious violations of human rights continue. Contested elections by multiple parties are not enough to ensure that all the attributes of modern democracy, including the protection of individual rights, will be put in place. However, introducing some of the institutions of democracy does sometimes make it possible to introduce others that are capable of addressing the lingering evils of authoritarian rule. One such institution is the pressure group.

In Latin America there has recently been an "explosion of nongovernmental human rights organizations"—over 3,000 by recent count. Guided by different concerns, the groups are learning to work together and to form alliances with investigative journalists to expose continuing abuses. They use computers in order to communicate with one another, to trace the flow of illegal monies, and to maintain secure records of repression, torture, the denial of habeas corpus, and other offenses against human liberties. Individual members provide personal support, often by moving in as protective companions, to those who are threatened for probing into and reporting violations.

These groups believe government corruption is so pervasive that it would be a mistake to turn human rights protection over to officialdom: "Governmental agencies lack the independence needed for public accountability." On the other hand, they believe in working for changes in the law, by lobbying legislators and providing information for the press and television. They frequently propose constitutional changes, seeking to eliminate any legal basis for future military arbitration or tutelage. The Inter-American Court in San José, Costa Rica, has been used to pressure offending nations not to repeat injustices.

Their work is far from complete, but thanks to these groups "the rule of law is being pursued with an intensity new to Latin America." Hope for true democracy is heightened by their activity.

Source: Edward L. Cleary, "Struggling for Human Rights in Latin America," *America* (5 Nov. 1994): 20. Reprinted by permission.

ore to an unrealistically low price that benefited a chief purchaser, Bethlehem Steel Corporation; ensured that abnormally low taxes would be paid to the Liberian government; and established several means of distributing profits to Swedish and American stockholders before allocating the remainder to the partner nations, including Liberia.[37]

As these three examples should suggest, sometimes certain groups grow so powerful that they usurp the power of constitutionally established governments. **Extraconstitutional power** is exercised when groups external to the government are able to exert *so much pressure* on the agents of government that the government has—or believes it has—*no choice but to comply*. In such cases the decision-making powers of government have been appropriated by powerful interests, and the government itself—that is, those persons who occupy all the constitutionally prescribed posts in government—no longer governs, or at least not exclusively. Now it often simply carries out the decisions made elsewhere. The two kinds of group that have most commonly assumed this degree of political power are business and organized religion. Here we discuss only the former.

BUSINESS AS AN EXTRACONSTITUTIONAL FORCE

The power of business to set government policy varies according to the kind of political system, the kind of economic system, and the nature of the popular culture, but it is found throughout the world. This is not a new phenomenon, although it accelerated a great deal in the twentieth century, and particularly after World War II. Even before the outbreak of World War I, major German industrial and financial leaders who had established close ties with Kaiser Wilhelm II were able to persuade him of the importance of raising the level of German armaments to unprecedented heights. These industrialists included the armaments manufacturer Friedrich Alfred Krupp, who "made good use of Wilhelm's favorite idea that Germany needed a strong army."[38] A similar relationship between Japanese shipping interests and the Japanese imperial government during the 1870s helped account for the rise of the Mitsubishi Company, whose power to resist government regulation (see p. 148) has made it another borderline case of extraconstitutionality.[39]

Even fully socialized systems have not proved to be immune to extraconstitutional business forces. In such systems, *business*, in the sense of independent commercial interests, ceases to exist; the state assumes control of the means of production, and the business of business is done by state-employed managers who are expected to remain subordinate to the state. However, they may nevertheless manage somehow to make policy on their own, for their own purposes, and when they do so they are assuming an extraconstitutional role.

Does it ever happen? Of course it does. Until the fall of communism in most of the former Soviet bloc, the evidence was hard to find simply because political infighting in such systems received so little publicity.[40] However, once the old system began to crumble apart, it became apparent that in fact one of the main reasons for the fall of communist regimes was public disgust with the use party officials made of the system for their own personal aggrandizement. According to Pavel Voshchanov, a spokesperson for Russian President Boris Yeltsin, when party leaders realized a market economy was inevitable, they began setting up independent commercial ventures for themselves as early as 1988. Voshchanov claims that "the managing department of the Central Committee alone had control of more than sixty major facilities, with a total value of 1.3 billion rubles ($18.6 million). Much more belonged to those groups on the lower levels—the provincial, city and district party committees."[41] Furthermore, the corrupt practices of these new "robber barons" have apparently continued during the Yeltsin presidency. According to a U.S. observer, the Russian leader has issued decrees facilitating the process by which "yesterday's communist bureaucrats are simply converting themselves into the CEOs and owners of the Russia of tomorrow."[42]

Similar processes appear to be at work in China, where senior party and government officials who benefit from nepotism, favoritism, and corruption are known as "princelings" by a resentful population. As China seeks to encourage free enterprise within the context of the continuing authoritarian rule of the Communist Party, some efforts have been made to bring such corruption to an end, but other forms are ready to take their place. According to Walter L. Keats, the ancient system of *guanxi* (relationships) that has always controlled Chinese interpersonal relationships is experiencing a revival, as party bureaucrats reveal confidential information to vendors with whom they have close relationships or allow them to ignore rules others must obey, all in exchange for favors that range from invitations to visits abroad to outright money bribes.[43] China has an unusually elaborate system for contending against such crimes. But when the criminals are themselves members of the government, who will guard the guards?

Another way private business may have an undue influence on government policy is simply to refuse to play—that is, to take its money and its business elsewhere when the home government is not to its liking. When Britain's Labour Party took power in 1945, it stimulated a flight of British capital into other nations' economies. The party itself was later to estimate that between 1947 and 1949 over £645 million (approximately $2.4 billion) left Britain. Less than half of that was actually invested elsewhere; the remainder was simply "hot" money, the party stated, "quitting Britain because its owners disliked the Labour Government's policy . . . or were engaged in currency speculation."[44] When socialist regimes fight back by imposing heavy penalties for transferring money out of the nation, private business may refuse to make significant levels of investment altogether, preferring to wait for an expected change of command back to procapitalist hands. In either case, the expected high levels of unemployment are likely to impose strong pressures on the government to modify any policies the private sector finds repugnant.

In contemporary times, the capacity of modern business to withdraw its marbles from the national game is greatly heightened by the emergence and development of the **transnational corporation (TNC)**, sometimes referred to as the **multinational corporation (MNC)**. The TNC is a cluster of businesses located in several different nations but owned and managed by the same people. Although they may have headquarters in a single nation (the United States and Japan are the first and second largest centers of transnational corporations), they carry out important management as well as production activities around the globe.[45]

TNCs are in some ways reminiscent of **cartels**, associations of businesses formed in the early twentieth century to establish national or international monopolies over particular raw materials or manufactured goods. However, despite their power, cartels depended in part on being able to maintain supportive economic and fiscal policies in the nations where they were headquartered. They were thus vulnerable to shifting political fortunes and the concomitant fluctuations in national policy. The modern TNC differs from the cartel in that it is more interested in expanding its profits than in establishing a monopoly, and it is a far more independent network of investment, research, productive, and distributive institutions. Some transnational corporations have become extremely large, with gross annual sales greater than the gross national products of many nations (see Table 7.1).[46]

The ease with which TNCs can transfer monies and activities from nation to nation—and the fiscal pressures they can bring to bear on both national economies and the private bank accounts of all-too-human government officials—can make it almost impossible for individual governments to bring them under the effective control of national policy institutions, or for labor unions, normally functioning within a single nation and subject to its regulations, to bargain with them effectively.[47] As a consequence, TNCs sometimes engage "in a variety of injurious actions that would have been violations of criminal, regulatory, or civil law in their home countries."[48] They have made illegal contributions to political parties, offered bribes to local officials, and refused to comply with the laws and regulations of the host nation. In one well-documented example, the International Telephone and Telegraph Company worked with the U.S. Central Intelligence Agency (CIA) to try to prevent the election of Salvador Allende as president of Chile and then, having failed in that endeavor, tried various means to remove him from power (a feat the CIA eventually accomplished on its own).[49]

Why should any polity allow so independent an entity to establish itself within its borders in the first place? The answer is that the advantages can be great, especially to less-developed nations. TNCs bring in technology otherwise unavailable and involve the host nations in new levels of international trade, with profit to many. They often establish fairer standards of treatment for workers and promote desirable social, political, and economic change. They take economic risks that indigenous commercial interests cannot afford, setting up in difficult conditions and forgoing profits for several years until the enterprise is well established.

But there are, of course, serious arguments against permitting the unchecked growth of TNCs. If they offer higher wages to skilled workers than the national average for comparable jobs, they may drive indigenous companies out of business. If they do not, they are perpetrating exploitation of cheap labor and often racist social patterns as well. The economic arrangements they make with the leaders of local governments often contribute to the evolution of a small wealthy elite and so to growing class conflict within the host nation. They prevent the development of the more diversified economy needed by the local population by insisting on contracts ensuring their own supply of raw materials and the host nation's excessive use of imported technology. They hinder the development of local expertise by bringing in too many foreign experts. They impede the development of self-sufficiency by encouraging false dependencies on foreign imports.

And, of course, they may simply insist on contracts that are harshly unfair to the host nation. (See the example of Bethlehem Steel, p. 150.)

Whether good or bad, however, TNCs are a global fact of life. They are one of the clearest signs of the increasing interdependence of the human polity and one of the most powerful forces helping to create that interdependence. Individual governments *do* have ways to curb their power, from driving hard bargains

TABLE 7.1   Ranking of Countries and Corporations According to Size of Annual Product, 1993

Rank	Economic Entity	$U.S. (billions)
1	United States	6387.7
2	Japan	3926.7
3	Germany	1903.0
4	France	1289.2
5	Italy	1135.0
6	United Kingdom	1042.7
7	China	581.1
8	Canada	574.9
9	Brazil	472.0
10	Russia	348.4
11	South Korea	338.1
12	Mexico	325.0
13	Netherlands	316.4
14	Australia	310.0
15	India	262.8
16	Switzerland	254.1
17	Argentina	244.0
18	Sweden	216.3
19	Belgium	213.4
20	Austria	183.5
21	Denmark	137.6
22	Indonesia	137.0
23	**GENERAL MOTORS**	133.6
24	Saudi Arabia	128.4
25	Turkey	126.3
26	Thailand	120.2
27	South Africa	118.1
28	Norway	113.5

29	**FORD MOTOR CO.**	108.5
30	Hong Kong	104.7
31	**EXXON**	97.8
32	Finland	96.2
33	**ROYAL DUTCH/SHELL GROUP**	95.1
34	Poland	87.3
35	**TOYOTA MOTOR**	85.3
36	Portugal	77.7
37	Greece	76.7
38	Israel	72.6
39	**HITACHI**	68.6
40	**IBM**	62.7
41	**MATSUSHITA ELECTRIC INDUSTRIAL**	61.4
42	**GENERAL ELECTRIC**	60.8
43	Malaysia	60.1
44	**DAIMLER BENZ**	59.1
45	Venezuela	58.9
46	**MOBIL**	56.6
47	Singapore	55.4
48	Philippines	54.6
49	**NISSAN MOTOR**	53.8
50	Pakistan	53.3

Note: Thirty-five of the next fifty economic entities are also corporations.
Sources: Country information is from *Britannica 1996 Book of the Year* (Chicago: Encyclopedia Britannica, Inc., 1996), pp. 792–96. Industry sales information is from *Hoover's Handbook of World Business, 1995–1996* (Austin, Tex.: Reference Press, 1995), pp. 28–29. Similar charts have been developed by many authors; to my knowledge the first one appeared in Abdul A. Said and Liuz R. Simmons, eds., *The New Sovereigns: Multinational Corporations as World Powers* (Englewood Cliffs, N.J.: Prentice Hall, 1975), pp. 214–15.

when original contracts are signed or must be renewed, to monitoring and screening investors and ownership, to rigorous taxation and investment policies, to outright nationalization.[50] But in the long run the only satisfactory solution for establishing sufficient controls over the extraconstitutional activities of transnational corporations may be the strengthening of transnational government—a topic we return to toward the end of the book.

SUMMARY AND CONCLUSION

Political organization exists throughout the human polity. Even where participatory politics is banned or confined to state-sponsored directive structures, the human need to articulate and act on behalf of shared interests will find a way to make itself felt by those in power. Types of organization may be as rudimentary as the East Bay Community Track and Field Association or as complex as a transnational finance corporation; as supportive to government as the latest Committee to Reelect the President or as hostile as the Red Brigades; as long lasting as the U.S. Democratic Party (which traces its origins back to the original struggle over ratifying the Constitution) or as short lived as an ad hoc coalition to seek asylum for a poet who is a political refugee from his homeland; as close to the grassroots as the Potrero Neighborhood Merchants Association for Fairer Taxes or as remote from its membership as the Coalition on National Priorities and Military Policy, a group whose policy decisions are made, like those of most public interest groups, by a narrow leadership corps. Wherever human beings congregate, groups will form, and sometimes some of these groups will seek to affect the operation of whatever government exists.

Institutions other than the constitutionally mandated ones sometimes usurp the policymaking roles a nation's constitution prescribes for particular government institutions. The power of the business world to do so varies according to the kind of political system, the kind of economic system, and the size of the business in question. Transnational corporations, giant businesses that operate in several nations at once, may be able not only to control the relevant policymaking in those nations but also to substitute their own decision-making processes altogether.

The forms of political organization we adopt inevitably influence the quality of life within individual nation-states and in the human polity at large. How well we are able to conduct our affairs, individually and collectively, depends to a large extent on how well our interests are articulated, compromised, and conveyed to those in power. When some interests are labeled out-of-bounds without fair hearing; when political organization takes the form of nontargeted rioting; when groups fall under the sway of leaders who use their resources for ends contrary to those of the membership; or when intragroup and intergroup compromises prove impossible to reach and maintain, the damage done will extend beyond those citizens whose interests are immediately affected. Unaccommodated interests, when they are seriously held, rarely dissipate, and the means used by the people who hold them to seek satisfaction are likely to grow progressively more disruptive to the entire political system. Nor do the disturbances that stem from failures of political organization necessarily stop at national borders. One of the chief causes of conflict in the human polity at large is the migration of unresolved internal disputes into the international arena, as representatives of the unaccommodated seek living space, material wealth, personal dignity, or whatever collective good they believe they cannot find in adequate supply at home.

Selected Readings

Alexander, Herbert E., and Rei Shiratori. *Comparative Political Finance among Democracies.* Boulder, Colo.: Westview Press, 1994. A comprehensive study of money in elections, with fourteen case studies from thirteen countries.

Berry, Jeffrey M. *The Interest Group Society*. 3rd ed. White Plains, N.Y.: Longman, 1997. An examination of the methods and influence of lobbyists in the United States, placed in the context of democratic theory and including chapters on the rise of issue networks and on the relationship between corporate wealth and political advocacy.

Cigler, Allan J., and Burdett A. Loomis, eds. *Interest Group Politics*. 3rd ed. Washington, D.C.: Congressional Quarterly Press, 1991. An examination of the role played by such groups as labor unions, the American Agriculture Movement and Common Cause in the U.S. political process, with a consideration of how such groups are adjusting to increased competition for congressional attention.

Clawson, Dan, Alan Neustadt, and Denise Scott. *Money Talks: Corporate PACS and Political Influence*. New York: Basic Books, 1992. How political action committees raise money and use political donations to influence public policy.

Gies, David L., J. Steven Ott, and Jay M. Shafritz, eds. *The Nonprofit Organization: Essential Readings*. Pacific Grove, Calif.: Brooks/Cole, 1990. An in-depth look at the functions, roles, institutions, issues, traditions, and values that shape nonprofit organizations, intended for managers and board members as well as for students.

Ginsberg, Benjamin, and Martin Shefter. *Politics by Other Means: The Declining Importance of Elections in America*. New York: Basic Books, 1990. An interesting look at paralysis in the U.S. government, which the authors suggest is due to the weakening of electoral politics.

Hiebert, Ray Eldon, and Carol Reuss, eds. *The Impact of Mass Media*. White Plains, N.Y.: Longman, 1988. A series of essays debating the role of the mass media in modern political and social systems.

Manzetti, Luigi. *Institutions, Parties and Coalitions in Argentine Politics*. Pittsburgh, Pa.: Pittsburgh University Press, 1994. A look at how special interest competition for resources has prevented long-term political and economic stability in Argentina.

Petracca, Mark P. *The Politics of Interests: Interest Groups Transformed*. Boulder, Colo.: Westview Press, 1992. A study of how and why people form interest groups and the role they play in the United States.

Walker, Jack L. *Mobilizing Interest Groups in America: Patrons, Professions and Social Movements*. Ann Arbor: University of Michigan Press, 1991. A theory of interest group formation and maintenance, emphasizing strategies and modes of mobilization.

Wilson, Graham K. *Business and Politics*. 2nd ed. Chatham, N.J.: Chatham House, 1985. A comparative examination of the relationship between business and politics in various countries—including the United States, the former West Germany, and Japan—which discusses the role of transnational corporations.

Notes

1. Such groups often decline almost as spontaneously as they form, once the crisis is past. The East Bay Community Track and Field Association never met again after its victory was won.
2. Jon Woronoff, *Japan as Anything but Number One* (Armonk, N.Y.: Sharpe, 1991), p. 159.
3. Kwame Nkrumah, *The Autobiography of Kwame Nkrumah* (Edinburgh: Nelson, 1959), pp. 40–83.

4. Jonathan Hartlyn, "Colombia: The Politics of Violence and Accommodation," in *Democracy in Developing Countries: Latin America*, vol. 4, ed. Larry Diamond, Juan J. Linz, and Seymour Martin Lipset (Boulder, Colo.: Rienner, 1989), pp. 305–6, 319–20.

5. This is the definition adopted by the members of the organized section on Parties and Other Political Organizations of the American Political Science Association. Reprinted by permission.

6. Robert Salisbury, "An Exchange Theory of Interest Groups," in *Interest Group Politics in America*, ed. Robert Salisbury (New York: Harper and Row, 1970), pp. 47–55. In this now classic work, Salisbury adopted a set of distinctions first made by Peter B. Clark and James Q. Wilson in "Incentive Systems: A Theory of Organizations," *Administrative Science Quarterly* 6 (Sept. 1961): 129–66.

7. Kay Lehman Schlozman and John T. Tierney, *Organized Interests and American Democracy* (New York: Harper and Row, 1986), p. 102.

8. Ronald J. Hrebenar and Ruth K. Scott, *Interest Group Politics in America* (Englewood Cliffs, N.J.: Prentice Hall, 1982), p. 18.

9. When Soviet consumers during the Stalinist years refused to spend their money on theatrical productions burdened with heavy political content and thereby forced the government to provide more entertaining fare, they were acting, claims David Lane, who invented the term, as an amorphous interest group. David Lane, *Politics and Society in the USSR* (New York: Random House, 1970), p. 251. We referred to this kind of individual action that inadvertently becomes group action in Chapter 6 (see p. 111).

10. This type of group and the following three are drawn from Gabriel Almond and G. Bingham Powell Jr., *Comparative Politics: A Development Approach* (Boston: Little, Brown, 1966), pp. 75–76. These authors use the word *anomic* to describe the groups we have here termed *spontaneous*. Although they say such groups lack "any set of regulating values or norms" (which would justify calling them anomic), in fact many of the examples they cite are groups that might claim with considerable justification that they are simply fighting for the avowed values of the society—racial justice, equitable distribution of the nation's wealth, patriotism, and so on. In any case, such groups usually defend some values and so are not normless, as the term *anomic* implies. *Spontaneous* is a better term for this kind of organization.

11. Anne Costain and W. Douglas Costain, "The Women's Lobby: Impact of a Movement on Congress," in *Interest Group Politics*, ed. Allan J. Cigler and Burdett A. Loomis (Washington, D.C.: Congressional Quarterly Press, 1983), pp. 191–216.

12. *Washington Post*, 19 Jan. 1991, A5, and 26 Jan. 1991, A13–18.

13. The last two have, of course, been strongly infused with Christian thought but cannot be said to have been inspired to form by it. For a study of social movements, see Cyrus Ernesto Zirakzedeh, *Social Movements in Politics: A Comparative Study* (Essex, England: Addison-Wesley/Longman, 1997).

14. Timothy Egan, "Industries Affected by Endangered Species," *New York Times*, 13 April 1995, A7.

15. For a recent review of consumer group activities, see Ardith Maney and Loree Bykerk, *Consumer Politics: Protecting Public Interests on Capitol Hill* (Westport, Conn.: Greenwood Press, 1994).

16. Marilyn Werber Serafini, "Senior Schism," *National Journal* 27, no. 18 (6 May 1995): 1089–93.

17. Andrew S. McFarland, *Common Cause: Lobbying in the Public Interest* (Chatham, N.J.: Chatham House, 1984), pp. 6–13; Carol Matlack, "Animal-Rights Furor," *National Journal* 23 (7 Sept. 1991): 2143–46; and Joan Biskupic, "NRA Gun-Control Supporters Take Aim at Swing Votes," *Congressional Quarterly Weekly Report* 49, no. 10 (9 Mar. 1991): 604–7.

18. Senator Boies Penrose, quoted in Carol S. Greenwald, *Group Power, Lobbying and Public Policy* (New York: Praeger, 1977), p. 144.

19. Herbert E. Alexander and Rei Shiratori, eds., *Comparative Political Finance among the Democracies* (Boulder, Colo.: Westview Press, 1994), p. 6. The connection between contributions and high appointments in the executive branch is even less hidden: U.S. Commerce Secretary Robert A. Mosbacher, who had been finance chairman of President George Bush's campaign, did not hesitate to protest publicly when he felt that too few other postelection appointments were being given to those who had made major contributions to the Republican victory.

20. Jane Fritsch, "Tobacco Companies Pump Cash into Republican Party's Coffers," *New York Times*, 13 Sept. 1995, A1, A12.

21. Quoted by Chuck Alston, "PACs' Independent Expenditures Slow Down," *Congressional Quarterly Weekly Report* 46 (5 Nov. 1988): 3186. The title of this article is misleading: The expenditures have not slowed down; what has slowed down is the rapid growth in the number of PACs, which mushroomed from 608 in 1974 to 4,009 in 1984.

22. Quoted in Alston, "PACs' Independent Expenditures Slow Down," p. 3186.

23. Sven Steinmo and Jon Watts, "It's the Institutions, Stupid! Why Comprehensive National Health Insurance Always Fails in America," *Journal of Health Politics, Policy and Law* 20, no. 2 (Summer 1995): 364.

24. Stephen Engelberg, "Business Leaves the Lobby and Sits at Congress's Table," *New York Times*, 31 Mar. 1995, A1.

25. Jane Fritsch, "The Grass Roots, Just a Free Phone Call Away," *New York Times*, 23 June 1995, A1, A11.

26. *Wall Street Journal*, 7 Dec. 1989, 1.

27. In a study with interesting implications for the focus of group efforts, Benjamin Ginsberg and Martin Shefter suggest that the focus of political battles in the United States has now shifted away from parties and elections to the media, congressional investigations, and judicial proceedings. See their *Politics by Other Means: The Declining Importance of Elections in America* (New York: Basic Books, 1990).

28. William Safran, *The French Polity*, 3rd ed. (White Plains, N.Y.: Longman, 1991), pp 110–24.

29. For an interesting recent study, see James A. Dunn Jr., "The French Highway Lobby: A Case Study in State-Society Relations and Policymaking," *Comparative Politics* 27, no. 3 (April 1995): 275–95.

30. Alfred A. Marcus, *Business and Society: Ethics, Government, and the World Economy* (Homewood, Ill.: Irwin, 1993), pp. 256–57. The largest Japanese conglomerate, Mitsubishi, owns "significant" portions of Mitsubishi Trust Bank, Tokyo Marine, Mitsubishi Heavy Industries, Mitsubishi Corporation, Mitsubishi Electric, Asahi Glass, Kirin Beer, and Mitsubishi Chemical. Other important *zaibatsu*, according to Marcus, are Mitsui, Sumitomo, and the banks Fuji, Sanawa, and Dai-ichi Kang.

31. Arthur F. Bentley, *The Process of Government: A Study of Social Pressures* (Chicago: University of Chicago Press, 1908); David Truman, *The Governmental Process* (New York: Knopf, 1951); and Robert A. Dahl, *A Preface to Democratic Theory* (Chicago: University of Chicago Press, 1956).

32. Michael Margolis, "Democracy: American Style," in *Democratic Theory and Practice,* ed. Graeme Duncan (Cambridge: Cambridge University Press, 1983), pp. 125–26. See also C. Wright Mills, *The Power Elite* (Oxford: Oxford University Press, 1957).

33. Douglas Farsh, "Vigilantes Retake Slums of Medellín," *Washington Post,* 7 Dec. 1991, A17.

34. Michael Parenti, *Democracy for the Few* (New York: St. Martin's, 1988), p. 144.

35. Ulf Sundhausen, "Indonesia: Past and Present Encounters with Democracy," in Diamond, Linz, and Lipset, *Democracy in Developing Countries,* pp. 138–39.

36. Daniel H. Levine, *Religion and Politics in Latin America: The Catholic Church in Venezuela and Colombia* (Princeton, N.J.: Princeton University Press, 1981).

37. Stewart Smith, *U.S. Neocolonialism in Africa* (New York: International Publishers, 1974), pp. 68–69.

38. Hans Jaeger, "Business and Government in Imperial Germany, 1871–1918," in *Government and Business,* ed. Keiichiro Nakagawa (Tokyo: University of Tokyo Press, 1980), p. 142.

39. Takeaki Teratani, "Japanese Business and Government in the Takeoff Stage," in Nakagawa, *Government and Business,* pp. 58–59.

40. In one of the few works by a disillusioned communist to reach a worldwide audience prior to 1989, *The New Class,* Milovan Djilas (a Yugoslav official who defected to the West in the 1950s) asserted that all communist bureaucrats, including those in managerial roles in industry, were directing public policy in their own, not the nation's, interests. They were able to give themselves, said Djilas, "special privileges and economic preference because of the administrative monopoly" they held in various economic enterprises, in sports and humanitarian organizations, and in other branches of the government bureaucracy. Milovan Djilas, *The New Class* (New York: Praeger, 1957), pp. 39, 46.

41. Pavel Voshchanov, "The Secret Business of the Communist Party," *World Press Review* 38 (January 1992): 22.

42. *Los Angeles Times,* 1 Mar. 1992, A1, A12.

43. Walter L. Keats, "Corruption and the China Trade," *China Business Review* (January/February 1988): 30. For a case study of an effort to bring down one family of "princelings," see Steven Mufson, "Web of Intrigue in Chinese Steel Firm Probe," *Washington Post,* 16 Mar. 1995, A29.

44. "Challenge to Britain," Labour Party Policy Statement, 1953, p. 6, cited in A. A. Rogow, *The Labour Government and British Industry, 1945–1951* (Ithaca, N.Y.: Cornell University Press, 1955), p. 36. See also Sidney Pollard, *The Wasting of the British Economy* (New York: St. Martin's, 1982), p. 88.

45. The United States's share in the "outward stocks" of foreign investment has, in fact, been on the decline, while those of Canada, Germany, Japan, and Switzerland have been rising. Charles W. Kegley Jr. and Eugene R. Wittkopf, *World Politics: Trend and Transformation,* 3rd ed. (New York: St. Martin's, 1989), p. 163.

46. Keith Cowling and Roger Sugden, *Transnational Monopoly Capitalism* (Sussex, England: Wheat-sheaf Books, 1987), p. 2.

47. Robert Reich, *The Work of Nations: Preparing Ourselves for Twenty-first-Century Capitalism* (New York: Knopf, 1991).

48. Raymond J. Michatowski and Ronald C. Kramer, "The Space between Laws: The Problem of Corporate Crime in a Transnational Context," *Social Problems* 34, no. 1 (Feb. 1987): 34.

49. Kegley and Wittkopf, *World Politics*, p. 170.

50. Kathryn Sikkink, "Codes of Conduct for Transnational Corporations: The Case of the WHO/ UNICEF Code," *International Organization* 40, no. 4 (Autumn 1986): 815–40.

8 Political Parties

In the summer of 1948, a young political-scientist-to-be sat by the radio, holding her breath and listening to the third roll call of the Republican convention. On the first two ballots, Ohio senator Robert A. Taft and former Minnesota governor Harold E. Stassen had prevented New York governor Thomas E. Dewey from getting a majority of the votes. After the second ballot, the anti-Dewey forces had asked for a recess. Now they were back, ready to go. Had they worked out a coalition to stop the New Yorker, or were they giving up? As the voice of the leader of each state's delegation came over the airwaves calling out that state's vote, the avid listener wrote down the numbers for each candidate, adding them as she went along. When one of them suddenly shot past the magic number of 548, she was able to shout, loud and clear, "It's Dewey!" a whole millisecond before the roar of a cheering crowd came out of the little brown box on the table beside her. Her math was as fast as anyone's that summer afternoon, long before calculators and computers were in common usage. Undistracted by the sight of flashing electronic bulletins or frantic reporters and delegates milling about, her mind filled with images of what a convention ought to look like, she experienced a sense of instant participation in U.S. political party life, via the media. It was wonderful.

In the summer of 2010, a political-scientist-to-be will sit by his combination television and home computer, holding his breath and watching the images on his screen, listening to the voices he hears, his hands poised above his keyboard. The images shift. Here are several men and women arguing animatedly around a table over which a sign reads, "Democratic Platform Committee." Here is a convention hall of Democratic delegates watching, on more screens, the men and women arguing. Here is an attractive older woman, the well-known governor of a southern state, carefully explaining what is to happen next. Now a question appears on the screen about the important issue of public policy the committee has been discussing, followed by four possible replies. The governor's voice says, "You have one minute to type in your response, delegates and telepollsters." After only a moment's thought, our hero forthrightly types: *c*. At the end of 60 seconds, the screen shows the tally: how many and what percent of all American voters registered to vote prefer policy choice *a*, *b*, *c*, or *d*; how many delegates at the convention make each choice; and the totals for each, with the winning response outlined in bright red.

Now cut back to the Platform Committee, so viewers can see its members looking at the results on their own large screen. Back to the governor: "Ladies and gentlemen, the Platform Committee will now continue its deliberations. Thanks to you, the committee knows what the Democratic delegates prefer and what the nation at large prefers on this important issue. But the final decision is their own. As soon as we know what they have decided, we will let you know." Cut for the commercial. Our political-scientist-to-be, one of those chosen to be part of the random sampling of the "nation at large," heaves a contented sigh and sits back in his chair. He has a feeling of instant participation in U.S. political party life, via the media. It is wonderful.

The 1948 example is a personal one, and I can tell you for a fact, it did indeed feel wonderful. And no doubt the 2010 version of participation via the media—or something similar—will also be filled with excitement and personal satisfaction. Yet although the media can and do give us such moments, their interaction with the U.S. political party system is fraught with controversy and, some would even say, with peril to democracy.

We return to this matter later in this chapter. However, political parties have not yet been taken over entirely by the media, even in the United States, and other questions require our attention first. In this chapter we consider the following topics: the difference between parties and interest groups, the functions parties are expected to perform, how parties are organized, who their members are, how they choose their candidates, how they prepare their campaigns, how they use the media to carry out their campaigns (and how the media use them), how they try to carry out their programs once in government, and, finally, the role of political parties today.

POLITICAL PARTIES AS A UNIQUE FORM OF POLITICAL ORGANIZATION

In Chapter 7 we identified three kinds of political organizations: interest groups, political parties, and violent revolutionary organizations. Why do political parties deserve a category—and here, even a chapter—of their own? In particular, what makes them different from interest groups?

Three characteristics, two always present and a third commonly so, distinguish the *political party*:

1. The members of a political party, not content with trying to persuade the government to act in a particular way, instead always seek to *place representatives in the government*.
2. To accomplish this goal, *the party nominates candidates to stand for election* in its name.
3. The political party almost always claims that, if successful, it will *exercise power on behalf of the general public*.

Sometimes interest groups seek to place their representatives in the government (by appointment to advisory boards, for instance, or to other important offices), put up independent candidates for elective office, and claim to act on behalf of the general public. Unlike interest groups, however, political parties never fail to manifest the first two of these three characteristics. And when an interest group assumes all three features, it is no longer a separate organization interested in pressuring government. It is an organization interested in taking part in government; it is a *party* to the action.

Besides puzzling over the difference between interest groups and parties, political scientists have puzzled over the **single-party system.** They have worried whether the single party—that is, a party that is the only party allowed in a political system—should be considered a party at all. Some have tried to write such parties out of their definitions: A party is "an organization of society's active political agents . . . who *compete* for popular support with another group or groups holding diverse views," says Sigmund Neumann, stressing that where there is no competition, there can be no true political party.[1] Similarly, Joseph Schlesinger has offered this definition of party: "The political organization which actively and effectively engages in the competition for elective office."[2] The point is an

In most multiparty systems it is not difficult to get a new party on the ballot. In France there are two environmental parties. Brian Lalonde (L), the leader of Génération Ecologie, competes with Antoine Waechter (R), who heads Les Verts ("The Greens"), as well as with the candidates of the major parties.

(Reuters/Christine Gunnet/Archive Photos)

interesting one but leaves the observer wondering—if a single party (which does, after all, meet the terms of the more standard definitions) is not a party, then what is it? Most writers are satisfied to count the single party as a type of party, and that is my approach here as well.

THE FUNCTIONS OF POLITICAL PARTIES

What is a political party's job? In practice, political parties perform a surprisingly wide range of functions, from providing holiday turkeys for the poor to making and carrying out a nation's foreign policy. Most commonly, however, parties are expected to conform to a somewhat more limited job description. Four functions appear on almost everyone's list of what a party does, or should do: leadership recruitment, interest aggregation, campaigning, and governing. We treat each of these in greater detail later in the chapter; here we simply offer brief explanations of each.

Leadership Recruitment

Even in eras when parties are widely scorned and other groups and individuals perform many of the functions formerly ascribed to them, the political party is still likely to be the structure that identifies potential leaders, brings them to public attention, and secures them the support necessary for taking public office. As we shall see, this is not always the case in the United States.

Interest Aggregation

A second major function of parties is **aggregating interests**—that is, serving as mediator for a wide range of politicized demands. To do this, parties must set up internal party procedures that permit different points of view—different *interests*—to be presented, discussed, compromised, and *aggregated*. Study groups, issue-oriented clubs, back room deals, and platform committees are some of the party structures that serve this function. The speeches of the parties' candidates, carefully addressing the various concerns of different groups whose support is being courted, are yet another instrument of interest aggregation.

Campaigning

Political parties normally play an important role in helping their candidates campaign for office. Even in today's world of mass media, political consultants, and direct mail advertising, the parties still play a part in ensuring that voters are registered, that they know the differences among the candidates, and that they know when and where to vote on election day. Where parties are strong, as in many western European nations, they may assume full responsibility for their candidates' campaigns, calling in media advisers, pollsters, and other professional experts only as they see fit.

Governing

Finally, the elected officials of victorious parties are usually expected to run the government and, in doing so, to make an effort to translate the party's program into legislative bills and thence into law. Of course, parties do not always perform these four functions, and when they do, they do not always perform them to citizens' satisfaction. To understand how they perform in practice, we need to look at them more closely. A good place to begin is *inside* the parties.

PARTY ORGANIZATION: IS INTERNAL PARTY DEMOCRACY POSSIBLE?

A political party is formed by individuals who want to acquire or maintain power in government and who seek to gain that power by convincing large numbers of citizens that the organization's candidates will serve as their representatives if elected. (For the transition from autocracy to party politics, see Box 8.1.) This commitment puts the political party in a special predicament, which can be

BOX 8.1   THE TRANSITION FROM AUTOCRACY TO PARTY POLITICS

- The king (or any autocrat) names a council of trusted advisers to assist him.
- The council becomes more and more powerful, perhaps because the king becomes more and more dependent on the resources it commands, perhaps because its members personally dominate a weak-willed monarch.
- The council bargains for and achieves a measure of power independent of the king's (to set taxes, say, or to raise armies), thus becoming a rule-making legislature.
- Factions develop within the legislature, differing on how and for what purposes it should exercise its power.
- Members of these factions seek external support for their side.
- Motivated by the hope of finding more such external support, the monarch and the legislators agree to the principle of elected legislators.
- The right to vote for legislators is extended to more and more of the populace, for the same motives elections were begun in the first place.
- Specific groups within the legislature set up external organizations to assist them in persuading the electors that the public interest will be served by their reelection.
- Challengers set up counterorganizations to persuade electors that the public interest will be better served by substituting their candidates for the incumbents.
- The external organizations outlive the candidacies of the legislators they first support.
- The leaders of the external organizations begin to make their own decisions about which candidates the organization will support—that is, *political parties seek to place their representatives in government by nominating candidates to stand for election in their names, claiming that power so won will be exercised in the public interest.*

Source: Kay Lawson, *The Human Polity*, 4th ed. (Boston: Houghton Mifflin Company, 1997). Reprinted by permission.

summarized in two questions: How can an organization represent "the people" unless it is open to the people and responsive to them? How can an organization subject itself to the fluctuating interests, fleeting passions, and unsophisticated methods of a constantly shifting band of uninformed enthusiasts and still get anything done? In a sense, the whole idea of a participatory organization is a contradiction in terms. The more participation, the less organization; the more organization, the less participation.

Is this conflict between the two goals to which all parties claim to be devoted unavoidable? Robert Michels thought it was and furthermore was convinced that the battle was dramatically uneven, with participation always sacrificed to efficacy. The person "who says organization, says oligarchy," claimed Michels, and he documented this "iron law of oligarchy" with a convincing study of European parties, in which he depicted the members as apathetic, hero-worshiping, transient, and incompetent, and the leaders as egotistically persuaded of their own indispensability—a set of characteristics many have claimed to find in parties in the United States as well.[3]

Other observers have agreed with Michels. Moisei Ostrogorski, who studied U.S. parties of the early twentieth century, went so far as to claim that the pretense of mass participation in fact lessened the opportunities for true participation. By admitting the "mob," Ostrogorski said, parties set up conditions that made it impossible to arrive at decisions in party meetings. The true work of the party was thus always done by the "wire-pullers," usually "the ward secretary surrounded by his ring of associates concocting the business of the party behind the scenes."[4]

Later on, Maurice Duverger provided grounds for a more positive view. If a party admits members freely but then requires their close affiliation, including payment of dues and attendance at meetings; if communication links are strong throughout the party structure; and if final decision-making powers are located at the top of the party in the hands of leaders chosen on the basis of their ability to perform important duties rather than on the basis of personal status, then, Duverger suggests, parties can hope to meet their dual obligation to be both representative and effective.[5] But very few parties in the United States or elsewhere live up to these high standards.

However, despite the forces that make internal democracy so difficult to achieve, the participatory impulse cannot be forever denied, as even Michels recognized when he acknowledged that "the democratic currents . . . are ever renewed" even if they "break ever on the same shoal" of oligarchy.[6] Parties that allow power to become excessively concentrated inevitably face a falling away of support, especially if their followers become convinced that the power so concentrated is no longer being exercised in their interest. The German Green Party emerged to protect the environment, but its members insisted that improving the environment means improving the political environment as well—that is, ensuring more democracy at the base—and the new party introduced a number of rules in the effort to prevent the rise of oligarchy (for example, the principle of *leadership rotation*; that is, the rule that no one should stay in elected office more than a single term).[7]

Other parties have sometimes attempted to resolve the dilemma of effectiveness versus participation by offering a kind of sham participation. The classic example is the old Soviet party congress, where all decisions were made in advance but a gathering of disciplined party activists could somehow be motivated to meet periodically and give their enthusiastic and unanimous consent. A case could also be made that contemporary U.S. or Canadian political conventions— or the annual meetings of the large central committees of European parties—provide very little more in the way of serious participatory input.[8] In many nations the average party militant simply works hard for candidates others have chosen, an observation that brings us to our next topic: the nature of party membership.

THE MEMBERS OF PARTIES

Ask a Chinese citizen if she belongs to a political party, and she will be puzzled only by the suggestion that there might be more than one political party to join. She will know for a certainty whether or not she belongs to the party. But ask an American if he belongs to a political party, and he is very likely to say, "Well, what exactly do you mean by *belong*, my friend?" What *does* it mean to belong to a party? Closeness of affiliation is not always easy to measure across cultural boundaries. Attending discussion meetings, learning party history, contributing a fixed amount of one's earnings to the organization, and enrolling one's children in an affiliated youth club may constitute a remarkably high level of commitment to party in Great Britain but would reflect a simple regimen of self-interest in China.

Duverger, as interested in this question as in forms of organization, named four levels of membership: sympathizers, adherents, militants, and propagandists.[9] A more common set of categories for membership in European parties today is simply supporters, adherents, and militants. The *supporter* always (or almost always) votes for the party's candidates; the *adherent* joins the party formally, filling out a membership blank and paying dues; the *militant* can be counted on to work actively for the party, performing such mundane chores as stuffing envelopes and distributing leaflets as well as preaching the party's cause at every opportunity.

Party membership in the sense of becoming an adherent is generally in decline, even in the European nations where it has been strongest in the past and even as the size of electorates (the number of qualified voters) has grown.[10] Jeremy Richardson argues that new interest groups and social movements are taking the place of parties now for citizens; that we have become "*consumers* of participation and activism" and that "a market" of participatory activities has now developed to meet our needs. There is now, he says, "a wide range of participatory organisations offering 'tailor made' opportunities for political activism. 'Brand loyalty' has decreased at the very time that new 'products' have arrived on the market-place." Richardson points out that the breadth of coverage offered by parties may make them the less desirable choice for citizens determined to donate their time or money to support a single issue, even though democratic theory calls for citizenship that is concerned about the public good more generally.[11]

Related to the question of closeness of affiliation is the question of reason for affiliation. The distinctions used by Robert Salisbury to categorize the motives of those who join interest groups—material, solidary, or purposive (see pp. 136)—do not fit quite as well for the study of those who join political parties. Other motives are clearly at work, such as a sense of loyalty (be it to a particular candidate or to the organization itself) and the pursuit of power—that is, the pleasure some take simply in being in a position to control the action of others (which, of course, is something one does gain in winning a position of party leadership or, better yet, public office). For parties, a different list is required. There are motives that are purely *personal* (here we may include the material and solidary motives mentioned by Salisbury but also the pure joy of exercising power over others); motives that have to do with one's *loyalty* to others; and, finally, the motive of *political conviction* (similar to the Salisbury notion of purposive motivation). As in the case of interest groups, it is, of course, possible and indeed likely that a person will have more than one kind of motive for joining a political party.[12]

Some have suggested that a briefer list covers all the motives of party members: They are either *amateurs* (sometimes called purists), motivated by conviction, or *professionals* (sometimes called realists), motivated by the quest for some form of personal gain.[13] Those who make this simple distinction nearly always favor the professional, who keeps his eye on the doughnut of success rather than on the hole of ideological purity. Ordinary citizens, however, sometimes naively wonder if party politics really suffers more from the intrusion of idealistic newcomers than from the cynical tactics of battle-weary veterans. In any case, amateurs have a way of eventually becoming professionals, especially in parties that know how to welcome and use their energy and enthusiasm at the outset.

Besides asking how closely affiliated members are and studying their reasons for joining, it is also interesting to consider what kinds of people join particular parties. Is the membership of the party as heterogeneous as the nation itself? The Democratic Party of the United States, the Rally for the Republic in France, the Congress Party of India, and the Partido Revolucionario Institucional of Mexico are all examples of parties that have succeeded in attracting supporters from all their nations' major social categories. Or is the party composed predominantly of the members of a single ethnic group (such as the predominantly Kikuyu Kenyan African National Union), a single religious organization (the fundamentalist Sokkagakkai of Japan), a single language group (the Swedish People's Party in Finland), or a single class (the Peasant Party of Romania)? The problem of communal parties has assumed new significance in recent years with the resurgence of ethnic nationalism in the new political systems of eastern Europe. Even when the overriding aim of an ethnic party is simply to protect its own peoples—as with the Hungarian Party in Romania, the German Minority Party of Poland, and the Movement for Rights and Freedoms (of ethnic Turks) in Bulgaria—the dangers of excessive fragmentation in newly forming democracies is very real.

THE SELECTION OF CANDIDATES

"Did he jump, or was he pushed?" The question can be asked about individuals found at the top of party organizations as well as about murder mystery victims found at the bottom of cliffs. It is often unclear whether those who become candidates for office do so because of special characteristics that permitted them to make the jump or because they were pushed (or pulled) by others eager to recruit a winner. An extrovert personality possessed of a strong intelligence and an equally strong appetite for power may be able to build a personal organization

capable of seizing the nomination. Control over a party's nominating processes may fall into the hands of a single autocrat (as Francisco Franco controlled the Spanish Falange) or a powerful lobby (as the railroad interests controlled California party politics at the turn of the twentieth century)—or simply remain the domain of its established leaders. In fact, in most cases the would-be candidate's personal traits and others' recruitment efforts interact so subtly that no one can be certain which is decisive. Here we look at each aspect in turn, remembering that in practice no such separation can be made.

Certain personal characteristics do correlate strongly with political leadership. Leaders usually come from higher socioeconomic backgrounds than do their followers, although what constitutes higher socioeconomic status may vary from culture to culture. Having been a tribal leader was very important to someone seeking to lead an African party well into the latter half of the twentieth century, although this qualification was usually combined with other, more modern indices of success, such as wealth, occupation, and education. Kwame Nkrumah took a chiefly title, Osagyefo, on assuming political leadership in Ghana, but he had also nearly completed the course of study for a Ph.D.

Leaders also have usually grown up in more politicized homes than followers, have adopted a particular party as their own at an earlier age, and are readier to adopt their parents' partisan affiliation. They have a stronger sense of political efficacy (a belief in their own power to influence the course of politics—but this is more likely to be a result rather than a cause of assuming leadership roles), hold views more uniformly in accord with the party's positions, and possibly are more neurotic than followers. (Fortunately for the followers, the evidence is mixed on this final point.)[14]

Rising to the top ranks of a political party, however, has at least as much to do with factors external to the individual. If a nation is divided and the party wishes to reach beyond such divisions, it must seek a leader who is not strongly identified with a particular subgroup or else set up a council of leaders drawn from all the important groups. If the electoral system offers a better chance to centrist candidates than to ideologues of either extreme, the parties are likely to choose their candidates accordingly.[15] On the other hand, if standing as a candidate is personally risky, as it may be in unstable societies where electoral defeat can bring imprisonment or exile, the party may well seek out its most committed firebrands. If the party has no chance of winning, it is also more likely to urge the nomination of women or of candidates of great ideological purity.

The presence or absence of major political issues also influences the kind of nominee a party seeks. If a particularly sensitive issue is at the forefront, the candidate's past and present pronouncements on that matter must be carefully reviewed. If the nation is in need of a drastic change in economic or foreign policy, the party may search for someone charismatic—that is, someone who has the gift of embodying the nation both at its traditional best and in its desired future state. The party formed to support French military hero Charles de Gaulle in 1958 was a dramatic case in point. More recent examples include Lech Walesa in Poland and Vaclav Havel in Czechoslovakia, two men who achieved prominence in the past in ways that lent them political legitimacy in a postcommunist world. And if the campaign is going to cost a great deal of money, far beyond that supplied by the nation's system of public financing, then the ability of a would-be candidate to rally financial support may turn out to be the characteristic that counts the most.

Of course, the kind of leader a party chooses also rests to a large extent on the nature of the party's nominating procedures. In some nations, such as England and France, the top party leadership has the right to "parachute" candidates in— that is, to give the nomination to someone who does not even live in the electoral district where the contest is being waged. In single-party systems it is common practice for the national party leadership to form a national list of candidates without specifying districts at all. (In such cases, being named to the list is tantamount to being elected.) Where local control is the rule, one must still ask whether final power rests in the hands of a small committee (as in Germany, Norway, and Sweden), is shared by all who pay dues (as in Belgium), or is distributed among all those who choose to attend the appropriate meeting and identify themselves as partisans (as in party caucuses in those U.S. states that do not choose delegates to the national convention by primary). Experience suggests that the lower the level of the party hierarchy involved in choosing the nominee, the more the candidate will represent local and special interests and the less he or she will adopt stances on national issues that attract wide popular support. Because candidates who cannot attract wide popular support are rarely winning candidates, we are back to the problem we encountered earlier: How can a party represent its followers and still do its job?

PREPARING THE CAMPAIGN

Preparing the campaign means more than finding the right candidates—or letting the candidates "find" the party. To do their job, parties also need money and a strategy. The latter includes a plan for developing a program but also the development and deployment of the technological expertise that constitutes so large a part of today's campaign.

Raising the Money

In the United States, most of the money collected for a political campaign is raised not by the parties but by the candidates, especially while they are seeking the nomination, and most of the funds so gathered come from individual contributions.[16] Once the nomination is in hand, most presidential candidates accept public funding (each major party candidate was entitled to $62.2 million for the general election campaign in 1996) and obey the requirement that they limit their spending to that amount. Independent expenditures (see Chapter 7) made by individuals and political action committees vastly increase the amounts of money spent in contemporary campaigns. Candidates who do not accept public funding (where that is available) are free to spend as much as they wish of their personal fortunes. Steve Forbes spent $16.5 million of his own fortune in 1995; although frontrunner Robert Dole raised and spent $21 million in the same time period, $2 million of that sum was spent on the costs of raising funds so as to qualify for matching funds under the terms of federal law.[17]

Despite the frenetic activities of the candidates, parties in the United States do still engage in fundraising themselves. Indeed, one of the key reasons for their continued importance regardless of voter disaffection is that they are able to raise and spend such monies legally and effectively. The Republican National Committee took the lead as early as 1962, when it first began making large-scale appeals by direct mail and collected $700,000. The Democrats were not long to catch on but have never been able to match the Republicans; by 1990, the Republicans were able to raise $207.2 million (86% in individual contributions), the Democrats $86.7 million (64% in individual contributions). Herbert Alexander estimates that a total of $471.2 million was raised for campaign purposes in 1990 and since that time the parties' role has been far from negligible.[18] Fundraising efforts other than direct mail now include special dinners, special "clubs" such as the Republican Eagles and the Democratic Business Council (in both cases, the "dues" are $15,000 per year).[19]

A major fundraising advantage the parties have over the candidates' own organizations is that U.S. federal law permits state and local party committees to raise and spend unlimited amounts of what is known as *soft money* for voter registration, get-out-the-vote drives, and grassroots campaign materials (signs, buttons, party newspapers, bumper stickers), as well as for the printing and distribution of sample ballots telling voters how to vote.[20] The parties have thus become the recipients of very large contributions that individuals and political action committees could not legally make to the candidates but that are, of course, made to work for those candidates just as well as if they *had* been contributed to them.

In many nations, parties need not "raise" money; they merely have to figure out how to make good use of that which is given them by the state. In France a party receives up to 6 million francs (about $1.2 million) for its presidential candidate's campaign expenses, provided that the candidate gains at least 5 percent of the vote on the first ballot. State funding is the most important source of funding for Norwegian parties and helps to make the parties roughly equal in resources. Germany has followed a path all its own. Having first decided that the direct financing of parties with public funds was unconstitutional, the German Supreme Court then ruled that it was acceptable for the state to reimburse the costs of campaigns for any party receiving 0.5 percent of the vote or more, a ruling particularly advantageous to smaller parties.[21] Later, the German legislature decided that parties that receive the least from private donations and membership fees should get proportionately more from the state.

Developing a Strategy

Of course, parties must also decide what to do with the money they raise. In addition, they need to plan the overall campaign. Determining the party's strategy depends on what role the party expects to play and what needs it expects to have. In nations where parties maintain control over their own nominations and are publicly funded and where paid advertising is kept to a minimum or forbidden, it is possible for parties to begin by formulating their programs. Individuals who hope to gain the nomination may work hard to influence the program, but technically the program comes first, candidate selection second. Where parties do not control the nomination, as in U.S. presidential elections, a party's own program-building activity will be much less meaningful; the program that counts will be that of the candidate who wins the nomination.

How do parties and candidates know what to put in their programs? In the past, it would have been assumed that they decided what they believed in and said so. But the art and science of figuring out what to say and where to say it is now highly dependent on a most sophisticated technology. According to Gary Selnow, the "twin engines" that "drive the political information machine" are public opinion polls and the database. But the engine that drives both of these, as Selnow also makes clear, is the modern computer.[22] Contemporary polling requires carefully crafted questionnaires, the selection of an appropriate sample of the population, and a complex process of data collection. Building a database means taking poll results and sorting out the electorate by almost every possible personal and political characteristic, including age, race, income, education, gender, partisanship and point of view on every conceivable question of the day—and, more and more important, proclivity to vote.

It is the computer that makes polling possible; it is the computer that creates the database out of the poll results. It is, of course, still a human being who tells the computer what to do. However, the guiding principle for that human being is now almost always the same: Figure out how to maximize the chances of the candidate. The goals of the candidate and the party cannot credibly be changed beyond all recognition, but emphasis can certainly be placed on those positions that best fit the voters' current desires. Different positions—on different issues—can be emphasized in different communities, over different media. The point is to win. Does this mean doing everything possible to attract as many votes as possible? The answer may seem obvious, but in fact, it is "no." As Paul Hernnson points out, "It makes more sense for candidates to allocate scarce campaign resources in the direction of large groups that vote in relatively large numbers than to direct those resources toward small groups that have low levels of voter turnout."[23] The tendency to ignore the habitual or probable nonvoter is now carried very far in the United States; according to Marshall Ganz, "As of election day, 63 percent of registered voters will not have been contacted by anyone. If, as is typical, only 60 percent of the eligible electorate [is] registered, 78 percent of the eligible voters in the district would never be contacted." Ganz does not accept this fact as calmly as other observers have; he believes that those who are not targeted to receive campaign messages are more likely to be of lower socioeconomic status than those for whom the message is designed and claims that "the introduction of the new political technologies has crippled the American attempt to combine equal voice in politics with unequal resources in economics."[24] Whether or not this is so, it seems unquestionable that the new technologies do not contribute to the democratic goal of rule by *all* the people.

Not every nation has gone as far as the United States in the direction of unrestrained targeting by computer science. Consultants and advertising agencies are widely employed, but in most nations the parties themselves and their leading candidates resist turning control fully over to such specialists. Parties in Austria incorporate outside consultants into internal decision-making structures in a formal and controlled fashion; parties in Germany and the Netherlands seek to develop in-house expertise—and some parties, such as the Swedish People's Party in Finland, the New Zealand National Party, the Austrian and German Green parties, and most Danish parties, are openly reluctant to use the new technologies at all and try to do without them as much as possible.[25]

EXECUTING THE CAMPAIGN: PARTIES AND THE MEDIA

Once everything is in place, the next step is to get the messages of the party's candidates to the voters. The candidate, his or her **surrogates** (persons who are close enough to serve as personal representatives of the candidate, such as a husband or wife, a sister or brother, or a grown child), other known political figures who support the candidate and are not currently running for office, and selected volunteers all put in long, grueling days speaking to as many groups and visiting as many institutions as time and energy permit and, especially in more local campaigns, going door to door.

Most important of all, however, and more important every year, is the campaign conducted via the media (see Box 8.2). Getting the media to cover the candidate's speech to the national meeting of the Businesswomen's Club or her visit to the workers in a garment factory is far more important than the immediate response of the businesswomen or the factory workers. But the media have some very special characteristics that must be taken into account by the parties. In the following pages we use the United States, where the new relationship is much more prevalent than in other nations, as our example. However, the same forces may be seen at work across the globe.

How Parties Use the Media

Whether or not journalists are motivated to report the activities of parties and their candidates aggressively, the simple fact that most media are profit-making businesses seeking to entertain strongly influences the ability of parties and politicians to convey their messages to potential voters and the ways they seek to do so. Four avenues are open to parties and their candidates seeking to reach the electorate via the media, although not all are open to all parties in all nations.

First, they may take advantage of the free time specifically allocated to them in most nations of the world (but not in the United States). Second, they may pay the media to carry their messages, in the form of paid advertising, although this is carefully limited or prohibited altogether in most nations, and is nowhere else so widely practiced as in the United States, where, since 1976 major-party candidates in general U.S. elections have normally spent close to half their total campaign budgets on preparing and buying political ads for television.[26] (However, the strategists for candidate Bill Clinton actually spent a fairly low proportion of his budget on network television ads and focused their advertising dollars instead on thirty-two targeted states, placing no ads in the media of *top-end* states —states where they had about a 30 percent lead at the beginning of the campaign).[27] On the other hand, Ross Perot introduced the highly costly *infomercial*, buying thirty-minute segments of time and using pie charts and diagrams to explain the specific details of his economic plan for the nation.[28]

A third way for parties and candidates to use the media is to attract free coverage. Government officials running for reelection or seeking to help those they wish to see win are at a great advantage, since they can often find ways to make campaigning look like the business of government. But even they, and certainly those who are not in office, will work hard to produce interesting political "stories" that can be told quickly and vividly, providing the well-designed *photo opportunity* combined with the well-prepared *sound bite*. A few seconds allowing the candidate to be filmed surrounded by adoring senior citizens at the annual picnic will bring out the television crews far more effectively than the preparation of a

BOX 8.2 MILESTONES IN THE DEVELOPMENT OF MODERN CAMPAIGN COMMUNICATION IN THE UNITED STATES, 1952–1994

1952   Richard Nixon's "Checkers" speech; first use by presidential candidates of televised spot advertisements.

1957   Supreme Court rules that broadcasters may not be held liable for content of campaign commercials.

1959   Enactment of exemptions to equal-opportunities provision of the Communications Act of 1934.

1960   First televised presidential debate; publication of the first *Making of the President* book, transforming press coverage of election campaigns; first use of election-night network news projections.

1961   First live televised presidential press conference.

1964   Redefinition of libel in *New York Times v. Sullivan;* first televised presidential adversary commercial; formation of News Election Service, permitting news organizations to acquire timely vote returns.

1968   First year of extensive coverage of national nominating conventions by networks; first use of exit polling by CBS.

1969   Publication of Theodore White's *The Selling of the President, 1968,* describing candidate control of campaign communication; attack by Spiro Agnew on the liberalism of the "northeastern establishment" press.

1972   Presidential primary process changed by Democratic Party reforms; Federal Elections Campaign Act takes effect.

1976   Federal Communications Commission reinterpretation of candidate debate regulation; spending limitations in effect during the presidential general election for the first time; network news offers regular primary-night news coverage.

1980   Exit polls used to project election results; extensive political advertising by political action committees.

1984   Networks reduce coverage of nominating conventions.

1988   Networks stop predicting the outcomes of elections before all polls have closed.

1992   Presidential candidates appear on talk shows and accept questions from callers. Independent candidate Ross Perot uses half-hour paid commercials to explain his program.

1994   Full Republican program reprinted in *TV Guide*.

Source: Adapted from Richard Joslyn, *Mass Media and Elections* (Reading, Mass.: Addison-Wesley, 1984), p. 6, plus recent additions. Reprinted by permission of the McGraw-Hill Companies.

200-page proposal to improve care for the elderly. The result, of course, is that very little substantive information is conveyed. According to Gary Selnow, "This highly visual and video-oriented society invests more in the illusion of television images than in the substance of reasoned analysis."[29]

Sometimes the second and third methods, paying and attracting the media, are actually combined. It is now more and more common in the United States for news broadcasts during election seasons to discuss political commercials as news. According to Kiku Adatto, 125 excerpts from such ads were shown on news broadcasts in 1988, but the question of whether or not the content of the ads was true was addressed less than 8 percent of the time: "Reporters became part of the campaign theater they covered—as producers, as performers, and as critics."[30]

Fourth, the parties now are more and more likely to use the ever more available alternative media, given the costs and the other limitations of the traditional media. Cable television permits access to smaller but more homogeneous audiences, which in turn permits delivery of better-targeted messages. Advertising on cable is far cheaper, which permits parties to use it more frequently and more repetitiously.[31]

Another form of alternative media is what Gary Selnow calls *direct-contact media,* media that allow the parties to go directly to the voters. Direct mail and the telephone are familiar forms of such contact, but use of electronic mail (e-mail) and of web pages on the Internet has been expanding by leaps and bounds in the past few years. The parties have not been slow to take advantage of the low cost of such media and of the possibility they offer for saying what they want to say, how they want to say it.[32]

How the Media Use the Parties and the Candidates

Nevertheless, the main outlets for political news remain the traditional media, and their journalists and broadcasters continue to turn to the parties and the candidates for stories that will fit the entertainment values that govern their profession. They follow candidates for office everywhere they go, sponsor frequent polls in order to keep their readers up to date on who is ahead, and do their best to give the campaign all the qualities of a long and intensely exciting horse race.[33] Personal qualities and histories are explored for dramatic, even melodramatic, effect, and no aspect of a candidate's life is considered out-of-bounds. Family life is often given inordinate attention. As Ann Grimes has noted, "One of the bigger myths in Presidential politics is that because he has an adoring wife who is willing to function as an elbow ornament, [the candidate] has a viable family life and a good marriage" and, further, that such assets will make a difference in how successful he will be in office if elected.[34] "I always accuse him of marrying me to give himself a respectable image," said Betty Ford of former president Gerald Ford.[35]

However, other motives besides providing entertainment are at work in determining what political news the media will present and how they will offer it. "Freedom of the press belongs to the man who owns one," says the cliché, and in choosing what to present, media producers and reporters may well be guided by the very normal desire to please the boss. The "boss" is now likely to be both more difficult to argue with and more powerful. Most owners of media own more than one agency, controlling either several examples of the same type or different agencies of different types. The same person may own a community's only

"NEVER MIND MY CONSTITUENTS—HAVE YOU
POLLED THE NETWORKS?"

(© Cole/Rothco)

newspaper, only television station, and only radio station, thereby controlling all the important information sources. This is the case in France, where at one time the conservative publisher Robert Hersant controlled 29 percent of the newspaper distribution, a major television network, and his own advertising company.[36] In the United States, 80 percent of all newspapers are owned by corporate chains.[37] The "boss" may not even be in the same country as the media he or she owns; as of 1994, the Fox television network was more than 99 percent owned by Rupert Murdoch's News Corporation, based in Australia.[38] Even alternative forms of broadcasting are not exempt from the processes of media globalization; of the ninety cable franchises awarded in Britain by May 1990, more than 89 percent went to American corporations.[39]

In any case, even when there is no **political bias** in the presentation of partisan news, we should beware, say Dan Nimmo and James E. Combs, of imagining we can learn the truth about politics simply by following media reports. They suggest that the development of mass **communications media** means the development of group fantasies about the nature of reality and argue that perhaps the required skills for citizenship are not those taught in civics texts—being interested and motivated to engage in political discussion and activity, acquiring political knowledge, being principled, and reaching choices by rational

BOX 8.3   SURVIVAL TIPS FOR WATCHING POLITICAL ADS ON TELEVISION

1. Be aware that the ad is designed to create an emotional response. Think about what mood the ad is trying to create, particularly with music and images.
2. Engage your intellect to examine the ad critically. Is there something that doesn't sound right? Does the ad raise more questions than answers?
3. Don't assume the commercial's information is accurate. Misleading and just plain untruthful ads often get on the air.
4. Don't figure that ads give you all the information you need. If you rely on political advertising to make a decision at the polls, you could be taken for a ride. Get more information from other sources: the *Voters' Pamphlet,* news coverage of the campaign, or knowledgeable friends whom you trust.

Source: Jeff Mapes, "Do Campaign Ads Really Work?" *The Oregonian,* 30 Oct. 1994, A1. Copyright © 1994, Oregonian Publishing Co. All rights reserved. Reprinted with permission.

thinking—but rather learning how to assess dramatic performances, fantasy themes, rhetorical visions, and melodramatic rituals. These skills might inspire us to demand more not only of parties, candidates, and journalists in the election melodrama but of ourselves as well.[40] (See Box 8.3, and the next time you watch a political commercial, see if you can use some of the techniques recommended there.)

How Citizens Respond

How *do* citizens respond to the information about politics available via the media? The question of media impact is a difficult one to study. Ask yourself what role the media played in your own choice in the last presidential election, and chances are you will be hard put to say. There is considerable evidence that U.S. citizens rely heavily on candidates' ads to "get some sense of what a candidate is like"; when asked, 62 percent either completely or mostly agree that "I often don't become aware of political candidates until I see their advertising on television." On the other hand, 74 percent say that news reports give them a better idea of where a candidate stands on the issues than do the ads, and 65 percent prefer news reports to ads for getting an "idea of what a candidate is like personally."[41] Canadians are somewhat less ambivalent: One-third of those polled would do away with ads altogether, and 77 percent believe there should at least be limits on party advertising; however, there seems to be, say André Blais and Elisabeth Gidengil, a majority conviction that ads "may sometimes play a useful role."[42]

Of course, we ourselves often do not know what role the various kinds of media play in helping us make distinctions between the parties or among the candidates, partly because the media seldom if ever reach us "unmediated." A medium is "an intervening thing through which a force acts or an effect is produced." The campaign news comes to us filtered not only through the commentaries of print and broadcast journalists but also through those of our friends and associates and, most important, through our own selective perceptions. We decide what we want to read or watch, and our choices are strongly conditioned by our desire to read or watch something that will confirm the beliefs we already hold; "good" news is news that tells us we were already right.

Furthermore, although those who pay attention to media coverage of campaigns tend to be better educated, more interested and active in politics, and more partisan, even they do not appear to remember much of what they watch, listen to, or read about. Studies in which television viewers have been interviewed show extremely limited recall. Two hours after a television network news show, viewers can normally remember only one of the twenty or so stories usually presented.[43]

At least in the United States, citizens do somewhat better at retaining personal information about candidates, including how well they are doing in the horse race. And they remember best of all favorable information about the candidates they prefer. Once the nominees are selected, over the course of the campaign Republicans become more and more favorable toward their candidate, Democrats toward theirs.

In any case, the parties themselves clearly believe in the power of the media. More and more, executing the campaign means taking it to the people via the media, and this in turn means accepting the profit-oriented demands of the media for stories that will attract viewers for their advertisers—or becoming paying advertisers themselves. Once the long electoral season is over, the parties claim it is they who will organize and conduct governments in our names, via their victorious candidates. We turn now to a consideration of whether or not this is so.

PARTIES IN GOVERNMENT

The idea that modern governments are run by political parties has been so widely accepted that the term *party government* has assumed the status of a concept, one that means government that is organized by the parties or, more specifically, the process whereby the leader of the party winning the most votes takes the top leadership role (be it president or prime minister), works with the advice of a cabinet formed of members of that party or of other parties that have agreed to work with the new leader, and sees his or her party's program translated into legislative bills, supported by party members or allies in the legislature, and made into the law of the land. But is party government really possible today?

In **multiparty systems** it is often necessary to form a ruling coalition by inviting leading members of different parties to take cabinet posts, thereby ensuring the support of their followers. When the parties take strongly different stands on major issues of the day, this can be a far from simple matter to resolve. No modern nation offers a better example of the intricacies of forming ruling coalitions than Italy, a nation in which the conservative Christian Democrats managed to remain in power for nearly forty years after World War II by the constant reshuffling of cabinet posts. In the late 1970s the party engineered the formation of a **minority government**, with cabinets composed of representatives of parties that had, altogether, only a minority of seats in the Chamber of Deputies—the communists, with 228 seats, could have brought the government down at any time but agreed to abstain in exchange for an unofficial but nevertheless significant say in all major issues. In 1981, as the communist vote was declining, the involvement of the Christian Democrats in a major political scandal forced them to share power with the small Radical Party to stay in power, and then, in 1983, it was the turn of the socialists to lay claim to a larger share of the pie, claiming and winning the prime ministership. In 1992, the legislative vote gave the four-party coalition that had been in power only 48 percent of the vote, and it was several weeks before the new cabinet could be formed.[44] Accumulating scandals and the ever more obvious and widespread power of the Mafia forced the Christian Democrats out of power altogether in 1994, when they won only 16 percent of the vote.[45] The new government was composed of three new center and center-right parties (Forza Italia, the Northern League, and the National Alliance), and it too was plagued by scandal and intercoalition squabbling, bringing it to an early demise. In 1996, the Italians formed their fifty-fifth government (cabinet) since the war, bringing in center-left as well as right-wing parties in the hope of having a strong enough majority to be able to move toward constitutional changes designed to end the chronic instability from which Italy has suffered so long.[46]

The Italian example is an interesting one because it is so often cited as proof that multiparty systems inevitably produce excessive fragmentation and are likely to lead to corruption as well. In fact, however, almost all of the world's party systems are multiparty (even in "two-party" United States and Great Britain, minor parties do exist and do sometimes win office, especially at the local level), and of course not all governments are unstable and corrupt. Nor are two-party systems exempt from these deficiencies: In 1993, the elected members of the opposition party in one of the world's few genuine **two-party systems,** that of Jamaica, refused to attend the sessions of that country's parliament on the grounds that the election that year had been so marked by fraud and corruption as to be invalid.[47] As the Italians seem to recognize, and as we consider further later in this book, government instability is likely to be a function of factors other than the number of parties—indeed, some argue that the absence of significant choice in a **party system** is more likely to produce discontent and instability than the difficulties of forming a government representative of a wide range of perspectives.

Even in different constitutional systems, however, effective party government is far from easy to establish. If the system allows for the separation of powers—and if electoral results sometimes place the legislative and executive branches of the government in the hands of different parties, as in the United States—then party government is possible only if each branch is run by well-disciplined party

TABLE 8.1   A Multi-Party System: The United States in the 1996 Presidential Election

Candidate (Party)	Popular Vote Total	% of Popular Vote
Bill Clinton (Democrat)	47,402,357	49.24
Bob Dole (Republican)	39,198,755	40.17
Ross Perot (Reform)	8,085,402	8.40
Ralph Nader (Green)	684,902	0.71
Harry Browne (Libertarian)	485,798	0.50
Howard Phillips (U.S. Taxpayers)	184,658	0.19
John Hagelin (Natural Law)	113,668	0.12
Monica Moorehead (Workers World)	29,083	0.03
Marsha Feinland (Peace and Freedom)	25,332	0.03
Write-in (Miscellaneous)	24,537	0.02
Charles Collins (Independent)	8,941	0.01
James Harris (Socialist Workers)	8,476	0.01
None of These Candidates (Nevada)	5,608	0
Dennis Peron (Grassroots)	5,378	0
Mary Cal Hollis (Socialist)	4,765	0
Jerome White (Socialist Equality)	2,438	0
Diane Beall Templin (American)	1,847	0
Earl F. Dodge (Prohibition)	1,298	0
A. Peter Crane (Independent)	1,101	0
Justice Ralph Forbes (America First)	932	0
John Birrenbach (Independent Grassroots)	787	0
Isabell Masters (Looking Back)	752	0
Steve Michael (Independent)	408	0

Source: Federal Elections Commission, "1996 Presidential Election Results," *Journal of Election Administration*, 18 (1997): 5.

loyalists, with policy outcomes the result of interparty as well as interbranch compromise. On the other hand, systems that allow only one political party do not guarantee that that party will actually govern. As power shifts in today's more centralized governments from legislative to executive hands, the leaders of political parties are hard pressed for means to assert control over their one elected representative in the executive branch (the president or prime minister), his or her numerous appointees, and the army of bureaucrats who remain in government regardless of the changing winds of politics. Single-party nations are not immune from this shift to executive power; if anything, the tendency to concentrate power is stronger in nations with long histories of authoritarian rule. The very forces that impel such a nation toward a single party in its early political

BOX 8.4   REGIME CHANGE

From Guerrilla Movements to Political Parties in Mozambique

Once independence was obtained from the Portuguese in 1977, the Mozambique Liberation Front (Frelimo), formerly a guerrilla movement, became the ruling party of that east African nation. Yet it was not long before Frelimo found itself the object of fierce resistance by another guerrilla movement, the Mozambique National Resistance (Renamo).

However, Renamo has recently followed the example of its bitter enemy and converted itself into a party working through the democratic process. The transformation began in 1992, when United Nations–led negotiations secured an end to the rebel fighting that had kept the nation at civil war for twelve long years. In 1994 the United Nations spent $17 million to provide Renamo with the vehicles, telephones, and fax machines that would enable it to carry out a meaningful campaign for office in that year's presidential elections, held under the international body's close supervision. When the movement-turned-party lost the presidency but made strong showings nonetheless in some of Mozambique's most populated provinces, the onetime warriors gave up armed struggle altogether and took their place in parliament.

Will the transformation hold? At present writing, municipal elections without U.N. supervision are on the calendar, and Renamo is expected to increase its share of power, especially in the north, where it is stronger. Frelimo is accused of having become corrupt and excessively bureaucratic, yet Renamo is said to lack the organization and trained personnel to be able to govern. The situation is volatile, especially as regime change continues, now in the economic domain, since the government has dropped its earlier socialist program and is moving briskly into privatization and capitalist development. Regime change almost always entails both political and economic change—it is a dynamic process, which once begun seldom comes to an immediate and tidy end. Mozambique is a case in point.

Source: Colin Barraclough, "From Rubble to Reform," and "Once-Bitter Foes Work Together," a two-part article in the *San Francisco Chronicle,* 13 Oct. 1997, A12, A15, and 14 Oct. 1997, A10, A12. Reprinted by permission.

struggles will serve to demote that party to a lesser role once an independent government takes hold.[48] (See Box 8.4.)

THE ROLE OF PARTIES TODAY

Political parties are held in low esteem in most nations today. Americans tend to rank parties near the bottom of any list of public institutions. Asked to give a letter grade to the performance of the two parties in the 1988 presidential campaign, a national sample gave both parties an average grade of C, and by 1991, 41 percent of Americans saw no difference between the parties in their ability to handle "the nation's most important problem" (whatever the respondent deemed that problem to be).[49] The citizens of other nations seldom show their parties more respect and sometimes show them less. Parties are viewed as selfish, dishonest, biased, and incapable of recruiting leadership of the quality citizens feel they deserve. Leftists imagine that parties work only for the elite members of society; elitists are certain they are the ignorant instruments of mobocracy.

The fact is that parties have almost always been held in contempt, and yet they continue to exist, be formed, and be reformed. If we dislike them so, why do we keep them? James Madison faced part of the answer squarely in Federalist Paper no. 10, when he recognized that the one thing worse than factionalism was a state that denied its citizens freedom of assembly.[50] The late shah of Iran acknowledged another aspect of the power of party when he formed a state-run party, the Rastakhiz, in a belated attempt to create a structure for rallying supporters. Charles de Gaulle discovered twice in his life that the forces of party could be stronger and more enduring than those of personal charisma. Both his retirements—in 1953 and in 1969—were hastened by the machinations of party. In 1980, independent candidate John Anderson found how little enthusiastic public response counted for in the United States without the multiplier effect of a major party's nomination; in 1992, independent Ross Perot, supported by millions of Americans but not by an organized party, lost heart for the battle and dropped out early in the race, only to announce in 1995 that he would try again, this time with a real political party of his own (despite the fact that to place a single candidate on the ballot in all states, a new party in the United States must collect over 750,000 signatures).[51]

Fully understanding why we keep forming institutions in which we place so little faith, however, requires sorting out two matters that are commonly confused. First, we do *need* political parties. We have already reviewed the reasons parties are formed in the first place and the many functions they traditionally perform. Second, we are not satisfied with the *kind* of parties we get. Few observers of political parties deny that they are guilty, at least on occasion, of all the sins of which they have been accused.

For some, the answer to this dilemma is simple: Reform the parties. Efforts at reform, however, often either place the powers of party in the hands of the reformers, who soon begin to perpetrate the very abuses they swore to eradicate, or else rob the parties of much of their capacity to perform their appropriate functions. The latter problem has been particularly pronounced in the United States, the Western nation in which political parties are the most severely regulated.[52]

Why is it so difficult to devise reforms that work? Part of the answer lies in the connection between parties and power. Party militants want to win elections in order to obtain specific rewards. Obviously, not all the men and women who seek such rewards do so at unreasonable cost to others. But then again, what seems reasonable to me may well strike you as self-serving and exploitative. As long as we have no universal agreement on the rightful distribution of power and the resources it commands, and as long as mere human beings stay in charge of political parties, we must expect that their performance will continue to be disappointing to many.

However, another part of the answer may lie in the fact that we may have been too quick to assume we know the procedures that make democracy work, including how best to organize and regulate our parties. Is it true that parties are impossible to reform, or have we simply not yet given the problem sufficient attention? Despite the fact that political parties are capable—at least in theory—of providing wide-ranging programs and popularly selected candidates and thereby giving citizens a serious link to all the work of their governments, our general dissatisfaction with their performance may soon reach the point of no return. But when we seek to organize in a way to reach our governments on behalf of more than a single cause, what alternatives do we have?

SUMMARY AND CONCLUSION

Political parties are a unique form of political organization, characterized by their effort to place representatives from their own membership in office, which they do by nominating candidates to stand for election in their name. Their principal functions are leadership recruitment, interest aggregation, campaigning, and governing.

Internal democracy is extremely difficult to establish within a political party because of the typical characteristics of members, leaders, and organizations themselves. Nevertheless, the effort to democratize parties seems to be an unending one, most recently epitomized by the new Green parties of Europe.

Party members may be supporters, adherents, or militants. The motives for joining parties may be summarized as personal objectives, loyalty, and political conviction; as in the case of interest groups, individuals may have more than one kind of motive. Some parties attract members from every sector of society, whereas others focus on the members of a particular ethnic group, religion, or language group. Candidates are chosen by a very wide range of methods throughout the world, and different qualifications are sought according to the conditions of the campaign to come.

Preparing the campaign requires raising funds and developing a strategy; in both cases, modern technologies play an ever more important part. Carrying out the campaign is more and more likely to be done via the media. To understand the role of the media in modern politics, it is important to understand their dependency on attracting as large an audience for their advertisers as possible and the effect this need has had on their presentation of political news, including political campaigns. Parties and candidates gain access to the media via legally required free time, paid advertising, free coverage, and alternative media such as cable television, direct mail, the telephone, electronic mail, and web pages on the Internet. Media reporters and editors use political news to attract as large an audience as possible and also to meet the demands of the owners, who may have specific political agendas of their own. Citizens have lately shown increasing interest in alternative media, including talk shows, but still tend to gather a large portion of what information they have about politics from paid ads, especially in the United States.

Once in government, the elected representatives of parties do not necessarily rule. They may be hampered by divided government, by their inability to form a governing coalition, by their own corrupt behavior, and/or by the excessive power of the civil service.

Parties are inevitably disappointing; we need them to make democracy possible, yet they are formed to gain power, and those who seek power have their own motives for doing so. Perhaps the only answer is to learn to accept our need for these puzzling and annoying organizations and give more serious attention to how to make them work for us and our democracies.

Selected Readings

Beck, Paul Allen. *Party Politics in America.* 8th ed. White Plains, N.Y.: Longman, 1996. A basic text that provides careful and readable coverage of the key topics in the study of U.S. political parties.

Duverger, Maurice. *Political Parties: Their Organization and Activity in the Modern State.* Trans. by Barbara and Robert North. New York: Wiley and Sons, 1954. One of the first comprehensive, comparative studies of political parties, with chapters on organization, membership, leadership, and the nature of party systems.

Hoftstadter, Richard. *The Idea of a Party System: The Rise of Legitimate Opposition in the United States, 1780–1840.* Berkeley and Los Angeles: University of California Press, 1972. One of the most interesting analyses of U.S. party history, tracing the slow legitimization of the idea of a competitive party system, as it reached fruition during the presidency of Martin Van Buren.

Katz, Richard S., and Peter Mair, eds. *How Parties Organize: Change and Adaptation in Party Organizations in Western Democracies.* London: Sage, 1994. Case studies of political party organization drawn from the United States and eleven European nations.

Lawson, Kay, ed. *How Political Parties Work: Perspectives from Within.* Westport, Conn.: Praeger, 1994. A collection of case studies illustrating the difficulties of achieving internal party democracy, the relationship between leadership and organization, the ways internal organization affects parties' performance, and how external events can cause change in their internal organization.

Michels, Robert. *Political Parties.* New York: Dover, 1915. The classical study of the rise of elite control (oligarchy) in all political organizations, even in those political parties most strongly dedicated to democratic procedures.

Schattschneider, Elmer E. *Party Government.* New York: Holt, Rinehart and Winston, 1942. Another classic in the literature, defending political parties as superior to interest groups as agencies of linkage in modern democracies.

Selnow, Gary W. *High-Tech Campaigns: Computer Technology in Political Communication.* Westport, Conn.: Praeger, 1994. An explanation of targeted communication and of the universal trend in political campaigning to focus on ever narrower audiences, with a concluding discussion of the effects of these technologies on American voters, the press, and the political system.

Ware, Alan. *Political Parties and Party Systems.* Oxford: Oxford University Press, 1996. A comparative introduction to the study of parties and party systems, with an emphasis on the parties of Great Britain, France, Germany, Japan, and the United States.

Notes

1. Sigmund Neumann, ed., *Modern Political Parties* (Chicago: University of Chicago Press, 1956), p. 395. Italics added. Copyright © 1956 by the University of Chicago. All rights reserved. Reprinted by permission of the University of Chicago Press.

2. Joseph Schlesinger, "Political Parties: Party Units," in *International Encyclopedia of the Social Sciences* ed. D. L. Sills (New York: Macmillan, 1968), 2:428.

3. Robert Michels, *Political Parties*, trans. Eden Paul and Cedar Paul (New York: Dover, 1959), p. 209."These former believers, these sometime altruists, whose fervent hearts aspired only to give themselves freely, have been transformed into sceptics and egoists whose actions are guided solely by cold calculation" (401).

4. Moisei Ostrogorski, *Democracy and the Organization of Political Parties*, vol. 1 (New York: Anchor Books, 1964), p. 177.

5. Maurice Duverger, *Political Parties: Their Organization and Activity in the Modern State,* trans. Barbara and Robert North (New York: Wiley and Sons, 1954), pp. 4–202.

6. Michels, *Political Parties*, p. 408.

7. Donald Schoonmaker, "The Challenge of the Greens to the West German Party System," in *When Parties Fail: Emerging Alternative Organizations*, ed. Kay Lawson and Peter Merkl (Princeton: Princeton University Press, 1988), pp. 41–75. This same party has, however, recently found it necessary to modify the rules intended to protect internal democracy in order to have greater continuity of leadership and program (Thomas Poguntke, "Goodbye to Movement Politics? Organisational Adaptation of the German Green Party," *Environmental Politics* 2, no. 3 [Autumn 1993]: 379–404).

8. For a study of this question in Canada, see John C. Courtney, *Do Conventions Matter? Choosing National Party Leaders in Canada* (Montreal: McGill-Queen's University Press, 1995).

9. Duverger, *Political Parties*, p. 82.

10. Richard S. Katz, "Party as Linkage: A Vestigial Function?" *European Journal of Political Research* 18 (1990): 143–61; and Richard Katz et al., "The Membership of Political Parties in European Democracies, 1960–1990," *European Journal of Political Research* 22 (1992): 329–45.

11. Jeremy Richardson, "The Market for Political Activism: Interest Groups as a Challenge to Political Parties," *West European Politics* 18, no. 1 (Jan. 1995): 116–39. See also Lawson and Merkl, *When Parties Fail.*

12. This reformulation of Salisbury's list is based on Kay Lawson, "Toward a Theory of How Political Parties Work," in *How Political Parties Work: Perspectives from Within*, ed. Kay Lawson (Westport, Conn.: Praeger, 1994), pp. 288–91.

13. This distinction is made by James Q. Wilson in *The Amateur Democrat* (Chicago: University of Chicago Press, 1963), passim.

14. Useful studies include Barbara Kellerman, *Political Leadership* (Pittsburgh, Pa.: University of Pittsburgh Press, 1986); Bryan D. Jones, ed., *Leadership and Politics: New Perspectives in Political Science* (Lawrence: University Press of Kansas, 1989); and

John W. Gardner, *On Leadership* (New York: Free Press, 1990). See especially chapter 14 in Gardner.

15. See Chapter 6 for a discussion of electoral systems.

16. Herbert Alexander, *Financing Politics: Money, Elections and Political Reform*, 4th ed. (Washington, D.C.: Congressional Quarterly Press, 1992), p. 50.

17. Stephen J. Wayne, *Road to the White House 1996* (New York: St. Martins, 1996), p. 45; *International Herald Tribune*, 7 Feb. 1996, 3.

18. Alexander, *Financing Politics*, p. 63.

19. Ibid., pp. 53–54.

20. Federal Election Commission, *Campaign Guide for Corporations and Labor Organizations* (Washington, D.C.: Federal Election Commission, 1994), pp. 45–51; Alexander, *Financing Politics*, pp. 65–366. FEC publications are available free of charge and may be obtained by dialing 800-424-9530 or (for immediate fax delivery) 202-501-3413.

21. David P. Conradt, *The German Polity*, 4th ed. (White Plains, N.Y.: Longman, 1989), pp. 123–24.

22. Gary W. Selnow, *High-Tech Campaigns: Computer Technology in Political Communication* (Westport, Conn.: Praeger, 1994), pp. 13–14.

23. Paul S. Hernnson, "Field Work, Political Parties, and Volunteerism," in *Campaigns and Elections American Style*, ed. James A. Thurber and Candice J. Nelson (Boulder, Colo.: Westview Press, 1995), p. 154.

24. Marshall Ganz, "Voters in the Crosshairs: Elections and Voter Turnout," *Current* (May 1994): 4–10.

25. Shaun Bowler and David M. Farrell, eds., *Electoral Strategies and Political Marketing* (New York: St. Martin's, 1992), pp. 226–28.

26. Thomas E. Patterson, "Television and Presidential Politics: A Proposal to Restructure Television Communication in Election Campaigns," in *Presidential Selection*, ed. Alexander Heard and Michael Nelson (Durham, N.C.: Duke University Press, 1987), p. 303.

27. Bruce I. Newman, *The Marketing of the President: Political Marketing as Campaign Strategy* (Thousand Oaks, Calif.: Sage, 1994), pp. 114–15.

28. Ibid., p. 83

29 Selnow, *High-Tech Campaigns*, p. 143

30. Kiku Adatto, "The Incredible Shrinking Sound Bite," *New Republic* 202, no. 22 (May 1990): 20–23.

31. Selnow, *High-Tech Campaigns*, p. 140

32. Ibid.

33. For a case study of the horse race phenomenon in the coverage of U.S. campaigns, see Henry E. Brady and Richard Johnston, "What's the Primary Message: Horse Race or Issue Journalism?" in *Media and Momentum: The New Hampshire Primary and Nomination Politics*, ed. Gary R. Orren and Nelson W. Polsby (Chatham, N.J.: Chatham House, 1987), pp. 127–86.

34. Ann Grimes, "The Making of a Bachelor President," *New York Times*, 6 Oct. 1991, sec. 4, 17.

35. Ibid.

36. *Le Monde,*, 18 Feb. 1987, 10. In other cases, large corporations control numerous media enterprises along with several other types of businesses. The General Electric corporation media holdings are large enough and successful enough to make it fourth in R. Craig Endicott's 1990 list, "One Hundred Leading Media Companies," *Advertising Age* 61, no. 26 (25 June 1990): 51–58.

37. Foreign Policy Association, "Media's Role in Shaping Foreign Policy," in *Great Decisions* (New York: Foreign Policy Association, 1991), p. 90.
38. *New York Times*, 30 Nov. 1994, 1.
39. Ralph Negrine, "The Media and the Public Interest: Questions of Access and Control," in *Controlling Broadcasting: Access Policy and Practice in North America and Europe*, ed. Meryl Aldridge and Nicholas Hewitt (Manchester, England: Manchester University Press, 1994), p. 58. For a general review of legislation designed to maintain diversity and competition in European broadcasting industries, see chap. 10, "Competition Policy and the Broadcast Industry in Member Countries," in Organization for Economic Cooperation and Development, *Competitition Policy and a Changing Broadcast Industry* (Paris: OECD, 1993).
40. Dan Nimmo and James E. Combs, *Mediated Political Realities* (White Plains, N.Y.: Longman, 1983), p. 69.
41. *The People, the Press and Politics, 1990* (Washington, D.C.: Times-Mirror Center for the People and the Press, 1990), p. 133, cited by William J. Keefe, *Parties, Politics and Public Policy in America*, 7th edition (Washington, D.C.: Congressional Quarterly Press, 1994), p. 142.
42. André Blais and Elisabeth Gidengil, *Making Representative Democracy Work: The Views of Canadians* (Toronto: Dundurn Press, 1991), pp. 113–26.
43. Richard Joslyn, *Mass Media and Elections* (Reading, Mass.: Addison-Wesley, 1984), p. 176.
44. *International Herald Tribune*, 7 Apr. 1992, 1.
45. For the 1994 shift, see Mark Donovan, "The Politics of Electoral Reform in Italy," in *The Politics of Electoral Reform*, ed. Pippa Norris, a special issue of *International Political Science Review* 16, no. 1 (Jan. 1995): 47–64; David Henderson, "Little Joy for the Italian Left," *New Statesman and Society* (1 Apr. 1994): 10; David I. Kertzer, "Italy Produces a Ballot-Box Revolution," *Baltimore Sun*, 3 Apr. 1994, 1E; and Mario Sznajder, "Heirs of Fascism? Italy's Right-Wing Government: Legitimacy and Criticism," *International Affairs* 71, no. 1 (Jan. 1995): 83–102.
46. *International Herald Tribune*, 1 Feb. 1996, 5, and 2 Feb. 1996, 1, 11.
47. Basil Wilson, "Fifty Years of Party Politics in Jamaica," *Everybody's* (July 1993): 15–18. Jamaica has had only two parties for over fifty years but has also had frequent periods of instability, particularly during the 1970s.
48. For an example, see Yahya M. Sadowski, "Cadres, Guns and Money: The Eighth Regional Congress of the Syrian Ba'th," M.E.R.I.P. *Middle East Report* 134 (July-Aug. 1985): 3–8.
49. *The People, the Press and Politics 1990;* and *Gallup Poll Monthly* 300 (September 1990): 32, and 308 (May 1991): 36.
50. Alexander Hamilton, James Madison, and John Jay, *The Federalist Papers* (New York: Mentor Books, 1961), pp. 77–84.
51. *New York Times*, 28 Sept. 1995, A11.
52. For details of state regulation of parties in the United States, see Kay Lawson, "How State Laws Undermine Parties," in *Elections American Style*, ed. A. James Reichley (Washington, D.C.: Brookings Institution, 1987), pp. 240–60.

IV THE WORK OF GOVERNMENT: LEGISLATIVE, EXECUTIVE, AND JUDICIAL FUNCTIONS

9 Making the Laws

Do you remember your first day in college? Chances are you spent most of that day trying to figure out the rules. All kinds of rules presented themselves to you: rules about which pieces of paper you had to have, where to exchange them for other pieces of paper, where to put your things, where to put yourself. Some rules were more compelling than others: If you are a young man receiving a government-backed loan for your education, you may have been required to demonstrate that you had registered for the draft in order to receive

that aid. Other rules were given quietly, and following them was clearly op-
tional: You learned without being told that there was or was not a specific way
to dress, to talk, perhaps even to sit and look about. In any case, there you were,
an independent human being with the ability to decide for yourself which rules
to follow and which to reject. Once you had sorted it all out, made your decisions, followed some rules to completion ("Here is the check for my tuition"),
adopted others as a pattern for your behavior ("I will be in my botany class by
8:10 every Monday, Wednesday, and Friday morning"), and rejected others ("I
don't care what the others do; I'm going to wear the clothes I have and that's
that"), chances are life began to seem a little bit easier. You knew what you were
doing.

What you went through in those first few days tells you a great deal about the
role of rules in our lives—including the role of those rules we call laws. A rule is
a guide to behavior. It may be a regulation established by persons in authority, a
principle of conduct that one sets for oneself, or simply something that normally
happens ("As a general rule, people in the United States eat three meals a day").
A law is a rule of the first category: a regulation established by persons in authority. But not all such regulations are laws. A **law** is a regulation established by
public authorities and backed by the collective power of the polity to which it applies. It is, in effect, a *plan*—a decision to handle a particular problem in a particular way—and a *commitment*, made by the entire polity when they acquiesce in the
authority of those making the plan, that the plan will in fact be carried out. Because it is so strongly backed, it is the most powerful kind of rule. We have the
power to act contrary to the law, but we do so at our peril.

The polity for which a particular law is made may range from the smallest village to the nation-state. (The uncertainty of enforcement of most international
law places it in a special category; see Chapter 13.) At the lowest level are local
ordinances, sometimes referred to collectively as **municipal law.** "The charge to
the university for providing police protection at university events shall be $35
per hour per officer" is a rule set by officeholders (perhaps a council, a board, a
mayor, or a sheriff) who have been granted the authority to make such rules
throughout a governmental domain (a village, township, city, or county), either
by other officeholders or by statute.

Laws are made at all levels of government, and rules with the force of law can
be made by any branch of government. We think of the legislative branch as the
lawmaking branch of national government, and quite rightly so; thus, the work
of legislatures is the central topic of this chapter. However, legislators are not our
only national lawmakers; rules issued by executives also have the force of law, although they may be called by a different name. "I have ordered the National
Guard to remain on twenty-four-hour duty at all campuses of the university
where disturbances have been reported" is a rule set by a chief executive. Such a
rule is often called a **decree** but may also be called an ordinance, an executive
order, or a decree law.

The pronouncements of judges are more likely to be rulings than rules, but these
too can have the force of law. "The right of students to use notes in university

examinations is not protected by the First Amendment; there was, therefore, no violation of the Constitution in the university's decision to withhold the degree" is a **ruling**, which is to say, an interpretation of a rule (such as a clause in a constitution, law, ordinance, decree, or executive order) that affects the applicability of the rule. A nation's constitution is a set of rules that has precedence over all other rules. The constitution and judicial rulings about the meaning of the constitution are together called **constitutional law.**

Some rules have the force of law even when made outside government. "Henceforth the party's policy is that only those veterans with three or more years' membership in the party are eligible for educational benefits" is a rule that may have the force of law if the party in question has unrestrained power to tell the legislature what laws to write and pass.

Finally, some rules are written to be laws from the very beginning. In 1976, the U.S. Congress ruled: "Institutions of higher education receiving financial assistance whether directly or indirectly [shall not] undertake any study or project or fulfill the terms of any contract containing an express or implied provision that any person or persons of a particular race, religion, sex, or national origin be barred from performing such study, project, or contract."[1] That rule, once entrenched in the U.S. Code, became part of the law of the land. Such laws can be reversed only by other, subsequent laws or by ruling of the U.S. Supreme Court that they are in some way contrary to the U.S. Constitution.[2]

This chapter is about the making of those rules that are called laws or that have the force of law. Our primary emphasis is on how laws are made in legislatures, but we also give some consideration to how executive and judicial agencies make law.

LAWMAKING IN THE LEGISLATURE

A **legislature** is an institution in which individuals gather with the primary purpose of making laws. It need not be an elected body, although it often is. It need not be a permanent body convened periodically—sometimes it is; sometimes it is not. A legislature is established every time a tribal chief, king, military commander, or the highest potentate in a theocracy summons some of the elders, nobles, senior officers, or higher clergy (respectively) to help work out policy on a matter of politywide concern. When the governor of a colonial territory appoints a few trusted individuals to form a legislative council, as was the British practice in the heyday of empire, that too is a legislature.[3]

The more familiar form of a modern legislature, however, is a permanent, periodically convened institution composed of officials elected for a limited term for the express purpose of making laws, such as the German Bundestag, the British House of Commons, the Japanese Diet, the French National Assembly, the Mexican National Congress, and the U.S. Congress. Even in this category there are numerous variations. The legislature's relationship to the executive branch and the individual legislators' relationships with their constituents vary significantly from polity to polity. Other differences include the number and nature of the individual houses of the legislature, the power of committees, and the customs and mores of the particular legislature.

THE RELATIONSHIP BETWEEN LEGISLATIVE AND EXECUTIVE POWER

Legislative power need not be separate from executive power. Indeed, it seldom is. Just how closely connected they are, and what the balance between them may be, depends on a nation's constitution and whether it prescribes a parliamentary system, a presidential system, or a blend of the two. The simplest way to make this distinction clear is to describe each of these three systems in turn. Figures 9.1 and 9.2 illustrate how a parliamentary system and a presidential system establish different relationships between legislative and executive power.

The Parliamentary System

In a **parliamentary system**, the legislature maintains extremely close bonds with the system's executive leadership and has significant power of its own. Because this system works very differently from the one you probably know best, it may help you to refer to Figure 9.1 while reading the next few pages. In the diagram, a solid arrow shows the direction of effective control of one body over another and a broken arrow indicates some degree of control, often varying according to political circumstances.

In a parliamentary system the same executive leadership directs the work of the legislature, called **parliament** and normally consisting of an upper house and a lower house, and the work of the **bureaucracy**. The bureaucracy includes all the departments or ministries of government; it is sometimes called the **administration**. That executive leadership is the **cabinet**—which is composed of the heads of the departments of government, usually called **ministers**, occupants of important appointive posts, such as the head of the national security agency, the top leader in the military forces, or an important prelate in a system where church and state are closely intertwined—and the chief executive, usually called the **prime minister**. The cabinet in a parliamentary system is often called the **government**, not because it is in fact the entire government but in recognition of the key role it does play.

Where do parliamentary cabinets come from, and what do they do? In the most typical form, the individual members of the cabinet are chosen by the prime minister but must be approved by the lower house (see p. 205 for the difference between the lower and upper houses of legislatures). To become prime minister, one must be a leader (usually the top leader) of a political party. If that party wins a majority of the seats in the lower house of the legislature, its senior leader will be asked to try to "form a government." If he or she can win the approval of the lower house of parliament for the cabinet proposed (and if the party has won the majority of seats in the legislature, such approval is virtually assured), then the new government is established and the party leader in question becomes the prime minister. The cabinet may be formed exclusively of members of parliament

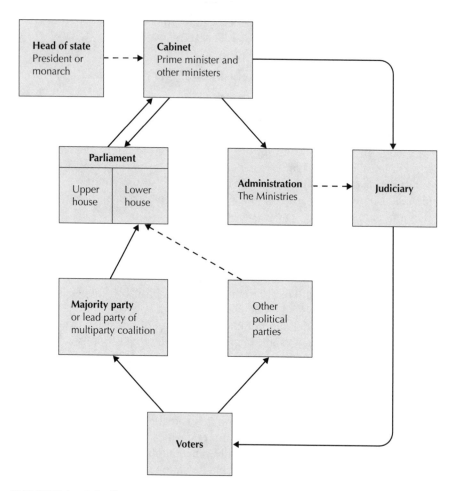

FIGURE 9.1   A Parliamentary System

(who may or may not be allowed to keep their seats in that body), or it may include some persons who have not been elected to any office whatsoever; the more common pattern is for cabinet members to be members of parliament as well.

In a parliamentary system, the person who asks the party leader to try to form a government is the nation's monarch or president (often referred to as the **head of state**). This is the most important role—or at least the most politically powerful role—that a monarch or a president can play in a parliamentary system; the other functions of the head of state are limited to the ceremonial or morally suasive. Even in this case, if the party leader leads a party that has indeed won a majority of seats in the lower house, the head of state can only follow a script written by others. Everyone knows that the majority party's leader must be asked to form a government and will succeed in doing so.

In *multiparty parliamentary systems,* however, where it often happens that no party wins a majority of the seats, the ceremonial leader may have an opportunity to exercise a very real influence on the course of events. In this case it is usually still expected that the leader of the party winning a plurality of seats will be given the first chance to form a government, often by asking leading members of various other parties to take posts in the cabinet in order to form a *coalition* government. If that cabinet cannot win the approval of the lower house, the same person may be asked to try again with a different cabinet, or the leader of another party may be asked to try. Sometimes a nation's politics are so fragmented that no single leader is considered dominant over all the others in a particular party; in that case, the job of trying to form an acceptable cabinet may be passed on to someone else in the same party. As a general rule, the more difficult it is to form a government (cabinet) that the lower house will accept, the more power will be exercised by the monarch or president in a parliamentary system, at least during this difficult period. However, even in cases where it is very difficult indeed to form a new government, the ceremonial leader customarily takes the advice of the nation's most astute and most powerful politicians in deciding whom to ask next.

Once formed, the new cabinet becomes the center of the entire governmental process in a parliamentary system. It assumes primary responsibility for the formulation of new legislation and accounts for the initiation of most new bills. Government bills (bills proposed by the cabinet) typically have precedence over bills proposed by individual members of parliament. In some systems, individual members are not allowed to introduce certain kinds of bills—for example, those that would require additional expense with no provision for additional revenue. At the same time, it is also the duty of cabinet members to see to it that the bills are properly carried out by the appropriate departments or ministries once they become law.

So far it may appear that once the legislature has approved a cabinet and a government is formed, the ordinary members of parliament will find themselves playing an insignificant role in the making of laws. Such an impression is not correct. Although most bills are initiated by the cabinet and all laws must be carried out through the administrative apparatus the cabinet controls, the members of parliament still have an important role to play in shaping the content of legislation. (We come back to this in discussing the role of committees.) No bill becomes law without the consent of at least the lower house of the legislature; more commonly, both houses must approve. Furthermore, it is usually possible for the legislature to put an end to the life of any cabinet. The most forthright way of doing so is by calling for a motion of censure or by voting negatively when the government itself calls for a **vote of confidence.** If a majority of the lower house votes for the motion (or against the government), the government is dismissed— or, in the term more often used, *dissolved.* However, this procedure normally means not only that the cabinet must resign but also that the members of the lower house will themselves have to face new elections. Since this is not always politically convenient, members of parliament often prefer to accept partial changes to the cabinet, engineered by the majority party's leadership. However, if it proves impossible to form a new cabinet that can command a majority, then elections must be held.

In sum, the parliamentary system is predicated on keeping the functions of government tightly interwoven. The link between legislative and executive functions is considered so important that one author has referred to it as the "buckle" that holds everything together and makes the system work.[4]

The Presidential System

The **presidential system** is characterized by weak ties between the legislative and executive branches and a shifting balance of power. The presidential system (illustrated in Figure 9.2) functions quite differently from the parliamentary system. It rests on the assumption that placing too much power in the hands of too few is dangerous to the liberty of citizens. The government is therefore divided, on the principle of the **separation of powers**, into three branches: legislative, exec-

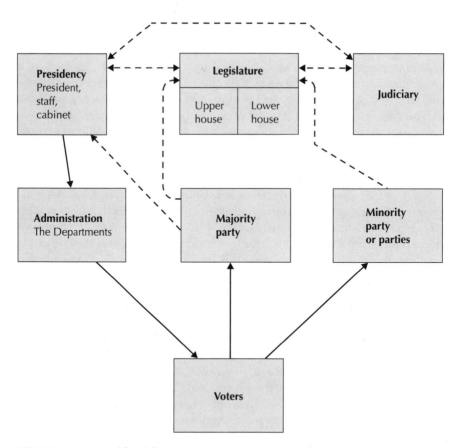

FIGURE 9.2   A Presidential System

utive, and judicial. Each branch is given a separate domain, a separate source of power (the chief executive and the legislators are elected independently; the highest judges are appointed), and the power to correct the abuses of the others. Under this system the relationship between the executive and legislative branches, which may and often do come under the control of members of opposing parties, is likely to be contentious and fraught with difficulty. Defenders of this system argue that such conflict is a small price to pay to protect the nation against the tyranny that might arise with more concentrated power.[5] But those who prefer parliamentary government point out that that system permits stronger parties, more frequent elections (when deemed necessary), and, most important, more cohesive government.

Key Differences between the Two Systems

Whatever side one takes in such a debate, it is important to understand four crucial differences between presidential systems and parliamentary systems: the different sources of executive power, the different roles of the executive in the initiation of legislation, the presence or absence of ceremonial leadership, and the different roles of political parties. Exact procedures vary, but the more usual patterns are as follows.

Source of Executive Power. In a parliamentary system, the prime minister is chosen first by a party (as party leader), second by the voters in a particular constituency (as their representative to the lower house of the legislature), third by the ceremonial leader (as a possible head of government), and fourth by the lower house of the legislature (as prime minister in fact). The other members of parliament are chosen by the voters. National legislative elections are always important: They determine the balance of power in both the legislative and executive offices.

In a presidential system, on the other hand, the president is chosen first by a party (as nominee) and second by the voters of the entire nation (as president).[6] The members of the legislature are also chosen first by the parties (as nominees) and second by the voters (as representatives) in elections that may or may not be held at the same time as the presidential election. In any case, the members of the legislature in a presidential system have terms of office different from that of the president and play no part in his or her selection. Presidential elections are normally considered far more important than legislative elections in a presidential system.

Initiation of Legislation. In a parliamentary system, the prime minister and the cabinet can and do initiate legislation. In a presidential system, the president and the members of the administration may initiate new legislation, but usually only indirectly, working through individual members of the legislature who agree to sponsor such bills. Those bills have no special priority over other bills proposed by the same or other individual members. However, we should not exaggerate the importance of this difference, since in practice the legislative leaders in a presidential system are usually extremely well aware of which bills have the backing of the president, and such bills will almost always receive greater and more favorable attention than bills sponsored by ordinary members.

Ceremonial Leadership. In a parliamentary system, the **ceremonial leader** plays a role in establishing the link between executive and legislative powers by calling upon the party leader most likely to gain the approval of the lower house to form a government. The ceremonial leader takes power either by right of birth or by election (but in either case, the choice of that official is far less important than the choices made in legislative elections). In a presidential system, the president is also the ceremonial leader.

Role of Political Parties. In a parliamentary system, the political parties choose the candidates for the legislature and choose their own leader in the knowledge that if enough of their legislative candidates are successful, that leader will become the prime minister. They also know that the leader will count on the votes of the successful candidates of the party, not only to take office, but also to carry out the party's program. This means that the party plays a far more critical role in parliamentary systems than in presidential systems. Furthermore, the constitutional link between executive and legislative power in parliamentary government forces a link between the party's candidates for executive and legislative power. This means a more unified party, better able to maintain party discipline in the legislature, more responsive to majority vote (unless there is a coalition government), and thus better able to combine legislative and executive power in implementing its program. In a presidential system, the political parties choose legislative and executive candidates separately, receive little encouragement from the constitutional system to operate in harmony, and are thus more likely to permit undisciplined voting in the legislature. The end result is that although the voters in a presidential system directly elect the president as well as the legislators, choosing between competing candidates from different parties, they do not have the advantage of knowing that strong and well-disciplined parties will hold their successful candidates responsible to the program on which they campaigned (hence the broken lines in Figure 9.2 from the parties to the presidency and the legislature).

The combined effect of these four differences between a presidential system and a parliamentary system is to make the ties between executive and legislative power much looser in a presidential system.

A third kind of relationship between the legislature and the executive may be called the **presidential-parliamentary system.** This system is characterized by strong ties between the legislature and the executive and a weak legislature. This system was invented by the French in 1958 and has since been adopted in several of the new nations of the third world, particularly those in Africa that were formerly under French colonial control. Under this system, the president chooses a prime minister, who must win the approval of the legislature's lower house for a cabinet, just as in a parliamentary system. However, the president has the power to appoint anyone at all as prime minister and to remove that person at will. The prime minister need not be a member of parliament, need not be a leader of a major party, and in fact need not even be a member of a political party. The prime minister forms a cabinet, which must be approved by the legislature, but, again, cabinet members need not be members of parliament or leaders or members of political parties. It is normal in this system for the president to be elected directly by the people; the prime minister and cabinet members need not have been elected at all. The constitution of a quasi-presidential system may also give the president the right to name the highest judges, rule the nation directly during states of emergency, and declare when such a state of emergency exists. This system permits the president to be a much stronger figure than does a typical parliamentary system. However, the prime minister retains the important powers of setting the government's daily agenda and overseeing both the formulation and the execution of policy—it is the prime minister who plays the most active role, but that role must be played in a way that is satisfactory to the president, to whom the prime minister reports and who has the power to remove him or her from power.

REPRESENTATION: LEGISLATORS AND THEIR CONSTITUENTS

We have just examined two versions of the legislature's relationship to the executive branch and briefly mentioned a third. Another key difference in legislatures around the world is seen in the relationship that legislators maintain with their constituents. One question all legislators must resolve is whether to act independently on the basis of what they personally believe to be correct principles or to attempt to carry out the will of constituents even when it runs contrary to those principles.

Any attempt to answer the fundamental question is likely to lead to a host of other problems. It is often difficult to know the will of constituents with certainty. It is not easy to treat all constituents as equals—some will be better informed and more articulate than others, some will be major contributors to the legislator's campaign fund, and some will be other powerful political leaders who helped the representative secure the nomination in the first place. Sometimes nonconstituents have a claim to legislative attention on the grounds of past favors, promises of future help, or the national importance of the causes they represent. Even if a legislator wishes to be loyal to his or her own constituents, it is often very difficult for that legislator to be sure that the will of the voters truly reflects their own interests. Furthermore, these interests may be extremely varied and not easily compromised. The interests of the whole (the community) are not always in accord with the sum of the interests of the parts (the individual citizens and groups), and both may be in conflict with the interests of the larger polity (the nation) of which they form a part.

Even when legislator inclination, constituency will, and national interests conveniently match, problems remain. These problems are related to the theme of interdependence we are pursuing throughout this book: How do international developments impinge on the proposed legislation, and what is the responsibility of the individual legislator to add "best interests of the human polity" to the list of objectives to be served?

Consider, for example, the problems the U.S. Congress had to wrestle with after the brutal repression of student demonstrations took place in China in June 1989. Many members of Congress believed that global protection of human rights required that the United States impose economic sanctions on China as well as issue strong statements of disapproval, whereas others believed such a move would do more damage to U.S. business interests in China than good to the cause of fostering democracy. In the final analysis, the latter camp prevailed. The United States severely criticized the Chinese government but limited more substantive response to a temporary ban on diplomatic visits between the two nations and on new loans to China by the World Bank and other international development banks. When the new Clinton administration put the question of human rights back on the agenda for discussion with the Chinese, it did not stay there long; by the end of 1994, the policy of linking trade benefits to human rights had again been openly abandoned.[7]

A further problem in securing fair representation is the inability of certain groups to elect persons like themselves to serve in their nation's legislative bodies. Sometimes this is simply a matter of voting rights; for example, it is only very recently that the majority black population of South Africa has achieved full voting rights, but that transition was swiftly followed by the transformation of that nation's legislature as well. Often, however, the problem is social and political rather than constitutional. Take a moment to read Table 9.1: In how many nations have women had the right to vote and to be elected for more than thirty years yet still not gained more than 15 percent of the seats in the legislature? What accounts for the slow progress of women in gaining full representation?

There is no easy cure for skewed representation where all have the vote, but remedies for corrupted representative leadership are even more difficult to devise. Two practices that offer some hope of protection are by no means foolproof. One is the establishment of independent watchdog agencies, such as the office of ombudsman in Sweden. It is the task of the ombudsman to expose (and presumably end) the more heinous abuses of the privileges of office.[8] Of course, such agencies do not always work as intended. Because such watchdog agencies are themselves part of the government they are expected to monitor and control, a stronger institutional safeguard against corruption rests in the existence of a wide range of political organizations outside government, although these may come to wield excessive and/or unbalanced power. Furthermore, protecting the right of free assembly that ensures the existence of a pluralistic political system is a task that inevitably devolves on government—that is, on the very officials whose actions we hope to guide and control. Institutions can take us only so far. There comes a time when we must rely on the quality of the men and women inside them.

TABLE 9.1   Women in National Legislative Office

Selected Countries	Date of Right to Vote	Date of Right to Be Elected	Percent of Women in Parliament, 1991
Algeria	1962	1962	2.4
Argentina	1947	1947	4.7
Australia	1901/1967[a]	1901/1967[a]	6.7
Bangladesh	1947	1947	10.3
Brazil	1934	1934	6.0
Bulgaria	1944	1944	8.5
Cameroon	1946	1946	14.4
Canada	1917/1918/1950[a]	1920/1960/1969[a]	13.2
Chile	1931/1949[a]	1931/1949[a]	5.8
China	1949	1949	21.3
Cuba	1934	1934	33.9
Czechoslovakia	1920	1920	8.7
Denmark	1915	1915	33.0
Ecuador	1946	1946	5.5
Egypt	1956	1956	2.2
El Salvador	1961	1961	8.3
Equatorial Guinea	1963	1963	0.0
Finland	1906	1906	38.5
France	1944	1944	5.7
Gabon	1956	1956	4.2
Germany	1918	1918	20.4
Greece	1952	1952	5.3
Hungary	1945	1945	7.0
Iceland	1915	1915	23.8
India	1950	1950	7.1
Indonesia	1945	1945	12.4
Iran	1963	1963	1.5
Iraq	1980	1980	10.8
Ireland	1918	1918	7.8
Israel	1948	1948	6.7
Italy	1945	1945	12.8
Ivory Coast	1952	1952	4.6
Jamaica	1944	1944	5.0
Japan	1945/1947[a]	1945/1947[a]	2.3
Jordan	1974	1974	0.0
Kenya	1963	1963	1.1
Korea (North)	1946	1946	20.1
Korea (South)	1948	1948	2.0
Kuwait	not yet	not yet	0.0
Laos	1958	1958	8.9

TABLE 9.1 *Continued*

Selected Countries	Date of Right to Vote	Date of Right to Be Elected	Percent of Women in Parliament, 1991
Luxembourg	1919	1919	13.3
Madagascar	1959	1959	6.5
Malaysia	1957	1957	5.0
Mexico	1947	1953	12.4
Mongolia	1923/1924[a]	1923/1924[a]	2.1
Morocco	1963	1963	0.0
Mozambique	1975	1975	15.7
Nepal	1951	1951	3.4
New Zealand	1893	1919	16.5
Nicaragua	1955	1955	16.3
Norway	1907/1913[a]	1907/1913[a]	35.8
Pakistan	1937	1937	0.9
Papua New Guinea	1975	1975	0.0
Peru	1950	1956	5.5
Philippines	1937	1937	9.0
Poland	1918	1918	13.5
Portugal	1931/1976[a]	1931/1976[a]	7.6
Romania	1929/1946[a]	1929/1946[a]	3.6
Rwanda	1961	1961	17.1
South Africa	1930/1984[a]	1930/1984[a]	2.6
Spain	1931	1931	14.6
Sweden	1918/1921[a]	1918/1921[a]	38.1
Switzerland	1971	1971	14.0
Syria	1949	1953	8.4
Thailand	1932	1932	3.8
Togo	1956	1956	3.9
Tonga	1960	1960	0.0
Tunisia	1959	1959	4.2
Turkey	1930/1934[a]	1930/1934[a]	1.3
United Arab Emirates	not yet	not yet	0.0
United Kingdom	1918/1928[a]	1918/1928[a]	6.3
United States	1920	1788	6.4
Venezuela	1947	1947	9.9
Vietnam	1946	1946	17.7
Zambia	1962	1964	5.1
Zimbabwe	1957	1978	12.0

[a]Where several dates are shown, full suffrage for all adult women came in several stages.
Source: Irene Franck and David Brownstone, *The Women's Desk Reference* (New York: Viking, 1993), pp. 806–7.

CAMERAS, COMMITTEES, AND CUSTOMS: OTHER VARIATIONS IN LEGISLATURES

The term *camera* originally referred to a chamber or a room and only later came to mean a device for taking photographs. Thus, when we say that a legislature is *unicameral* or *bicameral*, we are referring to the number of houses (chambers) it has. A **unicameral legislature** has one house, a **bicameral legislature** has two.[9]

Most legislatures have two houses to ensure that different interests—and different principles of representation—will have appropriate arenas of action. Normally the lower house is elected directly by the people, with each representative serving approximately the same number of constituents. Upper houses vary from system to system, but they are usually made up of elder statesmen, elected indirectly (for example, French senators are elected by local and regional government officials) and in office for a longer term than their counterparts in the lower house. In some nations the upper house consists entirely of appointed members, and in Great Britain it is composed of "lords," most of whom have little claim to glory beyond the fact that they have inherited titles of nobility. In *corporatist* states, one or both houses (if there are two houses) will be composed of representatives from different occupations and branches of industry, not from different regions (for example, the Corporazione of Italy under the rule of Benito Mussolini before and during World War II).

In most nations with bicameral legislatures, the lower house is far more powerful than the upper house; the upper chamber deliberates on all bills, but it is easily overridden by the lower house in the event of disagreement. There are, however, exceptions. The U.S. Senate—directly elected by the people since 1913—has always been at least coequal with the House of Representatives in the exercise of power.

The Role of Committees

Even in systems where the decision-making power of the legislature is weak or nonexistent, the actual work of turning bills into laws can be onerous and time consuming. The concerns of modern government range far beyond the expertise any single man or woman can acquire, yet legislators are expected to exercise an informed judgment about each piece of legislation that comes before them. This problem has no real solution, but the work of modern legislatures is made somewhat easier by the use of the **committee system**.

There are basically two kinds of committee systems. In some legislatures, such as the U.S. Congress, each committee has a specialized function, and only bills having to do with that specialization may be referred to it.[10] The Merchant Marine and Fisheries Committee of the House of Representatives deals with the merchant marine and fisheries and nothing else. This system of **specialized committees** permits legislators to develop more expertise on particular subjects, since they will consistently be concerned with bills relevant to the same subject matter.[11]

In other legislatures, such as the British parliament, a composite committee system exists. Specialized committees are established for some purposes, such as the British Specialist Select Committee for Agriculture, but other committees are general **standing committees** to which different questions may be referred. There are no permanent memberships on the standing committees, which are labeled simply by the letters of the alphabet: "When a bill is sent to committee, the Committee on Selection appoints sixteen to thirty members to serve on that committee to deal with that bill only. Thus although standing committee A may deal with several bills—totally unrelated to each other—during a given session of Parliament, the membership of the committee will change completely from one bill to the next."[12]

Although committee systems are one way to free legislators from having to consider every piece of legislation in depth, the workload of the individual committee member can still be very great. In many legislatures each committee has a paid staff to help the legislators who serve on it. In addition, individual legislators usually have some help from a staff of their own in determining what position to take on any bill that comes before the committees on which they serve or before the full house. Where no such aid is given, or where it is given in inadequate amounts, the individual legislator is inevitably more dependent on others' opinions about the merits of all bills presented. Because they need help in sifting through the masses of materials presented to them, poorly staffed legislators are likely to be more open to lobbying efforts by private groups or by representatives of other branches of the government than are those with adequate help. Lobbyists are always ready to offer interpretations of pending legislation, with supporting documentation, but their interpretations are likely to be anything but objective.

Customs and Mores

There are also significant differences in the customs and mores of the world's legislative bodies. Differences in style may seem to be of little importance, but they can have a strong influence on the course of government. Most African legislators are still influenced by the traditions of *palaver* (discussing each topic as fully as possible), consensus (doing everything possible to reach a unanimous decision rather than simply abiding by majority rule), and respect (especially for those elders who have achieved the status of "leaders of thought"), which were likely to prevail in the decision-making processes of earlier, smaller communities. In some Western legislatures occasional raucous outbursts by opposition deputies protesting government policy are considered acceptable behavior. The British House of Commons is particularly notorious for these spectacles, especially since its proceedings have been televised, a practice that seems to have heightened the intensity of verbal assaults by opposing members of parliament rather than lowering it. The new Russian parliament seems to have fallen into the same kind of behavior (see Box 9.1). At the same time, of course, losing one's temper is regarded as unseemly and counterproductive in many other parts of the world. In some legislatures a certain amount of friendly accommodation, even across party

BOX 9.1   REGIME CHANGE

Russia's Duma Adopts Western Ways

Ultranationalist leader Vladimir Zhirinovsky battling with Russian lawmaker Yev-geniya Tishkovskaya in session of the Duma, the lower house of the Russian par-liament.

(AP/Wide World Photos)

In September 1995 the Russian parliament debated the nation's position on the use of force by NATO in former Yugoslavia and the maintenance of sanctions against Serbia. The position of Andrei Kozyrev, foreign minister, supporting both the use of NATO force and sanctions, was supported by a few deputies. However, the followers of ultranationalist Vladimir Zhirinovsky were speedily able to turn the issue into a patriotic test case, stressing the strong cultural and religious ties between the Serbs and the Russians. Passions ran high—so high that a nationalist deputy assaulted a radical Orthodox priest, tearing a crucifix from his neck, after which Zhirinovsky picked a fight with a woman deputy who opposed his posi-tion, calling her "scum." Far from discrediting the nationalists, such behavior seemed only to serve their cause; the legislature voted 258 to 2 that their country should unilaterally lift United Nations sanctions against Serbia and impose them against Croatia, at the same time calling for an end to Russia's participation in NATO's Partnership for Peace program. Given the strength of presidential powers in the domain of foreign affairs, the vote was not binding, but the pressure on Boris Yeltsin was obviously increased, especially with parliamentary elections due at the end of the year.

Source: John Thornhill, "NATO Force Debate Sparks Duma Fight," *Financial Times,* 11 Sept. 1995, A1, 18. Adapted by permission from the *Financial Times.*

Autocratic lawmaking. Iraqi president Saddam Hussein makes all major policy decisions for his nation, despite the fact that his is an *executive*, not a *legislative*, office.

(AP/Wide World Photos)

lines ("We'll vote with you on *X*, if you will help us out on *Y*"), is seen as essential to good government; in others a tradition of strong party discipline ensures strict partisan voting on even the most minor matters.

LAWMAKING OUTSIDE THE LEGISLATURE

The lawmaking powers of formal legislatures have been progressively eroded in many polities. In some nations it is very clear that laws are effectively being made by the chief executive. It is almost part of the definition of **charisma** that the charismatic leader will have the final word (and sometimes the first and only word as well) on all matters of importance. Hereditary rulers have traditionally felt free to issue new and binding commandments in the form of law, with or without the advice of others. But even modern constitutions may be written to give a particular executive carte blanche in the making of laws. Thus, Kwame Nkrumah was made president for life in Ghana and explicitly given extensive powers in the legislative, judicial, and executive domains.[13] Other chief executives have not always gone through the niceties of seeking constitutional ratification of their usurpation of legislative power. In April 1992, Peru's President

Alberto Fujimori, who had already issued some 126 decree laws in his first twenty months in office and was in constant battle with the Chamber of Deputies, simply suspended the nation's democratic constitution, closed down the legislature, dismantled the judiciary, and assumed dictatorial rule. It was an *autogolpe*, which is to say (in Spanish), "a self-coup."[14]

More often, however, executive usurpation of the lawmaking function is a collective enterprise, not the act of a single person. Even Fujimori could succeed only because he had the support of a majority of military officials, business elites, and even of the general population (although 75 percent said they preferred democracy to dictatorship, the same percentage approved the takeover, apparently owing to a conviction that only autocratic rule would be able to address the nation's declining living standards and increased political violence).[15] In other systems, dictatorial takeover has often been the result of the military acting on its own to stage a coup and set up a ruling junta (team of leaders), which then makes all policy decisions by authoritarian means. When the army took power in Thailand in a military coup in 1991 and placed Prime Minister Chatichai Choonhavan under arrest, the military immediately wrote a new constitution and promised new elections but made it clear that in the meantime legislative powers—and all others—would remain in its own hands.[16] When the first round of legislative elections in Algeria in December 1991 gave victory to Muslim fundamentalists, the military took power immediately, forced President Chadli Benjedid first to dissolve parliament and then to resign himself, and set up a seven-person Constitutional Council to rule by decree.[17]

Legislatures do not always lose to executive dominion, but neither do they always maintain their powers even when they may appear to do so. In some polities, a pretense may be maintained that lawmaking is the job of the legislature, but in practice that body has progressively allowed the executive branch a larger and larger role in the exercise of that function. Such delegation of the lawmaking power may be overt and deliberate, taking place through formal processes and at a specified point in time. The U.S Congress, for example, has formally established independent regulatory commissions and given them the right to issue rulings with the force of law. In other cases, the delegation of power may take place slowly, almost accidentally, emerging in response to changing circumstances and the strength or weakness of particular leaders and particular institutional constraints.

Do legislators best serve those who elected them by handing over their powers to presumably more efficient executives in times of national danger? Certainly the practice is fraught with peril; it was, after all, the German parliament that gave Adolf Hitler his unlimited powers. Of course, it is true that legislative abandonment of responsibility has seldom been so extensive or had such dire results, but still it is important to remember that a nation's legislature is the one arena where representatives of all interests can be expected to meet as equals, struggle to find compromises, and formulate policy acceptable to all. The damage done to the political process by casually giving up those rights can never be deemed inconsequential.

. When rueful legislators do attempt to repossess the powers they have allowed others to usurp, they may well find it necessary to turn to a third branch of government, the judiciary, to adjudicate disputes that arise when they attempt to rectify what now appear to them to have been mistaken delegations of their powers. Similarly, embattled executives may seek judicial endorsement for maintaining powers they have become accustomed to exercising or to keep legislatures from invading what appear to them to be constitutionally protected executive functions.

Whichever side is the plaintiff, the ironic effect is likely to be that the judiciary itself becomes seriously involved in the making of laws. In no other nation is the judiciary so heavily implicated in the lawmaking process as in the United States. In that nation, justices routinely take it upon themselves to decide whether or not legislation conforms to the Constitution, a process known as **judicial review.** As most students of American history will recall, this power was not explicitly given to the courts by the Constitution but was effectively asserted by the first chief justice, John Marshall, in the 1803 case of *Marbury v. Madison.* It was a classic case of executive-legislative struggle in which the winner was the judiciary (see Box 9.2).

The power of judicial review is one that the U.S. judicial system has continued to develop. The current controversy over abortion illustrates the significance the process has assumed in great national debates. When the Supreme Court decided in the case of *Roe v. Wade* in 1973 that there was "a privacy right to abortion" in the Fourteenth Amendment's due process guarantee of personal liberty, state legislatures and lower courts throughout the nation found themselves faced with some very tough questions, defended pro and con by some very tough advocates: May and should a state legislature write laws either making abortion illegal under certain circumstances or reinforcing abortion rights? May and should a court find a particular state law relative to abortion unconstitutional? Should the opinions on this matter of candidates for judicial posts enter into the decisions of those charged with their appointment? The controversy has become one of the most bitter in the nation's history, and the form it takes is shaped by the right of judicial review.[18]

In more recent constitutions, the power of judicial review is explicitly included. The Japanese constitution, for example, gives the Supreme Court of Japan the "power to determine the constitutionality of any law, order, regulation or official act."[19] But in other nations, judges have no place at all in lawmaking. They are expected to assume that all legislation is constitutionally correct and then simply to adjudicate disputes that arise under existing law. Other nations allow a modified form of judicial review, as in France, where the leaders of the government (the prime minister, the president, and the presidents of the two houses of parliament) all have the right to ask a nine-person Constitutional Council to rule on the constitutionality of an act of parliament. Unlike the U.S. Supreme Court, the French Constitutional Council is not the highest appellate court; it has only limited functions, and it can review the constitutionality of legislation only on substantive, not on procedural, grounds. On the other hand, the Constitutional Council has the right to review acts of parliament before they be-

BOX 9.2   REGIME CHANGE

Lawmaking by Judges: The Case of *Marbury v. Madison*

When President John Adams lost his bid for reelection to Thomas Jefferson in 1800, he did what he could to fill the offices of government with members of the Federalist Party before leaving the presidency. But not all of the new appointments could be made official before he left office. One undelivered commission was the one that made William Marbury justice of the peace for Washington, D.C. Marbury asked Jefferson's new secretary of state, James Madison—whose job it was— to deliver the commission. Madison refused, saying the new government had the right to name its own appointee to fill the post. Marbury went to court, asking for a writ of *mandamus* (a court order forcing delivery of the commission), as was his right under the Federal Judiciary Act of 1789, and counting on the partisan sympathy of Chief Justice John Marshall, also a Federalist. But Marshall ruled for Madison, on the grounds that the Federal Judiciary Act of 1789 was itself an unconstitutional invasion of the appointment rights of the executive branch by the legislative branch.

Well satisfied, the new government accepted the ruling, but in doing so helped Marshall establish the precedent for **judicial review,** the right of the courts to review the nation's laws to ensure that they are in accordance with the Constitution. This gave the courts a power they had not in fact been given under the original constitution, and initiated a major regime change. By taking a power for himself and the U.S. Supreme Court which was far more important than maintaining his party's control over the minor office of justice of the peace for Washington, D.C., Marshall made it possible for the U.S. judiciary in general—and for nine nonelected men and women in particular—to exercise far more control over the course of U.S. legislation and policy than the founders had ever dreamed of giving them.

Source: Kay Lawson, *The Human Polity,* 4th ed. (Boston: Houghton Mifflin, 1997). Reprinted by permission.

come law, and its powers are carefully spelled out in the French constitution— two advantages denied the U.S. court.[20]

Assuming the power to scrutinize the work of the legislature is not the only way judges become involved in the making of laws. Under the terms of many nations' constitutions, the chief executive has the power to appoint the highest-ranking judges. Not infrequently, when the right of such an executive to issue a particular decree is challenged, the matter will end up in court. Judges who owe their appointments to powerful executives are unlikely to be fully impartial in their rulings at such times.

SUMMARY AND CONCLUSION

Oliver Wendell Holmes once said, "When I think of the law, I see a princess mightier than she who once wrought at Bayeux, eternally weaving into her web dim figures of the ever-lengthening past—figures too dim to be noticed by the idle, too symbolic to be interpreted except by her pupils, but to the discerning eye disclosing every painful step and every world-shaking contest by which mankind has worked and fought its way from savage isolation to organic social life." [21]

As Justice Holmes's compelling imagery suggests, the law never exists *ab ovo* (a useful Latin term meaning "from the egg"—that is, as if with no other beginning) but is made, and remade, in all kinds of places, for all kinds of purposes. Furthermore, contrary to Holmes (who was, after all, making an address to a bar association dinner and was not above flattering his audience), we have seen that it is not always made by those with the grace and authority of mighty princesses, or by those who are constitutionally responsible, or even by those who are responsive to the needs of ordinary citizens.

We have also seen that even when the lawmaking function is exercised predominantly in representative legislatures designed for that purpose, the exact division of labor is likely to vary. There may be one or two houses, specialized or nonspecialized committees, and a host of customs and mores unique to each nation to determine what laws can be made, how, and by whom.

In all probability, however, the right to make a nation's laws will not be held exclusively by the legislature but will be shared—to a greater or lesser extent—with others outside that body. The executive almost always plays a role in making as well as executing the law, and judges, party leaders, religious authorities, corporation heads, and military chiefs of staff may also feel obliged to join the work of lawmaking when the circumstances make it possible for them to do so.

Furthermore, when legislative power is shared with the executive, the balance of power between the two branches differs according to whether it is a democratic or a nondemocratic system. In a democratic system, it makes a great deal of difference whether we are talking about a parliamentary system, where power may be shared fairly equally; a presidential system, where power is likely to shift back and forth between the two; or a presidential-parliamentary system, where the executive tends to take and keep the upper hand. In all three such systems the question of who will make the law is decided in part permanently and deliberately, mandated by constitutional provision, and in part temporarily and almost accidentally, as legislators delegate others to perform tasks that were originally theirs—or simply allow such powers to drift into others' hands. In nondemocratic systems, on the other hand, legislators may share the right to make a nation's laws reluctantly and resignedly—or even give up such rights altogether—when an autocratic or oligarchic executive forcibly usurps powers that do not constitutionally belong to that branch.

In pointing out how active a role the executive plays in the making of laws, we have already had quite a bit to say about the executive powers of governments. It is time now to focus directly on that subject. Laws mean little or nothing until someone carries them out. What does it mean to execute the law? The next chapter is an attempt to answer that question.

Selected Readings

Congressional Quarterly Press. *Congress, A to Z: A Ready Reference Encyclopedia.* Washington, D.C.: Congressional Quarterly Press, 1993. A useful reference book describing the organizational structure of Congress, the legislative process, and important members and issues.

George, Stephen, ed. *Britain and the European Community: The Politics of Semi-Detachment.* New York: Oxford University Press, 1992. A collection of writings examining the domestic policy conflicts faced by the British government since Britain joined the European Community.

Hickock, Eugene W. Jr., and Gary L. McDowell. *Justice vs. Law: Courts and Politics in American Society.* New York: Free Press, 1993. The authors argue that controversial policy issues that should be addressed by Congress are being left to the U.S. Supreme Court to decide.

McWhinney, Edward. *Supreme Courts and Judicial Law-making: Constitutional Tribunals and Constitutional Review.* Dordrecht, Netherlands: Martinus Nijhoff, 1986. A comparative jurisprudential study of supreme courts and their lawmaking role in France, Canada, Japan, Germany, and the United States.

Rhodes, R. A. W., and Patrick Dunleavy. *Prime Minister, Cabinet and Core Executive.* New York: St. Martin's, 1995. An introduction to the roles of the prime minister and the cabinet in British government.

Spitzer, Robert J. *President and Congress: Executive Hegemony at the Crossroads of American Government.* New York: McGraw-Hill, 1993. A historical study of the relationship between presidents and Congress with a focus on the formation of policy and legislation.

Westlake, Martin. *A Modern Guide to the European Parliament.* London: Pinter, 1994. An in-depth study of the European Parliament and the changes it has undergone as a result of the ratification of the Treaty of Maastricht.

Notes

1. U.S. Code, 1976 ed., title XX, sec. 1145b.
2. Affirmative action laws were in fact changed by such procedures in the 1990s.
3. Michael Crowder, *West Africa: An Introduction to Its History* (London: Longman, 1977), p. 155.
4. "A cabinet is a combining committee, a *hyphen* which joins, a *buckle* which fastens, the legislative part of the state to the executive part of the state." Walter Bagehot, *The English Constitution* (London: Oxford University Press, 1867), p. 12. Italics in original.
5. In a comparative study of several presidential and quasi-presidential systems, Matthew Soberg Shugart has shown that the president's party's share of legislative seats tends to be reduced after midterm elections and in systems where electoral laws permit legislative candidates to function independently of their parties (that is, are "localizing rather than nationalizing"). "The Electoral Cycle and Institutional Sources of Divided Presidential Government," *American Political Science Review* 89, no. 2 (June 1995): 327–44.

6. The U.S. presidential system has an intermediate step: the Electoral College. Each state chooses electors, who meet and vote. It is now understood (and in many states, mandated by law) that the electors will all vote for the candidate who won the majority of that state's popular vote. The number of electors each state has is based on its population.

7. John Felton, "A Policy Confrontation on China?" *Congressional Quarterly Weekly*, 14 June 1989, 1564, and *New York Times*, 12 Nov. 1994, 6. In mid-1995, James B. Steinberg, director of the Policy Planning Staff of the U.S. Department of State, confirmed the new policy: "Russia and China are no longer our ideological or strategic adversaries," he said, adding, "While we feel deep frustration at our limited progress in securing human rights in China . . . we must make sure the response we adopt will help achieve our goal." *U.S. Department of State Dispatch* 6, no. 19 (8 May 1995): 392.

8. Ulf Lundvik, "Sweden," in *International Handbook of the Ombudsman*, ed. Gerald E. Caiden (Westport, Conn.: Greenwood Press, 1983), pp. 179–81.

9. This is also the sense of the word behind the phrase *in camera*, referring to proceedings of legislative or judicial bodies held in secrecy.

10. For the work of committees in the U.S. Congress, see Malcolm Shaw, "Committees in Legislatures," in *Legislatures*, ed. Philip Norton (Oxford: Oxford University Press, 1990), especially pp. 258–59.

11. For an interesting recent discussion of a similar system, see Austin Mitchell, "The New Zealand Way of Committee Power," *Parliamentary Affairs* 46, no. 1 (Jan. 1993): 9–19.

12. Alex N. Dragnich and Jorgen Rasmussen, *Major European Governments*, 7th ed. (Homewood, Ill.: Dorsey, 1986), p. 133. In a detailed study of the committee systems of eight nations, Malcolm Shaw has ranked the relative importance of these bodies to the work of their legislatures as follows (from most to least important): the United States, Italy (pre-1994), Germany (pre-reunification), Philippines (pre-1972), Canada, Britain, India, and Japan (pre-1993). On the basis of these eight cases, he demonstrates that committees are strongest in political systems where parties are weakest, where presidents are strongest (presidential or quasi-presidential systems), and where bills are debated in committee before being given full debate on the floor of the house. Shaw's findings suggest that committees, if given the chance to formulate the terms of debate in the absence of strong party leadership, can be effective ways for legislatures to reestablish some of the power otherwise lost to chief executives. Shaw, "Committees in Legislatures," pp. 237–67.

13. Henry L. Bretton, *The Rise and Fall of Kwame Nkrumah* (New York: Praeger, 1966), pp. 50–51, 107. Nkrumah's powers in other domains included the right to detain anyone he suspected of disloyalty without trial or appeal; the right to appoint and remove all judges of the superior courts; and the right to appoint, promote, dismiss, and discipline members of the civil service.

14. Cynthia McClintock, "Peru's Fujimori: A Caudillo Derails Democracy," *Current History* (Mar. 1993): 112–19.

15. Ibid.

16. *New York Times*, 2 Mar. 1991, A3.

17. *Washington Post*, 14 Jan. 1992, A16.

18. Steven Pressman, "Abortion Politics," *California Journal* 20 (Oct. 1989): 395–97;
Joan Biskupic, "Pennsylvania Case Portends New Attack on Abortion," *Congressional Quarterly Weekly Report* 50, no. 4 (25 Jan. 1992): 169–71. Note also the entry
of the courts into the latest battles over affirmative action law: See the decision
of the U.S. District Court of Appeals for the District of Columbia Circuit to prevent the Federal Communications Commission from giving companies owned
by women or minorities special advantages in the acquisition of licenses for new
wireless telephone and data services, mentioned in note 2 above. Andrews, *New
York Times,* sec. A22.
19. Theodore McNelly, *Politics and Government in Japan,* 2nd ed. (Boston: Houghton
Mifflin, 1984), p. 149.
20. For a good discussion of the Constitutional Council, see William Safran, *The
French Polity,* 4th ed. (White Plains, N.Y.: Longman, 1995), pp. 216–20.
21. Oliver Wendell Holmes, "The Law," an address before the Suffolk Bar Association Dinner, 5 Feb. 1885. Reprinted in his *Collected Legal Papers* (New York: Peter
Smith, 1952), p. 27. "She who once wrought at Bayeux" refers to Joan of Arc.

10 Running the Government: Executives and Bureaucrats

H ere you are, reading this book, trying to get caught up on your homework. Suddenly it occurs to you (and not for the first time, either): I'd like to stop all this studying and start doing. I'd like to be active in politics and get into government. And I'd like to be a real leader, too, not just one of those bureaucrats.

Well, why not? But let's be practical. Let's think this thing through. So take a piece of paper. First, jot down the steps you might take to get into a position of political leadership. Second, make a list of what you think your duties will be once you have arrived at the top.

Now let's give a little more thought to those poor despised bureaucrats. After all, it could just happen that you might never make it to the presidency, might even find yourself in a bureaucratic job. Isn't that a terrible thought? After all, what did any bureaucrat ever do for you?

Better turn that piece of paper over and add a few more notes. First, get it out of your system: Write down ten bad things that never would have happened to you (or a friend or a relative) if it hadn't been for "one of those bureaucrats." Now for the hard part: Write down ten good things that never would have happened *for* you (or a friend or a relative) if it hadn't been for "one of those bureaucrats." And, finally, the *really* hard part: can you think of anything good—for a *polity*— about having a bureaucracy? Put that piece of paper in a safe place, please. And then do me one more favor—read this chapter before you hit the campaign trail.

BECOMING A LEADER

There are four main ways to become a leader: by ascription, by appointment, by election, and by force. Although they may be combined in actual practice, we look at each separately.

Ascription

In some societies the route to power is open only to those who possess certain characteristics. If they are believed to have those characteristics (that is, if those characteristics are *ascribed* to them), they may become leaders; if not, they cannot. In the most extreme case, the characteristic is something one—and only one—person has by birth. The system of hereditary monarchy, which ensures that only one person can be "next in line," is the most obvious example; there are still over thirty reigning monarchs in the world (see Table 10.1). Of course, the word *reigning* must not be taken literally for those in Western parliamentary democracies (see Chapter 9), and indeed the marital shenanigans of the British heir apparent and his spouse provoked many in that nation to question whether an ascriptive monarchy really is appropriate in lands where the important decisions are all made by elected representatives.[1]

A slightly different definition of **ascription** is offered by Talcott Parsons and Edward Shils, who say it means assigning people to leadership positions (as well as giving them other forms of differential treatment) on the basis of their attributes (including the groups they belong to and the wealth they possess) rather than on the basis of anything they have accomplished.[2]

If this is confusing, then let's try again. What Parsons and Shils mean by ascription is simply that in some systems in order to be chosen for a leadership role you have to be the "right" sort of person, belong to the "right" group (ethnic group, kinship group, social club, geographic community, or other type of "collectivity") or have the "right" kind and quantity of belongings. In such societies, you belong to the pool from which leaders are chosen if you meet the appropriate ascriptive standards; if you do not, nothing you can do to show your ability to perform the job will make any difference.[3]

As Parsons and Shils point out, all polities—even the most democratic—specify and abide by some measure of ascription. Age is the obvious example. Despite biblical injunction and the occasional coronation of an infant, no people really allows a little child to lead them.[4] Criteria of race, ethnicity, sex, and geographic community are also very common, even in systems that claim otherwise. Write to me when the United States chooses an Asian woman from the small state of Delaware as its president, and I will happily eat my words.

As all this suggests, ascriptive criteria in most cases simply narrow the pool of possible leaders. Moving into a leadership role is still likely to depend on being appointed, being elected, or exercising force.

Appointment

Although some form of election, however rigged or manipulated it may be, is employed in choosing the top leadership of almost every nation, nearly every system fills a large number of its lesser leadership positions by appointment. When this happens, some of the interesting questions are: What kinds of posi-

TABLE 10.1   Ascriptive Power: Monarchs in the Modern World[a]

Bahrain:	Sheikh Isa bin Sulman al-Khalifa (emir since 1971)
Belgium:	King Baudouin Albert Charles Leopold Axel Marie Gustave (1951)
Bhutan:	The Druk Gyalpo Jigme Singhye Wangchuk, King of Bhutan (1972)
Brunei:	H. M. Sultan Haji Hassanal Bolkiah (1968)
Denmark:	Queen Margrethe II (1972)
Great Britain:	Queen Elizabeth II (1952)
Japan:	Emperor Akihito (1989)
Jordan:	King Hussein ibn Talal (1953)
Kuwait:	Sheikh Jaber al-Ahmad al-Jaber al-Sabah (1977)
Liechtenstein:	Hans-Adam II (1989)
Lesotho:	King Letsie III (1990)
Luxembourg:	Grand Duke Jean (1964)
Monaco:	Prince Rainier III (1949)
Morocco:	King Hassan II (1961)
Nepal:	King Birendra Bir Bikram Sha Dev (1975)
Netherlands:	Queen Beatrix Wilhemina Armgard (1980)
Norway:	King Harald (1991)
Oman:	Sultan Qaboos bin Said (1970)
Qatar:	Sheikh Khalifa bin Hamad al-Thani (1972)
Saudi Arabia:	King Fahd ibn Abdul Aziz (1982)
Spain:	King Juan Carlos I (1975)
Swaziland:	King Mswati III (1986)
Sweden:	King Carl XVI Gustav (1973)
Thailand:	King Bhumibol Adulyadej (1946)
Tonga:	King Taufa'Ahau Tupou IV (1965)

[a]As of 1993. There are also seven sheikhdoms in the United Arab Emirates, whose rulers were installed between 1948 and 1990.
Source: Derived from Geoffrey Smith, "Must Royals Take a Back Seat?" *World Monitor* (Mar. 1993): 36–41. Reprinted by permission.

tions are filled by appointment? Who gets to do the appointing? What motivates the appointing party to appoint one person rather than another?

Kinds of Positions Filled by Appointment. A great deal of variation is found from one polity to the next in the kinds of positions that are filled by appointed officials, but as a general rule we may say that the more specialized the position—that is, the more the job in question requires a high degree of a limited kind of expertise—the more likely it will be filled by appointment rather than by election. The voters of the German state of Hesse may be competent enough to choose their chief executive, the ministerpräsident, but the Hessian minister of finance must be chosen—or so the reasoning goes in the selection of specialists across the globe—far from the heat of electoral competition and as much as possible on the basis of expertise rather than personal attractiveness or other characteristics.[5]

There is another rule for determining which positions will be filled by appointment: The more autocratic the regime, the greater the use of the appointment power. The reason for this is obvious; one of the best ways to stay in power is to control who works for you and to make sure they understand to whom they owe their jobs. It is thus not surprising that Jerry Rawlings, who has twice taken over the government of Ghana by military coup, keeps the right to appoint high-ranking members of the civil and police services for himself. Nor are leaders of ostensibly democratic regimes immune to the temptation to enhance their power by using the power of appointment to the utmost. When Vladimir Meciar, head of the Movement for a Democratic Slovakia, managed to return to the position of prime minister in Slovakia in 1994 after having been removed earlier in the year, he quickly made sure his own supporters were put in charge of all the major appointive offices (including the Supreme and Constitutional Courts).[6]

Who Appoints? The simple answer to this question is that **political appointments** are made by those already in leadership positions. As usual, the simple answer is a little bit too simple. In the first place, sometimes the appointment is preordained by law and need not be made by anyone. This is the case when the law states that people who occupy one position are ex officio (that is, owing to the office) entitled to occupy another position. The governor of the state of California is always a member of the Board of Regents of the University of California. The voters elect the governor; the fact of being governor secures the incumbent appointment to the Board of Regents.

And even when appointments are made by other leaders rather than by force of law, the answer to the question "Who appoints?" is not always an easy one. It is often the case that more than one leader will be involved in the making—or the blocking—of a major appointment. Watching our own presidents anxiously awaiting senatorial confirmation of their choices for their cabinet or for Supreme Court vacancies gives us a recurrent example of appointments that require the concurrence of many individuals beyond the person whose job it is to suggest a nominee. Never was this clearer than in the 1991 confirmation of Clarence Thomas as justice of the U.S. Supreme Court by a vote of 52 to 48 in the U.S. Senate, after days of nationally televised debate over the testimony of law professor Anita F. Hill that Thomas had subjected her to continued sexual harassment when she was his employee.[7]

Motives Guiding Appointments. Suppose you have just been elected governor of your state and you have several important appointments to make when you assume office. While the world waits, an inquiring reporter asks you what motives will guide you in your choices. Having just won an election, you are probably smart enough to answer, "I am simply looking for the most capable man or woman to fill every single post." But both you and the reporter know full well there is more to it than that.

This is not to say, however, that finding qualified persons is of no concern to the leader with the power to appoint other leaders. Most elected or appointed officials have agendas they believe in and want the best possible people to help them carry them out. Furthermore, how well or how badly one's appointees perform inevitably reflects on one's own record in office.

But other motives are also at work. We have already considered (see p. 220) the motive of enhancing one's own control by filling appointive posts with as many supporters as possible. Appointing a particular person to high position may also send a special signal regarding what the executive intends to have happen next. When Russian president Boris Yeltsin appointed Yegor T. Gaider as acting prime minister in June 1992, his doing so was interpreted internationally as a signal of commitment to serious and rapid reform, because Gaider had been the chief architect of the nation's new economic reform program.[8] The appointment by the British of Chris Patten, a "political heavyweight" with the personal backing of Prime Minister John Major, to be governor of Hong Kong shortly before the 1997 deadline for the return of that colony to Chinese control, was seen as a way to send a strong message to the Chinese government regarding the British determination to protect its own interests. As one journalist put it, "Patten's resumé includes something the Chinese recognize as *guanxi*, or connections."[9]

The power to appoint is also the power to reward. Appointments frequently go to those who have worked hard (or contributed heavily) to secure the election of the officeholder. For many years the office of postmaster general in the United States traditionally went to the chairman of the party whose nominee won the presidency. Ambassadorships are often meted out to the close friends and associates of the chief executive—or to *their* friends and associates. When the late Pamela Harriman was appointed ambassador to France in 1993, the widow of Governor Averell Harriman of New York owed the honor partly to her reputation as someone who "knew and understood the inner workings of government," but her principal qualification was clearly her status as "the doyenne of Democratic politics and [as] a leading fund-raiser and donor."[10] Lower-level posts are also open to loyal supporters of party politics. Among Western democracies, the bureaucracies of Italy and Israel have been particularly open to political appointment, but the practice has not been unknown in the United States. It is said that Abraham Lincoln, on taking office in 1860, found it necessary to give 1,457 of the 1,639 available posts to party loyalists.[11]

Finally, an appointment may well be motivated by the desire to co-opt someone whose support one seeks but does not yet have. **Co-optation** is sometimes used on erstwhile enemies, as when newly elected Mexican president Ernesto Zedillo appointed a member of the opposition Partido Acción Nacional (PAN) as the new attorney general in 1995.[12] Others may use appointments to co-opt those who are not yet either friends or enemies but who would be useful to have as the former.

One of the advantages—for the appointing officer, not for the appointee—of placing someone in office by appointment is that the process often works both ways: The person appointed can also be removed. When José Lutzenberger, an outspoken advocate of environmental causes in Brazil, became a liability—"his outspokenness enraged conservatives and his distaste for administration alienated environmentalists"—he was dismissed from his post as secretary of the environment by President Fernando Collor de Mello just a few weeks before the United Nations Conference on Environment and Development held in Rio de Janeiro in June 1992.[13]

Election to Office

We have already given some consideration in Chapter 6 to the different rules and regulations that govern voting throughout the world, but our focus there was on what these differences meant to individual participation in the political life of a nation. In Chapter 8 we looked at elections again, this time focusing on political parties and the media. Here our concern is with election as a means of achieving a position of leadership and with how the nature of different electoral systems influences the quality of leadership as well as the quality of citizenship throughout the human polity.

The best way to understand how the circumstances surrounding elections influence the quality of leadership is to imagine yourself a candidate in various systems. Getting elected is not just a matter of getting the most votes. Write-in candidacies are seldom allowed, and where permitted they are seldom successful. You must get on the ballot to have a good chance of becoming a leader through the electoral process. This usually means that you must meet certain personal standards of age and residency. It may very well mean that you must have been nominated by an officially recognized political party—and not all parties find it easy to win and keep that recognition. In single-party systems the would-be candidate has only one place to turn.

In any case, winning a party's nomination means going through a completely separate battle for leadership status before you can even think about competing for government office. If who gets the nomination is controlled by a primary election, your job is to win votes at the polls. But if the party itself decides who its candidate will be—as is the case in most political systems, the American primary election being an exception—then winning the nomination usually means building a record of loyalty to the party and of hard work on its behalf. The party may expect you to have shown you can muster an adequate campaign fund and a personal organization of devoted followers—or perhaps such assets will be seen as liabilities, suggestive of excessive pride and independence. Then there are personal characteristics to consider. Winning the nomination is very likely to mean being a member of the gender, the religious group, and the ethnic group your party is looking for this year. It may mean having the right kind of family life as well as being a good speaker and reasonably attractive to look at—not to mention being smart enough, educated enough, tough enough, nice enough, and well balanced enough, to endure the ordeals of candidacy without having a nervous breakdown.

Or perhaps you are seeking a nonpartisan post. More than 50 percent of elected officials in the United States have gained their posts through nonpartisan elections—that is, elections in which parties are not allowed to participate.[14] Such elections are particularly common at the local level. In such a case you may still have to show support by presenting a petition signed by a minimum number of your fellow citizens who are willing to assert that the world (or at least Fairview City) will be a better place if you are allowed to run for office. To become a candidate, you must be able to get those signatures. In most countries you must also be able to pay a filing fee, which may or may not be refundable if you win a certain percentage of the vote.

The question of money is, of course, another major consideration. Campaigns are always costly, no matter where they take place. In some systems those costs are covered, wholly or in part, by the government. In others, the parties are able to cover a major portion of their candidates' expenses. Private interests may fill a candidate's coffers, but as we have seen, they are likely to expect something in return.

As should be clear by now, the preliminary stages of the electoral struggle are likely to eliminate vast numbers of able potential leaders from waging, much less winning, the battle for votes. But let us say that you have nonetheless managed to get on the ballot and amass the funds to run an adequate campaign. At this point, the features of the electoral system we discussed in Chapter 6 are likely to make themselves felt. If you are campaigning in a system in which extensive personal and impersonal restrictions are placed on the right to vote, you will have to be able to fit your appeal to the relatively narrow interests of the voting population. On the other hand, if you are campaigning in a large and heterogeneous system in which nearly every adult has the right to register and vote, you must be the kind of candidate who can find and take positions with a broad appeal and who is willing to let more divisive issues fall by the wayside.

Similarly, it makes a difference whether you are running in a single-member constituency or under a system of proportional representation (see Chapter 6). If you are one of several representatives to be chosen in your district and the candidate of one party among many, you will be busy calculating what percentage of the vote you or your party will have to win for you to gain office. If you are running in a single-member district, you will want to know if there are provisions for a runoff, and if so, what it will take for you to get into that runoff.

In short, the nature of the electoral system influences the calculations the candidate will make, the kind of campaign he or she will wage, and—given varying abilities to run the necessary kind of campaign—the quality of the leaders who are ultimately chosen.

Force

The reasons that have been given for taking power by force—or for trying to do so—are many and varied; but prime among them, even though rarely mentioned, is likely to be the belief that other routes to leadership are closed. Political systems that pose excessively narrow ascriptive criteria for the pool of potential leaders, that fail to use the powers of appointment to maintain and broaden support, that keep large numbers of voting-age adults off the electoral rolls, or that manipulate election results to suit the purposes of incumbent leaders are clearly more likely than others to be considered illegitimate and thus deserving of overthrow by force.

Often, of course, those who exercise force do so only in order to take (or repossess) power with little concern for moral justification. A time of rapid change often gives the advantage to those with the greatest armed might, as several of the former states of the Soviet Union have discovered in recent years: The governments of Tajikistan, Turkmenistan, Uzbekistan, Kazakhstan, and the Ukraine were all accused of using force to oppress dissent in the early 1990s.[15] At other times the decision to substitute force for other forms of power is more surprising: We have already noted (see Chapter 9) the case of President Alberto Fujimori, who, not satisfied with being elected to office, staged a coup against his own government.[16]

But not all assassinations, coups d'état, and revolutions have been motivated solely by the ambitions of those who ended up taking power. Sometimes the new leader does not take part in the act of force at all but simply finds a way to turn a complex situation to his or her advantage and then, once in power, shows little sign of sharing the values of those who accomplished the forceful overthrow of the previous government. Shakespeare's characterization of Mark Antony—as a bystander who publicly laments the murder of Julius Caesar by others while calculating how to turn it to his own advantage—has had more than one real-life parallel in the twentieth century.[17]

Indeed, assassinating a leader is often just one way to ensure that one's own life will be forfeit and that the next head of state will turn out to be someone ready to carry out the murdered leader's program. U.S. president Lyndon Johnson, Egyptian president Hosni Mubarak, and Nigerian supreme military commander Olusegun Obasanjo all came to power as a result of the murderous acts of others, and all made every effort to carry on the plans of the leaders they replaced. Any innocent successor who shows signs of doing otherwise is likely to be in serious trouble—remember that Andrew Johnson, who came to power when Abraham Lincoln was assassinated and who then began to take a softer line with the defeated South than Lincoln's supporters believed their fallen hero would have done, was the only president ever to be impeached by the U.S. House of Representatives.[18] The principle applies to leaders in the other branches of government as well. When the Mafia crime syndicate had a well-known Sicilian judge assassinated in 1992 for his unrelenting efforts to bring its leaders to trial and imprisonment, the result was to catalyze anti-Mafia sentiment among the general population of that beleaguered Italian island as never before.[19]

A successful coup d'état or revolution (revolution provokes a far more extensive change than a coup, which is largely confined to changing the top leadership of a regime) is a more effective means of ensuring that leadership will be transferred into sympathetic hands, if not into those that held the gun. Political coups are led by politicians of all political persuasions: Fidel Castro of Cuba, the Ayatollah Ruholla Khomeini of Iran, and Vaclav Havel of the Czech Republic all came to power as the result of successful coups d'état or revolutions. In 1992, the Algerian military backed a coup designed to prevent a Muslim fundamentalist takeover of the democratic government—but that takeover would have been via democratic elections! [20]

However, coups d'état do not always produce the expected results. One of the most remarkable stories of achieving power by force can be found in the career of Boris Yeltsin, president of the Russian Federated Republic in the new Commonwealth of Independent States. The force that brought Yeltsin to power was not his; it was, in fact, exercised by persons in deep opposition to everything he stood for. But when Yeltsin and his supporters succeeded in rousing sufficient public support to doom the efforts of right-wing plotters to overthrow the government of then Soviet president Mikhail S. Gorbachev, it was he who proved the hero of the day and the ultimate winner of power, not the visibly shaken Gorbachev, whose inability to predict and prevent his own arrest by the rebels led to the further diminishment of his already shaky reputation. In the unraveling of the coup, the government *did* fall, but not into the hands of those who had instigated it.[21]

Wars are seldom fought simply to place certain people in power, but it is not unusual for them to be waged to remove an existing leadership, as the first step to ensuring a more favorable policy toward the invading nation. Iran invaded Iraq in the summer of 1982 with the avowed purpose of "liberating" that nation from the "infidel" rule of President Saddam Hussein, and many believed—erroneously, as it proved—that the United States would not end its intervention in Arab politics during the Gulf War of 1991 until it had finished what Iran had left undone.[22]

In some situations the threat of force is sufficient to change the occupants of leadership roles. A minimum of force was exercised in the ouster of Ferdinand Marcos from the presidency of the Philippines in 1986; the knowledge that the U.S. government expected him to leave and was ready to add its military might to the limited arms of his local opposition if necessary was quite sufficient to persuade the corrupt and unpopular Marcos to depart. The departure of the communist leaders of eastern Europe was also accomplished in most cases by the threat rather than the exercise of violence against their persons, the 1989 Christmas Day execution of Romanian President Nicolae Ceauşescu providing the noteworthy exception.

WHAT CHIEF EXECUTIVES DO

We take it more or less for granted that the most important person in any political system is that nation's **chief executive** officer, be it president or prime minister or head of the military junta. However, when you stop and think about it, isn't it a little bit strange—at least in democratic systems—that so much emphasis should be placed on that one leader? After all, in democratic systems the chief executive is simply supposed to see to the carrying out of laws that others have made, right?

Wrong. We have already seen that in nation after nation the chief executive plays an important role in initiating and formulating the bills that the legislature will eventually enact into law and in rallying public support for the policies that

Chief executives also speak to other nations on behalf of the interests of their own country. Here South African president Nelson Mandela speaks in London in July 1996, seeking to promote British business interest in investing in his nation.

(AP/Wide World Photos)

are explicit or implicit in those laws. The chief executive's role as chief executor of the laws is almost always less significant than his or her role as partner in the making of those laws. And it is the combination of those roles—a combination normally found only in chief executives and their immediate staffs—that gives these leaders the power they have.

It is, however, the second aspect, the literal "executing" role of chief executives, that concerns us here. And having said that the executing role is less significant than the legislating role, I must immediately make clear that it is nevertheless a far from negligible task. The three principal *executive* tasks of the chief executive are to make appointments, oversee the bureaucracy, and guide public opinion. We have already covered the first (pp. 218–22); we turn now to the other two.

Overseeing the Bureaucracy

Once they have made their appointments, chief executives are responsible for keeping a constant eye on the activities and accomplishments of the people they have appointed. Overseeing that bureaucracy—the public employees whose job it is to carry out the laws of the land—is a task normally shared (not always easily and cooperatively) by the chief executive and the legislative committee responsible for the particular laws being carried out. Carrying his or her share of the surveillance burden is one of the most difficult and thankless tasks any president, prime minister, or other chief executive must face. Contrary to what might at first be expected, the problem is not just making sure that enough work gets done; it is also trying to keep too much useless work from being done. Bureaucrats are very much like other workers; some simply want to get through the day with as little effort as possible, but others—perhaps the majority—want to do their work well, so well that they will be praised, promoted, and put in charge of other bureaucrats. Hard-working bureaucrats do not want to be overseen; they want to be encouraged to do more of what they think they do best.

These very natural human tendencies are found in nearly every workplace but cause special problems when the workplace is a government office. In government, one important aspect of the normal relationship between management and the workforce is reversed. In private business, the managers have usually been around a lot longer than most of the people they manage; in government, the newcomers are more often found in management and the oldtimers in the workforce.[23] The new executives are imposed on the bureaucratic workforce by a powerful outside body that usually has little expertise in the actual business of government—that is, by the voters or the leaders of a coup d'état.

Having the right to bring in new management—which is what voters do every time they elect a new president or change the balance of power in a parliament and thereby force the selection of a new prime minister—is an essential element of the democratic process. Even when the new management is brought in by force, it can sometimes produce salutary results if the ousted government was more authoritarian and more remote from the people's will than its successors are. In any system, new managers may be more up to date in their area of specialization, more politically sophisticated, and more in touch with the popular will than the managers they replace. On the other hand, the imposition of new management by nonexperts can also mean that inexperienced and temporary top managers will be unable to exercise full control over an experienced and self-aggrandizing workforce.

Chief executives cannot oversee every department personally. There were, for example, 2,971,357 people employed in the U.S. federal government in 1994.[24] Their natural inclination is to establish some sort of administrative office to help with the task or to ask the legislature to set up such an agency. This is especially true when new problems must be solved: Consider the proliferation of environmental agencies at the state and federal level when the seriousness of environmental hazards to the planet's and our own well-being began to be recognized. Or consider the creation of the Treuhandanstalt ("trustee agency") in Germany at the time of that nation's reunification, an agency whose sole mission was to oversee the transfer to private ownership of the more than 8,000 state-owned enterprises in eastern Germany.[25]

Guiding Public Opinion

Another chore that falls to chief executives is one for which they are often far better qualified: rallying the public in support of the decisions they or other government leaders make. Making one's way to any nation's top executive post almost always means mastering the art of persuasion. Richard Neustadt has pointed out the importance of this role for presidents of the United States; an American president must, he says, "be effective as a teacher to the public." Neustadt identifies four ways presidential teaching is different from classroom teaching. First, there is no captive audience; most of the "students" live far away and are preoccupied with their own lives. Second, these students pay attention only when they are already concerned about the matters the president wants to teach them about. Third, the president teaches more by doing (or not doing) than by talking. Fourth, their evaluation of the president's past performance always influences how susceptible citizens will be to the efforts of the chief executive to teach them anything new.[26] Neustadt could have added a fifth difference, one that perhaps seemed too obvious to mention: The position of the presidency gives its occupant a unique combination of prestige, power, and visibility, advantages that go far to overcome the disadvantages suggested in the first four points.

Although Neustadt is probably right that presidents teach more effectively by doing than by talking, chief executives around the world do offer a good deal of direct explanation to the voters, openly explaining the virtues of the policy in question and asking for support. Thus, when Great Britain was about to join the effort to force Iraq from Kuwait in the 1991 Gulf War, Prime Minister John Major personally explained why he believed this to be necessary; the cost of war, he said, would be "less than that of failing to defend principle."[27] When Jean Chrétien, prime minister of Canada, decided it was time to take steps to reduce that nation's mounting public debt, he spoke first through his finance minister, Paul Martin, who said the debt must be brought down "come hell or high water."

Then he went himself on a morning television news show, *Canada A.M.*, to prepare his listeners for the cuts he believed were essential, telling them bluntly, "Too many people have become too dependent on government."[28] Executives may also seek to prevent the development of unrealistic expectations. When former president Jimmy Carter visited North and South Korea seeking to facilitate their reunification, South Korean president Kim Young Sam spoke through his press secretary, Park Chin: "On the surface, what Mr. Carter [said] looks positive. Of course, we have heard many of these things before. Still, it seems momentum has been created."[29]

Sometimes the message the chief executive tries to get across has less to do with future policies for which he or she seeks public support than with an effort to place the effects of past policies in the best possible light. This tactic, popularly known as "spin control," depends heavily on creating spectacles that both attract the media (see Chapter 8) and carry the "right" message. It isn't easy to do, since the media are just as likely to make news out of the effort to spin as to carry the message itself—John Anthony Maltese tells how in his early months in office Bill Clinton was castigated as a "tax and spin" president, despite his carefully nonpartisan appointment of Republican commentator David Gergen as his "communications director."[30]

Refusing to Execute

In one of those paradoxes that make governments work better while confusing the people who observe them, it is common constitutional practice to give the government officials whose duty is to carry out the laws the power to refuse to do so. Chief executives very often have the right to refuse to sign—that is, to **veto**—the acts of legislatures as well as to interfere with the carrying out of judicial decisions by pardoning men and women who have been found guilty and sentenced to imprisonment or capital punishment.

Sometimes the **executive veto** is absolute, but more commonly it can be overridden if the legislature can muster the votes to pass it again by a large enough majority. According to Richard Watson, U.S. presidents have traditionally used the veto to protect the executive against legislative encroachment on its powers, to protect the constitution, or to prevent the introduction of new laws that appear administratively unworkable, fiscally unsound, or simply unwise. He points out that the U.S. Congress has not been reluctant to overrule the president. The record was set during the tenure of Harry Truman, when 37 percent of that president's vetoes were overturned by a second vote.[31]

Vetoing a bill checks the power of legislatures; a **pardon** issued to someone convicted of a crime checks the power of the judiciary. The executive right to pardon is normally extensive in theory but quite limited in practice. Pardons can be granted to those convicted of ordinary crimes when new and unusual circumstances are uncovered after the sentencing, but under such circumstances it is much more likely that the convict's lawyers will simply seek a new trial. Pardons are more commonly granted for political reasons—either to bring the governmental process into closer accord with public opinion or to curry political favor openly with particular individuals or groups. Although the latter motive is never openly acknowledged, it is often very clear, as when Argentinean president Carlos Saul Menem signed presidential pardons in late 1990 for seven of the men who had been leading protagonists of that nation's "dirty war" of internal repression in the mid-1970s. Menem was under such heavy pressure from the military to free the men that he did so despite the fact that their activities had led to the loss of over 9,000 lives and despite the anger he knew the pardons would provoke at home and abroad.[32]

THE BUREAUCRACY

If you are attending a community college, a state college, or a state university, you deal with bureaucrats every time you pay your school fees. Regardless of what kind of college you are attending, you may be paying those fees at least in part with a government loan or with financial aid from the government. You may have been to see government bureaucrats recently to arrange your transportation: to get a driver's license, a student bus ticket, or a license for your bicycle. Many of you have registered to vote. Some of you are paying income taxes. Some are married, some are divorced, and some of you have had to register the births of your children. In every case it was necessary to fill out the proper papers with the government.

The same or similar experiences are common to the lives of everyone in the human polity. A young Paraguayan decides to pursue his studies at the National University of Paraguay and fills out the necessary papers. An Indian mother decides to take the rewards offered by her government for joining its sterilization program and signs the appropriate form. A Canadian veteran decides to buy a larger house in Moosejaw, Saskatchewan, and applies for the government loan her military service has entitled her to seek. An Albanian alcoholic agrees to work on his problem and signs himself into the government hospital for treatment.

Not all bureaucratic experiences are initiated by citizens. Some of us get arrested for crimes we may or may not have committed, get drafted into armies we would prefer not to serve in, or have our paychecks garnisheed for taxes we failed to pay. If we live under a heavily authoritarian government and dare to express dissent, we may find agents of government taking over our property, getting us fired from our jobs, and even subjecting our bodies to confinement and torture.

But even if our experiences have been much less traumatic, almost all of us resent having to go through the normal bureaucratic procedures: standing in lines, submitting to interviews, filling out forms, identifying ourselves by numbers, signing everything in triplicate. **Bureaucracy** means, first and foremost, "administration of government," but it also means "governmental officialism," and the adjective **bureaucratic** is usually interpreted to mean "following an inflexible routine." When pressed, we will probably agree that we need government to help us solve some of our individual and collective problems (although we will disagree among ourselves about how much help we need) and also that we believe in "equal protection under the law"—that is, in having the laws applied to all of us in the same way. But shouldn't there be a better way than "inflexible routine" and "governmental officialism" to accomplish these goals?

Before we can consider how the world's bureaucracies might be improved, we need to know more about how they operate now. We need to look at the work of the bureaucrats, considering who they are and how they do their jobs in various nations, before we can properly consider the interesting question of whether or not there is any way to have "administration of government" without "inflexible routine."

The Work of Bureaucracy

As the work of governments grows ever more complex, the world's bureaucratic workforces grow ever more elaborate and specialized. Special agents are required for everything from inspecting nuclear power plants to supervising the artificial insemination of prize heifers on ranches receiving government subsidies. Books must be kept on expenditures of all kinds, for political campaigns in Iowa's First Congressional District, for laying transcontinental gas pipelines in Russia, for shipping kangaroos from Australia to the world's zoos. Of course, not all bureaucratic activity is domestic; a vast array of bureaucratic officialdom is devoted to foreign affairs. In our increasingly interdependent world, some nations, such as Japan and the United States, even maintain special bureaucratic corps to help foreigners develop international trade.[33]

The activities of bureaucrats, however diverse, have in common the fact that they all involve the efforts of bureaucrats to *implement* government policy. To accomplish this broader goal, it is not enough, however, simply to do the job called for by policy. Bureaucrats must also gather the funds to pay for the work of government, disburse those funds to the other bureaucrats or private-sector entrepreneurs who do that work, and see to it that no laws or rules are broken in the process. These three more specialized tasks of bureaucrats are worth a closer look.

Collecting Revenue. Bureaucrats collect the revenue necessary to do the work of government. They write up the tax forms and instruction booklets for all kind of taxes; personal income taxes, corporate income taxes, import and export duties, license fees, inheritance taxes, and taxes on purchased goods are a few of the more common ones. Taxes are levied even on illegal activities; until the practice was recently ruled unconstitutional by the Supreme Court as a form of double punishment, farmers convicted of marijuana farming in Montana were taxed "$100 an ounce or 10 percent of market value, whichever is greater."[34] Bureaucrats not only levy taxes; they also process the penalties, settle disputes (although, as in the Montana case, final appeal may be made to the judicial branch of the government), and help prepare legislation to change the laws governing the collection of taxes and other revenues.

Disbursing Government Funds. Bureaucrats also disburse government monies. They prepare the government's budget, and once it has acquired any necessary ratification from other branches or offices of the nation's government, they carry it out. They are the ones who purchase raw materials and finished goods (including all those necessary for the nation's defense establishment); pay bills; meet payrolls; process applications for government loans; pay interest on government bonds; give political parties and their candidates whatever help with campaign expenses they are entitled to by law; pay price supports to farmers; pay a wide range of social benefits, from welfare to family allowances to full medical coverage; support the United Nations and its affiliated agencies; and send foreign aid to other nations. In nations with socialist or mixed economies, bureaucrats distribute financial support to state-owned enterprises. (For the role of Eastern European bureaucrats in the transition from state-owned to private enterprises, see Box 10.1) Bureaucrats even manufacture the nation's money in the first place.

Sometimes, of course, goods rather than money are disbursed. The United States sends surplus food abroad, but the bureaucrats of poorer nations also distribute (and redistribute) goods, especially land; the bureaucrats in the Ministries of Agriculture and Construction in Ethiopia have been major (and sometimes conflicting) actors in the massive distribution of new lands to thousands of peasants suffering from drought and famine in the Wollo and Tigraye regions of that nation.[35]

Preventing or Punishing Infractions of the Law. Bureaucrats are also expected to see to it that the rules a government sets for the personal behavior of its citizens are obeyed—or at least that infractions meet with the prescribed sanctions. Some of these rules, such as laws determining what acts constitute criminal behavior, apply to everyone; others apply only to those entering into particular relationships with government.

Whether the rule is intended to prevent crime, to protect the environment, or to meet some other social goal, if it is a rule made by government, it will be the work of some bureaucrat to see that it is obeyed or to call the malefactor to account. Police officers, prosecuting attorneys, and prison administrators are bureaucrats who try to enforce laws against criminal activity; health inspectors, welfare "snoops," and government safety commissioners are bureaucrats who try to enforce laws concerning other forms of activity that policymakers have decided are desirable or undesirable. The line between the two kinds of policing is not always easily drawn; serious infringement of rules set to accomplish social goals can lead to prosecution for criminal behavior.

Subdividing the Work of Bureaucracy. Max Weber, one of the first serious students of bureaucracy, believed that in the ideal bureaucracy all tasks would be assigned carefully on the basis of *specialization* and *hierarchy.* Everyone would do the job for which he or she was best suited, every job would be specific and limited, and every bureaucrat would occupy a clear-cut place in the chain of command, with no confusion as to who had authority over whom.[36]

BOX 10.1   REGIME CHANGE

The Role of Bureaucrats in the Transition from Communist to Capitalist Economies

The regime changes that took place in the nations of eastern Europe during the 1990s placed unusually difficult burdens on the bureaucrats of these states. Although almost everyone was keen to make the switch to pure capitalism as rapidly as possible, the very difficulties that did so much to help bring the communist system down—economic mismanagement and poor competitiveness in the global market—made it difficult to find private buyers, at home or abroad, for state-owned enterprises (SOEs). During the first five years of regime change, only a fraction of each nation's industry found its way into private hands.

What can a bureaucratic manager do under such conditions, knowing that privatization is the goal yet obliged in the meantime to keep production flowing and employees paid? The difficulty was compounded by counterproductive government policies: Price controls on food and other goods were removed, causing inflation to soar, which in turn meant that demand was reduced. As a result, production was cut back, unemployment grew, business bankruptcies increased, and tax revenues from SOEs declined drastically, producing "large budget deficits and a vicious cycle of cutbacks in public spending, further declines in consumer demand, more reductions in industrial output and thus state revenue, and still greater cutbacks."

Nevertheless, some SOEs have been working hard to meet the challenge, striving to "streamline their product lines, update production, improve quality control, introduce modern cost accounting, and . . . search for new markets." Furthermore, these states are clearly having second thoughts about the policy of treating the firms they still own as if they were already privatized, denying them support when they get in trouble. In actual practice, the left hand *does* know what the right hand is doing and tries to help. State subsidies have continued to flow to "technically bankrupt" SOEs that provide crucial employment, put otherwise idle equipment to work, and are among the nation's major exporters. Some analysts now argue that since it is unlikely that the SOEs are going to disappear overnight, it is time to rationalize and legitimize this continuing state assistance. The state's role, they say, must be brought into the open, and clear-cut standards and goals for obtaining aid must be imposed. Only thus can the move to capitalism be combined with sufficient concern for the welfare of the citizens of these states during this transition.

Source: Alice H. Amsden, "Eastern Europe: Putting Some Government Back in Manufacturing," *Technology Review* 98, no. 5 (July 1995): 56. Reprinted with permission from Technology Review, published by the Association of Alumni and Alumnae of MIT, copyright © 1998.

Even Weber might be surprised if he could see how seriously modern bureaucracies have taken his advice regarding specialization. Consider, for example, the fine distinctions made between the jobs of Oven-Press Tender I and Oven-Press Tender II in the U.S. government (see Box 10.2). States that take direct control of industrial development must make an even broader range of distinctions; con-

BOX 10.2   IS TOO MUCH BUREAUCRACY SLOWING US DOWN?

573.685-042   OVEN-PRESS TENDER (asbestos prod.) I

Tends hot press and related equipment that hardens asbestos disc pads for use as brake linings; positions metal die plate on roller-type conveyor, picks up stack of asbestos disc pads from table, and places individual pads into wells of die plate. Discards broken or defective pads. Pushes filled die plates onto racks of hot press. Starts machine that automatically closes press to heat-treat pads for specified time and opens press at end of press cycle. Pulls die plates from press onto conveyor. Removes cured disc pads from die plates, using knockout device that forces pads from plates. Loosens stuck pads with rubber mallet and tosses pads into storage container. Sprays empty die plates with silicone solution, using spray gun, to prevent pads from sticking to plates during heat-treating process. GOE 06.04.19 PD M 08 09 15 17 EC 07 M1 L1 SVP 4 SOC 7675

573.685-046   OVEN-PRESS TENDER (asbestos prod.) II

Tends hot press that hardens asbestos disc pads for use as brake linings; pushes metal die plates filled with asbestos disc pads onto feed elevator of machine. Presses buttons to open press, move die plates from elevator into press, and closes press. Observes timer lights, dials, and pressure gauges on control panel of machine to determine end of press cycle. Presses buttons at end of cycle to simultaneously open press and move cured disc pads from press onto discharge elevator. Pushes die plates from elevator onto roller-type conveyor, using metal rake. GOE 06.04.19 PD M 08 09 15 EC 07 M1 L1 SVP 4 SOC 7675

Source: U.S. Department of Labor, Employment and Training Administration, *Dictionary of Occupational Titles,* 4th ed. supplement (Washington, D.C.: U.S. Government Printing Office, 1986), p. 38.

---

sider the posts assigned in the cabinet of the Chinese government, and imagine the vast responsibility of each minister in this nation of over 1 billion citizens (see Box 10.3).

Obviously, overspecialization can hinder effective performance by individuals who dare not step past the limits of their own job description. It can also make meeting Weber's second recommendation—keep the lines of authority clear—very difficult. States with highly specialized bureaucratic structures almost always find it hard to maintain clear lines of authority. The very principle of specialization suggests that the person doing the job knows best how it should be done—better than any alleged superior. As Weber himself noted, "The trained permanent official is more likely to get his way in the long run than his nominal superior [when the latter] is not a specialist."[37] Furthermore, specialization and

BOX 10.3   MINISTRIES IN THE CHINESE CABINET

Agriculture	Public Health
Chemical Industry	Public Security
Civil Affairs	Radio, Film, and Television
Coal Industry	Railways
Communications	State Commission for Economic
Construction	Restructuring
Culture	State Commission for Economic
Electronics Industry	Trade
Finance	State Commission for Education
Foreign Affairs	State Commission for Family
Foreign Economic Relations	Planning
and Trade	State Commission for Nationalities
Forestry	Affairs
Geology and Mineral Resources	State Commission for Physical
Internal Trade	Culture and Sports
Justice	State Commission for Planning
Labor	State Commission for Science and
Light Industry	Technology
Machine Building Industry	State Commission for Science,
Metallurgical Industry	Technology, and Industry for
National Defense	National Defense
Personnel	State Security
Posts and Telecommunications	Supervision
Power Industry	Water Resources

Source: Arthur S. Banks, ed., *Political Handbook of the World: 1993* (Binghamton, N.Y.: CSA Publications, 1993), p. 167. Reprinted by permission of the publisher.

hierarchy are difficult to combine, because those who specialize do not always respond well to proposals that they coordinate their work with that of other specialists. Specialization is thus likely to lead to the proliferation of bureaucratic units with overlapping jurisdictions. Resentful of competition, the person in charge of each unit may well become extremely jealous of his or her own authority, insisting on control of everything that happens within that unit and refusing to cooperate with other units in any way that might impair that authority.

Who Are the Bureaucrats?

Although we often think of bureaucrats as white-collar workers standing behind a counter with a grill or seated behind a desk, in fact any employee of a large organization is a bureaucrat, and any employee of government can therefore be called a *government bureaucrat*, including the engineers, teachers, janitors, and other specialized employees who work on the government's payroll. In practice, however, it is more useful to say that a **bureaucrat** is someone who does the administrative work of government—that is, who has responsibility for interpreting and implementing government policy, whether as the cop on the beat or the highest-ranking minister.

Taking on the role of bureaucrat also means taking on the *bureaucratic style*. To do their work, bureaucrats have developed a set of norms to guide them. The important principle here is *fairness*—or *the appearance thereof*. Whether or not the concept is enshrined in the constitution, as in the case of the United States (see the Fourteenth Amendment), every nation at least gives lip service to the ideal that the laws must be applied with equal force to every citizen; this is the *sine qua non*, the minimal requirement, of bureaucratic fairness. To accomplish this goal, bureaucrats attempt to follow the law to the letter—that is, to carry it out exactly and explicitly. Because most laws are written in language open to a wide range of interpretations, the bureaucratic solution is to write a set of rules detailing exactly how each law is to be carried out and then to attempt to follow these rules without exception. This can lead to an appearance (and in some cases a practice) of rigid, inhuman, and even ridiculous behavior on the part of some bureaucrats—the kind of behavior that leads us to use the word *bureaucratic* as a pejorative. When we ordinary citizens want something perfectly reasonable from a government office and are told by a clerk, "I'm sorry, but according to the rules it simply cannot be done," our normal response is to feel angry and frustrated and to storm out muttering, "Bureaucratic!" as if it were one of the worst terms of opprobrium. But the next time you are tempted to do that, you might stop to consider that this determination to stick to the rules *does* have its positive side, *does* mean that the clerk has been taught to adhere loyally to the principle of equal protection under the laws. There certainly may be better ways to protect that principle, but most of us would agree that protecting it is worth a few inconveniences.

How to Become a Bureaucrat

There are basically two routes to a bureaucratic position: You may be given a political appointment, or you may be hired on the basis of merit. We have discussed political appointments at length (see pp. 219–22). When bureaucrats are hired on the *basis of merit*, a number of different methods may be employed to determine the most meritorious applicant for the job. Years of experience in related tasks, years of education in relevant fields of study, and level of performance on tests designed for the job in question are some of the criteria most commonly employed.

The use of tests was common practice long before the emergence of modern bureaucracy. Passing rigorous examinations was the most honorable path to advancement for administrators in ancient China.[38] Under the Russian czar Alexander I, the law required candidates to pass examinations in Russian, mathematics, Latin, and modern languages before they could be promoted to "collegiate assessor, the eighth rank, or state councillor, the fifth rank."[39]

Specialized training for government work has become more and more important in the modern age, and without such training the elected official is likely to find it more and more difficult to interact effectively with the bureaucrats he or she is expected to guide. Some polities have established special schools to train those who aspire to high bureaucratic position. France has an entire system of *grandes écoles* (literally, "great schools") for educating its public servants, and those who are able to pass the rigorous entrance examinations for the National School of Administration (ENA) are almost always assured of a high government post upon graduation. Such training has become important for those who seek high elective posts in France as well; almost all French presidents, prime ministers, and major cabinet ministers in recent years have been either *Enarques* (the popular term for ENA graduates) or graduates of other *grandes écoles*.[40]

Success in Third World bureaucracies is also likely to depend on suitable expertise, in particular a background in global economic affairs. Nicephore Soglo, the president of Benin, was himself an official of the World Bank, and, as Victoria Brittain points out, the presidents of Cameroon, Congo, Gabon, Ivory Coast, Senegal, and Zaire have all tended to seek out "techno-politicians" with "years of experience in multi-lateral agencies" for senior appointive positions.[41]

Of course appointment by political patronage is still widely practiced in every nation in the world. However, it is rare that the executive making the appointment fails to consider the actual capabilities of the would-be bureaucrat. A new British prime minister is expected to appoint only parliamentary members of his or her own party to all the paid positions associated with the cabinet, but members of parliament who lack administrative competence for the post in question are as unlikely to be chosen as those who are deficient in personal loyalty.[42]

TOO MUCH GOVERNMENT? OR TOO LITTLE?

We human beings are difficult to please when it comes to the operation of our governments. We don't like it when the garbage is not collected, when our roads develop potholes, or when our unemployment benefits run out. We are deeply dismayed when government aid in times of natural catastrophe is slow to arrive, when "nothing is done" about inflation, or when our armies are defeated in foreign wars. On the other hand, we resent seeing our paychecks whittled away by taxes, we don't like to stand in line, we hate to fill out forms, and we detest having to answer the questions of bureaucratic busybodies. And some of us are sure that government benefits are going to all the wrong people—to "welfare cheats" or "exploiting capitalists."

Even when we admit that a bureaucratic system is a necessary part of any modern government, that after all it makes no sense to elect officials to make government policy if no one is in place to ensure that the policy is carried out, still we tend to hold the very idea of bureaucracy in contempt. Is this because we have too much bureaucracy in our lives? Or because the job of bureaucracy is poorly done? Or is it because our expectations of what can and should be done by government bureaucrats are simply unrealistic?

As you probably expect, the answer is a combination of all three, and the exact proportions in that combination vary from polity to polity.

Too Much Government

Duplication and waste are found in every domain of human effort. We need only take a critical look around our own homes to find embarrassing examples of waste—food we allowed to spoil, magazines we bought and never read, notes we made and then forgot to consult. And all of us have been known to engage in overkill—making three copies where one would do, checking ten books out of the library when we knew perfectly well only three of them were likely to be useful for that missing section in the term paper we had to write, or reminding a good friend over and over not to forget an important appointment.

What accounts for such behavior? Without troubling our fellow social scientists the psychologists for an answer, we can speculate that such behavior will be most pronounced when four conditions prevail: relative affluence (we can afford a little waste), a strong desire to reach relatively limited and particular goals (so we give tasks pertinent to those goals excessive energy and attention), nonaccountability (no one else pays much attention to these useless and wasteful activities), and failure to use common sense (we "just didn't think").

All four conditions are all too likely to prevail in the normal bureaucratic setting. First, bureaucrats find themselves in the happy position of spending other people's money—a circumstance that can easily bring a sense of relative affluence. Citing instances of rank extravagance in the Agency for International Development, Sheila Kaplan suggests the ruling motto appeared to be "Why Pay Less?"[43]

Second, most bureaucrats occupy highly specialized roles. If they are ambitious, their hopes for promotion are likely to rest on demonstrating superior performance of specific tasks. Their jobs seldom require them—or permit them—to consider means of accomplishing overall policy goals that might entail shifting energies and expenditures away from their own narrow domains. Like specialists in any large organization, they seek to use every possible means to create a praiseworthy record of accomplishment, even at the cost of duplication and waste.

Third, bureaucrats are very difficult to hold accountable. Their claims of expertise are often well founded, and their ultimate bosses—temporary elected officials—cannot always deal with them in terms that command their respect. Furthermore, any efforts to improve accountability may simply stimulate greater waste, as reports fly back and forth and efforts are made to meet—or to give the appearance of meeting—standards of efficiency set by those too remote from the tasks being performed.

Finally, it often seems especially difficult for even the best-intentioned bureaucrats to operate according to the dictates of common sense. This difficulty flows in part from two other problems in the bureaucratic world that we have already mentioned: the need to succeed within a narrowly defined domain and the absence of true accountability. Under these circumstances, the typical bureaucrat tends to operate strictly according to the rules, regardless of how patently ridiculous or unproductive the consequences of doing so may be.

Too Little Government

It is no paradox to say that we can have both too much and too little bureaucracy. At the same time that bureaucrats are busily duplicating their activities and wasting their energies, they may also be failing to do what really needs to be done—that is, putting the laws and rules that are supposed to govern the nation into actual practice. Probably more social problems persist because of a failure to implement laws already on the books than because of an absence of such legislation. Yet sometimes the failures of implementation are owing to the nature of the laws themselves. As we saw at the beginning of Chapter 9, laws are merely plans, and, like all plans, they can never be entirely complete, can never foresee all contingencies, and need elaboration and modification when it comes time to carry them out. What we so easily label *bureaucratic inefficiency* may result simply because agency officials are being asked to carry out tasks so large under conditions so difficult that normal standards of efficiency are simply impossible to meet.[44] The failure of the U.S. Food and Drug Administration to take steps to implement serious regulation of the tobacco industry prior to the appointment of David Kessler as its new commissioner in 1990 has been an interesting case in point. "We just didn't want to fool with tobacco," said a former official of the agency, stressing the power of two forces: the smoking habit and the industry itself.[45]

It would be naive, however, to deny that bureaucratic misimplementation—or nonimplementation—can also be deliberate. To understand why this is so, it is important to realize that the more power shifts to the executive branch, the more those affected by public policy shift their lobbying efforts to that branch. Bureaucrats are subject to a wide range of temptations to abandon the rules of strict neutrality that supposedly govern their work. They may be bribed to carry out their roles in ways the groups they are supposed to be regulating desire. Or they may simply find that it is suddenly remarkably easy to gain membership to distinguished private clubs or to book good seats for the theater. Perhaps they will be offered a chance of lucrative employment in the private sector when they leave government, if they have done their job "well" in the meantime.

But the most common means lobbyists employ in dealing with bureaucrats is one that is entirely legal and, on the face of it, merely supportive and useful. As already noted in Chapter 7 (p.143), they simply provide the bureaucrats with information. The information they offer will not be effective if it is too blatantly biased or inaccurate, yet inevitably it will be one sided and partial. Nevertheless, bureaucrats all over the world welcome the help and often depend on it. Close ties develop between the regulator and the regulated; the lobbyists become the "clients" of the regulators, exchanging information and services for a form of policy implementation that is sympathetic to their needs.[46] And like all good merchandisers, the bureaucrats take care of their clients, subtly (and sometimes not so subtly) shaping their interpretations of the law in such a way as to minimize inconvenience to those they oversee, even when the net result is a clear violation of legislative intent. Some have gone so far as to lobby Congress on behalf of those whose behavior they are supposed to regulate, as when U.S. Interior Secretary Manuel Lujan asked Congress to waive a key requirement of the proposed Endangered Species Act in order to save the lumber industry (instead of the spotted owl).[47] When such a pattern of misimplementation evolves, ordinary citizens suffer from both too much and too little bureaucracy. Too much is done for a privileged few, and too little is done to carry out laws originally intended to apply with equal force to all.

The widespread prevalence of this problem of **bureaucratic drift**—drift away from control by elected representatives of the people they serve and drift toward control by the very persons and organizations they are expected to guide and supervise—has led to a number of attempted reforms. In the United States, the General Accounting Office (GAO) audits the spending of other bureaus, and the Office of Management and Budget (OMB) has a management section that continually reviews the leadership, organization, and overall effectiveness of all programs submitting requests for funding. Such offices are, however, themselves part of the bureaucratic apparatus and thus are inevitably susceptible to the same viruses that sometimes infect their fellow bureaucrats. More promising means of holding bureaucrats responsible to the general public must come from the public itself. When well informed by responsible news media, well socialized to accept and carry out the duties of citizenship, and well equipped with a strong party system capable of keeping elected representatives aware and accountable to their interests, the people themselves are the surest means of ensuring bureaucratic responsiveness to the public will, as expressed in the law of the land.

SUMMARY AND CONCLUSION

This brief introduction to the many questions involved in the study of executive and bureaucratic government may have given you some further ideas about the questions we raised at the beginning of the chapter. You know now that when you are trying to persuade others to accept you as their leader, it would be helpful to have at least some of the ascriptive criteria commonly looked for in those chosen for positions of power, even if you are more interested in figuring out how to earn the approval of those who choose leaders on the basis of their proven abilities. But what kind of abilities? Will you try to develop the specialized expertise more commonly associated with taking office by appointment, or will you work instead to master a wide range of information, to make friends with all kinds of people, and to exhibit the mixture of personal stability and charm that are the essential attributes of the elected officeholder? You are probably not giving serious thought to the idea of taking power by force. Besides the fact that it is likely to be contrary to your moral principles, this tactic has a very poor record of success in recent years.

As you no doubt knew before you opened this book, the jobs of chief executives go well beyond carrying out the law. Indeed, one of their most important roles is to appoint and supervise others who will do the actual job of implementation. Another important task is to find ways to guide the formation of public opinion, using the prestige and visibility of your office to rally support for policies you believe in. You may be wondering how you would use the powers of the veto and the pardon, powers that can be used to prevent decisions made by others from being enacted.

But perhaps you will never be a top executive but will instead become a bureaucrat, a public servant with direct responsibility for interpreting and implementing government policy. As we have seen, the chores of the much-maligned bureaucrats are many and varied. Not only must they take the necessary steps to carry out policies made by others but they must also take responsibility for collecting and disbursing the revenue that makes the government's work possible and for preventing or punishing infractions of the law. So complex is the work of bureaucracy that it must be subdivided and parceled out into the hands of specialists. However, the greater the specialization, the more difficult it is to maintain clear lines of authority, because those who specialize accept the guidance of nonexperts only reluctantly.

It is possible to have too much government, but it is also possible to have too little. Duplication and waste prevail under conditions of relative affluence, intense need to reach relatively limited and particular goals, relative nonaccountability, and refusal to follow the dictates of common sense. However, poor implementation of policy can also be the result of procedures that produce conflicting results, pervert the intention of the policymakers, or regulate the activity in question right out of existence. It can be caused by inappropriate response to lobbying by an agency's "clients," by plain inefficiency, or by the overwhelming difficulty of the task.

The numerous problems associated with executive and bureaucratic government make public administration one of today's most challenging professions. Nowhere is there more need for well-qualified, well-motivated, and *persistent* men and women. Nowhere are there greater opportunities to bring about change that will have an important and salutary impact on the lives of millions. The fact that the hurdles to doing this are so many and so high only makes the challenge that much greater.

Perhaps the real question to ask today is where we will find the men and women ready and able to meet that challenge. You may simply be more certain than ever that political leadership is not for you. But please do not be too quick to dismiss the idea. After all, those who do lead have not yet shown us remarkable success in solving all the problems of the human polity. Leadership is one of the developing arts and sciences, not a fixed craft. You may have more to offer than you imagine and an ability to acquire the skills and knowledge you currently lack. After all, you *are* a student of the science of politics.

In any case, even though not all of you will join the ranks of government, all of you have reason to hope for the best possible performance by those who do. When executives and bureaucrats fail to implement policy in accordance with the laws we have set, we do have another place to turn. The function of judicial bodies is to adjudicate the disputes that arise under the implementation of the law. We examine these bodies and their work in the next chapter.

Selected Readings

Bass, Bernard M. *Stogdill's Handbook of Leadership.* 3rd ed. New York: Free Press, 1990. A comprehensive study of styles of leadership, their applications, and their implications.

Casamayou, Maureen Hogan. *Bureaucracy in Crisis: Three Mile Island, the Shuttle Challenger, and Risk Assessment.* Boulder, Colo.: Westview Press, 1993. Personal interviews and public testimony are used to illustrate how bureaucratic failures contributed to these two catastrophes.

Foley, Michael. *The Rise of the British Presidency.* Manchester, England: Manchester University Press, 1993. The author argues that personal political leadership has become increasingly important to the role of prime minister in Great Britain and compares the British prime ministership to the U.S. presidency.

Kingdom, J. E., ed. *The Civil Service in Liberal Democracies.* London: Routledge, 1990. A comparison of the civil service in six European nations and the United States.

Glentz, Harris. *Heads of State and Governments: A Worldwide Encyclopedia of Over 2300 Leaders, 1945 through 1992.* New York: McFarland, 1994. A useful source for detailed biographical information on heads of government worldwide.

Kerbel, Matthew Robert. *Beyond Persuasion: Organizational Efficiency and Presidential Power.* New York: State University of New York Press, 1991. An in-depth look at the components of presidential power in the United States.

Machiavelli, Niccolo. *The Prince.* New York: Appleton-Century-Crofts, 1947. Writing in the early sixteenth century, Machiavelli laid out pragmatic rules for taking and maintaining power without regard for the rights of others or for any other principles of moral behavior.

Neustadt, Richard E. *Presidential Power.* New York: Wiley, 1960. The classic study of the U.S. presidency, with insights still applicable today.

Watson, Richard. *Presidential Vetoes and Public Policy.* Lawrence: University Press of Kansas, 1993. A historical view of how presidents have used the veto to influence policy, including examples from recent presidencies.

Notes

1. Michael Elliott, "Why the Monarchy Must Go," *Newsweek,* 11 Mar. 1996, 24, international edition. Not only in the West—and not only in the interests of democracy—have the powers of the monarch been limited: In Cambodia the kingship has traditionally been elective, but the new constitution now says the monarch must be "a member of the Khmer Royal Family, aged at least 30 years, coming from the bloodline of the King Ang Duong, Norodom or Sisowath." William Shawcross, *Cambodia's New Deal* (New York: Carnegie Endowment for International Peace, 1994), p. 53.

2. Talcott Parsons and Edward Shils, "Orientation and Organization of Action," in *Toward a General Theory of Action,* ed. Talcott Parsons and Edward Shils (New York: Harper and Row, 1951), p. 82. Their exact definition of ascription is "the norma-

tive pattern which prescribes that an actor in a given type of situation should, in his selections for differential treatment of social objects, give priority to certain attributes that they possess (including collectivity memberships and possessions) over any specific performances (past, present, or prospective) of the objects." (Copyright © 1951 by the President and Fellows of Harvard College. Reprinted by permission of Harvard University Press.) This is a good example of the use of unnecessary jargon in the social sciences ("social objects" means people!), and I have taken the liberty of providing a translation.

3. The opposite of ascription, according to Parsons and Shils, is "achievement: the normative pattern which prescribes that an actor in a given type of situation should, in his selection and differential treatment of social objects, give priority to their specific performances (past, present or prospective) over their given attributes (including memberships and possessions), insofar as the latter are not significant as direct conditions of the relevant performances." Ibid., pp. 82–83.

4. See Isaiah 11:6, *The Holy Bible* (Boston: Massachusetts Bible Society, 1965), p. 655.

5. For the Hessian example, see David P. Conradt, *The German Polity*, 4th ed. (White Plains, N.Y.: Longman, 1989), p. 217.

6. Samuel Abraham, "Early Elections in Slovakia: A State of Deadlock," *Government and Opposition* 30, no. 1 (1995): 86–100. In this century no one has understood and used the powers of appointment for the purposes of autocracy better than Generalissimo Francisco Franco during the thirty-nine years he ruled Spain. Franco selected, appointed, and dismissed the prime minister and all ministers at will and saw to it that the occupants of other significant offices were appointed by his own appointees. Any official who had significant power to exercise did so only so long as he remained in the favor of the generalissimo. Since Franco's death in 1975, Spain has adopted a much more democratic constitution, in which appointive offices such as the president's cabinet, high judicial offices, and the Constitutional Court are carefully specified and regulated.

7. *Congressional Quarterly Weekly Report*, 49, no. 42 (19 Oct. 1991): 3026–33.

8. *International Herald Tribune*, 16 June 1992, 1.

9. Benedict Brogan, "Heavyweight in Hong Kong Ring," *The Herald* (Glasgow), 25 Apr., 1992, p. 9; Anthony Blass, "Burke's Heir," *Far Eastern Economic Review*, 22 Oct. 1992, pp. 25–26.

10. *New York Times*, 24 Mar. 1993, A7.

11. Eva Etzioni-Halevy, *Bureaucracy and Democracy* (London: Routledge and Kegan Paul, 1983), p. 164.

12. *Wall Street Journal*, 8 Sept. 1995, A11. For the widespread use of co-optation in Mexico, see also César Cansino, "Mexico: The Challenge of Democracy," *Government and Opposition* 30, no. 1 (1995): pp. 60–73.

13. *New York Times*, 11 Mar. 1992, A7.

14. Xandra Kayden and Eddie Mahe, *The Party Goes On* (New York: Basic Books, 1985), p. 43.

15. Adrian Karatnycky, "The Comparative Survey of Freedom: 1994—Freedom in Retreat," *Freedom Review* (Jan.–Feb. 1994): 4–9.

16. *Los Angeles Times*, 7 Apr. 1992, A1.

17. "Here comes his body, mourned by Mark Antony: who, though he had no hand in his death, shall receive the benefit of his dying." William Shakespeare, *Julius Caesar*, act 3, scene 2, lines 45–47.

18. Murray Clark Havens, Carl Leiden, and Karl M. Schmitt, *The Politics of Assassination* (Englewood Cliffs, N.J.: Prentice Hall, 1970). Johnson was impeached by the House but not found guilty by the Senate and so stayed in office.

19. Judge Giovanni Falcone was assassinated in Sicily on May 23, 1992. For the response of the Italian public, see *Le Monde*, 26 May 1992, 3; and *New York Times*, 26 May 1992, A3.

20. Edward Gonzalez, *Cuba under Castro: The Limits of Charisma* (Boston: Houghton Mifflin, 1974); Amin Saikal, *The Rise and Fall of the Shah* (Princeton: Princeton University Press, 1980); and Kim Murphy, "Algeria Struggles to Retain Democracy—But Can It Survive after Being Voted Out?" *Denver Post*, 1 Feb. 1992, 19A.

21. *Los Angeles Times*, 21 Aug. 1991, 1, A8–A16, and 22 Aug. 1991, 1, A7; *Current Digest of the Soviet Press* 43, no. 51 (22 Jan. 1992): 1–6.

22. "A Quest for Vengeance: Khomeini's Legions Invade Iraq and Threaten the Whole Arab World," *Time*, 26 July 1991, 18–25.

23. To be sure, private business does hire new executives from time to time and does not always promote from within. But in such cases the new executives are hired by those already in place and can be expected to have similar values and priorities. In government, however, the new executives periodically taking over the top positions are not hired by those already hard at work.

24. U.S. Bureau of the Census, *The Statistical Abstract of the United States*, 115th edition (Washington, D. C.: U.S. Bureau of the Census, 1995), p. 350.

25. *The Europa World Year Book*, vol. 1 (London: Europa Publishers, 1992), p. 1177.

26. Richard E. Neustadt, *Presidential Power* (New York: Wiley, 1961), p. 100.

27. *The Times* (London), 16 Jan. 1991, 5.

28. Craig Turner, "Canada's Leader Takes Aim at National Debt," *Los Angeles Times*, 22 Oct. 1994, A2.

29. T. R. Reid, "Two Koreas' Leaders Seek First Summit," *Washington Post*, 19 June 1994, A1.

30. John Anthony Maltese, *Spin Control: The White House Office of Communications and the Management of Presidential News* (Chapel Hill: University of North Carolina Press, 1994), pp. 232–39.

31. Richard A. Watson, *Presidential Vetoes and Public Policies* (Lawrence: University Press of Kansas, 1993), pp. 133–51. For a comparative study of the veto power, see George Tsebelis, "Decision Making in Political Systems: Veto Players in Presidentialism, Parliamentarism, Multicameralism and Multipartyism," *British Journal of Political Science* 25, no. 3 (July 1995): 289–325.

32. *New York Times*, 30 Dec. 1990, A9. "This is the saddest day in Argentine history," said former president Raul Alfonsin, under whose administration the men had been brought to trial and sentenced a mere five years earlier.

33. Ku Tashiro, "Japan," in *Public Administration in Developed Democracies*, ed. Donald C. Rowat (New York: Marcel Dekker, 1988), pp. 380–82.

34. *Washington Post*, 7 June 1994, A6.

35. Alemneh Dejene, *Environment, Famine and Politics in Ethiopia: A View from the Village* (Boulder, Colo.: Rienner, 1990), pp. 95–109.

36. Weber also believed that the rules of bureaucratic behavior should be clearly set, should be impersonal—that is, apply to all without favoritism—should be based on written documents, and should apply only at work; the private and public spheres should be clearly distinct. Max Weber, *Essays in Sociology*, trans. and ed.

H. H. Gerth and C. Wright Mills (New York: Oxford University Press, 1958), pp. 196–97.

37. Max Weber, *The Theory of Social and Economic Organization*, trans. by A. M. Henderson and Talcott Parsons (Glencoe, Ill.: Free Press, 1947), p. 338.

38. Pao Chao Hsieh, *The Government of China* (Baltimore: Johns Hopkins University Press, 1925), p. 143; E. A. Kracke Jr., "Region, Family and Individual in the Chinese Examination System," in *Chinese Thought and Institutions*, ed. John K. Fairbank (Chicago: University of Chicago Press, 1959), pp. 251–68.

39. Edward C.Thaden, *Russia since 1801: The Making of a New Society* (New York: Wiley, 1971), p. 51.

40. William Safran, *The French Polity*, 4th ed. (White Plains, N.Y.: Longman, 1995), pp. 243–45.

41. Victoria Brittain, "Democracy Takes a Few Steps: The Charismatic Populists are Gone," *World Press Review* (Aug. 1991): 14–16.

42. Dennis Kavanagh, *British Politics: Continuities and Chance*, 2nd ed. (Oxford: Oxford University Press, 1990), p. 203.

43. Sheila Kaplan, "Porkbarrel Politics at U.S. AID," *Multinational Monitor* (Sept. 1993): 10–15. According to Kaplan, this U.S. agency authorizes not only the payment of excessively high fees for expertise and materials but also the hiring of "advisers" who are in fact "on the lookout for overseas business" in the nations where they are doling out advice.

44. For general discussions of the problems of implementation, see Cathy Marie Johnson, *The Dynamics of Conflict between Bureaucrats and Legislators* (Armonk, N.Y.: Sharpe, 1992); and Edward C. Page, *Political Authority and Bureaucratic Power* (London: Wheat-sheaf Books, 1985). For a detailed study of the implementation of a single law, see Michael C. LeMay, *Anatomy of a Public Policy: The Reform of Contemporary American Immigration Law* (Westport, Conn.: Praeger, 1994).

45. *Wall Street Journal*, 22 Aug. 1995, A1, A5.

46. Joseph La Palombara first explained this form of clientelism in *Interest Groups in Italian Politics* (Princeton: Princeton University Press, 1964), chap. 8.

47. *New York Times*, 21 Feb. 1992, A12.

11 Justice under the Law

In every system of government, three tasks must be performed: Laws must be made, laws must be carried out, and some effort must be made to see that justice is done in the process.

Few qualities of human existence are more deeply valued than justice, although we are not always aware how much it means to us. Ask your friends to list eight or ten great goods of human existence in order of importance (give them *love* and *friendship* as examples if they need help getting started), and chances are that most of them will not even mention *justice*. However, this may simply be a sign that people you know have never felt that they have been treated unjustly by the legal system.

Suppose, however, that one of your friends was Cuban poet Maria Elena Cruz Varela, who was forced to eat copies of her dissident poetry, then dragged by the hair down four flights of stairs and into the street, arrested, and later sentenced to two years in prison for her membership in the opposition group known as Criterio Alternativo.[1] Or perhaps the good friend you ask is Fauzi Saado, a Lebanese refugee in the German town of Huxene, just after he has sat in court listening to Judge Walter Stoy reduce the charges against the three neo-Nazi skinheads who set his home afire—declaring they were "youthful offenders" (the youngest was 18; the others were 19) who had been drunk and had not intended to kill anyone, and sentencing them to a maximum of five years' imprisonment—despite the fact that the result of their rampage was serious injury to two of the Saado children, leaving one of them deformed for life.[2] Or suppose you asked your question of 27-year-old Jerry Dewayne Williams, who was sentenced in 1995 to twenty-five years to life imprisonment for having stolen a slice of pepperoni pizza from a group of children. The sentence was mandatory under California's new "three strikes" law, which applies to any person with two previous convictions (of which one was for a serious or violent felony) who then commits a third crime—Williams the pizza thief "qualified."[3] Might we not expect Varela, Saado, and Williams to be more likely to include *justice* on their lists? We sometimes learn how much we cherish fair treatment under the law only when we encounter what appears to us to be its very opposite.

WHAT IS JUSTICE?

Most of us are likely to say that an injustice has been done when we believe that we ourselves or those for whom we feel compassion have not been treated fairly *by people in positions of authority*. Not all acts of fair treatment are acts of justice, just as not all rules are laws. **Justice** is a possible result of decisions made by those who have been granted authority to determine what constitutes fair treatment. In the case of governments, justice means *fair treatment under the law*. These five simple words contain a wealth of meaning. Treating people—that is, meting out rewards and punishments—*under the law* means showing respect for the most fundamental principle of human rights: the rule of law. Only by establishing laws that apply equally to all do those in power gain legitimacy in the minds of those over whom they rule. There can be no belief in the possibility of justice without the prior establishment of the principle of the rule of law. There can be no justice without a body of law to guide the judges.

However, the mere existence of a body of law and of properly credentialed judges in no way guarantees that justice will prevail. No one who has studied the 1857 Dred Scott decision of the U.S. Supreme Court can doubt that those who have been given the authority to determine what is just may make errors of judgment.[4] All we have said so far is that just government is a product that *may* result from the decisions of those who are formally authorized to determine how the laws shall be applied.

What, then, do we mean by *just?* The answer is not easy. What seems just to me may seem highly unjust to you. The California state attorney general saw nothing wrong with sending someone to jail for a minimum of twenty-five years for stealing a slice of pizza: "We at least can think our children can sit down in peace in broad daylight, without a 6-foot 4-inch, 220 pound ex-con threatening them and taking away food from them," said Daniel E. Lungren, and presumably there were other Californians who agreed.[5] Justice is a relative term. A decision is considered *just* if it meets a society's current standards of what constitutes fair treatment under the law.[6] Such standards evolve from tradition, from religious belief, from moral codes, and sometimes from simple pragmatic need. It may be just to hang a man for stealing a horse when the community's very survival depends—or seems to depend—on the government's ability to protect cattle ranching. (For further examples, see Box 11.1.)

Are we treading dangerous ground here? Yes, indeed; but then, nobody promised you easy solutions to tough ethical questions when you took up the study of politics—at least I hope nobody did. Most of us do not want to manifest the cultural arrogance of the British colonial authorities who ruled that African chiefs could mete out justice on the basis of native law and custom as long as their decisions were not "repugnant to humanity"—we know that no one people or race has an innate right to determine what is or is not to be considered moral by another. Most of us accept the principle of **cultural relativism**—the idea that each society sets its own standards in accordance with its own culture and that what is correct in one society may be repugnant in another. But when we apply that principle to our considerations of justice, we may get the uncomfortable feeling that our own values are slipping away as guides to reality. Are we obliged to consider just the laws that sanction slavery because most people in a slave-owning society find them so? Must we agree that torture is an acceptable punishment for political dissent if we know that those so punished would use the same means if they themselves could acquire power? Should we accept as a mere statement of fact the information that in some Arab societies women may be divorced by the simple word of the husband but have no equivalent right themselves—and that there is little or no evidence the women themselves find this practice unjust?

This problem of cultural relativism in the determination of what is just is one of the most difficult problems in the human polity. There is no simple solution to the ethical dilemmas it poses for us, but observing certain precautions can help us find our way. First, we must be careful not to assume that the standards of justice of ordinary men and women around the globe are actually as different as the laws made by the powerful sometimes suggest. Has anyone, for example, really studied the beliefs of ordinary citizens in a slave-owning society, of divorced women in an Arab state, or of the men and women who have been tortured for their political beliefs?

Second, it is important to distinguish between making an evaluation of a given practice and assuming the right to impose change. Surely I have the right to my

BOX 11.1   REGIME CHANGE

Can Justice Be Done after Regime Change?

One of the most difficult problems a nation must face after serious regime change has taken place is what to do about unjust acts that the former regime either instigated or condoned.

The dilemmas are numerous. Sometimes bringing the malefactors to justice is simply too dangerous. When civilian rule replaces that of the military, as has often been the case recently in Latin America and Africa, there is seldom any guarantee that the military will remain docile. When the forces opposed to the rule of General Augusto Pinochet in Chile were about to take power in 1989, the old general (in power since 1973) made his position crystal clear: "The day they touch one of my men, the rule of law ends." In Argentina when three military uprisings protested trials called in the 1990s to determine the guilt of those accused of ordering the torture and murder of political opponents in the previous regime, the new and supposedly democratic regime called off the trials and even pardoned some of those who had already been convicted.

But even when the military is safely under control, there are other obstacles to making sure that justice is finally done. Sometimes the criminals are dead or very old before regime change is sufficiently advanced to make bringing them to justice otherwise possible; many of those responsible for the worst offenses of the Stalinist era escaped retribution by the mere passage of time. In other cases simply too many people are probably guilty; complicity is "so widely shared that trials would add literally millions of new cases to already overburdened and understaffed courts." Sometimes the acts now deemed criminal were not so at the time: Tapping telephones and barring students from attending colleges for their political beliefs were both legal in East Germany. Or the act in question, though undeniably heinous, may have been carried out at the command of superiors: Border guards who shot citizens trying to get across the Berlin Wall usually did so on direct order from their officers.

All kinds of difficulties present themselves when states judge the past and those who gave it its form. Does contemporary Bulgaria have the right to try former officials who sent government funds to Third World communist movements? Should the former head of the East German secret service have been sentenced to prison in 1993 for his part in murders committed in 1931 on the basis of evidence gathered by the Nazi government, possibly using torture?

Achieving post hoc justice is thus no easy task for the new and would-be democratic regime. It is all very well to say that "the best way to deal with the past is to treat it according to the democratic standards [the new regimes] have supposedly embraced." However, a few questions remain: What exactly are those standards in cases like the above? How can newly appointed (or newly reformed) judges be expected to know and apply such standards? And is it really possible to apply them when so many victims and victims' relatives are clamoring for nothing more, and nothing less, than "simple justice"?

Source: Tina Rosenberg, "Overcoming the Legacies of Dictatorship," *Foreign Affairs* (Spring 1995): 134.

negative opinion of public whipping as a punishment for adultery, say, whether or not I have the right (or the power) to move in and take the whip away. Third, let us remember that as the world shrinks, we may be evolving toward an international code of justice. It may be that your own great-grandchildren, finding this book in the attic and thumbing through it idly, will find this discussion old-fashioned and unnecessary, having grown up in a world in which there are no longer significant differences in what different people find just or unjust throughout the human polity. We ourselves may hasten that day by working with other peoples to create a shared vision of a just world toward which all (ourselves very much included) might resolve to strive. Acknowledging cultural relativism need not mean abandoning hope for a better world.[7]

In the meantime, different conceptions of justice do exist, and different systems have been developed for the administration of justice. Yet even now there are certain similarities across the globe in the way the job is done. Whatever the standards of justice, in every polity there are people whose job it is to make certain that the laws of the land are just and that they are justly administered. To some extent, this is a job shared by everyone in government. Lawmakers (legislators) and law implementers (executives) are expected to carry out their functions in a manner consistent with those standards. But human nature being what it is, those who make and execute the laws may not always themselves be just. For this reason, most polities have established an institution of government, the **judiciary**, whose particular function it is to see to it that the citizens receive fair treatment under the law. The job of *assuring* justice is first and foremost the work of judges—not legislators, not executives. In this chapter we explore the judicial function. There can be no judiciary without a body of trained, authorized judges, so we begin with a consideration of the ways judges are chosen throughout the human polity. Then we explore the question of judicial independence. How free are judges from political intervention, and what are the consequences for the political systems within which they carry out their functions? Then we review and explain the principal systems of law used in the administration of justice. We conclude with an overview of regional variations in the rule of law.

CHOOSING CREDIBLE JUDGES

Implicit in the very idea of a judicial system is the conviction that there must be some place where final decisions on political and governmental matters can be made, and made so as to command respect and obedience. For this condition to be fulfilled, the people who make such decisions must know and respect their society's system of law and standards of justice. But it is not enough for them to have this knowledge and respect. They must be believed to have it; they must have legitimacy in the eyes of the public. Such legitimacy is traditionally achieved by three means—by appointing only those whose past careers seem likely to have given them that knowledge and respect, by giving the right of appointment to government officials who are themselves respected because of the importance of the offices they occupy, and by surrounding the judicial role with the physical accoutrements of dignity and stature.

Experienced Judges

In some nations, no one can become a judge who has not followed a clearly defined educational and career path. In others, those who have the power to appoint judges can appoint whomever they please but are expected to choose only those with obviously relevant experience. In Germany, law students must choose at the end of their studies whether to become a judge, prosecutor, civil servant, notary public, or private lawyer. Those who decide to become judges must go through a three-year probationary period, but after completing that successfully they are given a judgeship with lifetime tenure and security. Once made, the decision is fixed—German lawyers do not later become judges, and German judges do not decide to leave the bench and take up lawyering. By the time the German judge achieves appointment to one of the high federal courts, he or she is likely to have acquired a wealth of experience.[8]

In Great Britain, the young man or woman bent on a legal career does not have to decide between being a lawyer and being a judge but rather between being a *barrister*, a lawyer qualified to appear as an advocate in court, and being a *solicitor*, a lawyer qualified to do the paperwork in law offices. Most of those who become barristers have solidly middle-class or upper-class origins and have attended private schools for their secondary education and then the more prestigious universities and law schools (such as Oxford, Cambridge, and the Inns of Court in London). British judges are chosen from the ranks of practicing barristers.[9]

In other nations, however, it is legally possible to become a judge with no formal training or experience whatsoever. This is the case in the federal court system in the United States, where it is not even necessary to be a lawyer to become a federal judge. And in Denmark two ordinary citizens serve alongside one professional jurist as judges in municipal courts and rule on lesser, but still criminal, cases; in appeals from municipal court cases to a high court, three citizen judges participate with three jurists.[10]

Respectably Chosen Judges

Who is to say who is to say? Never is it more important to find the right answer to this question than in determining who will choose the men and women who are to say what is just. The answer varies a great deal from polity to polity. Nearly all German judges are appointed by the state ministers of justice and are considered civil servants and thus part of the bureaucratic hierarchy, promoted on the basis of recommendations from superiors. They have middle-class or upper-middle-class backgrounds; only 6 percent come from working-class families. German reunification has played a part in recent judicial recruitment: Many of the judges in former East Germany were considered "poorly prepared for Western styles of judicial and legal practice or . . . compromised by past political connections" and have been replaced by judges from former West Germany.[11]

In other systems, all but the highest judges are appointed by the judges themselves. In Mexico, the Supreme Court judges appoint all the judges for the lower courts and elect their own chief justice.[12] In Canada, the federal government controls the appointment, salary, and tenure of judges.[13] In Zambia, Kenya, Malawi, Senegal, and the Ivory Coast, judicial commissions composed of the nation's chief justice, representatives of the bar association, and officials from the executive branch advise the president in the appointment of judges. Malawi, however, actually has two judicial systems: traditional and magisterial. Certain criminal cases are heard in the traditional courts and are judged on the basis of traditional law by judges who are also traditional chiefs.[14] In Israel, appointments are made by a highly prestigious nine-member appointments committee; tradition requires that at least one religious leader serve on the high court and that women be well represented.[15]

Legislators often play an important role in the appointment of judges. U.S. presidents must get senatorial ratification of all appointments they make to the federal judiciary. When such appointments become controversial, not only the senators but the general public may well become involved.

Dignified Judges

Making sure that judges have appropriate qualifications and are appointed through time-honored official procedures is clearly a reasonable way of ensuring

"Lights! Camera! Justice!"

their credibility. A third method seems less logically defensible yet may be even more effective. It is common practice to surround the judicial office with all possible material attributes of seriousness and high purpose. Almost everywhere, judges are expected to wear special somber apparel, to speak carefully, and to refrain from laughter or other signs of lightheartedness (no matter how humorous or even laughable the proceedings in the courtroom may occasionally be). A sergeant-at-arms or bailiff reminds everyone in the courtroom to rise when the judge enters and to maintain appropriate behavior. In Britain and several other nations in the British Commonwealth, it is still the custom for judges and the barristers who plead cases before them to wear powdered wigs.

Although such practices still prevail, the dignity of the court has nevertheless suffered in recent years from a more modern phonemon: the invasion of the camera. The difficulty of maintaining a sober atmosphere when a trial is receiving constant publicity and can be followed minute by minute on the screen was made all too amply apparent in the O. J. Simpson case in the United States, when a black sports hero was accused of killing his wife and another man. The knowledge that they were being watched clearly influenced the behavior of everyone in the courtroom. Typical media comments were, "There is no question that both the prosecution and defense . . . overtly played to the gallery," and "The judge and the lawyers on both sides seem unable to curb their appetite for attention."[16] The media, often accused of covering trials irresponsibly and biasing the jurors (whose isolation from their coverage is never likely to be complete), defend themselves on the vague grounds of the "people's right to know" and, in the United States, on the basis of the First Amendment. News media cameras and microphones are now permitted in forty-seven states in the United States. The same kind of coverage is possible in Canada, with one important exception: The judge always has the right to order a news blackout if he or she believes the case will be too sensational, and this is often done. Even a Canadian editor who favors changing the law acknowledges the damage done to the dignity of the courts by the presence of the camera eye: "The circus aspect to some trials is disturbing," he says, and adds, "To see evidence related to a trial on *Eyewitness News* is, shall we say, inelegant."[17]

AN INDEPENDENT JUDICIARY: THEORY AND PRACTICE

There is no liberty, if the judiciary power be not separated from the legislative and executive. Were it joined with the legislative, the life and liberty of the subject would be exposed to arbitrary control; for the judge would be then the legislator. Were it joined to the executive power, the judge might behave with violence and oppression. There would be an end of everything were the same man or the same body, whether of the nobles or of the people, to exercise those three powers, that of enacting laws, that of executing the public resolutions, and that of trying the causes of individuals.[18]

French political philosopher Charles Montesquieu's eloquent statement is usually taken as the basis for the principle of separation of powers that is embedded in the U.S. Constitution. But his arguments on behalf of separating the judicial

Challenging the legal system. Dr. Jack Kevorkian (C), flanked by his attorneys, faces criminal charges in his determination to establish the right of individuals to medically assisted suicide and of doctors like himself to provide that assistance. Is the judicial system out of touch with the public on the issue of euthanasia?

(Reuters/Corbis-Bettmann)

branch from executive and legislative functions have a special cogency. **Judicial independence** means that the judiciary is protected—usually by constitutional guarantees—from interference by the other branches of government in the conduct of its work.

As we saw in Chapter 9, even in parliamentary systems—in which the executive and legislative functions are closely joined—the judiciary often maintains a significant measure of independence. The constitution of the Federal Republic of Germany declares without equivocation, "The judges shall be independent and subject only to the law" and are perceived as simply "neutral administrators of the law."[19] Even where such independence has been violated in practice—as in India, when Prime Minister Indira Gandhi was accused of making openly political appointments to the highest courts—the principle of judicial independence is accepted as legitimate.[20] Only openly authoritarian systems fail to offer the judicial process at least a semblance of protection from interference by others in power.

The arguments for an independent judiciary come easily to mind. If judges can be removed from office for unpopular decisions, they are likely to try harder to please the people who have that power of removal than to determine what constitutes the fair application of the law. If judges' decisions can easily be set aside or overthrown, the painstaking, expensive, and time-consuming judicial process becomes an empty exercise. If judges must always rule as instructed by those in high executive office, regardless of the clear meaning of existing law or the principles of fair practice, they will be helpless to foster respect for the law, for those principles, or for the political system itself.

However, there are also some interesting arguments against the establishment of an entirely independent judiciary, even in democratic systems of government. Judges are almost always appointed rather than elected, so it can be argued that they should not be able to set aside the will of the people by selective interpretation of the laws written by the people's elected representatives. The argument against judicial review of laws regulating abortion largely revolved around this question, with some going so far as to claim that in this matter the U.S. Supreme Court had perpetrated "an unconstitutional abridgment of . . . fundamental rights."[21] Such arguments have become less common with the emergence of a more conservative court and consequent uncertainty about which way the court will "jump" on a particular abortion-related statute; however, this very uncertainty has complicated the lawmaking process, helping to make legislative debate on the issue "more varied and more contentious than any in recent memory."[22]

A second argument against absolute judicial independence is that the powers this gives to judges are difficult to limit by law and are consequently likely to be extended ever further. Such *judicialization* or *judicial activism* is most likely in liberal democracies, argues C. Neal Tate, who shows how the process is now well underway in the recently democratized Philippines.[23] Although this trend may have been originally inspired by an effort to extend the protection of individual rights, there is no guarantee that judges who overstep traditional bounds will always be on the side of the common man or woman, or even on the side of the highest law of the land. In the United States, for example, federal appeals courts have long taken for granted their authority to review juries' decisions to make "excessive" awards of damages, but some attorneys argue that the reexamination clause of the Seventh Amendment to the U.S. Constitution actually forbids judicial review of any lower case decision in which a jury has ruled (except under conditions that do not apply to this kind of case).[24]

A third argument is made on the simple grounds that beneath their impressive robes judges are, after all, mere human beings. There is always the chance that they will begin to manifest the various frailties of the species yet be impossible to remove from power. Some observers of the U.S. court system have suggested a constitutional amendment limiting federal judgeships to a single ten-year term, and indeed in most other nations such limitations do exist.

Finally, we have said that what is considered just depends on each polity's particular standards. When those standards change, the society's judges—often socially isolated by virtue of their lofty and engrossing occupations—may be among the last to recognize what has happened. If it is impossible to remove judges who are out of touch with the evolution in the thinking of ordinary men and women, it may be equally impossible to ensure that justice will be done.

The arguments against unlimited judicial independence have inspired some polities to choose judges by election, particularly those at the lower levels of the court system. Although the general public usually approves of judicial elections, the judges themselves would almost always prefer to reach office by appointment, citing the difficulties of maintaining accountability to two masters: the voters and the law.[25]

GUIDELINES FOR ADJUDICATION: THE KINDS OF KINDS OF LAW

As we noted earlier, normative standards of what is just vary from culture to culture. So do the kinds of law in which those standards are given legal expression—laws that guide the rulings of jurists whose job it is to determine what constitutes fair treatment. Here we consider first the different kinds of law that have emerged in human history and then the kinds of law that are dominant in the various "legal cultures" presently found throughout the human polity (see Figure 11.1).

Before we begin, however, a word of caution is in order. Trying to understand the different kinds of law can be difficult until we grasp that there are "kinds of kinds"—which is to say, there is more than one way to categorize the kinds of law we human beings have devised. We find out about these different "kinds of kinds" when we ask different questions. If we ask the question, "Are laws based on discovered truth or on commonsense pragmatism?" then we are likely to hear about the difference between *natural law* and *positive law.* But if we ask, "Are laws always written and codified by officially designated lawmakers, or do they emerge more gradually over time, as judges decide thorny questions in the courtroom?" then someone will be ready to explain to us the difference between *statutory law* and codes of law on one hand and *common* (or "judge-made") *law* on the other. Or perhaps we wonder, "Is there a difference between laws that determine what punishments fit what crimes and laws that are designed simply to settle disputes and provide retribution?" In that case we will be told: Yes, there is *criminal law* and *civil law.* Finally, it may occur to us to ask, "Is there a body of law that governs the relationships between nations, separate from the law that governs relationships within them?"—thereby stimulating someone to tell us all about the difference between *domestic law* and *international law.*

The task for beginners would be considerably easier if there were well-known names for these kinds of kinds of law and if scholars would always make clear exactly what kinds they are talking about. Unfortunately, commentators tend to jump about from one kind to the other without raising any signals and even to use the same terms to identify quite different distinctions. We try to avoid that pitfall here. To help you find your way, we take up each kind of kind of law in

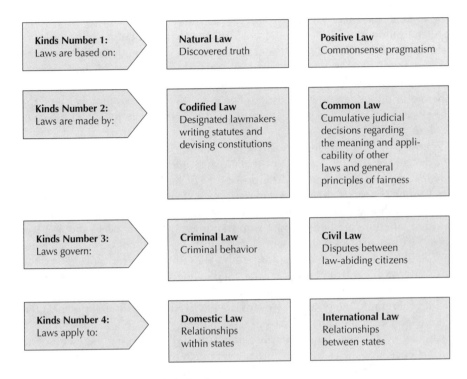

FIGURE 11.1   The Kinds of Kinds of Law

turn, give them names that signal (even if somewhat roughly) what each is about, and keep our usage of these terms consistent throughout.

Law's Relationship to Truth: Natural Law versus Positive Law

Life on this planet is sometimes extremely perplexing. How did we get here? Are we here for a reason or just by accident? How should we spend our time here? And what, if anything, happens next? These questions all fall within the domain of philosophy and theology—that is, the domain of metaphysics. However, the third question, "How should we spend our time here?" is also partly the domain of law, which determines what conduct is not permitted as well as what acts must be performed.

This overlapping of the worlds of law and metaphysics has led some philosophers to believe that philosophy should instruct law. If philosophy or religion can tell us in general how we should spend our time on earth, then we ought to be able to deduce the particular rules we should follow—or so say those who believe there is such a thing as **natural law**. We ought to be able to discover the laws that already exist in nature, which have been, some would add, implanted there by a divine creator. The idea of natural law can be traced back to the Greek and Roman Stoic philosophers and particularly to the ideas of Marcus Tullius Cicero, who argued that there was a universal law of nature, discoverable by "right reason" and binding on all.[26] Islamic law is still largely based on the philosophy of natural law. The *qadi* (judge) is expected to reach a decision by considering first "the claims of God"—the rulelike statements of law contained in the Qur'an— and second the Traditions, statements about what the prophet Mohammed actually said or did in determining justice. The judge then seeks to discover how the present case is analogous to a situation cited in these basic texts and rules accordingly.[27]

Those who have argued for **positive law**, or law made by humans, usually have not denied the various precepts of their society's dominant religion or philosophy. What they *have* denied is the possibility of discovering laws in that way. They argue instead that laws are and must be made pragmatically, to meet given ends. Laws should be clearly *promulgated* (announced), as should the punishments or other sanctions applied to those who transgress them. Such laws should be in accord with the society's moral principles, but they should not be seen as having the weight and authority of absolute truth. They should be recognized, say the positivists, as the instruments of mortal, fallible humans who are simply attempting to establish order on the basis of their empirical experience.[28]

In recent times, the positivist view of law has been dominant. But the idea that natural law exists and can be discovered has had great appeal in the past. If it can be argued that the law represents absolute truth of divine origin, then who dares to challenge any law as unjust? Throughout much of human history, the principles of natural law were used to bolster the authority of autocrats. Kings succeeded to power, it was argued, only because it was the will of a divine being that they do so. Thus, their decrees had divine sanction and had to be accepted without question. Even when the "divine right of kings," as this theory is called, led to patently outrageous abuses of power, uncompromising believers in natural law argued that the edicts of kings must be obeyed.

However, such abuses inevitably led other political thinkers to look for arguments that would permit the dethroning of tyrants without denying the existence of natural law. In the seventeenth century, John Locke found such an argument. Natural law was given, said Locke, for the preservation of humankind and to ensure the public good of society. Its commands were binding on sovereigns and legislators as well as on ordinary men and women; when those in power acted in a manner contrary to those purposes, it was a sign that they themselves were contravening natural law. In such a case, it was the right and indeed the duty of the people to replace their rulers with those who would act more in accord with the strictures of natural law.[29]

How Law Is Formalized: Common Law and Codified Law

Many of those who puzzle about the nature of law are content to leave the question of its relationship to truth unresolved and do not feel the need to categorize law as either natural or positive. For them, a more important question is how the law was established. The categories that matter to them are common law and codified law. Other variations in how law is formalized include equity law, statutory law, and constitutional law.

When the Roman empire grew to include vast numbers of peoples, each with its own established laws, problems developed in maintaining peaceful relationships throughout the land. What was normal practice in one province might be a serious crime in another. Simply imposing Roman law on everyone could have created as many problems as it solved. The Roman answer was to establish special courts to hear cases involving disputes between inhabitants of different territories. The judge (known as a *praetor peregrinus*, or judge for foreigners) would then consider the legal principles of both lands, look for common ground between them, and—failing that—propose a solution based on *equity*, that is, a solution based on an abstract notion of fairness. These decisions frequently served as precedents for succeeding cases. Eventually, in the sixth century C.E., Emperor Justinian ordered Roman jurists to codify the body of law that was emerging in this way. The result, known as the "law of the peoples" (*jus gentium*), was the "first comprehensive compilation of the rules of any legal culture."[30]

The Roman solution offers good illustrations of several of the ways laws can be established. When the judges for foreigners took it upon themselves to declare what was just, then took note of one anothers' decisions and treated them as **precedents**—that is, as examples to be followed in succeeding cases—they were building a body of "judge-made law," a kind of law that would later be known as *case law* or **common law**. Common law has both the virtue and the flaw of flexibility. In most systems it is only as fixed as the judges want it to be, which means that unfair decisions can be set aside relatively easily—but so can those that are fair. None of the participants can be certain when the judge's ruling will be *stare decisis* ("let the [previous] decision stand") or when he or she will decide that previous decisions do not really apply to the case at hand.

Today common law is particularly "common" in northern Europe and the United States. The evolution of the legal system of the Republic of Ireland offers an interesting example of the twists and turns possible over the centuries. Some Irish law finds its roots as far back as the customs of the seventh century, when Ireland was composed of separate kingdoms and fiefdoms and the law and its application were in the hands of a small group of teachers and judges. Conquest by the English led, especially after 1800, to a body of English-Irish common law, much of which remained operative after independence was granted in 1922. Beginning with the 1924 Courts of Justice Act, the newly free republic revised its laws to suit itself but often used English law as its model nonetheless. Since 1973, judges have been influenced by European Union law, but Irish courts continue to be required to follow precedents, so long as the earlier decisions "meet the requirements of aptness and similarity."[31]

Not surprisingly, a body of common law often emerges—or is extended—when a nation must deal with remarkably new and challenging circumstances, circumstances that existing laws simply fail to cover.[32] When, during the Watergate scandal of 1972 to 1974, the U.S. Congress became persuaded that some-

thing had to be done about the infusion of large sums of private money into political campaigns, it passed the Federal Election Campaign Act of 1974. This act
imposed rigorous requirements for the disclosure of the sources of all political
funds and imposed strict limits on both contributions and expenditures for campaigns. It also raised almost as many questions as it answered, such as: When does
a contribution become an expenditure? How can spending and contribution limits be reconciled with rights of free speech? The result was a series of court cases,
usually brought by people who had been affected by the Federal Election Commission's interpretation of the act. These cases have in turn produced an interesting contemporary example of the building of common law.

Another development in common law is taking place right now, as cases are
being brought before the courts of several modern nations that involve the new
problem of computer theft. Ingenious *hackers* (computer hobbyists) can now
crack code after code and enter the secret systems of governments and business
corporations, and the courts are under heavy pressure to interpret existing laws
in such a way as to halt such practices. As they do so, they will be further extending the reach of the common law, although whether the precedents thus established will be codified in the future remains to be seen.[33]

Codified law is a body of law that has been set down in writing, as Justinian
directed his jurists to do in the sixth century. It may draw on many sources;
edicts, treaties, decrees, legislative enactments, and the substance of common
law decisions are all grist for the mill of the codifiers, who may themselves write
new law to eliminate contradictions or to fill gaps in the material before them.
Codified law need not be permanently fixed, but changes in a code of law are usually made more formally than are changes in common law. The Roman code was
modified again and again over the centuries until, early in the nineteenth century,
Napoleon ordered a new systematization of law throughout the empire he had
built for France. The Napoleonic code was built on the Roman code, as were subsequent modifications of that code, such as the code of the German Empire of
1900 and the Swiss code of 1907.[34]

Equity law is a form of law that developed as a way of compensating for another difficulty that arises from common law. Common law can usually be applied only after a crime or a damaging act has occurred. In a typical example of
equity law, a judge might decide that waiting for an anticipated act to occur before deciding whether it is legal would do irreparable harm and might therefore
issue an order forbidding the intended act. The act in question might be one performed by a private party (for example, your landlord may plan to install insula-
tion materials to which you are violently allergic) or by government (for
example, the Highway Department's bulldozers are bearing down on your cherished elm tree because they want to widen your street). The most frequent modern legal action invoking equity comes in the form of an **injunction** issued to
suspend proceedings until one party or the other has had time to prepare a fuller
case.[35]

Statutory law includes all legislation, treaties, executive orders, and decrees as well as codes of law. As we noted, law codes usually incorporate whatever statutory law exists at the time of codification. But the other forms of statutory law continue to be written, day after day, year after year. New statutes may or may not be incorporated into an existing code. In some nations, such as Norway, judges have at their command a rich tradition of common law, supplemented by a wide-ranging and ever-changing body of uncodified statutory law. Special forms of statutory law, such as **administrative law** (the rules and decisions of administrative agencies) and **admiralty and maritime law** (for cases having to do with shipping and waterborne commerce), are sometimes considered to be altogether separate forms of law.[36]

A **constitution** is itself a special form of law, often referred to as the "highest law in the land." **Constitutional law** is law that has evolved in cases that require independent judicial interpretation of the provisions of a constitution (such as all cases of judicial review). As such, constitutional law can be seen as a form of common law.[37]

Different Law for Different Acts: Criminal Law and Civil Law

Another way to subdivide the kinds of law is to consider the acts of the parties in the case—or rather, the alleged acts. Is someone claiming that a crime against the public order has been committed and must be punished by society? Then the judge must decide the applicability of the appropriate **criminal law** to the case. Or is someone alleging that one individual has acted unfairly toward another in a way that damages only that individual—not the society at large—and that some form of retribution must be made to the individual who suffered the damage? In that case, the judge will turn to **civil law.**

Civil law covers cases dealing with such matters as divorce, child custody, inheritances, and contracts. Criminal law covers any act that is considered an offense against society, from the most serious cases of rape, arson, or murder to the most petty infraction of parking regulations. The line between civil law and criminal law is not always clear; some acts can be considered simultaneously offenses against society, requiring punishment, and offenses against individuals, requiring restitution. One way to decide which form of law applies is to consider the circumstances. An act that was intentional or reckless may be deemed criminal, while the same act may be subject only to civil law if it results from negligence or accident.[38]

A separate but related distinction is made between crimes with victims and such victimless crimes as gambling and possession of marijuana. It is sometimes argued that "victimless" crimes should be subject to neither criminal penalty nor civil retribution, because there is no nonconsenting victim in such cases. However, most polities have decided that at least some of these activities do constitute offenses against the society at large and should be punished as such—that is, under criminal law.[39]

Ordinary citizens who have occasion to deal with the courts are likely to find the distinction between civil law and criminal law more important than any other. The rules of proceeding and the range of possible outcomes vary radically according to whether a civil or a criminal case is under consideration, so much so that it is common to establish two entirely separate systems of courts.

The Scope of Law: Domestic Law and International Law

A final categorization of kinds of law derives from the territorial scope of any law. The most obvious distinction here is between **domestic law**, the body of laws that nations apply only within their territories, and **international law**, the law that applies in relationships between nations, or between the citizens of one nation and either the government or individual citizens of another nation.

We examine the provisions of international law more carefully in Chapter 13. Here we consider two essential differences between domestic law and international law. First, domestic law has much greater legitimacy than international law. Domestic law evolves from the beliefs and culture of a particular society and is therefore likely to be accepted as reasonable and understandable by most of the members of that society. But international law is not based on the culture of those to whom it applies, and its dictates may draw on notions of fairness that are puzzling, unfamiliar, and even repugnant to those to whom they are supposed to apply.

Second, domestic law is much easier to enforce than international law. The weapons and armies of the world are almost entirely under national, not international, control, even when they are temporarily on loan for the peacekeeping missions of international organizations. Furthermore, the strength of nationalistic sentiment is such that any effort at armed enforcement of an unpopular settlement is always likely to deteriorate into simple warfare between nation-states. The Korean conflict in the 1950s makes an excellent case in point.[40]

Nevertheless, both the body of international law and the machinery for arriving at settlements under that law do exist, and they do "work" more often than might at first be expected. Karl Deutsch suggested that international law prevails (when it does) because "it serves the nations to coordinate their mutual expectations and behavior *in their own interest.*"[41] It is in every nation's interest, for example, for all **diplomats** to receive special attention and privileges, as outlined in the Vienna Convention of 1961. This often includes immunity from arrest except in the most serious cases. In recent years, however, there have been incidents suggesting to some that such privileges are being abused beyond endurance. In one case, shots fired from the Libyan embassy in London on a crowd of demonstrators killed a British policewoman. The response to this kind of case has been not to change the law regarding diplomatic immunity but to insist on its more careful and more measured observance. Diplomats *"are not* immune from the laws of the country where they are accredited," Grant V. McLanahan reminds us, "but only from the usual methods of enforcement." Host nations are now more likely to "institute preventive measures, issue systematic warnings, and announce possible penalties to diplomats"; those who go too far may now well find themselves expelled altogether.[42]

The slow but steady strengthening of the European Union has brought new considerations regarding the scope of international law to its member states. The

EU writes laws to which these states are expected to conform, even when their domestic laws may conflict. The Treaty of Maastricht (see Chapter 13) brought the dilemma home to the French in 1992. Although committed to endorsement of the treaty, the logical French had to admit it required commitments from them that were expressly forbidden not merely by domestic law but by their national constitution. What to do? The answer was clear: The French revised their constitution to make it possible to approve the treaty.[43]

Even when a nation is opposed to some provision of international law, and has the strength to be able to flout it with seeming impunity, responsible leaders are usually aware that the situation may be drastically changed at some later date. "Most nations do well," said Deutsch, "to consider the possibility, and indeed the probability, of role reversal in the future."[44]

There are, of course, also differences in the scope of law *within* nation-states. Municipal ordinances, county rules, state or provincial law, and national legislation all vary in the territorial extent of their coverage. However, local law within nations, a topic we return to in the next chapter, must always be consistent with national law and, except in rare instances, can always be overturned at the national level. The difference between domestic and international law is in that respect a different kind of difference (a different kind of kind).

SUMMARY AND CONCLUSION

As we have seen, the meanings and means of justice vary throughout the human polity. In general, we may agree that justice means "fair treatment under the law," but in practical terms justice is whatever a particular society believes it is. Still, it is important not to exaggerate the differences among various systems' notions of justice; the ordinary men and women of the world may have more shared beliefs about what is just than their systems of law would suggest. Even when we do not agree with one another, our new interdependence forces us to understand and accommodate one another's conception of justice—if only to permit us to do business with one another. Nevertheless, we can reserve the right to apply our own standards in evaluating other systems, once we have made a serious effort to understand why and how other polities have developed their own values about law and justice, acknowledged their right to do so, and firmly rejected the ethnocentric assumption that we ourselves know all the answers and therefore have the right to impose our views on others.

The means of establishing just government also vary. Every nation tries to choose credible judges by appointing only experienced people to that post, by giving the right of appointment to people who are themselves respected by virtue of the office they occupy, and by surrounding the judicial office with the physical accoutrements of dignity and stature—but each nation determines for itself what constitutes appropriate experience, respectable officeholding, and sufficiently impressive judicial insignia. Similarly, despite the obvious connection between keeping judges free from political restraint and protecting individual rights, there is no widespread agreement that the judiciary should be independent of the other branches of the government or, if so, how independent it should be.

In carrying out their work, the judges of the world draw on several kinds of kinds of law. Sometimes law is categorized according to how close it is believed to be to absolute truth, sometimes according to the process by which it is created and formalized, sometimes by the kind of act to which it applies, and sometimes by the territorial extent of its coverage. In every nation, the application of the law is inevitably uneven, whether by deliberate intent (more common in hierarchical systems) or by the accidents of interpretation (more common in democratic states). The application of the law becomes more personal, as well as more arbitrary, the closer we move to the local level. Indeed, most people have direct experience of government of any type only at that level. To broaden our understanding of the nature of that experience, we turn our attention now to local and regional government.

Selected Readings

Belliotti, Raymond A. *Justifying Law: The Debate over Foundations, Goals, and Methods.* Philadelphia: Temple University Press, 1992. A critical survey of the works of leading legal minds and of the different schools of legal thought.

de Cruz, Peter. *A Modern Approach to Comparative Law.* Boston: Kluwer, 1993. An introduction to the comparative study of law and legal systems.

Edelman, Martin. *Courts, Politics and Culture in Israel.* Charlottesville: University Press of Virginia, 1994. An examination of Israel's many legal systems and the difficulties such multiplicity causes for the development of a modern democracy, urging their reconciliation in a written constitution that includes a bill of rights.

Katz, Alan M., ed. *Legal Traditions and Systems: An International Handbook.* Westport, Conn.: Greenwood Press, 1986. Includes chapters on legal systems around the world ranging from Italy to Bangladesh.

Litan, Robert E., ed. *Verdict: Assessing the Civil Jury System.* Washington: Brookings Institution, 1993. Essays on the civil jury system in the United States, providing historical background as well as a thorough analysis of the contemporary system.

Lobban, Michael. *The Common Law and English Jurisprudence 1780–1850.* Oxford: Clarendon Press, 1991. A discussion of the intellectual history of law and the formation of the legal framework in Britain in the late eighteenth and early nineteenth centuries.

Lynn, Naomi B., ed. *Women, Politics and the Constitution.* Binghamton, N.Y.: Haworth Press, 1990. The authors contributing to this volume discuss the role the U.S. Constitution has played in women's history and in the development of women's rights.

Smith, Christopher E. *Courts and Public Policy.* Chicago: Nelson-Hall, 1993. This useful reference book synthesizes scholarly arguments and findings on judicial policymaking and discusses the constitutional scope of judicial authority and practical questions about the policymaking capabilities of the court.

Tate, C. Neal, and Torbjorn Vallinder. *The Global Expansion of Judicial Power.* New York: New York University Press, 1995. A study of the increasing power of the judiciary throughout the world.

Notes

1. *New York Times*, 8 Dec. 1991, 3.
2. Tamara Jones, "Germany's Troubles," *Los Angeles Times*, 7 Mar. 1993, 14.
3. *New York Times*, 5 Mar. 1995, 21.
4. In 1857 the Supreme Court ruled that Dred Scott, a slave who had claimed freedom after being taken to a free state, was nevertheless still a slave, arguing that "Congress could not deprive persons of any kind of property anywhere in the United States [and] that the old Missouri Compromise itself, which had set boundaries to slavery, had been unconstitutional all along." William Miller, *A New History of the United States* (New York: Dell, 1968), p. 196.
5. Just for the record, let it be noted that Williams was in fact 6 feet 5 inches tall and weighed 185 pounds. *New York Times*, 5 Mar. 1995, 21.
6. See John Rawls, *A Theory of Justice* (Cambridge: Belknap Press, 1971), pp. 1–16.
7. For an interesting contemporary discussion of this age-old problem, see Christina M. Cerna, "Universality of Human Rights and Cultural Diversity: Implementation of Human Rights in Different Socio-Cultural Contexts," *Human Rights Quarterly* 16, no. 4 (Nov. 1994): 740–52. Cerna concludes that "international norms dealing with rights that affect the private sphere of human activity will take the longest time to achieve universal acceptance" (p. 752).
8. David P. Conradt, *The German Polity*, 5th ed. (White Plains, N.Y.: Longman, 1993), p. 179.
9. "Judicial System," in *Twentieth-Century Britain: An Encyclopedia*, ed. F. M. Leventhal (New York: Garland Publishing, 1995), p. 417.
10. Stanley Anderson, "Lay Judges and Jurors in Denmark," *American Journal of Comparative Law* 38, no. 4 (Autumn 1990): 839–64.
11. Conradt, *The German Polity*, p. 179; and Thomas Reynolds and Arturo Flores, "Germany," *Current Sources of Basic Codes and Legislation in Jurisdictions of the World: Western and Eastern Europe* 2, (Rothman AALL publications series no. 33 (May 1995): 3–4.
12. Scott B. MacDonald, "Latin America," in *Legal Traditions and Systems: An International Handbook*, ed. Alan M. Katz (Westport, Conn.: Greenwood Press, 1986), p. 207.
13. Gregory S. Mahler, *Comparative Politics* (Cambridge, Mass.: Schenkman, 1983), p. 99.
14. Harvey M. Feinberg, "Africa," in Katz, *Legal Traditions and Systems*, p. 14; and U.S. State Department, Bureau of Public Affairs, "Malawi," in *Background Notes* (Washington, D.C.: U.S. State Department, Bureau of Public Affairs, 1989), pp. 1–5.
15. Asher Arian, *Politics in Israel: The Second Generation* (Chatham, N.J.: Chatham House, 1985), p. 182.
16. Charles S. Clark, "Courts and the Media," *Congressional Quarterly Researcher* (23 Sept. 1994): 819–35; and Marc Fisher, "Simpson Ad Nauseam? Tell It to the Judge," *International Herald Tribune*, 23 May 1995, 1, 3.
17. Clark, "Courts and the Media," p. 831.
18. Charles Secondat Montesquieu, *Spirit of the Laws*, ed. Franz Neumann, trans. Thomas Nugent (New York: Hafner, 1949), pp. 151–52.
19. Conradt, *The German Polity*, pp. 179. On the other hand, the Constitutional Court, which has the power of judicial review, is seen by Conradt as having an "explicitly political character," since "both state and party/political factors" play an important role in the selection of its members (p. 183).

20. Robert L. Hardgrave Jr., *India: Government and Politics in a Developing Nation*, 3rd ed. (New York: Harcourt Brace Jovanovich, 1980), pp. 78–79.

21. "Introduction to This Issue," *Judicature* 65 (Oct. 1981): 177.

22. Thomas P. Carr, Karen J. Lewis, and Michael J. Matheron, "Waiting for Roe II," *Congressional Research Service Review* (Sept. 1991): 5–6.

23. C. Neal Tate, "The Judicialization of Politics in the Philippines and Southeast Asia," *International Political Science Review* 15, no. 2 (1994): 187–97.

24. Jonathan S. Massey and Kenneth J. Chesebro, "Challenging Federal Appellate Review of Damage Awards: Lawyers Should Cite the Forgotten Second Clause of the Seventh Amendment," *Trial* 31, no. 5 (May 1995): 52.

25. *New York Times*, 12 Feb. 1992, A1.

26. Marcus Tullius Cicero, with an English translation by Clinton Walker Keyes, *de Re Publica, de Legibus* (Cambridge: Harvard University Press, 1966), passim.

27. Lawrence Rosen, *The Anthropology of Justice* (Cambridge: Cambridge University Press, 1990), pp. 41–42. Rosen notes, however, that the qadi's decision must also have "the general agreement or consensus of the community," since the prophet is believed to have said, "My community will not agree in error."

28. One of the earliest proponents of positive law was John Austin, in his *Lectures on Jurisprudence* (London: Murray, 1869). This view of the law emerged simultaneously with a more positive approach to all social phenomena—using the word *positive* with its dictionary meaning of "concerned only with real things and experience; empirical; practical." In this regard, see the work of the nineteenth-century philosopher Auguste Comte, in *Auguste Comte and Positivism*, ed. Gertrud Lenzer (New York: Harper and Row, 1975).

29. See John Locke, *Two Treatises of Government* (New York: Hafner, 1947), pp. 188–94; and Richard Hooker, *Of the Laws of Ecclesiastical Polity* (New York: Dutton, 1958), pp. 187–201. For an interesting discussion of these questions, see Lloyd L. Weinreb, *Natural Law and Justice* (Cambridge: Harvard University Press, 1987).

30. Henry Ehrmann, *Comparative Legal Cultures* (Englewood Cliffs, N.J.: Prentice Hall, 1976), p. 14. See also W. W. Buckland, *The Main Institutions of Roman Private Law* (Cambridge: Cambridge University Press, 1931), pp. 1–24; and H. F. Jolowicz, *Roman Foundations of Modern Law* (Oxford: Clarendon Press, 1957), pp. 6–21.

31. Thomas Reynolds and Arturo Flores, "Ireland," *Current Sources of Basic Codes and Legislation in Jurisdictions of the World: Western and Eastern Europe* 2, Rothman AALL publications series no. 33 (May 1995): 1–5.

32. Theodore F. T. Plucknett, *A Concise History of Common Law* (Boston: Little, Brown, 1956), p. 83.

33. Of course, existing criminal law amply covers those who use such tactics to obtain other persons' credit card numbers and personal security codes for automated bank teller machines, a new form of fraud now costing credit card corporations hundreds of millions of dollars per year. *New York Times*, 9 Apr. 1992, A25.

34. Ehrmann, *Comparative Legal Cultures*, p. 14. Codified law is sometimes also referred to as *civil law*, although that term is commonly used to identify law developed to settle disputes (as distinguished from criminal law). To avoid confusion, I use *civil law* only in its most common meaning. I have drawn heavily from Ehrmann's excellent work in this chapter, but I think his use of *civil law* to refer to "the codified systems of continental Europe" is unfortunate and confusing to novice legal scholars.

35. Plucknett, *Concise History of Common Law*, p. 675.

36. C. John Colombos, *International Law of the Sea*, 6th ed. (New York: McKay, 1967), sections 47–50; Richard B. Stewart, "The Reformation of American Administrative Law," in *Federal Administrative Agencies*, ed. Howard Ball (Englewood Cliffs, N.J.: Prentice Hall, 1984), pp. 30–37.

37. E. C. S. Wade and A. W. Bradley, *Constitutional Law*, 5th ed. (London: Longman, 1955), p. 7.

38. David M. Walker, *The Oxford Companion to Law* (Oxford: Clarendon Press, 1980), pp. 316–17. Political scientists, following the work of Gabriel Almond, sometimes refer to the judicial function as the "adjudication of disputes." A moment's careful consideration of the kind of cases that fall under criminal law, however, should make it obvious that this definition trivializes the work of the courts.

39. Joel Feinberg, *Harm to Others* (New York: Oxford University Press, 1984), pp. 12–13.

40. Bruce Cummings, *The Origins of the Korean War* (Princeton: Princeton University Press, 1981), pp. 101–29.

41. Karl Deutsch, *The Analysis of International Relations* (Englewood Cliffs, N.J.: Prentice Hall, 1968), p. 162.

42. Grant V. McClanahan, *Diplomatic Immunity* (New York: St. Martin's, 1989), p. 16.

43. *Le Monde*, 16 June 1992, 1, 11; *International Herald Tribune*, 20–21 June 1991, 4. The amendment authorizes transfers of sovereignty for the purpose of establishing a single European currency and a common foreign, security, and visa policy and to permit European Union citizens residing in France to vote in local elections.

44. Deutsch, *The Analysis of International Relations*, p. 163.

PART

V ALTERNATIVE ARENAS OF GOVERNMENT

12 Accessible Government: Local and Provincial Politics

Take me to your leader," says the charming but obviously well-armed extraterrestrial visitor. Assuming you decide to comply, what do you do next?

Take her home to meet Mother?
Take her to the chief of police, the mayor, or the county commissioner?
Take her to the governor?
Take her to the president?
Take her to the United Nations secretary-general?

Of course, you would like to take her to the president, but chances are you will decide to settle for a local government official. When we need government in a hurry, for a particularly urgent problem, we turn to local government. Ask yourself what level of government you would turn to in the following slightly more realistic emergencies:

You see the sky filling with black smoke a few blocks from your home.
You see a stranger taking valuables from your absent neighbor's home.
Your rural county's only doctor has collapsed of a heart attack on your doorstep.
You find a lost child.

If you think these examples are too carefully chosen, try this exercise: Make your own list of the first twenty emergencies, common to the human condition, that come to mind. Cross out the ones you would try to deal with without contacting any government agency (but be careful—hospitals are often city or county owned and operated). Then figure out in what percentage of the remainder you would be likely to turn to *local* government agencies. Even in this day of vastly expanded federal power, I will bet you a subway token that in well over 50 percent of the emergencies that require government assistance your first move will be to contact a local government body.

THE NATURE OF SUBNATIONAL GOVERNMENT

Subnational government is any government less broad in its extent and applicability than an entire nation. Only in the twentieth century has the distinction between national and subnational government become worldwide, or nearly so. When human beings lived in small communities, all government was local, and those who led the government were likely to be leaders in other domains as well, such as religion and hunting. Even today many nation-states have populations no larger than those of cities—and rather small cities at that (see Table 12.1).

Most nations, however, are too large to be served by a single level of government. Some problems cannot be solved the same way throughout the realm. Some problems do not manifest themselves everywhere. And above all, some problems require attention from people on the scene who are well acquainted with the local community.

All this is simply common sense. But these obvious and noncontroversial statements inevitably raise questions that may lead to debate and confusion. First, what specific kinds of problems require the attention of subnational units of government? Second, what should be the division of power among the various levels of government in a nation-state? Third, what kind of intermediate levels of government are required to meet a society's needs for governance? Fourth, what kind of institutional structures are appropriate to local government? Fifth, how can the quest for grassroots citizen involvement, most easily accommodated where local government structures are strong, be balanced against the need for centralized

TABLE 12.1   World's Largest Cities and Smallest Nation-States, by Population

Largest Cities	Population	Smallest Nation-States	Population
Tokyo-Yokohama	27,245,000	Nauru	10,000
Mexico City	20,899,000	Tuvalu	10,000
São Paulo	18,701,000	San Marino	24,000
Seoul	16,792,000	Liechtenstein	30,000
New York	14,625,000	Monaco	31,000
Osaka-Kobe-Kyoto	13,872,000	Saint Kitts and Nevis	41,000
Bombay	12,101,000	Marshall Islands	54,000
Calcutta	11,898,000	Andorra	64,000
Rio de Janeiro	11,688,000	Antigua and Barbuda	65,000
Buenos Aires	11,657,000	Seychelles	72,000

Source: *The World Almanac and Book of Facts, 1995.* Copyright © 1994 by K-III Reference Corporation, Mahwah, N.J. 07495.

planning and allocation of resources, a function that must fall to the national government?

Different nations have given different answers to these questions, and individual nations do not always give the same answers in every era—or region. One way to address the first two questions—what kinds of problems to refer to subnational governments and how much power to give these governments to handle those problems—is to adopt a unitary, federal, or confederal system of government. In the next section we examine the difference between these three ways of dividing the work of government. In the two following sections we examine some of the answers that have been given to the third question, what kind of intermediate structures are needed, and the fourth question, what institutional structures are appropriate for local governments.

Before we begin, however, let us clear up two matters of terminology. Political scientists sometimes use the word *local* to refer to any subnational government body and sometimes to refer only to the governments of cities or still smaller units. We follow the latter practice here and label *intermediate* or *provincial* any government body that is narrower than an entire nation yet wider than a city in the scope of its coverage—such as the American state, the French *département*, or the Swiss canton. The term **subnational government** refers to both intermediate and local units of government.

The use of the word *federal* can also be confusing, since U.S. citizens often refer to "the federal government" when what they really mean is the national (or central) government. We try to avoid that common yet understandable error. Here, *federal* has only the meanings assigned to it in the next section.

UNITARY, FEDERAL, AND CONFEDERAL POLITICAL SYSTEMS

We may agree that it is necessary to have more than one level of government to meet our immediate national and international needs for the exercise of collective power, but we still have to decide which tasks to assign to each level and how much power to give it. In a **unitary system** all the powers of government are reserved to the central government. That government may delegate the exercise of those powers to such subunits as counties or departments, but any such delegation can be revoked at any time. In a **federal system** of government, on the other hand, certain powers are reserved to the central government, but others are constitutionally reserved to the governments of the nation's constituent parts—that is, to the states, provinces, or cantons. Finally, in a **confederal system**, the units are actually independent states that have decided to join together in a formal alliance, acting as a single unit for some limited purposes but not for others.

Unpopular federalism. Here Quebec separatists demand that their province be set free from Canadian federalism by marching in a giant "Yes" parade in Montreal in October of 1995. Although the separatists lost in the subsequent referendum, it was by a very narrow margin.

(Reuters/Archive Photos)

All three systems have clear advantages and disadvantages. In a federal system, the national government is, at least in theory, freer to deal with national issues. Citizen participation is made easier by the existence of several levels of government, some close at hand. Governmental experiments (primary elections, welfare aid, and abolition of the death penalty are examples in the United States) can be tried out and modified in a limited setting. And when new groups seek statehood or cantonhood, additional units can be added with no disruption of the system.[1]

In a unitary system, on the other hand, laws are much more likely to be uniform throughout the nation, and representation is more likely to be equal throughout the nation. (Provisions for equal representation of every constituent unit in a federal system regardless of the number of its inhabitants, as in the U.S. Senate, inevitably creates disproportionate representation.) It is less likely that some parts of the nation will have greater tax revenues than others. Finally, in a unitary system, no sphere of independent power is capable of blocking the execution of national policy, and there is no difficulty keeping the lines of authority clear.

A confederal system lacks most of the advantages of either federal or unitary government. It does, however, provide a structure for harmonious interaction on a limited number of matters for peoples for whom single nationhood is not yet—or is no longer—tolerable. It is often a transient system, for systems on the way to greater unity or greater independence but as such can provide an extremely useful set of institutions.

However, which system a nation adopts is likely to depend far less on the careful weighing of such pros and cons than on the conditions prevalent at the time the new nation comes into existence. If the demands for unified action in the face of a hostile world are extreme and if authoritarian leadership is accepted as the norm—two conditions prevailing when most of the older nations of Europe and Asia were formed—a unitary system is likely even when the peoples joining together have very different backgrounds and customs. When a number of Gallic tribes united under the bold leadership of Vercingetorix in an effort—vain, as it proved—to resist the advance of Julius Caesar and his armies in 52 B.C.E., that was the beginning of modern France. The forceful imposition of nearly forty years of communist rule on most of eastern Europe was maintained by creating unitary states, with power strongly concentrated at the top. China is another example of a unitary state created by force in which all power is exercised at the center. According to that nation's constitution, each province's government is the administrative arm of the central government; whatever powers it has may be revoked at any time. National bodies have the power to annul "those local regulations or decisions of the . . . provinces, autonomous regions and municipalities . . . that contravene the Constitution, the statutes or the administrative rules and regulations" of the central government, as well as "to exercise unified leadership over the work of local organs at different levels throughout the country."[2]

If a nation-state is to be created out of what have been largely independent units, each with a separate political culture and separate bases of economic and military power, if the motive to join together is strong but no unit or individual

BOX 12.1   REGIME CHANGE

Can Federalism Bring Peace to Former Yugoslavia?

The effort to bring peace between Bosnia-Herzegovina and Serbia focused heavily on the search for a federal solution. Plans accepted by both sides in November 1995 called for a federated Bosnia, divided into two separate territories. One territory was to be a Serbian "republic" in the northeast, occupying 49 percent of the territory of the new federation, while the other was to be a Muslim-Croatian federation controlling 51 percent of the nation. Each territory was to have the right to "develop special ties to neighboring countries." The presidency would be a collective body, with two-thirds of its members from the Bosnian-Croatian federation and one-third from the Serbian "republic."

Can there be a "republic" within a federation? For that matter, can there be a federation within a federation? Will the Serbian republic simply become, de facto, a state of neighboring Serbia, especially after it has developed its "special ties to neighboring countries?" Is there any reason a federal solution, however fine tuned, should work any better now than it did in the former Yugoslavia, itself a federal state? None of these questions can be answered yet; all we can say is that the efforts to achieve peace in this beleaguered land involve some of the most complex federal proposals yet devised within the human polity.[3]

Source: Kay Lawson, *The Human Polity*, 4th ed. (Boston: Houghton Mifflin Company, 1997). Reprinted by permission.

---

has the force to impose unity against the will of the others, and, finally, if not everyone is sure that a single polity is possible or desirable, federalism may be the answer. Federalism is a complex form of government, but that very complexity may be what it takes to make government work in a complex situation. Consider the proposals made to resolve the problems in the former Yugoslavia (see Box 12.1). Although they cover nearly half of the world's land surface, only about one-tenth of the world's nations have federal governments.[4] Table 12.2 lists eleven major federal systems and their constituent units.

The **confederation** is a form of limited unification that is now in the process of being reinvented. Until the recent astonishing transformations in the map of the world, the standard example of a confederation was drawn from history. The thirteen American colonies were far from certain they wanted to be even as closely allied as federalism requires, and the first U.S. constitution, the Articles of Confederation, called only for a partnership among nearly independent equals. The earliest U.S. political parties were named, significantly, the Federalists and the Antifederalists, signifying those who argued for and against "a more perfect union." The Swiss provided another historic example, having joined together in the thirteenth century as a loose confederation of cantons but deciding eventually to form a federation, in 1848.

Lately, however, we have witnessed the emergence of new confederations—or quasi-confederations. Europe itself is assuming the form of a confederation and

TABLE 12.2   Eleven Major Federal Systems

Nation	Number and Name of Units
Australia	6 states, 2 territories
Brazil	26 states, 1 federal district
Canada	10 provinces, 2 territories
Germany	16 states
India	25 states, 7 union territories
Mexico	31 states, 1 federal district
Nigeria	30 states, 1 federal capital territory
Russia	21 autonomous republics, 49 oblasts, 6 krays
South Africa	9 provinces
Switzerland	20 cantons, 6 half-cantons
United States	50 states, 1 federal district

Source: *The World Almanac and Book of Facts, 1996* (Mahwah, N.J.: Funk and Wagnalls, 1996), pp. 740–831, passim.

may someday even become a true federation, a United States of Europe. The breakup of the Soviet Union meant the breakup of a federation, but the nation of Russia, once again an independent entity, is itself a confederation, at least on paper. However, the latter example is also useful to remind us that not every contemporary state fits clearly into one of the three categories of unitary, federal, or confederal. Theoretically, Russia contains twenty-one "autonomous" republics, designated as "independent participants in international and foreign economic connections," a status that comes very close to suggesting a confederation. In practice, however, it has become clear that these republics (which account for 29 percent of the nation's territory and 15 percent of its population) are not at all autonomous. Neither Tartarstan nor Chechnya has ever opted to be part of Russia, and the oppressive military response to the efforts of Chechnya to break away and form a genuinely independent state has made clear how little independence has actually been granted to these units. Since 1991 President Boris Yeltsin has seesawed on the question of regional powers, attempting to curry the favor of regional leaders in his struggle with the Russian parliament and other opponents in Moscow.[5] But his ability to take away at will what has been given makes it clear that in many respects Russia more closely fits the definition of a unitary state.

INTERMEDIATE LEVELS OF GOVERNMENT

What kind of intermediate levels of government are required to meet a society's needs for governance? The answers given have been many and varied. Choosing between a federal and a unitary system is only the first step. Both federal and unitary states require subnational units. True, only in federal systems do such units have complete responsibility in certain domains, and in actual practice national governments are increasingly exercising broader control over subnational units even in federal systems. Nevertheless, there remains a significant scope for the exercise of state (or cantonal or provincial) power in every federal system. Furthermore, even though the policymaking powers granted subnational units in unitary systems can readily be revoked, in practice such units typically have a considerable measure of independence as long as they operate within national guidelines. And in both federal and unitary systems, subnational governments bear the heavy burdens of administering policies made either by them or at the national level.

Provincial Government

Much of the real work of government is carried on at intermediate levels. All but the world's smallest nations have some level of intermediate government between the central government and municipal government. In federal systems they are usually called states, provinces, or cantons. In unitary systems the more common name is department. Be careful, however—the name itself is not a sure guide to the kind of system under study. The French, for example, whose government is strictly unitary, use the word *canton* to refer to the constituency from which are elected representatives to the *departmental* level of government (there is no cantonal level of government any more than there is a congressional district level of government in the United States), and when they talk about life in "the provinces," they do not mean "in the *départements*" but rather anywhere in France that is not Paris. And of course, the word *state* is often used to refer to the nation-state, as is the word *republic* (but the latter was also the name for the subdivisions of the Soviet Union). To keep confusion down to a minimum, here we use the term *provinces* to mean all intermediate governments that are directly above the local level yet still below the level of the national government, trusting you to remember that this includes American counties and states, Canadian provinces, Israeli administrative departments, Swiss cantons, French *départements*, British counties, and numerous other units.

Whatever its name and whatever its powers, the provincial government occupies a difficult position in any nation's hierarchy of governmental bodies. Normally it has come into being because its inhabitants have some qualities or needs in common that are not shared by the rest of the nation. The provincial government must strive to protect its inhabitants' interests, whether the system is federal or unitary. The government of the Canadian province of Quebec seeks to maintain a fair balance between its majority population, which is of French extraction, and the British-descended minority, while at the same time ensuring that the rights of its French-speaking people are protected within Canada at large. Even where the boundaries have been drawn by imperialistic conquest, breaking up formerly united peoples, as in Africa, or by nature, following rivers or mountain ranges, or by ruler-wielding bureaucrats (look at the straight-edge boundaries of the U.S. state of Colorado), a sense of common identity often builds within the unit. With that identity comes a shared set of goals requiring purposeful government action.

At the same time, the provincial government often lacks both the powers and the resources to meet those goals. It must struggle with both central and local governments to recruit the leadership, acquire and keep the rights of taxation, and rally the degree of popular support that will permit it to meet the demands placed on it by those governments as well as by its own inhabitants. Its struggle with national government is likely to be particularly difficult and frustrating, as that body becomes ever more powerful and uses its powers of taxation to redistribute a nation's wealth in accordance with national policy.

On the other hand, provinces seldom accept the yoke of central control without a struggle. If the situation becomes intolerable, and circumstances suggest the plan is plausible, a province may even seek to set itself up as a separate nation, as has been the case with the Republic of Chechnya in the new Russian Federation.[6] More commonly, when a provincial government, or one of its agencies, is particularly dissatisfied, it seeks to gain the support of one branch of the national government in curbing what it views as the excesses of another. In the United States, the courts often play a particularly important role in this regard, adjudicating disputes between the levels of government. Another approach that may work is to rally public opinion against national policy. For example, when a local environmental protection agency in Siberia opposed the Russian government's agreement to give Weyerhaeuser Corporation, a U.S. timber company, access to some 1 million hectares of Siberian forest land, it was able to gain sufficient international publicity for its cause to slow the project down. Still, when the province is up against international business as well as its own national government, as in this case, the scales may seem unfairly weighed against it. Weyerhaeuser has undertaken its own extensive public relations campaign and is now providing funding for a local research institute that was originally one of the strong opponents of the logging plan. The company is expected to "go into Siberia towards the end of the century."[7]

Provincial governments also struggle with each other in their incessant quest for a greater resource base. This aspect of the problem is further complicated by the fact that needs, goals, and even political identity patterns are constantly shifting among constituent units. States that were on opposing sides in a historic civil war may find themselves embattled partners in the struggle to get a fair share of revenue allocation from a burgeoning oil industry now developing in other states—states that may themselves have been enemies but are now united in their efforts to protect a new source of wealth.

Regional Government

One answer to the shifting dilemmas of provincial government is to establish yet another intermediate level of government: the *region*. A region is usually formed by grouping provincial units. **Regionalism** is intermediate government just below the level of the national government and above the level of the province. Occasionally a region is formed *within* a single province, but even then it usually is responsible only to the national government. There are two kinds of regional government, distinguished by the scope of their coverage and also to some extent by how permanently each appears to be embedded in the nation's political system.

Structural Regionalism. In the first kind, **structural regionalism**, provincial units are grouped in regions by constitutional fiat. Regional assemblies, normally composed of elected representatives from the provincial level, meet to deal with matters of regional significance and concern. This kind of regionalism is normally established by constitutional amendment, and the regions thus created are expected to be permanent additions to the body politic. As an example, under the Fifth Republic, France has been divided into twenty-two regions, most of which are made up of several of the republic's ninety-six departments. Each region has its own council, charged with "assuming the burden and receiving the benefits of [the region's] share in the national economic plan."[8] Established by the followers of Charles de Gaulle when the Fifth Republic was created in 1959, the new regions were considerably strengthened by the socialists when they came to power in 1981. The socialist government quickly moved to establish direct elections to the regional councils and to eliminate the requirement that they submit all their deliberations to a regional prefect for approval. These changes have been maintained as the Gaullists have regained control of the French parliament (from 1986 to 1988 and again in 1993).

Structural regionalism has also been used to permit minority nationalities living in compact communities to exercise some degree of autonomous power. China has five autonomous regions: Guangxi Zhuang, Nei Menggu (Inner Mongolia), Nijgxia Hui, Xinjiang Weiwuer (Uighur), and Xizang (Tibet). Although power is still rigorously controlled from Beijing, regional identity permits symbolic remnants of cultural-historical distinctiveness—such as the "Nine Leagues and Forty-Seven Banners" of Inner Mongolia—to be retained (see Figure 12.1).[9]

Functional Regionalism. The second kind of regional government, **functional regionalism**, is more limited in scope. It is usually not a permanent structure established constitutionally but rather a short-term statutory solution to current problems that may or may not endure. Such regional governments are normally established to deal with only a single problem, such as the development of electricity, the conservation of water resources, or other specific policy areas not easily accommodated by municipal, provincial, or national centers of government. The Bay Area Air Quality Management District (BAAQMD), established to limit air pollution and offensive odors in the San Francisco Bay Area, is an example of such particularized regionalism. The district maintains a professional and effective staff, and investigates some 7,000 pollution complaints per year. It maintains a toll-free complaint hot line and investigates all complaints, if possible within forty-five minutes of the call.[10]

Particularized regionalism develops within provinces as well as above the provincial level. Beginning as early as 1910, the U.S. Bureau of the Census recognized the need to identify urban regions, a need that quickly became particu-

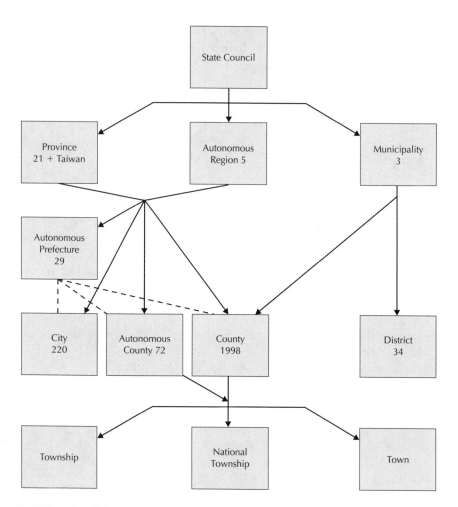

FIGURE 12.1   China's Governmental Structure

Source: Eileen Martin Harloff and Cuiyi Wei, "Present Day Local Government in China," *Planning and Administration* 16 (1989–92): 115. Reprinted by permission of the International Union of Local Authorities.

larly pronounced in the domain of transportation, since both goods and people move regularly across municipal and provincial borders. The answer was to create Regional Transportation Authorities, ranging from New York's Metropolitan Transportation Authority (MTA) to the Metropolitan Atlanta Rapid Transit Authority (MARTA) to the San Francisco Bay Area Rapid Transit District (BART). All are government bodies empowered to deal with transportation problems within their special jurisdictions.[11]

One of the problems with functional regional governments, however, is the difficulty citizens (and sometimes even other government officials) may have in remembering that they exist. Suppose you were annoyed by one of the following problems:

- the water has a bad taste
- the subway is *always* late
- there are never enough picnic tables available in the park
- traffic control on the bridge you drive across is poorly designed and is costing you precious study minutes every day
- your local library never gets the books you order on interlibrary loan in time for the papers you have to write

In all these cases, it might well be that the best way to draw attention to the problem—especially if you live in a large metropolitan area—would be to register a complaint with the appropriate functional regional government. Would you know which one to call? Take a look at the list in Box 12.2. Pick one of the problems just listed and imagine yourself living in Oakland, California, one of the cities in the San Francisco Bay area. Which agency would you call?

The reasonable answer, regardless of which problem you selected, is probably, "None of them." Your first call should almost certainly be to your own local city hall, in order to find out whom to call next. However, functional regionalism is definitely on the rise. One of your questions to city hall should be "Is there a regional agency that handles matters like this?"

LOCAL GOVERNMENT

The structures of local government are, if anything, even more varied than those of intermediate or national government. Human beings live in all kinds of aggregations, from isolated hermitages to small farms, from compounds or small villages to suburban settlements, from towns to medium-sized cities to major metropolises of several million inhabitants. With such immense variety, what does it take for government to be "local?" Is a nearby city hall serving millions more local than a distant county seat serving a mere handful of ranchers?

Here we interpret **local government** to mean any government that can be physically known to each and every citizen. Local government is government that citizens can quite literally get in touch with—and vice versa. It may be a hard day's drive away, but the ordinary citizen can achieve some degree of personal access to local government, if only to hand over his or her tax payment to a bored bureaucrat. It may be possible for some citizens to acquire the same degree of access to other levels of government, but local government is close and accessible to everyone. (That being the case, you may find it useful to take a break in your reading and go visit some unit of local government yourself. Attending a town meeting, interviewing a mayor or city manager, or just watching your local board of education in action is an excellent way to learn how meaningful this level of government can be to citizens affected by its action.)

Local governments, like provincial and national governments, have rule-making, rule-applying, and rule-adjudicating functions to carry out. However,

BOX 12.2   REGIONAL GOVERNMENT IN THE SAN FRANCISCO BAY AREA: AGENCIES AND PURPOSES

Alameda–Contra Costa Transit District (AC Transit). Purpose: Public bus transit Association of Bay Area Governments (ABAG). Purpose: Areawide comprehensive planning; cooperative action among Bay Area governments

Bay Area Air Quality Management District (BAAQMD). Purpose: Air pollution control

Bay Area Dischargers Authority (BADA). Purpose: Collection of data on aquatic wildlife and quality of water; assessment of the effect of pollution on San Francisco Bay

Bay Area Rapid Transit District (BART). Purpose: Rail rapid transit system

Bay Conservation and Development Commission (BCDC). Purpose: Regulation of filling, dredging, and changes in existing uses of the bay and shoreline

East Bay Dischargers Authority (EBDA). Purpose: Wastewater disposal

East Bay Municipal Utility District (EBMUD). Purpose: Water supply, wastewater treatment, management of public use lands

East Bay Regional Park District (EBRPD). Purpose: Provision of open space, regional parks, trails, recreational opportunities, and environmental education for the public

Golden Gate Bridge, Highway and Transportation District (GGBHTD). Purpose: Operation and maintenance of Golden Gate Bridge, bus, and ferry systems

Metropolitan Transportation Commission (MTC). Purpose: Comprehensive regional transporation planning; allocation of state and federal transportation funds

Midpeninsula Regional Open Space District (MSORD). Purpose: Acquisition and preservation of open space lands for low-intensity recreation and greenbelt

Regional Water Quality Control Board (RWQCB). Purpose: Protection of the quality of surface and ground water

Source: Jane Bergen, League of Women Voters of the Bay Area, *Decision Makers: Directory of Regional and Inter-County Agencies 1995-1997,* 15th ed. (Lafayette, Calif.: League of Women Voters of the Bay Area Education Fund, 1995). Reprinted by permission of the League of Women Voters of the Bay Area.

local government is typically under the control of provincial government—even in federal systems, since the federal principle is never extended to the grassroots. Consequently, mayors, chiefs, councils, and boards all carry out these functions only at the sufferance of higher authorities.

Rule Making at the Base

The form local government takes is usually determined by the national or provincial governments. The most common rule-making body at the local level is the **elected board** or **council**. Each French commune has its *conseil municipal.* Each

Chinese county has a County People's Congress. Each of the main islands of the Cook Islands has an elected Island Council.[12]

These local legislative bodies normally make rules (commonly referred to as *ordinances*) that apply to the local matters over which the central government has delegated them the authority to rule. When national matters assume deep importance locally, a local council may well be tempted to overstep these bounds. A number of U.S. city councils, for example, have taken it upon themselves to declare their cities "nuclear-free." Is nuclear policy always a matter for national policymaking only? Not necessarily, says Albert Donnay, director of Nuclear Free America: "Cities do have a right to regulate what goes on within their border for their own self-interest." The federal government, in sharp disagreement, has taken the matter to court.[13]

However, the more common problem facing local legislative bodies is not how to acquire more or broader rule-making power but rather how to acquire greater resources to finance the programs they would like to carry out under the powers they already have. The tax base of local governments is always limited;

A neighborhood meeting in Austin, Texas. The most common problem facing neighborhood groups with specific demands and their local legislative bodies is how to acquire the resources they need to finance the programs they would like to carry out.

(Bob Daemmrich/Stock Boston)

the demands of citizens for local government response to their daily needs are not. Local communes constantly seek new sources of revenue to finance programs that higher levels of government have assigned to their domain.

In Norway, for example, local government is responsible for providing day care centers, basic education, and primary health care for the elderly. However, the local authorities rely on grants from the central government and income taxes for almost all their revenue, and it is the national government that determines what the income tax rate will be. Property taxes provide 10 percent of total revenue, but these too are limited by national law. Thus, when national growth rates in the overall economy decline or stagnate, the tax base is weakened and central government grants are reduced. At such times, local governments in Norway find it difficult to meet their obligations; they bear the responsibilities for key aspects of social welfare but lack the resources to carry out their functions well.[14]

Even Orange County, California, one of the wealthier communities in the world, found itself desperately low on cash at the end of 1994 when several Wall Street brokerage houses refused to renew short-term loans of $12 billion that the county had borrowed in order to develop an investment portfolio worth $20 billion. Unable to repay the loans, the suddenly impoverished government declared bankruptcy.[15] Although it may be hard to work up much sympathy for Orange County, the problem exists throughout the human polity, with more painful results in the poorer nations of the world. In Mexico, says Daniel C. Levy, "municipalities depend on states and the national government regarding leadership and funds, and funds are very unevenly disbursed; most municipalities lack income beyond very small appropriations and fees from licenses and fines."[16]

Rule Application at the Base

There is great variation in how local rules are carried out and by whom. The chief executive at the local level may be a traditional *chief* entitled to his post by his place in the kinship system, a *mayor* elected by the people or by the rule-making council, a *city manager* hired by that council, or a *civilian* or *military administrator* appointed by the national government or by the government of a conquering nation. The powers of each of these leaders may be extensive or merely ceremonial. In earlier times, African chiefs sometimes ruled autocratically, but they were more often limited by the knowledge that they could be removed from power if they went too far beyond the will of those they governed. Ashanti chiefs, for example, always knew they could be "destooled"—that is, have the symbol of power, typically a three-legged stool on which no one ever actually sat, taken from them. In contemporary Africa, the chief has often become a merely ceremonial figure, although that status in itself may help him achieve appointment as a modern paid administrator.

The bureaucratic apparatus available for carrying out local rule is similarly varied. City hall may be an elaborate edifice such as the Hotel de Ville in Paris or the kitchen table of a part-time mayor in an Appalachian town. Public service may be more or less personal, more or less efficient, and more or less humanitarian, but in all cases the problems of limited funds, limited powers, and unlimited demands are likely to make themselves felt.

On the other hand, not all local communities have the same response to limited funds, not even within the same nation. Robert Putnam argues that it makes a great deal of difference whether or not the community has strong traditions of civic engagement of any kind. According to Putnam, when citizens routinely take part in their community life—such as reading the local newspapers, joining music or literary societies, or taking part in a soccer club—local government is likely to work well. Civic engagement produces social capital, creates a reservoir of trust, and makes it possible to get things done even when resources are limited. Anticipating an argument, Putnam insists such communities "did not become civic simply because they were rich. . . . They have become rich because they were civic."[17] He seems to suggest that solutions to the problems of local communities lie in their own hands, regardless of national or provincial funding, regardless of levels of affluence within the community, and regardless of any history of political oppression. (For some interesting figures on the second point—levels of affluence within the community—see Table 12.3.)

A more promising approach to improving the effectiveness of local government may be contemporary efforts that combine local and provincial or national government resources and expertise to combat a local problem experienced in numerous communities throughout a nation. Violence by and against young people became that kind of problem in the United States in the early 1990s, a time when the adolescent homicide rate doubled, when gunfire became a leading cause of teenage death, and when more than 60 percent of persons arrested and charged with crimes were between the ages of 13 and 29.[18]

The sense of crisis that such conditions reasonably produced has been met with a variety of responses attempting to draw on all possible resources. In crime-beleaguered Las Vegas, local and state officials work together to provide counseling, social services, dispute mediation, and other services in local centers, some of which are in buildings provided by private persons. The state of Missouri has set up an Intensive Case Monitoring program that assigns (and pays) college students to tutor, counsel, and "keep a close watch" over juvenile delinquents. The state of Washington has fourteen violence-prevention projects funded with a combination of federal, state, and local resources. Such efforts have yet to be evaluated for long-term results, but recent statistics suggest that nationwide the problem remains severe: Even as the crime rate among adults is falling, the rate for those below the age of 25 has been on the rise.[19] It should come as no surprise that those who work in juvenile justice at the local level continue to clamor for more state funds.[20]

Rule Adjudication at the Base

No question of local government is more sensitive than the resolution of disputes. When crimes are committed, reputations are besmirched, or contracts are

TABLE 12.3   Differences in Income in the Ten Largest U.S. Cities[a]

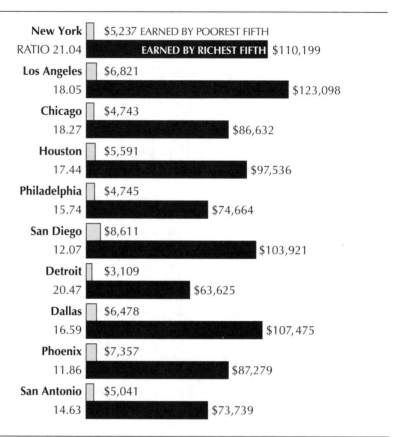

New York	$5,237 EARNED BY POOREST FIFTH
RATIO 21.04	EARNED BY RICHEST FIFTH $110,199
Los Angeles	$6,821
18.05	$123,098
Chicago	$4,743
18.27	$86,632
Houston	$5,591
17.44	$97,536
Philadelphia	$4,745
15.74	$74,664
San Diego	$8,611
12.07	$103,921
Detroit	$3,109
20.47	$63,625
Dallas	$6,478
16.59	$107,475
Phoenix	$7,357
11.86	$87,279
San Antonio	$5,041
14.63	$73,739

[a]Median annual incomes of the poorest fifth and richest fifth, with difference expressed as ratio (e.g., $5,237 is 1/21.04 of $110,199).
Source: *New York Times,* 26 Dec. 1994, A20.

violated, tempers flare and the human heart reaches out for help—social help. Whether or not that help will be available depends in large part on the local judicial apparatus.

Technically, the local police are not part of that apparatus; their job is simply to carry out the rules. In practice, however, the police are often both the first and the last agency of local justice with which the citizen comes into contact. Typically, police officers arrive on the scene, attempt to calm tempers and impose order, and suggest solutions. Although most police are careful to carry out these duties within the limits of the law, some are not; police racism, brutality, and corruption are widespread evils. Comments made during and after the 1992 riots in Los Angeles following the jury's verdict in the case of Rodney King suggest that the massive and costly explosion of anger was caused not merely by the patent unfairness of that one decision but also by the sense of despair so many felt to think that police brutality against persons of minority race was somehow acceptable to white Americans.[21] When "justice is done" on the spot, by a uniformed and armed agent of the executive branch of government, it must be perceived as truly just by all concerned.

Of course, the police do not always have the final judicial word, and it matters a great deal what other, more formally juridical bodies are available at the local level. In many villages, especially those more remote from large centers of population, the lowest level of the judicial branch is a local notable with minimal training and credentials who has been assigned to "keep the peace" by settling minor disputes. In U.S. small towns this may be the justice of the peace; the Nuer people of the Upper Nile River valley used to assign one of their members to be the "leopard skin chief"; and in China, neighborhood committees deal with first-time offenders who have committed minor crimes, seeking to reeducate them, and turn offenders over to public security units only if the deviant act is repeated.[22]

What if the matter is too weighty for such relatively informal adjudication or the decision seems unsatisfactory and unfair to one of the parties? At this point almost every government provides some way of linking local judicial functions to the national court system. Whether the dispute goes to a municipal criminal court, a small claims court, or a nearby national appeals court, a line is being crossed—away from relatively autonomous local justice and into a national network of courts, appeals, higher courts, and "courts of last resort" (which may not be courts at all; chief executives sometimes personally fulfill that function). Nations that cannot establish such links from local to national systems of justice are not, finally, sovereign states. They are little more than loose confederations— otherwise they would not leave final authority in such an important domain in the hands of local fiefdoms. The effort in the United States to eliminate "vigilante justice"—that is, justice administered by bands of armed men self-appointed to hold others accountable to what they conceived society's norms of righteous conduct to be—was thus a key step in nineteenth-century nation building.[23] Similarly, the Constitutional Council of Nigeria had to find a way to persuade northern Nigerian authorities that citizens in their region had the right to appeal decisions of the Islamic local courts to the secular national court system. Making such links is no easy matter. American vigilantes often had to be treated as criminals themselves before the authority of the national system could be established; in Nigeria the Constitutional Council had to agree that the national courts would include judges well versed in Islamic law, and even then consent was tacit and grudging during that nation's most recent experiment with civilian rule.

SUMMARY AND CONCLUSION

Subnational government is government we cannot do without, even if it is also government we cannot always make work in comfortable tandem with national politics. Most polities are simply too large and too complex to be served adequately by a single level of government. It always helps, and is often essential, to have local authorities who understand and can respond to purely local needs, even if the resources must be obtained from higher levels of government.

In a unitary system, all the powers of government are reserved to the central government but may be temporarily delegated to such subunits as states. In a federal system, certain powers are constitutionally reserved to the government of the nation's constituent parts, although the tendency in recent years has been for the national government to assume an ever stronger role. In a confederal system, largely sovereign states maintain a loose association that permits coordinated action on a limited number of matters.

A federal system can free the national government to deal with the more important national issues, allow citizens more meaningful participation at a lower and more immediate level of government, permit governmental experimentation on a limited basis, and allow for the addition and subtraction of constituent units with relatively little turmoil. A unitary system often provides its citizens with more uniform laws, provides for more equal representation and disbursement of government monies, has clearer lines of authority, and avoids the development of independent spheres of power. A confederal system sometimes offers a useful transitional structure as peoples move closer together or further apart.

Local government is government that can be physically known to each and every citizen. Its rule-making functions are normally carried out by elected bodies acting within the constraints imposed by higher levels of government—particularly the economic constraints of a severely limited power to tax or otherwise raise revenues adequate for the services their constituents demand. Local justice is often rendered by an executive agency, the police, and that agency may be responsible to national rather than local authorities, further complicating the relationship between the two. Once the more formal local judicial system is brought into a dispute, the crucial question becomes the nature of the link between that system and the national judiciary. Establishing some such link is essential for maintaining the sovereignty of the state at large.

As we have seen, subnational governments are essential components of the human polity. Indeed, because they are the governments we have most immediate access to, they are the governments we would most like to see assume a truly human face. But local and provincial government officials occupy a difficult terrain, caught between the multitudinous hopes and aspirations of the citizens they live among and the distant centers of national power whose purposes they must serve to serve their own. If they do not always respond as we might wish, there is nothing to stop us from scorning them in private, and those of us living in systems with free elections may do so openly—blithely throwing the rascals out from time to time. However, before grasping the momentary satisfactions of democratic empowerment, we might sometimes do well to consider the limitations under which they labor and ponder whether those we propose to send to city hall or to the provincial capital in their stead will be any better able to overcome the constraints inherent in the very principle of divided government power. In the next chapter we turn to yet another set of constraints operating on government officials—at local and provincial, but especially at national, levels— the nature of relationships among all the nations of the world.

Selected Readings

Beer, Samuel Hutchison. *To Make a Nation: The Rediscovery of American Federalism.* Cambridge, Mass.: Belknap Press, 1993. A readable study of the origins of federalism in the United States.

Bennett, Robert J. *Local Government in the New Europe.* New York: Halstead Press, 1996. An examination of local government systems and the process of political decentralization throughout Europe.

Berry, Jeffrey M., Kent E. Potney, and Ken Thomson. *The Rebirth of Urban Democracy.* Washington, D.C.: Brookings Institution, 1993. How citizens in five major U.S. cities collaborated with their governments to bring about positive change in their communities.

Burgess, Michael, ed. *Canadian Federalism: Past, Present and Future.* New York: Leicester University Press, 1991. Essays on the evolution of Canadian federalism.

Cairns, Alan C. *Charter versus Federalism: The Dilemmas of Constitutional Reform.* Montreal: McGill-Queen's University Press, 1992. The role of the constitution in Canadian society, with an emphasis on how the Charter of Rights and Freedoms introduced in 1982 has affected the relationships between the national government and the provinces.

Lewis, Norman. *Inner City Regeneration: The Demise of Regional and Local Governments.* Buckingham, Pa.: Open University Press, 1992. The author argues that local governments in the United States suffer from a "legitimation deficit" and lack of the power and resources to cope with the socioeconomic decline of older cities.

Mabileau, Albert, et al. *Local Politics and Participation in Britain and France.* Cambridge: Cambridge University Press, 1990. A collection of essays exploring the ways in which reforms in local government and administration have changed opportunities for French and British citizens to participate in government.

Michelmann, Hans J., and Panayotis Soldatos, eds. *Federalism and International Relations: The Role of Subnational Units.* Oxford: Clarendon Press, 1990. Essays on the performance of federal systems as actors in international relations with cases including Australia, Austria, Belgium, Canada, Germany, and Switzerland.

Schumaker, Paul. *Critical Pluralism, Democratic Performance and Community Power.* Lawrence: University Press of Kansas, 1991. Focuses on the policymaking process at the community level of government and examines how decisions about the distribution of public resources are made.

Notes

1. The Brazilian federal constitution allows the states of that nation to divide or join with others freely, a right that is quite frequently exercised—as recently as 1988 a former Brazilian territory, Fernando de Noronha, became part of the state of Pernambuco. See "Brazil," in *Political Handbook of the World,* ed. Arthur S. Banks (New York: CSA Publications, 1991), p. 82.

2. Article 67, sec. 8, and Article 89, sec. 4, General Principles of the Constitution of December 1982 adopted by the Fifth Session of the Fifth National People's Congress. From "The People's Republic of China," in *The Europa World Year Book*, vol. 1 (London: Europa Publishers, 1994), pp. 781, 783.

3. *New York Times*, 1 Nov. 1995, A9; and *San Francisco Examiner*, 1 Nov. 1995, A16.

4. Ivo D. Duchacek, *The Territorial Dimension of Politics within, among, and across Nations* (Boulder, Colo.: Westview Press, 1986), p. 68.

5. Colin Campbell, Harvey Feigenbaum, Ronald Linden, and Helmut Norpoth, *Politics and Government in Europe Today*, 2nd ed. (Boston: Houghton Mifflin, 1995), pp. 496–99.

6. Andrei Shoumikhin, "The Chechen Crisis and the Future of Russia," *Comparative Strategy* 5, no. 1 (1996): 1–10.

7. Divish Petrof, "Siberian Forests under Threat," *Ecologist* (Nov.–Dec. 1992): 167–70.

8. Henry W. Ehrmann and Martin A. Schain, *Politics in France*, 5th ed. (New York: HarperCollins, 1992), pp. 370–84.

9. Eileen Martin Harloff and Cuiyi Wei, "Present Day Local Government in China," *Planning and Administration* 16 (1989–92): 115.

10. Noga Morag Levine, "Between Choice and Sacrifice: Constructions of Community Consent in Reactive Air Pollution Regulation," *Law and Society Review* 28, no. 5 (1994): 1051–53.

11. For an argument that new regional agencies in transportation and other areas of government are needed now, see *Los Angeles Times*, 19 Jan. 1990, A24.

12. Except the island of Rarotonga, which is divided into three tribal districts (*vaka*). *The Europa World Yearbook, 1991*, vols. 1 and 2, 32nd ed. (London: Europa Publishers, 1991).

13. *New York Times*, 8 Sept. 1989, A10, and 22 Dec. 1989, B6. In April 1990, a federal district judge ruled that a 1988 ordinance proclaiming Oakland, California, a nuclear-free zone "interfered with the Federal Government's constitutional authority over national defense and atomic energy." *New York Times,*, 18 Apr. 1990, A11.

14. Rune J. Sørensen and Arild Underdal, "Coping with Poverty: The Impact of Fiscal Austerity on the Local Budgetary Process in Norway," *Scandinavian Political Studies* 16, no. 1 (1993): 58, 59. See also Gunnar Rongen, "Efficiency in the Provision of Local Public Goods in Norway," *European Journal of Political Economy* 11 (1995): 253–64.

15. *New York Times*, 7 Dec. 1994, 1, C5.

16. Daniel C. Levy, "Mexico: Sustained Civilian Rule without Democracy," in *Democracy in Developing Countries: Latin America*, vol. 4, ed. Larry Diamond, Juan J. Linz, and Seymour Martin Lipset (Boulder, Colo.: Rienner, 1989), p. 470.

17. Robert D. Putnam, "The Prosperous Community: Social Capital and Economic Growth," *Current* (Oct. 1993): 4–9.

18. Carla Nielsen et al., "Youth Violence," *State Government News* (Aug. 1994): 20–35. In 1991, 27 out of every 100,000 persons in Calhoun County, Florida, were children killed by gunfire. Other cities have lower rates, but it is hardly reassuring that the figure was "only" 3.9 per 100,000 in Cook County, Illinois, 5.6 in Baltimore, 2.6 in Las Vegas, 6.6 in the Bronx, 4.7 in Dallas, and 4.8 in Los Angeles.

19. *New York Times*, 6 May 1966, A1.

20. Nielsen et al., "Youth Violence," p. 23.

21. "Don't white folks . . . believe in justice?" wondered one African-American commentator. "After all, they're the ones who created the Constitution and the Bill of Rights." *New York Times*, 1 May 1992, A12; see also *Los Angeles Times*, 2 May 1992, A2, A20, and 3 May 1992, A1, A14. For a general study of the role of the police as mediators in neighborhood disputes, see Wayne A. Kerstetter, "Who Disciplines the Police? Who Should?" in *Police Leadership in America*, ed. William A. Geller (Chicago: American Bar Association, 1985), pp. 149–82. Of course, police brutality is a problem in other countries besides the United States. For stories regarding abusive behavior by police in Japan, Canada, and Mexico, see *Washington Post*, 30 Apr. 1990, A13, A19; *Christian Science Monitor*, 31 July 1991, 4; and *New York Times*, 1 Apr. 1992, A3.
22. See E. E. Evans-Pritchard, "The Nuer of the Southern Sudan," in *African Political Systems*, ed. M. Fortes and E. E. Evans-Pritchard (London: Oxford University Press, 1940), pp. 291–94; James C. F. Wang, *Contemporary Chinese Politics: An Introduction*, 2nd ed. (Englewood Cliffs, N.J.: Prentice Hall, 1985), p. 123.
23. For a contemporary example of vigilantism, this time in Venezuela, see Diana Jean Schemo, "Lynch-Mob Justice Growing in Poor Sections of Caracas," *New York Times*, 12 May 1996, A4.

13 International Relations

Once upon a time, when we were young and not so foolish, my husband, our small son, and I spent a year living on a boat moored on the Seine, in the heart of Paris. The boat was one of several small but livable craft rented out to an international community of young people like us, newly arrived in Paris, ready for adventure, and unwilling to move into any of the dingy apartments we could otherwise afford. In the midst of this enthusiastic group lived one middle-aged woman, the mother of a young Englishman, who had come along to "keep boat" for him. She, unlike the rest of us, was less than thrilled with her accommodations. She didn't mind the low ceilings, the butane heaters, or even the way the dishes rattled in the galley every time a barge went by. But she was sure she would never be able to bring this nautical home up to her own standards of cleanliness. "Because you know, my dear," she told me in her haughtiest British tones, there in the middle of Paris, "foreigners are always so dirty."

Some of us are never foreigners, at least not in our own eyes. Either we never travel, or when we do we move through the world so immersed in our own sense of nationhood that we never really see the world at all. Such uncompromising chauvinists go beyond patriotism. They believe not only that their nation is the best nation but that it is the only one that really matters. In some cases, they suffer from **xenophobia**, the fear or hatred of anything foreign or strange.

This book is dedicated to the principle that all nations, and all their citizens, matter. The human polity is the composite of all the world's polities. But is there really such a thing as "the human polity?" Is there a whole that is greater than—or at least different from—the sum of the parts? Throughout this book we have discovered a number of similarities in the politics and government of the world's nations and a number of signs of their interdependence. But by and large we have continued to treat different nations as distinct and separate entities. Here we look more closely at the interrelationship among polities, the *inter-nation* relationships, or, in short, at **international** relations. Although these relationships almost always stem from the efforts of individual nations to expand or defend their territorial, material, and cultural goods, they have inevitably produced a vast web of global interdependence. It is this web of interdependence that gives substantive content to the idea of a human polity.

In this chapter we begin by examining an important contemporary issue of international politics—human rights—and then consider the ways such politics are conducted, including the organizations and treaties that give international relations structure and coherence and the rules of law and force that govern behavior in the world arena. By chapter's end we should be in a better position to assess the extent to which the citizens of the world may be starting to conceive of themselves as global compatriots—rather than just themselves, the good guys, versus the others, the dirty (or primitive or pagan or war-mongering or fanatical or oppressive) *foreigners*.

A CONTEMPORARY ISSUE OF INTERNATIONAL POLITICS: HUMAN RIGHTS

Whether a nation's policies are focused on foreign or domestic affairs, whether they are openly belligerent or only indirectly influential on other nations' destinies, the growing interdependence of individual polities has so extended the scope of international politics that almost *any* course of action undertaken by a single nation will have some influence on the well-being of one or more other nations. The proliferation of arms, the protection of human rights, the rise of ethnic nationalism, and the ever more serious need to protect our environment are only a few of the problems requiring our urgent, global attention. To understand the impact of our increasing interdependence in international relations, it is helpful to take a longer look at one of the key issues in global politics today, the protection of human rights.

The violation of human rights by governments that imprison, torture, and execute their own citizens is a major issue in international relations. Often these citizens' only offense has been political dissent. The military weapons and methods now available to control domestic populations have made tyranny more fearsome than ever before; even the most determined band of dissidents is a poor match for the strength of the modern police state. When dictatorships are ruthless in the execution of policies designed to eliminate protest, the only hope for their oppressed citizenry may be to appeal to more powerful external forces—that is, to other nations and to world opinion.

The Universal Declaration of Human Rights, adopted in Helsinki, Finland, in 1975, states that everyone has the right to "life, liberty and security of person." The exercise of political power to deny these basic rights is certainly not a new phenomenon in human history, but the scale of punishments meted out to those who attempt to exercise such rights has reached truly horrifying proportions as twentieth-century technological efficiency is exhibited in the instruments and strategies of oppression. China's swift and bloody suppression of the student-led democracy movement in 1989 deeply dismayed a watching world, as did the revelations that in the Philippines Fernando Marcos had ordered some 50,000 persons to be arrested, detained, and, in many cases, tortured and killed.[1] Elsewhere—out of camera range, as it were—other appalling events have been taking place in the past quarter of a century. Over 500,000 people were killed by the Indonesian army, assisted by gangs of youths belonging to a fundamentalist Muslim party, in the nine months following the attempt of dissidents to overthrow the government in 1965. In Cambodia under Khmer Rouge rule (1975–79), between 1 and 3 million people were killed in a series of purges that began with the highest officers of the preceding government and worked steadily downward through lower officials, intellectuals, teachers, students, members of ethnic minorities, and finally even members of the current government who were considered less than 100 percent loyal to the leadership. The numbing statistics go on: up to half a million killed in Uganda during the eight-year rule of President Idi Amin (1971–79); 5,000 political opponents killed in a single Ethiopian city in a three-month period (November 1977–February 1978); more than 80,000 killed in Burundi in the spring of 1972; 11,712 noncombatants killed in El Salvador during 1981; as many as 20,000 persons described as "the disappeared" in Argentina between 1976 and 1984; about 20,000 Hindu Tamils killed in Sri Lanka since 1983; and over 25,000 persons killed from 1980 to 1992 in the fighting between members of the Sendero Luminoso (Shining Path) guerrilla movement and three successive Peruvian governments.[2]

Every one of these numbers is made up of a series of individuals—of human lives. A man or woman or child woke up, considered the day ahead, got dressed, ate whatever breakfast was available, and sallied forth to death. Such assassinations and massacres are not only committed outside anything that can be called the law; they are for the most part entirely unwarranted even on grounds of fear of opposition. Whole ethnic groups or social classes are labeled undesirable. Their most innocent and nonpolitical members are killed indiscriminately along with the dissenters—and, of course, those who have dissented have frequently done so only by means that would be considered legitimate and fair in polities that respect human rights. Furthermore, these figures—far from complete—say nothing of the even greater numbers of people who are imprisoned and tortured by such governments. Nearly half of the 184 nations that make up the United Nations (UN) are believed to be holding in prison people whose only offense is their beliefs or origins. Since 1979, 60 nations have been accused of practicing torture.[3]

It is widely recognized that such wholesale contempt for human life and liberty can be curbed only by concerted international action, and a wide range of international remedies has been sought. Declarations and covenants abound: The Nuremberg Charter, the Geneva Conventions, the International Covenant on Civil and Political Rights, the American Convention on Human Rights, the African Charter on Human Rights, and the European Convention on Human Rights are the six most widely cited. Although their high-sounding language may seem a weak defense against ruthlessness on the scale we have just reviewed, these covenants provide the necessary definitions and distinctions on which to base more substantive intervention. (For example, they set standards for fair trials, for legal use of the death penalty where serious crimes have been committed, and for "acceptable" killings during times of war and other armed conflicts.) The UN Human Rights Commission (UNHRC) is devoted to the protection of human rights, and regional organizations such as the European Parliament, the Inter-American Commission on Human Rights, and the African Commission on Human and Peoples' Rights have also sent fact-finding missions and published reports identifying abuses of human rights.[4]

One of the most powerful international agencies in the struggle to protect human rights is a private group, Amnesty International. Founded in 1961 and awarded the Nobel Peace Prize in 1977, this organization has emphasized wide publicity for human rights violations and has organized international visits and letter-writing campaigns as a way of bringing pressure to bear on governments responsible for human rights violations (see Box 13.1).

BOX 13.1   AMNESTY INTERNATIONAL: FIGHTING FOR HUMAN RIGHTS WITH PRIVATE MEANS

Amnesty International, a private organization based in New York City, describes itself as "a worldwide movement working impartially for the release of all prisoners of conscience, fair and prompt trials for political prisoners, and an end to torture and executions." One way the organization works is to send its members a monthly "Freedom Writers" newsletter, telling of two or three cases of human rights violations that the organization has investigated. Members are asked to write protest letters to the authorities responsible for the unfair trials, imprisonment, and/or torture being endured, and to send short postcards of encouragement to the victims as well. Addresses are provided, as well as sample letters that can be used. Here is a typical case, reported in the July 1996 newsletter:

> **Zhao Lei** and her husband **Bai Weiji** are serving prison sentences of 6 and 10 years respectively for "illegally providing national secrets to a foreigner." The information they reportedly provided—news articles and reports on economic and foreign policy—would not be considered secret in many other countries. Bai Weiji had worked for the Foreign Ministry but lost his job when he organized workers to support the pro-democracy demonstrators in Tiananmen Square in 1989. Zhao Lei is also a former employee of the Foreign Ministry. She and her husband have a five-year-old daughter. Please send cards [addresses of Zhao Lei and Bai Weiji are given].

Usually the newsletter has some good news to report as well, although not every case has a happy ending. Here are some "Case Updates."

- **Kelthoum Ahmed Labid El-Ouanat** of Morocco/Western Sahara (May 1996 *Freedom Writer's Bulletin*)—Released from prison along with five co-defendants.
- **Wafa' Wasfi Ahmad** of Kuwait (October 1994 *Freedom Writer's Bulletin*)—Released from prison.
- **Jose Luis Grave de Peralta Morell** of Cuba (February 1994 *Freedom Writer's Bulletin*)—Released from prison.
- **Zikrayat Mahmud Harb** of Kuwait (August 1993 *Freedom Writer's Bulletin*)—Released from prison.
- **Thomas Wainggai** of Indonesia (May 1991 *Freedom Writer's Bulletin*)—Died on March 12, 1996, while being transferred from prison to a hospital.

Amnesty International also holds annual regional conferences throughout the world; works on special problems (for example, a worldwide campaign to help refugees in 1997); sends its representatives to meet with government officials; publishes an annual report and *Amnesty Action,* a quarterly newspaper, in addition to the newsletter; and raises private funds to pay for its actions. It limits itself to "state-backed human rights violations" and does not focus on abuses perpetrated by individuals.

Sources: *Freedom Writer's Bulletin* (July 1996); *Amnesty Action* 19, no. 1 (Winter 1996); and *New York Times,* 16 July 1995, A10.

THE ACTORS IN INTERNATIONAL POLITICS

Who participates in international politics? The answer that first comes to mind is a simple one: individual nations. But it is more and more common for private groups as well as nation-states to work actively in the international sphere, and even nations must act through individuals. Who, then, are the key actors in international politics? In a certain sense, all of us are. We may act openly, taking part, for example, in a letter-writing campaign denouncing the continued imprisonment of a Chinese dissident, or telephoning the office of a chief executive to say how deeply we approve or disapprove of a particular treaty or (more likely) act of war. But even our private acts help influence the course of world events. The decisions an individual consumer makes about whether to take her vacations by air, train, or car have their impact, however small, on whether or not the United States will decide to upgrade its railway system to European standards by importing a rapid train system from France, Japan, or Germany (presently the three leaders in this industry). The unwillingness of a Japanese farm community to sacrifice its land for the building of a new international airport shapes that nation's ability to engage in foreign trade. Your own readiness or reluctance to register for the draft or to urge others to do so must be taken into account when your nation's leaders calculate their preparedness to use military means to secure the ends they seek.

Similarly, the acts of a wide range of public officials help shape the course of international relations. Local politicians, for example, may work hard to create conditions that will convince foreign investors to establish production facilities—and create jobs—in their communities, even when they would prefer to be able to do without the foreign capital. Jyoti Basu, chief minister of the Indian state of West Bengal, recently toured the United States and Europe with twenty-seven of Calcutta's top industrialists to publicize the city's political stability, skilled workforce, local democracy, falling birthrate and rising literacy. A lifelong communist who has held his office for eighteen years, the 82-year-old Basu has accepted the pressures of global capitalism. "I am forced to do certain things," said the minister, conceding that, given present circumstances, "when PepsiCo came here and took over a sick company . . . it was very good. I'm not interested in their drinks but they've done good work in Punjab with food processing."[5]

Legislators and executives at the provincial level can also be significant actors in international relations. They can create conditions that foster or impede the development of export commodities, the demand for imported goods, the growth of defense industries, the willingness to accept refugee populations, or the establishment of cultural ties. National legislators perform all these roles as well and often have the further responsibility of approving treaties, declaring wars, and appropriating the funds to carry out a nation's international commitments. As we have already noted, chief executives normally play a leading role in establishing as well as executing foreign policy, aided by a more or less vast bureaucratic apparatus devoted to that task. Nor is it uncommon for judges to have their say in this domain, ruling the terms of particular treaties valid or invalid or judging the behavior of citizens lawful or unlawful according to its conformity with international agreements that have become the law of the land.

In recent years private groups and enterprises have taken an increasingly active role in international politics. In the European context, such organizations are referred to as *Eurogroups.* Although some authors, such as Ernst B. Haas, predicted that the growth of supranational bodies would lead automatically to federations of national interest groups, in practice most national associations have not yet been willing to provide either the necessary funding or the necessary spirit of transnational cooperation to give such activities effective power. The result has been, especially in the realm of private business, a determination to go it alone. As Andrew McLaughlin, Grant Jordan, and William A. Maloney have shown, in such cases individual businesses do not hesitate to bring their own "distinct corporate interests" into the international arena.[6]

Nevertheless, among the various participants in international affairs, members of the world's executive branches and departments still hold the lead in making and carrying out the decisions that shape relations among nations.

ORGANIZING INTERNATIONAL POLITICS

Two factors making political relations between nations difficult are the unpredictability of significant economic, social, and political events and the impossibility of foreseeing the impact of such events on international relations. Gathering good intelligence helps reduce the element of surprise, and maintaining diplomatic relations improves the international community's chances of responding effectively to sudden crises. Another way the nations of the world attempt to gain some mastery over the course of history is by making pacts with one another—agreeing to engage in certain activities or promising to do so in the event of certain other developments. Such pacts may be made between as few as two nations. They may take the form of regional organizations, and such associations may make and remake the terms of their relationship with further pacts. Or the pacts among nations may assume worldwide proportions.

Treaties: Functionally Limited Pacts

The **treaty** is a time-honored means of organizing the relations between nations. The Stele of Vultures, a document that records the terms of peace insisted upon by Eannatum of Lagash in Babylonia after he defeated the city-state of Umma, was written nearly 4,500 years ago. Another almost equally ancient treaty that archaeologists have discovered is a friendship treaty between the city-states of Lagash and Uruk. The best known of the ancient agreements is the treaty made 3,200 years ago by the Hittite king Hattusilis III and Ramses II of Egypt after the battle of Gadesh.[7]

Treaties are made for a wide range of reasons. They may be intended to offer assurance to the signatories that if one of them is attacked the others will come to its aid, as in the North Atlantic Treaty signed by the United States and eleven other nations in 1949, in which the partners agree to consider an armed attack against one or more of them in Europe or North America an attack against them all. The role—and possible expanded membership—of NATO has been under serious discussion since the fall of the Soviet Union and the end of the Cold War. Will those against whom the alliance was formed now join it as cooperative members? Will the alliance become an agency for keeping or restoring peace in the world's trouble spots? Or are other functions likely to develop? At the present time, it seems reasonable to predict only that the functions of this institution are likely to continue to change in response to changing circumstances, while the body itself remains in place.[8]

Treaties may also be made in an effort to reduce the chance of war, as in the series of arms limitations agreements between the United States and the Soviet Union toward the end of the Cold War. Treaties may be made at the conclusion of a war, spelling out the terms of dominion of one nation over another, as when the Fulani people conquered the Mande people of West Africa in the middle of the eighteenth century and demanded that the Mande respect the laws of Islam or turn over their land to those who did.[9] Or the terms of peace may be considerably less demanding, as at the conclusion of the Gulf War, when little more was actually demanded of Iraq than its withdrawal from Kuwait and its leader, Saddam Hussein, was allowed to remain in power.[10]

Treaties are also made for purely peaceful purposes, often in the realm of international trade. The scope of such treaties may be broad indeed; the principal signatories (Canada, the United States, and Mexico) of the North American Free Trade Agreement (NAFTA) have a combined population of 370 million people and gross domestic product of $6.8 trillion. The main provision in NAFTA is a schedule of tariff reduction on manufactured goods that will lead to their total elimination by the year 2009. The signatories are still unsure what the long-term effects on their economies will be, especially in the case of Mexico, where some see the likelihood of vastly increased foreign investment as making that nation the main beneficiary of the treaty and others insist that poorer Mexicans will be forced out of their own economy, losing their land and their jobs to the economic "readjustments" made necessary by the treaty.[11]

Treaties may also be much more limited in scope, such as those that settle border disputes between two nations or clarify the conditions under which the citizens of one nation may visit or emigrate to the other. Yet even such limited pacts may well have wide significance. When Germany and Poland signed a 1991 treaty fixing the borders between them, they were seeking to end centuries of debate, mistreatment of each other's emigrating citizens, and frequent armed aggression. The signing of this treaty was seen as a key moment in the creation of a "common European house" in the postcommunist era.[12] (See also Box 13.2.)

Regional Organizations

Often even the simplest treaties entail the establishment of some form of organization to carry out their provisions. More elaborate treaties necessitate more elaborate structures, and if these in turn prove successful, they sometimes inspire the formulation of further treaties and further structures. In some cases the

BOX 13.2   A PEACE TREATY IS MADE

TEXT OF THE AGREED BASIC PRINCIPLES ENDORSED BY THE FOREIGN MINISTERS OF BOSNIA AND HERZEGOVINA, CROATIA, AND SERBIA AND MONTENEGRO, SEPTEMBER 8, 1995.

1.   Bosnia and Herzegovina will continue its legal existence with its present borders and continuing international recognition.

2.   Bosnia and Herzegovina will consist of two entities, the Federation of Bosnia and Herzegovina as established by the Washington Agreements, and the Republica Srpska (RS).

2.1   The 51:49 parameter of the territorial proposal of the Contact Group is the basis for a settlement. This territorial proposal is open for adjustment by mutual agreement.

2.2   Each entity will continue to exist under its present constitution (amended to accommodate these basic principles).

2.3   Both entities will have the right to establish parallel special relationships with neighboring countries, consistent with the sovereignty and territorial integrity of Bosnia and Herzegovina.

2.4   The two entities will enter into reciprocal commitments (a) to hold complete elections under international auspices; (b) to adopt and adhere to normal international human rights standards and obligations, including the obligation to allow freedom of movement and enable displaced persons to repossess their homes or receive just compensation; (c) to engage in binding arbitration to resolve disputes between them.

3.   The entities have agreed in principle to the following.

3.1   The appointment of a Commission for Displaced Persons authorized to enforce (with assistance from international entities) the obligations of both entities to enable displaced persons to repossess their homes or receive just compensation.

3.2   The establishment of a Bosnia and Herzegovina Human Rights Commission, to enforce the entities' human rights obligations. The two entities will bide by the Commission's decisions.

3.3   The establishment of joint Bosnia and Herzegovina public corporations, financed by the two entities, to own and operate transportation and other facilities for the benefit of both entities.

3.4   The appointment of a Commission to Preserve National Monuments.

3.5   The design and implementation of a system of arbitration for the solution of disputes between the two entities.

Source: *U.S. Department of State Dispatch* 6, no. 37 (11 Sept. 1995): 679–80.

A treaty made in the hope of ending war. The presidents of Serbia (Slobodan Milosevic), Bosnia (Alija Izetbegovic), and Croatia (Franjo Tudjman) sign the Dayton accords, November 1995.

(Mikhail Schultz/Sygma)

process thus begun can lead to the formation of new states, as formerly distinct entities move from functional cooperation to national integration. It is easy enough to find historical examples; contemporary Italy, Germany, and Switzerland were all formed after a long period of treaty making between independent principalities. But can it still happen today? What are the chief regional organizations of today? What are the chances that new national entities will emerge from them?

The list in Box 13.3 answers the first question. Here we examine some of the possible answers to the second question by looking at two examples: the European Union and the Organization of African Unity (OAU).

The European Union. A condition of the Marshall Plan, initiated by the United States after World War II to assist in the rebuilding of Europe, was that the recipients work out a single plan for the distribution of any aid received. In response, French foreign minister Robert Schumann proposed the creation of a single authority to control the production of coal and steel. In 1952, France, former West Germany, Italy, Belgium, Luxembourg, and the Netherlands signed the European Coal and Steel Community Treaty (ECSC). This was no simple treaty; although its terms covered only coal and steel, the well-known intention of at

BOX 13.3   MAJOR REGIONAL ORGANIZATIONS FORMED SINCE WORLD WAR II

1945	League of Arab Nations (actually established in March 1945, but probably legitimate to consider it as post-war)
1947	Economic Commission for Europe (ECE)
1948	Organization of American States (OAS)
1949	Council of Europe
1949	North Atlantic Treaty Organization (NATO)
1949	Council for Mutual Economic Assistance (COMECON)
1952	Australia, New Zealand, United States Security Treaty Organization (ANZUS)
1952	Nordic Council
1955	Warsaw Treaty of Friendship, Cooperation and Mutual Assistance
1955	Western European Union
1957	Council of Arab Economic Unity
1957	European Economic Community (the Common Market)
1960	Central American Common Market (CACM)
1960	European Free Trade Association
1961	Organization of Economic Cooperation and Development (OECD)
1963	Organization of African Unity (OAU)
1967	Association of Southeast Asian Nations (ASEAN)
1968	Organization of Arab Petroleum Exporting Countries (OAPEC)
1969	Andean Community of Nations
1973	Caribbean Community (CARICOM)
1975	Economic Community of West African States (ECOWAS)
1989	Asia-Pacific Economic Co-operation
1991	Commonwealth of Independent States (CIS)
1991	Southern Common Market (MERCOSUR) (Argentina, Brazil, Paraguay, Uruguay)
1992	Council of the Baltic Sea States (CBSS)
1992	European Union (evolved from European Community)
1992	Southern African Development Community (SADC)
1993	Common Market for Eastern and Southern Africa
1994	Organization for Security and Co-operation in Europe (evolved from Conference on Security and Co-operation in Europe—CSCE, 1972)
1995	North American Free Trade Agreement (NAFTA)
1998	Pacific Community (evolved from South Pacific Commission, 1947)

Source: *The World Factbook 1995* (Washington, D.C.: Central Intelligence Agency, 1995), pp. 485–521; and *The Europa World Year Book, 1998,* vol. 1 (London: Europa Publications, 1998), pp. 1–313. Reprinted by permission.

least some of the signers was to develop eventually a wider-ranging European Common Market—and possibly even a single European nation, roughly equal to the Soviet Union and the United States in territory, population, and natural resources.

In the first years of the ECSC's existence, the partners made rapid progress toward these goals—so rapid that in 1957 the Treaty of Rome was signed, creating the European Economic Community (EEC). The EEC abolished all customs duties among the member countries and established a Council of Ministers, an Executive Commission, and a Court of Justice. Ten years later, in 1967, a European Parliament was added. However, for the first twelve years of its existence the parliament was a nonelected body with no legislative functions, and it was not until 1979 that the member states first held direct elections to this body.

Nevertheless, by the end of the 1980s the EEC included twelve members (Denmark, Greece, Ireland, Portugal, Spain, and the United Kingdom having joined the earlier six), and these twelve had agreed that as of 1992 they would eliminate all internal commercial, financial, and customs barriers, thereby creating a truly common market. As of February 1992, the twelve put the final touches on the Treaty of Maastricht, named after the small Dutch town in which they met. The treaty went far beyond the trade agreements originally envisaged. It called for massive changes in the nature of the community, laying out in detail the steps to be taken toward a new Economic and Monetary Union (EMU) and a new political union (European Union). In the very near future, said Maastricht, Europe would have a single currency, a common foreign and defense policy, and common citizenship.

It was not easy to get all the representatives to agree on the details, and then the new treaty had to meet the test of several referenda and failed the first by a narrow margin, when the Danes voted against it on June 2, 1992.[13] The Irish voted yes by a very large margin a few weeks later, but the positive French vote in September was by a very slim majority. Some important changes were made in the treaty, and Denmark reversed its vote in the following year. In 1994, four other nations voted on whether or not to seek to join the union: Austria voted yes heartily (66.4% approving), Finland was reasonably enthusiastic (56.9% in favor), Sweden agreed but rather reluctantly (52.2%), and Norway, in a vote that raised a new record for voter turnout, said no (by 52.3%).[14]

The road to unity is obviously not an easy one and there have been important setbacks, but progress nonetheless seems steady and sure. Ignoring dire warnings from a cynical new world that the effort to combine social protection with economic progress and fiscal stability is hopelessly out of date in an era of unrestrained free-marketeering, the old world continues to build a yet newer world, a united Europe.[15] By 1995, very few of the 373 million citizens of Europe thought of themselves as purely European; about a fourth of the Belgians, Germans, French, and Luxembourgers were ready to say they were "European first" and their own nationality second, and in every nation but Britain about 50 percent said that although they were their own nationality first, they were "European second." One analyst suggests that Europeans are after all accustomed to a sense of dual nationalism (for example, the Welsh who are British, the Bretons who are French, the Basques who are Spanish) and that it may be easier for them than it might be for others to accept the idea of divided loyalty and divided sovereignty.[16]

The Organization of African Unity. The Organization of African Unity was formed in 1963, when thirty-one heads of African states met in Addis Ababa, Ethiopia. There was little agreement at this first meeting as the dignitaries present argued among themselves about whether the new organization should immediately form a common market and work to establish some form of pan-African union, take a much more gradual approach toward the same ends, or focus primarily on lending "unconditional support" to the African peoples still under colonial rule. The last position ultimately prevailed, as eloquently stated by Algeria's president, Ahmed Ben Bella: "Let us all die a little, so that the peoples still under colonial domination may be free and African unity may not be a vain word." The OAU took this mission as its prime reason for existence.[17] By 1983 twenty more nations had gained independence—many of them significantly aided by efforts of OAU member states—and joined the organization; and by 1991 there were fifty-one member states in the OAU.

Besides holding annual meetings, the OAU also organizes meetings on problems of special import, often in conjunction with the United Nations.[18] One such meeting was the International Symposium on Refugees and Problems of Forced Population Displacements held in Addis Ababa, Ethiopia, in 1995. There are now approximately 7 million refugees in Africa, ten times the number twenty-five years ago. The OAU identified the root causes as including not only armed conflict and arms proliferation but also natural disasters, the failures of governments, and poverty so severe that about two-thirds of Africa's population lives below the poverty line and thirty of the poorest countries in the world are on that continent.[19]

Working out of such desperate circumstances, it is little wonder the OAU has found it difficult to meet its own past commitments, in all domains. Yet the organization insists that Africans must "continue to sit down and take care of the problems themselves" and shows little tendency to blame postcolonial exploitation of their resources by First World nations for the fact that Africa is "the only region in the world likely to experience an increase in absolute poverty over the next decade."[20]

Most of the states belonging to the OAU have also pursued their goals through other bodies, such as the United Nations Economic Commission for Africa (ECA) and several smaller regional associations. There are now more than thirty regional associations in Africa. Among the most important are the sixteen-member Economic Community of West Africa (ECOWAS), focusing almost exclusively on economic ends, and the nine-member Southern African Development Coordination Conference (SADCC), still dedicated first and foremost to the independence of all African peoples.

The United Nations

No dream has held greater appeal for humankind than the dream of a united world. Confucius imagined a "Grand Union," Dante yearned for a world monarch, the anarchist Mikhail Bakunin sought a "United States of the World" based on "the right of voluntary union and the right of voluntary separation," and Marxists hoped that "the International Republic of Soviets" might one day be established.[21] Today a World Order Models Project (WOMP) periodically convenes, bringing together scholars from all the world's continents, who attempt to devise what they refer to as "relevant utopias"—that is, plans for a world order that are rooted in present reality and so will not be dismissed as mere wishful thinking.[22]

But however strong the appeal of the idea of world government is, at present the institution of the nation-state remains the clearly dominant form of human organization. Intergovernmental organizations that attempt to deny this reality founder or fail to materialize. The ones that take it as a given are more likely to achieve a modicum of success. The United Nations is an example of this kind of more realistic international organization.

The people who drafted the United Nations Charter were conscious of the need to recognize the continuing strength of nationalism and thereby avoid the fate of the League of Nations, the world's previous effort to establish international cooperation.[23] The new charter made it clear that no nation would be expected to commit its forces to a military action without internal deliberations and assent. It also avoided repeating what had proved to be another mistake of the league; instead of granting all nations equal voting power, as the league had done, the UN Charter gives the five major world powers (the United States, Russia, China, Great Britain, and France) permanent membership in the organization's strongest "action body," the Security Council, and provides each with the right of veto.[24]

The UN Charter, adopted in San Francisco in 1945 by fifty-one member states, is thus not the blueprint for a world state, nor is it intended to function as one. It is instead a set of rules governing a truly *international* organization, in which each nation's sovereignty is recognized and accepted. The United Nations was established to help preserve international peace and to foster international cooperation in addressing the social and economic problems that plague the human polity. The organization has six governing organs and a wide range of committees, programs, and agencies (see Figure 13.1).

The General Assembly. All the 184 member states of the United Nations are entitled to representation in the **General Assembly**. According to the United Nations's own description, this body discusses and makes recommendations on "any questions or any matters within the scope of the present Charter," controls the budget, and elects members to the five other governing organs. Originally intended to play a subordinate role to the Security Council, the General Assembly has become increasingly important in recent years, as the unwillingness of the

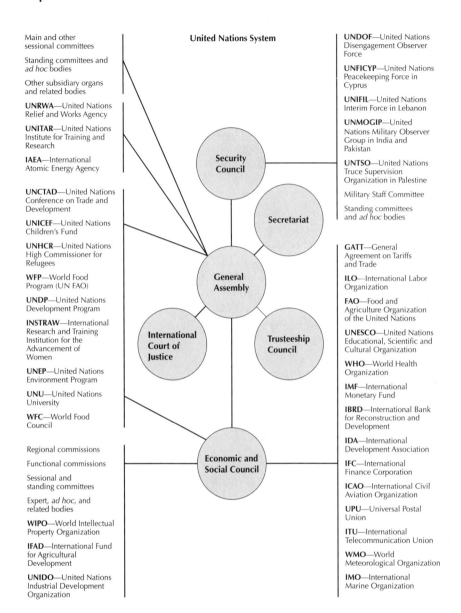

Main and other sessional committees

Standing committees and *ad hoc* bodies

Other subsidiary organs and related bodies

UNRWA—United Nations Relief and Works Agency

UNITAR—United Nations Institute for Training and Research

IAEA—International Atomic Energy Agency

UNCTAD—United Nations Conference on Trade and Development

UNICEF—United Nations Children's Fund

UNHCR—United Nations High Commissioner for Refugees

WFP—World Food Program (UN FAO)

UNDP—United Nations Development Program

INSTRAW—International Research and Training Institution for the Advancement of Women

UNEP—United Nations Environment Program

UNU—United Nations University

WFC—World Food Council

Regional commissions

Functional commissions

Sessional and standing committees

Expert, *ad hoc*, and related bodies

WIPO—World Intellectual Property Organization

IFAD—International Fund for Agricultural Development

UNIDO—United Nations Industrial Development Organization

United Nations System

Security Council

Secretariat

General Assembly

International Court of Justice

Trusteeship Council

Economic and Social Council

UNDOF—United Nations Disengagement Observer Force

UNFICYP—United Nations Peacekeeping Force in Cyprus

UNIFIL—United Nations Interim Force in Lebanon

UNMOGIP—United Nations Military Observer Group in India and Pakistan

UNTSO—United Nations Truce Supervision Organization in Palestine

Military Staff Committee

Standing committees and *ad hoc* bodies

GATT—General Agreement on Tariffs and Trade

ILO—International Labor Organization

FAO—Food and Agriculture Organization of the United Nations

UNESCO—United Nations Educational, Scientific and Cultural Organization

WHO—World Health Organization

IMF—International Monetary Fund

IBRD—International Bank for Reconstruction and Development

IDA—International Development Association

IFC—International Finance Corporation

ICAO—International Civil Aviation Organization

UPU—Universal Postal Union

ITU—International Telecommunication Union

WMO—World Meteorological Organization

IMO—International Marine Organization

FIGURE 13.1   The Structure of the United Nations

Source: United Nations publication.

Security Council members to cooperate with one another and the veto power of that body's five permanent members have combined to produce successive stalemates in its deliberations. The General Assembly requires a two-thirds majority to decide on the most important matters, but that has on occasion proved easier than getting the Security Council to move of its own accord.[25]

Until 1970, the United States and its Western allies effectively controlled the General Assembly. When checked by Soviet vetoes in the Security Council, this bloc of nations could usually find a means to have its way on major issues. Since that time, however, power in the assembly has shifted away from the Western world, and it is now more likely for blocs and counterblocs of small, medium, and large states to form and reform as the assembly moves from issue to issue. The Western powers have shifted their focus to other subsidiary bodies (see below).

The Security Council. The role of the **Security Council** is to maintain international peace and security. Besides its five permanent members (China, France, Russia, the United Kingdom, and the United States), the Security Council has ten members elected for nine-year terms according to rules that ensure geographic representativeness. The Security Council has the right to discuss any situation that threatens international peace, to make recommendations for the resolution of disputes, to require members to apply sanctions against other states, and to make recommendations concerning the regulation of national armaments. On substantive matters, all five permanent members plus four other member states must vote affirmatively—that is, each permanent member has the right to veto any proposal before the council.[26]

The Economic and Social Council. The fifty-four members of this body are elected by the General Assembly for three-year terms. Here, too, every effort must be made to ensure geographic representation. The function of the **Economic and Social Council** is to promote international cooperation in economic and social matters. The council is assisted by a large number of functional and regional commissions, such as the Population Commission and the Western Asia Commission, and by a wide range of specialized agencies, such as the World Health Organization (WHO), the International Monetary Fund (IMF), the United Nations Educational, Scientific, and Cultural Organization (UNESCO), and the General Agreement on Tariffs and Trade (GATT).[27]

The Trusteeship Council. The Trusteeship Council was originally established to assume the role formerly held by the League of Nations Mandate System after World War I. Eleven territories taken from Germany, Italy, and Japan after World War II (by no means all the world's colonies) were placed under its supervision, and the council was directed to promote their political, economic, social, and educational advancement while fostering "their progressive development toward self-government or independence." The council's task was so limited—and has been accomplished so thoroughly—that little remains to be done by this body. Its members are China, France, Russia, the United Kingdom, and the United States.[28]

The International Court of Justice. The fifteen judges of the **International Court of Justice** (often called the World Court) are elected by the General Assembly and the Security Council for nine-year terms. All must be from different nations. The court has jurisdiction only over cases the members agree to refer to it, but it may give advisory opinions when requested to do so by other UN bodies. The court has sought to establish a reputation for fair and expert deliberation and thus to win compliance with its decisions but has not been entirely successful in either respect. The United States has been among those nations choosing to comply with World Court rulings only when convenient; a July 1987 ruling outlawing military and financial support for guerrillas opposing the Sandinista government in Nicaragua was repudiated on the grounds that the court had no legal jurisdiction over continuing armed conflicts.[29]

The Secretariat. The Secretariat is the bureaucratic apparatus of the United Nations. It is headed by the secretary-general, who is appointed by the General Assembly on the recommendation of the Security Council, and who is assisted by a worldwide staff of 23,000 persons.[30] The secretary-general has the additional responsibility of bringing to the attention of the organization any matter that seems to threaten international peace.[31]

How Successful Is the United Nations? Any evaluation of the United Nations, as of most human labors, is likely to be based on the evaluator's hopes for it. Those who believed the United Nations would be a means of keeping perfect peace have been disappointed. Belligerent parties have often ignored its recommendations. Open acts of aggression have been condoned and even encouraged. The organization has never had an enforcement capability sufficient to serve as a genuine deterrent to aggression. It played almost no role in ameliorating or resolving the most serious conflict that has emerged since its birth, the Vietnam War.[32] Its peacekeeping mission in the former Yugoslavia was widely ruled a failure. In other conflicts the United Nations has found itself enmeshed in situations it can neither leave nor resolve: Blue-helmeted peacekeeping forces have been in the mountains of Kashmir since 1949, in Cypress since 1967, on the Golan Heights since 1974, and in Lebanon since 1978.

But real successes have also been achieved. For years, the UN presence in the Middle East helped keep that trouble spot from triggering superpower confrontation. The organization made key contributions to a number of arms control measures: the partial nuclear test ban treaty, the banning of nuclear weapons from outer space and the seabed, and the Nuclear Nonproliferation Treaty. More recently the UN Observer Mission in El Salvador (ONUSAL) monitored a ceasefire and was involved in the entire restructuring of that nation's governing

The United Nations at work. Here a United Nations Special Commission inspection team consisting of fifty persons representing fifteen nationalities carries out an investigation of Iraq's largest chemical weapon production facility. Inspectors from the Netherlands are measuring the volume of nerve agent in a container.

(UN/DPI)

and socioeconomic structures at the end of its civil war. The UN Transitional Authority in Cambodia (UNTAC) supervised and verified the withdrawal of Vietnamese forces in 1992 and helped repatriate and resettle some 350,000 displaced Cambodians; it also eliminated millions of land mines, monitored human rights, and organized and supervised a national election in which 90 percent of the registered voters were able to take part in 1993.[33]

By their very nature, peacekeeping (or, perhaps more accurately, peace-establishing) missions are risky, complicated, costly, and unsure. Over a thousand men and women from more than forty countries have died while in the service of UN peacekeeping forces. The struggles emerging at the end of the Cold War era have greatly increased both the demand and the difficulty of success—by mid-1995, nearly 80,000 UN troops were involved in over 17 peacekeeping operations. In 1993 alone, the United Nations spent $3.7 billion on peacekeeping.[34]

The United Nations has also worked assiduously to improve the world's economic and social conditions. The World Health Organization virtually eradicated smallpox by 1980. The UN Relief and Works Agency has helped millions of refugees. The UN Human Rights Commission investigates situations in countries where human rights violations are believed to occur, and other UN agencies are also active in this domain. Its Commission on the Status of Women, ECOSOC, the General Assembly, the UNHRC, and the United Nations Development Program Governing Council have all been active in working to improve the condition of women around the globe. Other agencies with important humanitarian and pragmatic accomplishments to their credit include the Food and Agriculture Organization (FAO), the International Telecommunication Union, the International Maritime Organization, the World Meteorological Organization, the International Civil Aviation Organization, and the International Atomic Energy Agency.[35]

But although every nation in the world has benefited in one way or another from such activities, the United Nations has nevertheless been disappointing to many. The shifting terms of the global economy naturally produce confusion and anger, and sometimes that anger is directed against the United Nations as well as against competing nations. Those who are negatively affected argue that the United Nations should broaden its interpretation of "unfair trade practices" and act to restrict practices in other nations that are making the old terms of trade impossible to maintain.[36] Others are simply ready and eager to make the most of the new opportunities and would like the organization to work in ways that are useful to them. Yet another group of UN watchers can be found among those who are concerned that the emerging global economy may create a global underclass containing the less fortunate members of all our polities; they believe the United Nations must work against that likelihood. In figuring out where they stand on these questions—and on the role they would like to see played by the United Nations—U.S. citizens would do well to keep in mind that their own nation is by far the strongest member not only of the United Nations but also of such increasingly powerful international bodies as the International Monetary Fund, the World Bank, and the GATT (see Chapter 4). Its power is not likely to be severely affected by adverse votes in the General Assembly for a long time to come.

Meanwhile, despite the bad press and its sometimes genuinely disappointing performance, the United Nations continues to win strong support across the globe. An important accolade came in 1988 when the body won the Nobel Prize for peace, but this support has also been reflected at the level of ordinary citizens in the opinion polls that have been conducted by the agency in twenty-five nations every year since 1989. Recent polls have shown a strong awareness of the existence of the United Nations (at or above 90% in over half the countries)—even though less than 50 percent of the population in twenty-two of the twenty-five nations could remember having been taught about it in school. More significant, a strong plurality of the respondents assessed the organization's performance as good (far fewer said it was poor; many said they did not know if it was good or poor). The main reason offered by the minority who thought the United Nations was performing poorly was that it did not have enough power and authority to do its job properly; others saw the organization as too dependent on great world powers and political blocs. It may be something of an exaggeration to claim that there has always been "general agreement by [the] peoples of the world that the United Nations is the only hope for international peace and security and that it is an essential institution for the advancement of social and economic development," but that the United Nations is "truly a symbol and instrument for peace and human progress" seems difficult to deny.[37]

THE CONDUCT OF INTERNATIONAL POLITICS: LAW VERSUS FORCE

The actors in international politics may be elected officials, diplomats, or secret agents. They may work individually or within complex organizational structures. In any case, their behavior—where it is not purely careerist and self-serving—is likely to be guided by respect for two often contradictory principles: the rule of law and the rule of superior force. In international relations guided by respect for law, the final appeal in any dispute is properly made to the World Court, where the principles of international law are developed and applied. In relations between nations that are governed by respect for superior force, the final appeal is likely to be to strength in battle—to warfare. The net result of the world's mixed adherence to these two principles is the web of power relationships at any given time: victor to defeated, colonizer to colonized, superpower to satellite, peer to peer.

International Law

The international actor guided by respect for the rule of law must sometimes make a difficult choice between national and international law. If the two are in conflict, the choice is very likely to be made in favor of the national law; at the present time, the surest protector of the cultural identity and military security of any state remains that state itself. Yet even the most resolutely autonomous state can no longer fail to recognize the need for a modicum of global social order. New conditions that threaten the internal order of all nations but can only be solved on a global scale—such as international terrorism, control of outer space, exploitation of marine resources, the need for restraints on transnational corporations, and pollution of the biosphere—force the evolution of new international law, and it is often only by showing respect for such law that the nations of the world can have any hope of there being sufficient order and prosperity to permit them to pursue their separate ends. One of the clearest signs of how well this principle is now understood appeared in 1994 when the writers of the new Russian constitution expressly included treaties and customary international law in their domestic legal system. In areas such as human rights, the writers of the constitution formulated Russian domestic law by making direct reference to international law.[38]

Thus the body of international law continues to grow, gradually receiving greater and greater acceptance. The International Law Commission, an auxiliary of the United Nations General Assembly, has taken on the job of codifying international law in a wide range of fields. More specialized groups, such as the International Labour Organization and the Intergovernmental Maritime Consultative Organization, have helped to spell out accepted principles of law in their respective domains. Drawing from established customs, generally accepted principles of law, and specific treaties or conventions, the writers of international law have established rules to govern relations between nations. These rules cover such matters as the recognition by states of one another's sovereignty (including the granting of diplomatic immunity), the establishment of frontiers on land and water, the acquisition and loss of territory, the human rights of aliens and citizens, the making of treaties, the responsibilities of international organizations, the arbitration of third parties in international disputes, the conditions for the legal use of force, and the conditions governing nuclear testing.

Warfare: The Politics of Force

> When you see millions of the mouthless dead
> Across your dreams in pale battalion go,
> Say not soft things as other men have said,
> That you'll remember. For you need not so.
> Give them not praise. For, deaf, how should they know
> It is not curses heaped on each gashed head?
> Nor tears. Their blind eyes see not your tears flow.
> Nor honour. It is easy to be dead.[39]

The attitude of Charles Sorley, later killed at the age of 19 in the Battle of Loos in World War I, was not typical of the young men Britain sent to fight in that war. He refused to accept that it is sweet and proper to die for one's country (*dulce et decorum est pro patria mori*). A more common response in those days—and still not unknown in our own cynical times—was that of Sorley's fellow poet in arms, Rupert Brooke.

> Now, God be thanked who has matched us with His hour
> And caught our youth, and wakened us from sleeping,
> With hand made sure, clear eye and sharpened power
> To turn, as swimmers into cleanness leaping.
> Glad from a world grown old and cold and weary.
> Leave the sick hearts that honour could not move,
> And half-men, and their dirty songs and dreary,
> And all the little emptiness of love![40]

What causes human beings to prefer to settle disputes by the use of armed force? Theoreticians of war suggest almost as many plausible explanations as there have been wars. We consider only the following condensed list, giving each rationale for war the name of the author or scholar most commonly associated with it.

The Rupert Brooke Argument. War provides an opportunity to exercise some of the finer human qualities not called for in peacetime: self-sacrifice, courage, heroism, and devotion to a cause larger than oneself.

The Thomas Hobbes Argument. War is the natural condition of humankind; the state of nature is a time of "war of all against all."[41]

The Carl von Clausewitz Argument. War is the continuation of politics by other means. This often-cited argument from the early nineteenth century reads in full, "War is not a mere act of policy but a true political instrument, a continuation of political activity by other means. What remains peculiar to war is simply the peculiar nature of its means."[42]

The Sigmund Freud Argument. Humankind is innately, genetically predisposed to aggressive behavior as a way of discharging accumulated stress, asserting leadership, supplanting parents or breaking free of the restraints they impose, or relieving boredom.[43]

The Karl Marx Argument. War is a way of acquiring economic benefits from other states. The victors acquire access to raw materials, living space, cheap labor, expanded markets.[44]

The C. Wright Mills Argument. War is a way to acquire economic benefits from one's own political system. The industrialists who make war-related materials and the professional warriors who seek an opportunity to prove their worth combine forces in a "military-industrial complex" to manipulate public opinion and pressure elected officials to take the path of war.[45]

The Margaret Mead Argument. War is a cultural habit that, once learned, is passed on from generation to generation. If children are taught to engage in simulated acts of violence, exposed to stories in which violence plays an important part (whether they are told by grandmothers or broadcast on television sets) and encouraged to emulate the bellicose acts of their elders, their society will tend to settle conflicts with other states by means of war.[46]

Beyond Arguments: The Control of War. It is impossible to state with certainty what causes war, but we can say with considerable confidence that the Thomas Hobbes argument is wrong. There is a good deal of evidence that earlier societies were, on the average, less warlike than so-called modern states—that the incidence and severity of wars has, paradoxically, increased with the evolution of civilization. This phenomenon seems to be related to the development of fixed settlements and the consequent need to assert and expand control of territory. The technological advances that began in the fifteenth century have steadily improved (if that is the word) the capacity of humans to slaughter one another and have led to ever greater expenditures on arms and ever greater numbers of men and women serving in the military. Thus, it is no surprise that by far the greatest share of the work of diplomats, regional organizations, and the United Nations is devoted directly or indirectly to the attempt to avoid, limit, or end wars. For most of the twentieth century, war theoreticians tended to recommend one of two approaches to the men and women who are employed in this most crucial task. Unfortunately, the assumptions on which both are based are not always matched by reality, as the maelstrom of change, often violently produced, into which we have been spun at century's end makes all too clear.

The first approach to the control of war is to encourage the mutual development of the power to make war. A world in which every nation is fairly equally armed should, the theory goes, be a world in which no nation would dare risk armed attack. Struck by the relative peacefulness of Europe during the latter part of the nineteenth century, war historians pointed out that during those years the powers of the major European states were in rough equilibrium, and for this happy situation they coined the term **balance of power**. (Others have since pointed out that it was also a period when these states were directing their military efforts elsewhere, particularly in expanding imperialistic control over the land masses of Africa and Southeast Asia; when the United States was rent by a most terrible civil war, and when revolutionary leaders competed with imperial and military dictatorships in setting new records for bloodshed in Latin America. Nevertheless, the balance-of-power theory gained considerable credence.)

After World War II and the development of nuclear bombs, it became fashionable to speak of **deterrence** rather than balance of power. The idea of being able to prevent war by building such a massive and threatening arsenal of nuclear weapons that no one would dare attack seems at first fundamentally different from the idea of establishing a power equilibrium. But in practice deterrence theory seems to have become balance-of-power theory written in megatons. As we have seen, for forty years the two major superpowers relied on the fact of each other's power as well as their own; because the Soviet Union had its own arsenal of nuclear weapons, the United States could count on it to understand the probable meaning of particular U.S. advances in defensive or offensive weaponry and to be suitably "deterred"—and vice versa. Other nations accepted the argument and sought either to shelter under the protective wing of one of the superpowers or to develop their own deterrence force.

Even before the collapse of the Soviet Union, however, it was quite clear that balanced nuclear power might deter nations from engaging in nuclear warfare but had little or no impact on their willingness to engage in conventional warfare. We were very much back where we started, minus the billions of dollars and thousands of sleepless nights squandered on the nuclear nightmare. Russia has been working hard to unload the Soviet nuclear arsenal, but other nations are scrambling to take up any slack, both in nuclear and conventional arms. The United States is slowly decreasing its own military establishment, including its nuclear stockpile but nevertheless now maintains an apparently vast superiority to all other nations. What has happened to the balance of power?

According to a recent analysis that draws on several recent studies, what has happened is that deterrence simply no longer works: "A great power's capability and credibility, backed by the threat of the use of superior military force, is quite often insufficient to deter," say Don M. Snider and Gregory Grant. But it is not only classical deterrence strategy that no longer seems to apply. Snider and Grant identify five central strategic concepts—deterrence, collective security, power projection (e.g., declaring readiness to defend allies), forward presence (stationing forces outside the United States), and reconstitution (rebuilding diminished military capabilities rapidly in times of crisis)—and point out the inadequacies of each in the new world created by the dissolution of the Warsaw Pact, the withdrawal of Soviet armies from eastern Europe, the reunification of Germany, the breakup of the Soviet Union, and the fracturing of polity after polity into warring factions of nationality versus nationality, guerillas versus regular army, ins versus outs. The problem now is not as simple as how to keep two superpowers from engaging in nuclear war; it is how to prepare to respond at any and all times to "disparate crises and regional contingencies."[47] The struggles we are witnessing today provide clear and painful illustration of how badly we need new thinking on the important problem of bringing peace to our planet.

SUMMARY AND CONCLUSION

Contemporary issues of international politics are multiple and complex. The proliferation of arms, the protection of human rights, the international impact of ethnic nationalism, and the ever more serious need to protect our environment are only a few of the problems requiring our urgent, global attention. Treaties and regional organizations formed around the globe bind us to one another in economic, cultural, and defensive agreements that strengthen not only our interdependence but also our ability to meet our social and material needs while discouraging would-be aggressors. Lawyers steadily clarify and augment the body of law that gives us a means of resolving our international disputes peacefully and fairly. Social scientists study the possible causes of war and develop new methods for resolving conflicts. Some write books like this, hoping to make it ever more obvious that in today's world *we* must mean all of us, if it is to have any meaning at all.

Of course, none of this is enough. Our problems are immense, and the amazing events of recent years have not lightened our load, however heartening this era of dramatic change may have seemed at first. In the next chapter we look at some of the major developments in recent world politics, both those that we know very well and those that are taking place more gradually, but perhaps with even greater impact on our lives. We try to face candidly the ones that undermine our hopes for the future of the human polity, as well as explore the ones that give us hope.

As we take on the challenges of this final chapter, perhaps it will help us to bear in mind that we have been working on the task of settled, social civilization for only 5,000 years. If anthropologists are correct that our species took its present form about 35,000 years ago, then it took us 30,000 years (give or take a millennium) just to get to that point. Still, however rapid our recent progress has been when viewed metahistorically, we may not have a great deal of time left.

Given the success of the perverse efforts we have made to develop the means of destroying ourselves altogether, it is possible that the advances we have made in the last 5,000 years may prove to be too little, too late. Then again, the very magnitude of the "success" we have achieved in preparing for our own destruction may force us not only to save ourselves but also to create a stable and harmonious international order while we are about it.

Selected Readings

Bledsoe, Robert L., and Boleslaw A. Boczek. *The International Law Dictionary.* Santa Barbara, Calif.: ABC-Clio, 1987. Defines international political concepts and describes various international treaties.

Diehl, Paul Francis. *International Peacekeeping.* Baltimore: Johns Hopkins University Press, 1993. Provides a historical background to international peacekeeping and examines recent peacekeeping operations to determine the elements necessary for success.

Ellis, Anthony, ed. *Ethics and International Relations.* Manchester, England: Manchester University Press, 1986. A series of articles on ethical aspects of international relations that discusses topics including the applicability of the word *moral* to state entities, international intervention, and nuclear deterrence.

Forsythe, David P. *The Internationalization of Human Rights.* Lexington, Mass.: Lexington Books, 1991. A discussion of the protection of human rights in international law, the United Nations, the Organization of African States, the United States, and private international organizations such as the Red Cross.

Hartung, William D. *And Weapons for All.* New York: HarperCollins, 1994. A detailed study of U.S. arms trade policies, making clear how international, political, and industrial factors contribute to the proliferation of U.S. weapons worldwide.

Lundestad, Geir, and Odd Arne Westad. *Beyond the Cold War: New Dimensions in International Relations.* Oxford: Oxford University Press, 1993. A collection of writings on the future of world politics.

Schiavone, Giuseppe. *International Organizations: A Dictionary and Directory.* New York: St. Martin's, 1993. Provides profiles of over 200 international organizations.

Segal, Gerald. *The World Affairs Companion: The Essential One-Volume Guide to Global Issues.* New York: Simon and Schuster, 1991. An analysis of key issues in international affairs, with useful maps and charts.

Notes

1. Mel Gurtow, *Global Politics in the Human Interest* (Boulder, Colo.: Rienner, 1988); *Time International* (22 June 1992): 19.
2. Amnesty International, *Political Killings by Governments* (London: Amnesty International Publications, 1983), pp. 15–25; *International Herald Tribune,* 22 June 1992, 1, 4; *Time International* (22 June 1992): 38.
3. Jonathan Power, *Amnesty International: The Human Rights Story* (New York: McGraw-Hill, 1981), p. 6. Incidents of torture in recent years have been reported for Turkey, China, Syria, India, Peru, the former Soviet republic of Georgia, Israel, and Myanmar. See *Country Report of Human Rights Practices for 1991* (Washington, D.C.: U.S. Government Printing Office, 1991); and Jeri Luber, "Cruel and Usual Punishment," *New York Review of Books* (10 July 1989): 34–35.

4. For a sober and thoughtful study of the problems facing the most recently created of these organizations, see Claude E. Welch Jr., "The African Commission on Human and Peoples' Rights: A Five Year Report and Assessment," *Human Rights Quarterly* 14, no. 1 (Feb. 1991): 43–61.

5. Hamish McDonald, "The Big Switch: Calcutta's Ruling Communists Give Capitalism a Chance," *Far Eastern Economic Review* (29 June 1995): 58–61.

6. Andrew McLaughlin, Grant Jordan, and William A. Maloney, "Corporate Lobbying in the European Community," *Journal of Common Market Studies* 31, no. 2 (June 1993): 191–212.

7. J. A. Thompson, *The Ancient Near Eastern Treaties and the Old Testament* (London: Tyndale Press, 1963), pp. 9, 11.

8. Stanley R. Sloan, "NATO's Future in a New Europe: An American Perspective," *International Affairs* 66, no. 3 (July 1990): 495–511.

9. Ousmane Poreko, "Evolution sociale chez les peuls du Fouta-Djalon," *Etudes Guinéennes, Les Recherches Africaines* 4 (Oct.-Dec. 1961): 78.

10. For relevant articles on Iraq's continuing military power after the war, see *International Herald Tribune*, 30 June 1991, B1; and *New York Times*, 16 Apr. 1992, A3, A20.

11. Andreas Falke and Hung Q. Tran, "NAFTA and the European Union: Two Important Economic Regions with a Solid Basis for Cooperation," *Deutschland* (Oct. 1994): 18–21; John Ross, "Mexico: Historic Turning Point," *Global Exchanges* (Summer 1994): 1–6.

12. *Washington Post*, 18 June 1991, A12.

13. *Le Monde*, 16 June 1992, 7.

14. Pertti Pesonen, "Three Nordic Referenda on EU Membership," *Scandinavian Review* 82, no. 3 (Winter 1994): 4–11.

15. For a typical example of new world naysaying, see Walter Goldstein, "EC: Euro-Stalling," *Foreign Policy* 85 (Winter 1991–92): 129–47.

16. "More-or-Less European Union," *Economist* (26 Aug. 1995): 46.

17. Seth Kitange, "Towards a Pan-African Community," *Africa News* 20, no. 13 (28 Mar. 1983): 5.

18. The terms of association between the OAU and the UN were formalized in UN Resolution 48/25 in November 1993. See Department of Public Information of the United Nations, "Cooperation between OAU and the UN System," *Yearbook of the United Nations 1993*, vol. 47 (Dordrecht, Netherlands: Martinus Nijhoff, 1993), pp. 304–6.

19. Peter Tran, "The OAU/UNHCR International Symposium: Refugees and Problems of Forced Population Displacements in Africa," *Migration World Magazine* 23, nos. 1–2 (Jan.-Apr. 1995): 23–27.

20. This assessment, made by the World Bank in 1993, is cited in ibid.

21. Quoted in Gerard J. Mangone, *The Idea and Practice of World Government* (New York: Columbia University Press, 1951), pp. 3–9.

22. For the concept of world governance, see James Dilloway, *Is World Order Evolving?* (New York: Pergamon Press, 1986); Samuel S. Kim, *The Quest for a Just World Order* (Boulder, Colo.: Westview Press, 1984); and Meghnad Desai, "Global Governance," in *Global Governance: Ethics and Economics of the World Order*, ed. Meghnad Desai and Paul Redfern (London: Pinter, 1995), 6–21.

23. In fact, the league's language calling for collective action against aggressor states was extremely vague and required near unanimity among the members. As a result, the clauses were seldom invoked, and never successfully in any major conflict.

24. Robert E. Riggs and Jack C. Plano, *The United Nations: International Organization and World Politics* (Chicago: Dorsey, 1988), p. 38.

25. Peter Calvocoressi, "Peace, the Security Council, and the Individual," in *Diplomacy at the U.N.*, ed. G. R. Berridge and A. Jennings (London: Macmillan, 1985), pp. 22–24; and Thomas Hovet Jr. and Erica Hovet, *A Chronology and Fact Book of the United Nations, 1941–1985* (Dobbs Ferry, N.Y.: Ocean Publications, 1986), pp. 143–46.

26. The ten nonpermanent members of the Security Council must include five members from Africa and Asia, one from eastern Europe, two from Latin America, and two from western Europe and other states. Riggs and Plano, *The United Nations*, pp. 38–39. See also *Background Notes: United Nations* (Washington, D.C.: U.S. State Department, Bureau of Public Affairs, 1994), p. 2.

27. *Background Notes*, p. 2.

28. *Ibid.* The last territory under the control of the Trusteeship Council, the Federated States of Micronesia, was granted internal self-government on November 3, 1986, but the United States, which provides over 90 percent of government revenue and pays compensation for its continuing military presence, still controls some aspects of its foreign affairs.

29. *New York Times*, 1 Aug. 1987, A3.

30. *Background Notes*, p. 1.

31. Hovet and Hovet, *Chronology and Fact Book of the United Nations*, p. 163.

32. Riggs and Plano, *The United Nations*, p. 346.

33. Steve Burback, "The Blue Helmets: A History of United Nations Peacekeeping Forces," *Special Warfare* (Jan. 1994): 2–6.

34. Ibid.

35. *Background Notes*, pp. 1–12.

36. Jagdish N. Bhagwati, *The World Trading System at Risk* (Worcester, England: Harvester Wheatsheaf/Simon and Schuster, 1991), p. 20.

37. Fred Babi, Gerhard Haensel, and F. Lwanyantika Masha, "Public Opinion in the World about the United Nations," *Review of International Affairs* 42 (10 May 1991): 12–15.

38. Gennady M. Danilenko, "The New Russian Constitution and International Law," *American Journal of International Law* 88, no. 3 (July 1994): 451–70.

39. Charles Sorley, "Sonnet," from *Marlborough and Other Poems* (Cambridge: Cambridge University Press, 1916), p. 69. Quoted in Giovanni Costigan, "British Poetry of World War I," in *War: A Historical, Political and Social Study*, ed. L. L. Farrar Jr. (Santa Barbara, Calif.: ABC-Clio, 1978), p. 249.

40. Rupert Brooke, "1914," in *Collected Poems of Rupert Brooke* (New York: Dodd/Mead, 1915).

41. Thomas Hobbes, *Leviathan* (Oxford: Basil Blackwell, 1960).

42. Carl von Clausewitz, *On War*, ed. and trans. Michael Howard and Peter Paret (Princeton: Princeton University Press, 1976), p. 87.

43. Roy L. Prosterman, "The Study of Lethal Human Conflict," in Farrar, *War*, pp. 14–17. It should be noted that Prosterman rejects all of these explanations except the quest to assert leadership, "Together, the frustrated, status-protecting, ideology-affirming leaders, and the obedient, ideology-accepting followers, make war" (p. 18). Prosterman also identifies Freud with the Thomas Hobbes argument, but elsewhere Freud argued along the lines described here, in a fashion more consistent with his general trend of analysis.

44. Karl Marx, "The German Ideology," in *The Marx-Engels Reader*, ed. Robert C. Tucker (New York: Norton, 1972), pp. 115–16.
45. C. Wright Mills, *The Power Elite* (New York: Oxford University Press, 1956).
46. Margaret Mead, "Alternatives to War," in *War: The Anthropology of Armed Conflict and Aggression*, ed. Morton Fried, Marvin Harris, and Robert Murphy (Garden City, N.Y.: Natural History Press, 1968), pp. 215–28.
47. Don M. Snider and Gregory Grant, "The Future of Conventional Warfare and U.S. Military Strategy," *Washington Quarterly* 15, no. 1 (Winter 1992): 203–28.

14 Regime Change in the Human Polity

Prague is the capital of the Czech Republic, the larger and more western part of what used to be Czechoslovakia, in central Europe. It is a very old city that has weathered many crises and many battles. A great old castle looms on a hilltop on its western edge, and the river Vltava runs through it. On the eastern side of the river is the Old Town, and further east yet is the New Town. Franz Kafka, whose novel *The Castle* tells far more about the negative aspects of modern bureaucracies than you found in Chapter 10, lived in Prague—you can go there and visit his tiny house, just below the castle. And when you roam around the city, you will see some of the world's most dazzling examples of every form of architecture: Roman, Gothic, baroque, rococo, neoclassical, art nouveau, modernist, and contemporary.

But if you drop your eyes down from the castle heights, and down too from the turrets, towers, and spires of the bridges, churches, and other wondrous buildings, what you will see in Prague today is: A hot dog stand. A young man selling toys. A shop selling souvenirs. A tour guide inviting you for a boat ride on the river. And yourself, the traveling student, multiplied a thousand thousand times. Prague is open to the world, and the world has discovered Prague—again. Capitalist enterprise runs rampant in its streets and up the sides of neon-lighted hotels. The city is alive, the money flows, the times are good.

Or thus it appears in Prague. The countryside does not look quite the same. As your train chugs in from the west, you are immediately struck by how utterly decrepit the rail yards are, and although the countryside is green and beautiful, the small towns you wind through on your way do not look much better. The people you see seem poor, but you notice they do not look sad or oppressed, just matter-of-fact as they go about their lives. Later someone may tell you, as someone did me, "Regimes come and go; the Czech peasant knows how to take it all in stride."

Regimes come and go. We live now in an era of massive regime change, from communism to democracy and capitalism, from single-party authoritarianism to multiparty democracy. What does it mean? Is it the triumph of democracy or the triumph of capitalism? Or is it both? What does it mean for individual lives? Surely not every citizen can "take it in stride"—not, for example, when regime change means massive ethnic cleansing, or genocide, as in former Yugoslavia or parts of Africa. And even in nations where the impact is less violent, regime change has its effects, produces its winners and its losers, gives the wheel of fortune a mighty spin. What is really going on?

Of course, we cannot fully answer such a question, but perhaps we can take a few steps in the right direction. In this chapter we consider some of the key questions posed by the effort to establish democracy and capitalism where they did not exist before. We look at some of the more striking kinds of regime change recently experienced—at nations that have moved from communism to capitalism and democracy (and at some that have moved partway back again), at those that resist such a change but find themselves making certain compromises nonetheless, and at nations busily setting up the outward marks of democracy whose conversion may be less total than it at first appears.

But we do not stay at the level of the nation-state. We take a look as well at the impact on the individual, and on particular groups as well, such as the newly rich, the newly poor, and those newly uncertain what the future will hold. We give special attention to the impact of regime change on women. We examine the effects of regime change on the citizens of stable democracies: Are they becoming more isolationist, refusing to take on problems that are not theirs? Or is the humanitarian instinct gaining ascendancy?

We move as well to a perspective above the individual and above the nation-state: What is the impact of massive regime change on the human polity at large? Has it strengthened (or was it caused by) the forces pushing us toward globalization? What new roles has it given to international institutions, not only those we studied in Chapter 13 but also private international organizations, including multinational businesses? Will it eventually produce a new system of international government composed of transnational regimes? Is it a first step toward the ultimate regime change, an international government that works? We can do no more than begin to touch on the answers. But leaving important questions open is a good idea for an introductory text. What would be the point of an introduction that was also a conclusion? There is, after all, a whole world of political science out beyond this book.

ESTABLISHING DEMOCRACY

The most striking characteristic of contemporary regime change is the fall of communism in state after state and the establishment of capitalism. The second most widespread change is the transformation of noncommunist but nonetheless authoritarian states into multiparty political systems. There are now more than a hundred nations with competitive elections in which at least some civil and political rights are protected.[1] More than thirty nations began the move to democracy between 1974 and 1990.[2] This is not, therefore, just a time of massive economic change; it is the hour of democracy.

But shifting to democracy cannot be done merely by deciding to do so. Many questions about democracy have never been fully resolved. What, after all, *is* a democracy and what can we count on that kind of political system to do?

To begin with, we must always keep in mind that democracy is a political system, not an economic one. Although often present together, democracy and capitalism are far from synonymous, and indeed some scholars argue that the latter necessarily limits the possibility of fully achieving the former. In any case, the literal meaning of *democracy* is simply "rule by the people." In contemporary practice, it is often assumed that the way people rule is by voting in "free" elections—that is, elections with a secret ballot, universal suffrage (all or nearly all adult men and women are eligible to vote and allowed to vote without coercion or restriction), and more than one political party in the competition. A typical definition reflecting this certainty that free elections are all but synonymous with democracy is the one offered by Philippe C. Schmitter and Terry Lynn Karl: "Modern political democracy is a system of governance in which rulers are held accountable for their actions in the public realm by citizens, acting indirectly through the competition and cooperation of their elected representatives."[3]

Other authors have been more demanding. In addition to free elections, Robert Dahl lists effective participation, control of agenda, and enlightened understanding as necessary criteria.[4] Peter Merkl agrees that parties and elections are "common structural attributes and criteria" of democracy but adds civil, political, and social rights: Citizens in democracies have the right to petition government, to exercise free speech (including access to a free press), and to assemble and organize for democratic political purposes.[5] George Munda Carew, focusing on regime changes in the multiethnic political communities of Africa, points out that free elections are not sufficient to prevent unfair treatment of minorities; a true democracy must also respect "the fairness principle" and function within a "culture of solidarity, fellow feeling and fair play."[6]

Even when a regime meets the more difficult criteria set for democracy, we should not expect heaven on earth. Overall, the physical quality of life is clearly better in democracies (see Figure 14.1), but many have argued that the quality of life permits the establishment of democracy, not vice versa. Democracy does not guarantee social or economic equality or even a decent standard of living for all. It does not eliminate immorality or corruption: "Democratic politics involves, almost always, lots of unsavory characters, people whose views one finds unattractive, even antidemocratic, certainly unpalatable."[7] There is no solid evidence that democracies are more efficient economically or administratively than other forms of government, nor are they likely to "appear more orderly, consensual, stable or governable than the autocracies they replace."[8] Ensuring freedom of choice does not ensure its exercise; democratic government is not enough to protect us from the pressures of social conformism.

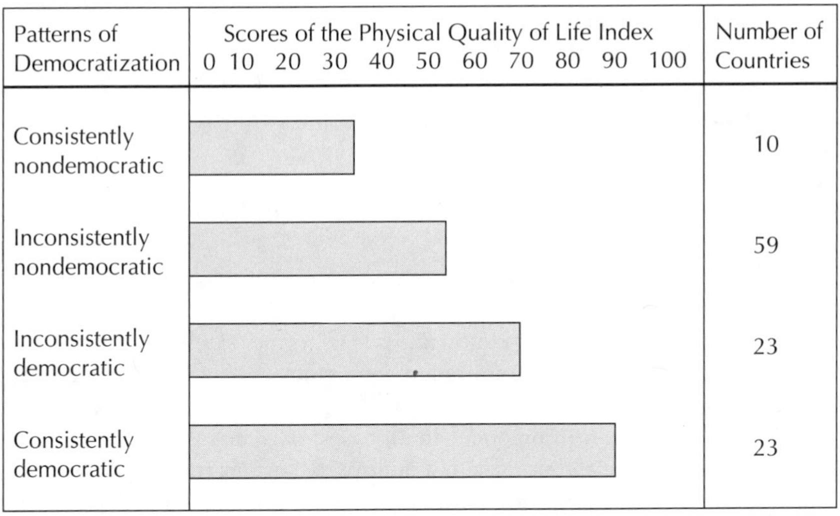

Patterns of Democratization	Scores of the Physical Quality of Life Index 0 10 20 30 40 50 60 70 80 90 100	Number of Countries
Consistently nondemocratic		10
Inconsistently nondemocratic		59
Inconsistently democratic		23
Consistently democratic		23

FIGURE 14.1   Patterns of Democratization and the Physical Quality of Life

Source: Dol Chull Shin, "Political Democracy and the Quality of Citizens' Lives: A Cross-National Study," *Journal of Developing Societies* 5 (Jan.–April 1989): 37. Leiden, The Netherlands: Brill Academic Publishers. Reprinted by permission.

Democracy does, however, have one indisputable advantage. It provides a more peaceful way of processing conflict and effecting change than can be found in any other existent system: "Democracies have the capacity to modify their rules and institutions consensually in response to changing circumstances"— when we are on the losing side, the processes of democracy help us to "lose peacefully."[9] The contribution democratic processes make to peaceful adjudication of disputes carries over into the international arena; although democracies go to war, they rarely fight each other: one author goes so far as to assert that since 1816 "no democracy has fought another democracy."[10]

There is now a widespread conviction that all nations should adopt the democratic model. However, as Georg Sorensen reminds us, "Democracy does not fall from heaven. It is brought about by individuals and groups, by social actors, who fight for it."[11] Charles Tilly wonders if trying to promote democracy is not like trying change the weather: "We can more or less understand the weather and its wide variation in different times and places, perhaps even affect it in small ways. However . . . no one seriously talks about promoting good weather."[12]

KINDS OF TRANSITIONS

Nevertheless, the major form of regime change in recent years has been from authoritarian to democratic. This change has taken place in two kinds of authoritarian systems, communist and noncommunist; in the former it has been accompanied by a change to a capitalist economic system. But not all regime change has been to democracy; as we illustrate, in some cases communist states have shifted a long way toward free market capitalism while making little or no political change. (And as the case of Peru reminds us, sometimes regime change can go in the opposite direction altogether, from democracy to authoritarian rule; see Chapter 9.)

Transitions from Communism to Democracy and Free Market Capitalism

The changes produced by the fall of communism beginning in 1989 have been the most dramatic and have seized the lion's share of the world's attention. All the component states of the Soviet Union and all the former satellites of that state in eastern and central Europe have shifted to democracy and have introduced a capitalist economic system.

What does this mean in practice? In all cases, it means the overnight introduction of competitive elections with a multiparty system and the slightly more gradual (and more partial) introduction of a market economy and private enterprise. What it does not mean is that all the former elites have been banished from power. Some of them have never left power, whereas others have begun to find their way back under new party labels. The changes have been radical, but the changes themselves have changed. At the same time, those communist nations that have so far resisted overt radical regime change—China, North Korea, and

North Vietnam as well as Cuba—have also been making some surprising changes, particularly in the nature of their economies. Let us examine this complex pattern of change in somewhat closer detail.

Of course, every case is different, but a brief examination of the recent history of Poland gives us some interesting illustrations of the kinds of changes that have taken place in eastern and central Europe. Poland is an interesting case because the move toward democratization began long before the fall of the Berlin Wall in 1989 and the rapid sequence of revolutionary overthrow of other communist regimes in the succeeding months. The trade union Solidarnosc and the Catholic Church had been putting pressure on the communist leadership for many years, and that leadership had been making concessions to that pressure, including the introduction of quasi-free elections in June of 1989. It surprised no one when Lech Walesa, the leader of Solidarnosc and an electrician by trade, became the president of the new regime in 1990; when the new Sejm (the lower house of the Polish legislature) was turned over to a strong anticommunist majority; and when the nation embarked on a vigorous promarket reform program. Yet a mere three years later, in September 1993, the parties with roots in Solidarnosc were soundly defeated and their leaders were ousted from parliament; in the presidential elections of 1995, Walesa himself lost his bid for reelection and was replaced by a former communist.[13]

What caused the shift back to leaders and ideas that seemed to have been so thoroughly discredited? There were a number of causes. One was the failure of Solidarnosc to hold together. Once the enemy, the former communist party, had been vanquished—and the enemy's best friend, the Soviet Union, had fallen apart—Solidarnosc lacked the focus that had held it together, and internal power struggles tore it apart. The two principal factions were led by President Walesa and his erstwhile ally, Tadeusz Mazowiecki, prime minister in the first Solidarnosc government. The split began almost immediately after victory, when the two men ran against each other in the 1990 presidential election. The new electoral system, commendably open and democratic, also played its part; anyone could form a party, and it sometimes seemed as if everyone did. By 1992 Poland had over 132 parties; by 1995, the number had grown to over 200. "Only" twenty-nine parties won seats in the 1991 elections to the Sejm, but the strongest of these had only 12.31 percent of the vote and sixty-two seats.

Another cause was that the new economic system, rather than bringing the optimistically expected instant improvement to the lives of the Polish people, imposed new rigors on most of them. The reform program of Finance Minister Leszek Balcerowicz was pushed forward vigorously, some said ruthlessly. Price controls were eliminated, and the market became the basis of all major economic activities. Although the state industrial sector did not disappear overnight, privatization flourished: Over 900 state-owned companies were sold off, and by 1995 the private sector accounted for 45 percent of the country's gross domestic product (GDP), employed 60 percent of the labor force, and included 1.5 million firms. Positive results were readily apparent: Inflation was reduced to a "mere" 38 percent by the end of 1993 (having reached 640% at the beginning of 1990), and economic growth moved into the highly respectable 4 percent to 5 percent range. Foreign aid was pouring in, 50 percent of the nation's foreign debt was canceled, and the International Monetary Fund (IMF) was offering some $700 million in loans.

But as we have seen in other cases, what looks like national economic recovery to outsiders may look like something very different to those inside who are stuggling to make ends meet. There were more goods available but less money to buy them with: By 1993 the average real wage was 25 percent below the 1989 level (the drop was 40% for industrial workers and 66% for farmers), public employees' wages were fixed (regardless of inflation), unemployment was at 15.7 percent (above 20% in thirteen of the forty-nine provinces), and a third of the people, many of them elderly, were living below the poverty line. All told, these categories, consisting of those least able to take advantage of the reforms and the newly free market, account for well over 50 percent of the Polish population.[14]

By 1993 the political tide was beginning to turn. There were 7,213 strikes in April and May of that year, and on May 28 the Sejm voted the existing cabinet out of power. President Walesa called for new elections, and in September the two formerly communist parties, the Democratic Left Alliance (SLD) and the Polish Peasant Party (PSL), won 171 and 132 seats, respectively, in the 460-member body, as well as 73 of the 100 seats in the Senate.[15]

The improvement in the national economy continued: By 1995 annual Polish exports were at $20 billion, imports at $23 billion, and Western foreign investment at $1 billion. The situation for some of the general population also improved: By the end of 1994, unemployment fell slightly (to 14%), real wages rose slightly (by 3.4%), and inflation was down to 22 percent.[16] But this was not enough to give Lech Walesa—who had lost credibility not only by the unsatisfactory performance of the economy but also by adopting an increasingly coarse and demagogic style—a second term in the presidency. At the end of 1995, Aleksander Kwasniewski, the leader of the Democratic Left Alliance, forced Walesa into a runoff, and in December of that year the former communist won, taking 51.7 percent of the vote.[17]

Had Poland returned to communism? Not at all, said Kwasniewski: "Communism is a thing of the past. It is not possible for it to return and there is no sense in its coming back."[18] Kwasniewski, described as a "deep-dyed, deideologized pragmatist," claims he is too young (41 years old at the time of his election) to be held responsible for the errors of the past regime and has an upper-middle-class family income. He is, he says, a social democrat. Although he favors reducing unemployment, building inexpensive municipal housing, and "taking into account the interests of labor veterans," he supports the entry of Poland into NATO and the European Union, promises to continue the market reforms, and is expected to continue the policy of fighting inflation, reducing state spending, encouraging privatization, and bringing in more foreign capital.[19]

Transitions from Communism toward Free Market Capitalism

The pressures for change exerted by an ever stronger international market economy are also being felt in still-communist nations like China, North Korea, North Vietnam, and Cuba. In these nations massive political regime change has not yet taken place, but economic changes have been profound.

Such changes began in the three Asian states long before the fall of the Berlin Wall. The beginning of China's economic reform dates back to 1978, and in fact 1989 brought a three-year setback, as the Tiananmen uprising on behalf of democratic politics in June of that year persuaded Chinese leaders to adopt more conservative economic policies as well as to heighten political oppression.[20] Despite this temporary slowdown, the economy of the People's Republic of China grew by more than an average of 9 percent per year from 1978 through 1995, with particularly spectacular growth since 1990; the gross domestic product in 1993 was $545 billion.[21]

The decision to compete in the world market has brought massive change to China, but so far it has not brought serious political change.[22] The communist party-state still rules. This means, in turn, that the economic system has not simply become a free enterprise system; it is what the Chinese call a "socialist market economy." Foreign investment has grown, and so has the private sector, but according to David S. G. Goodman, the most spectacular growth has been in what is known as the "collective sector." This sector includes collectively owned enterprises that are heavily controlled by—but for the most part not owned by—the state. They now account for 35.7 percent of the gross value of industrial output (the state accounts for 52.9%, private enterprise for 5.7%, and "other and foreign-involved" for 5.7%), and the official prediction is that they will account for 47.7 percent by the year 2000. Goodman identifies six kinds of collectives, from large-scale enterprises to local government collectives to share-based cooperatives. What they have in common is that "each must operate within the market economy but is also inextricably part of the party-state."[23] This dual identity shapes every form of economic development in China: Acquiring raw materials, securing bank credits, and finding markets still depend on personal connections with state officials. Is this a socialist market economy, as the Chinese claim? Or is it a transitional hybrid economy resulting from the effort of a massive authoritarian system to maintain total political control while effecting the transition to capitalism? And will economic change eventually force matching political change? It will be interesting to watch and see what the answers to these questions will be.

Transitions from Noncommunist Authoritarian Rule to Democracy

Transitions from noncommunist authoritarian rule to democracy have taken place in Italy and Germany after World War II and in Portugal, Spain, and Greece more recently.[24] But the most massive changes have taken place not in Europe but in Africa and Latin America.

Multiparty elections in Africa. Here Ivory Coast women vote at a polling station north of the capital of Abidjan in the October 1995 presidential election.

(AFP/Bettmann)

In Africa. In the first twenty years (roughly 1960 to 1980) after achieving political independence from colonial rule, most of the new African states were ruled by single-party or military dictators, often supported by the former colonial powers in exchange for continuing privileged access to these nations' cheap labor and raw materials. But in the 1980s regime change came to Africa, and by the mid-1990s multiparty elections had been introduced in a majority of African political systems: In 1996 alone, national elections were to be held in eighteen countries, and eight more were scheduled for 1997.[25]

What caused the change? Certainly world opinion played a part. So did domestic opinion as "declining living standards . . . arbitrary and bad government, corruption and a breakdown of law and order" caused Africans to lose patience with their rulers.[26] But this is a good time to remember the words of Georg Sorensen, who has insisted that what causes the introduction of democracy is the determination of the powerful to establish it (see p. 324).

In the African case, two sets of the "powerful" were at work. The first were the organizers of the "structural adjustment" programs of the World Bank and International Monetary Fund. Able to promise massive loans in exchange for economic liberalization (improving conditions for foreign investment) and political reform (introducing free elections that, besides introducing formal democracy, could also be expected eventually to loosen the grip of the autocrats), these international powers made a strong appeal to the second group of power holders, internal elites whose grip was becoming shaky as their nations' increasing fiscal decline reduced the resources they required (such as foreign exchange, local currency, and government contracts) to make the necessary patronage rewards to their supporters.[27] Although the dramatic events in eastern Europe and the Soviet Union and the more gradual shift from military to parliamentary rule in Latin America heightened global certainty that "democracy and capitalism are progressing irresistibly, and in tandem," close observers have pointed out that in Africa as elsewhere in the world there are reasons to doubt that the truth is as cheerfully simple as that.[28]

First, the move to democracy in these regimes is not only led by elites; it has often been less than popular with the general population, because it is linked with efforts to impose the austerity programs demanded by the IMF as part of structural adjustment. Second, although leaders may change, they continue to be members of the African elite; "lawyers, university lecturers, bankers, businessmen, professionals, and former officials of international institutions" predominate in the new governments and in the parties.[29] Furthermore, elections do not necessarily produce leadership change. Clever autocrats also know how to make "adjustments." When protests escalated in his country in 1990 and international pressures grew, the late Félix Houphouet-Boigny of the Ivory Coast moved swiftly to master the new situation. He "announced a suspension of many of the planned austerity moves, legalized opposition parties, and called presidential and legislative elections for October and November. . . . Thanks to this swift initiative, [his party's] advantages as the state party, and the opposition's fragmentation, [he and his party] won the elections handily."[30] (For another example, see Box 14.1).

Even the most dubious observers admit, however, that things have changed in Africa. Openly autocratic rule is no longer acceptable in most nations, opposition parties do exist, the press seems freer to criticize those in power, and associations such as trade unions and women's groups are taking a renewed interest in the political game. It may still be only a game and one that has little real meaning yet for the vast majority of Africa's population. Continuing and severe economic hardship plus ethnic rivalries that can erupt in mass violence make the task of democratic consolidation more difficult in Africa than in Europe.[31] But something has changed. It is too soon to be certain the change will hold, and deepen, but it is also too soon to be certain that the change will fail.

In Latin America. The situation in Latin America is similar to that in Africa in several respects. As in Africa, this continent also experienced a massive turn away from dictatorship in the 1980s; over two-thirds of Latin American people were living under military rule in 1979, but by 1993 "not a single military regime remained in Central or South America or the Spanish-speaking Caribbean"[32] (see Table 14.1). As in Africa, a severe need for economic bailout (in this case owing largely to the impossibility of keeping up payments on foreign loans—that is, to the international debt crisis discussed in Chapter 4) helped convince endangered elites they would have to accept neoliberal economic strategies of reducing gov-

BOX 14.1   "FREE ELECTIONS" IN THE SUDAN

The Islamic military government in the Sudan, led by Lieutenant General Omar Ahmed al-Bashir and the National Islamic Front, a fundamentalist party led by Dr. Hassan al-Turabi, staged its own version of "free" elections in 1995. Political parties were allowed to form but not to campaign. Forty-two candidates registered for the presidency, and 900 for the 275 seats in parliament. Candidates were given twelve days to campaign in a nation one-fourth the size of the United States. The government paid for and printed one piece of campaign literature for each candidate for the presidency and allowed each candidate one fifteen-minute spot on the state-owned television and radio station. Each candidate was also given a symbol (examples included a fan, a table, an elephant, a rifle, a razor blade), because the government insisted there were too many illiterate people to allow words on the ballots; officials in polling places were allowed to "help" voters tick off the "right" symbol if they were confused.

To no one's surprise, the principal opposition parties called for a boycott and General Bashir was reelected president, winning 4,181,784 of the 5,525,280 votes cast. According to the cheerful victor, the results made it clear that "the Sudanese people had decided to move ahead along the path of popular consultative democracy." According to the opposition, only 5 percent of the population had voted.

Sources: *New York Times,* 11 Mar. 1996, A5; "Sudan," *Defense and Foreign Affairs* (Mar. 1996): 14.

ernment regulation, privatizing public enterprises, and shrinking the size of the state in order to qualify for further foreign aid and loans.[33] As in Africa, democracy has been "pared to the bone" and is largely limited to its "electoral dimension," leaving social needs "at the bottom of the agenda."[34] As in Africa, certain groups, generally those already better placed in the social system, have prospered with the change, while the poor have grown poorer. As in Africa, intermediary representative groups (opposition parties, trade unions, other associations of civil society) have not yet gained sufficient strength as "channels of interest mediation [to be able to] renegotiate with society the terms of political representation."[35] And finally, as in Africa, although the overall results have been dubious and disappointing, one can find some grounds for hope, as we indicate below.

There is, however, one key difference in the nature of Latin American regime change, and that is the far more powerful role of the military, both before and after the changes that have taken place. Although military regimes were in power in many nations on both continents throughout the 1960s and 1970s, those in Latin America were far less limited by poverty and the inhibiting conditions of postcolonial trade and aid than were their African counterparts; at the same time, these nations were far more determined to "obliterate the political left and roll back decades of labor gains" (few such gains had yet been made in Africa).[36]

The exceptional power of the Latin American military did not come to an end with the introduction of formal democracy, and the new governments have been described as keen to avoid "any policy initiative that might provoke a new military coup." Although they have sometimes reduced the size of the military, they have often granted immunity, explicitly or tacitly, to members of the armed forces known to have engaged in extreme acts of oppression during their time in power, incorporated many of the antidemocratic and anti–civil libertarian institutions and practices of the past regimes into contemporary constitutions, and given the military a range of powers that more established democracies would never countenance. The result, according to Brian Loveman, is that these are "protected" democracies—which is to say, regimes in which the military is given the role of "protecting" the new system from its own "excesses" and/or in which the civilian authorities have accepted military definitions of what constitutes such an excess. Loveman concludes that in most of these nations military coups are no longer a threat, because they are not necessary: "Protected democracy provides a handy legal rationale for the military to assert themselves in a variety of acceptable ways. . . . Beneath the veneer of elected civilian government, both authoritarian legal institutions and a political mission for the armed forces have been consolidated"[37]

Nevertheless, as in Africa, the new regimes do provide some grounds for hope. They may not have had "any significant effect on the great and increasing inqualities" of their economies or societies, and it may be true that "the dice are probably loaded in favor of repeated iterations of shaky and relatively short-lived democracy and ever-uglier authoritarian rule," as Guillermo O'Donnell sadly observes.[38] Yet O'Donnell himself is willing to hope he may be wrong and bases that hope on the fact that "most political and cultural forces of any weight now attribute high intrinsic value to the achievement and consolidation of political democracy." He reminds us that when democracies are first established anywhere, it is usually with a great deal of pessimism, uncertainty, and even reluctance. Like Sorensen, he points out the importance of the motives of elites—it is, he says, when the main political, social, and religious forces conclude "that the

TABLE 14.1   Transitions to Civilian Government in Latin America

Ecuador	1979	Uruguay	1984
Peru	1980	Brazil	1985
Honduras	1982	Guatemala	1986
Bolivia	1982	Chile	1990
Argentina	1983	Paraguay	1993
El Salvador	1984		

Source: Brian Loveman, "'Protected Democracies' and Military Guardianship: Political Transitions in Latin America, 1978–1993," *Journal of InterAmerican Studies and World Affairs* 36, no. 2 (Summer 1994): 106.

costs of trying to eliminate each other [exceed] the costs of tolerating each other's differences" that true democracy has a chance.[39] Although the grounds for hope seem slight indeed, perhaps that moment is on its way in Latin America.[40]

REGIME CHANGE AND THE INDIVIDUAL

It is time now to examine a few of the more significant kinds of changes that can occur in private lives when regimes come and go.

Winners versus Losers: The Newly Rich, the Newly Poor

The shift to democracy may be limited to electoral formalism in many nations; the shift to capitalism is, however, likely to have far-reaching effects almost immediately. Of course, authoritarian communism did not eliminate economic inequity, and most noncommunist authoritarian states did not even seriously aspire to do so; what is new under worldwide market capitalism is not that such inequities exist but that different people are getting rich—and getting poor.

We have not said much in this chapter about regime change in Russia, partly because the process in that complex land is so unpredictable that tomorrow's headlines are likely to contradict any generalizations we might venture today. However, in recent years Russia has provided us with a wealth of examples to illustrate the impact on individual lives of a sharp shift to free market practices. Economic liberalization, including drastic cuts in public spending and extensive privatization of state-owned firms, has proceeded at a rapid pace, while overall productivity has taken a sharp dip (down 36% between 1989 and 1993) and inflation has only recently begun to come under control.[41] Such macrolevel changes do not fail to touch the lives of individuals. There are exciting opportunities for those well positioned to take advantage of them. Oleg Polumordvinov, who sells Japanese electronic space heaters and other appliances he buys in Vladivostok, happily reports a "kind of trading frenzy," and his fellow trader Alexandr V. Levin, who buys Russian pig iron, lead concentrate, and raw materials for Japan and sells Japanese consumer goods, forklifts, trucks, and electronics to Russia, is also enthusiastic: "When you succeed, wealth multiplies very quickly."[42] Thirty-six-year-old Nikolai Panchenko would surely agree: His new house in Zubchaninovka is a "colossal, turreted, walled-off brick mansion" complete with enormous bedrooms, a sauna and swimming pool in the basement, stained glass windows upstairs, and a marble entrance hall with a massive crystal chandelier. Prior to the fall of the Soviet state, he and his father were engaged in illegal speculation in consumer goods; Panchenko senior spent nine years in prison for selling sheepskin hats and nylon raincoats. But now Nikolai's 77-year-old father "watches with satisfaction as [his son] expands his business, opening a food store, dealing in car parts and importing consumer goods from Europe—all of it legal."[43]

That's nice for the Panchenkos and the other successful traders, but not everyone fares so well. Take the case of Viktor Popov, one of the world's leading

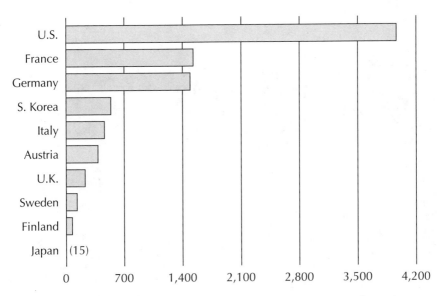

FIGURE 14.2   Foreign Investment in Russia. Value of Investments between January 1990 and September 1993 (in $US Millions)

Source: Elisabeth Rubinfien, "Divide and Conquer: Russia Demands a Regional Approach," *Central European Economic Review* 2, no. 2 (Spring 1994): 12.

experts in cell biophysics since the mid-1970s, whose laboratory now has less than 5 percent the funding it used to have, with "no money for equipment, for new journals, for computers," and who is one of several leading Soviet scientists seeking to supplement their incomes by tutoring U.S. high school students during the summer.[44]

Enterprising capitalists assisted by foreign investors and investments are frequently winners in the new regimes (for the extent of foreign investment in Russia, see Figure 14.2). Others, like Vera Simyonova, a 38-year-old cleaning woman, are out-and-out losers. Simyonova was never wealthy, but the food packages and other state assistance she used to receive from the old centrally controlled economic system now no longer come her way. Her monthly income of 200 rubles is far below the poverty line (1,900 rubles a month). To support herself and her developmentally disabled 14-year-old son she now goes, with hundreds of others like herself, to the outdoor market in the town of Tishinsky every day to try to sell whatever personal belongings she can, including canned food in her cupboard left over from the days of subsidized prices. Simyonova is not a fan of regime change: "Under Brezhnev," she says, referring to the days when hardliner Leonid Brezhnev was the Soviet leader, "everything was cheap. We could live."[45]

I miss Communism. There was nothing to buy, but at least I could afford it.

The Christian Science Monitor
Los Angeles Times Syndicate

(Danziger/© *The Christian Science Monitor*)

Women and Regime Change

As the case of Vera Simyonova and her son suggests, women and children are often particularly vulnerable to the impact of regime change on individual lives. Lynne Haney summarizes some of the changes in eastern Europe: the closing of child care centers and curtailment of maternity leave spending as part of cuts in government spending; the emphasis on the role of women as consumers in the new market economies (fashion magazines, home improvement guides); the spread of pornography as a result of the new freedom of the press (and the new license to focus on profit at the expense of other values); and the tendency of the new democratic parliaments to consist almost exclusively of men.[46]

As regime change has led to a reduction in number of government employees, women workers in the public sector have often been fired in disproportionate numbers. Over two-thirds of Russia's unemployed are women, and women are far more likely than men to be required to take extended holidays without pay or at the minimum wage or to leave the workforce altogether. In an interview given in 1993, Gennady Melikyan, Russia's labor minister, was unconcerned: "Why should we employ women when men are out of work? It's better that men work and women take care of children and do housework." Foreign observers have noted that "sexual harassment in the workplace is rampant in today's Russia," but although there are laws in place against such acts, cases that are reported are normally neither denounced nor investigated.[47]

BOX 14.2   REGIME CHANGE

Women before and after Regime Change in Poland

Walbrzych, Poland—The workers of the state-owned Porcelana china factory went on strike in 1980 against the evils of communism and in favor of political liberation. In 1993, the workers of the privately owned Porcelana china factory went on strike against the evils of capitalism and in favor of women's liberation.

The first strike took a decade to show results. The second might take longer. Communism was no picnic, but it gave women standing at work and security at home.

Now they have got stress at work and strife at home. Poles are so aggrieved at how capitalism has been thrust on them that in September they voted the old order's descendants back into power. Polish women have reason to feel more aggrieved than most.

The two-month strike . . . was about layoffs and low pay. The company agreed to think those things over, and work resumed in August. But at root, the strike was also about ownership: The women of Porcelana believe they got a better shake from the state. [Their boss] wholeheartedly agrees: "Day care. Holiday resorts. Subsidies for single mothers," he says. "These women got all kinds of assistance. It was a custom. A habit. They got soft treatment from management. Now they have lost these grants. This factory pays only for work done."

Source: Barry Newman, "Women in Poland Find Little Liberation in Shift to Democracy," *Wall Street Journal,* 19 Nov. 1993, 1, A11. Reprinted by permission of The Wall Street Journal, © 1993 Dow Jones & Company, Inc. All Rights Reserved Worldwide.

It should be remembered, however, that women's role was far from idyllic under communism. Although women entered the labor force en masse, they still spent nearly three times longer on household tasks than did men and held the lower-skilled and lower-paid jobs. In Hungary, they earned on average only 72 percent of what men were paid for equal work. In the Soviet Union, vocational training schools were segregated and provided different kinds of training for girls and boys. And one author insists, Polish men still "kissed women's hands, [but] never did a jot of housework."[48]

Furthermore, most women did not change their image of themselves during the communist era in ways that are familiar to Western women. According to observers, they needed to work and enjoyed working, but they were usually ready to agree with those who claimed that work was less important to a woman than to a man. Lynne Haney quotes a Hungarian sociologist she interviewed in 1987: "I know what to do at the workplace. I do it without concern. My husband is so concerned about work. Not me. . . . This struggle does not concern me."[49]

Such attitudes, carried forward into the present period, have clearly made it more difficult for women to fight for rights that are now ever more reduced. But there are a few signs of change. In her postrevolution research, Haney found some younger and better-educated Hungarian women who "flirted with notions of equality," and Barry Newman notes that in Poland, where the overall situation is much the same (see Box 14.2), some women are becoming owners of small businesses, women academics have succeeded in changing the law calling for their mandatory retirement at age 60 and have begun to introduce women's studies courses, and women's magazines now run stories advising readers, "Don't be afraid of success."[50]

REGIME CHANGE AND INTERNATIONAL INSTITUTIONS

Whatever the experience of citizens inside regimes, most observers agree that the problems raised by change on such a massive scale cannot all be solved by individual resourcefulness or by individual nations. As we have noted several times, international forces are involved in facilitating the economic and political changes under way. Fortunately, such forces are also involved in trying to correct the mistakes that have been made and bring relief to those whose lives have been shattered. Of course international institutions and groups are themselves affected by the scope of change—the roles they play are seldom what they were before 1989. Here we consider, briefly and in general terms, the impact of regime change on international government organizations, international nongovernment organizations, and international business.

International Government Institutions

The international government organizations most profoundly affected by the sweeping regime changes of the past few years have been the previously "subglobal" economic organizations such as the IMF, the World Bank, and the General Agreement on Tariffs and Trade (GATT). All now boast virtually universal membership and have, as we have seen, played a very strong role in shaping the economies of the new regimes. The number of countries seeking IMF funds to rehabilitate their economies has risen to ninety (from sixty-three in 1989). The powerful agency continues to operate with no public or professional scrutiny; its meetings are closed, and the minutes are not made public—even the amount of money the fund has to lend is never announced.[51]

Other groupings that have no aspirations to universality, such as the European Community, the Organization for Economic Cooperation and Development (OECD), and the Association of South East Asian Nations (ASEAN), have also been able, since 1989, to broaden their membership and to look ahead to yet a wider scope for action, as political reasons for declining membership have disappeared and the economic necessity of not being left behind has become ever more apparent.[52]

As we saw in Chapter 13, the United Nations has had a difficult time in the post–Cold War years, unprepared as it was to assume so massive and so difficult a peacekeeping role in lands where regime change was the first step to civil war. But its efforts to meet the challenge have met with some success, as we have seen, and it has often been particularly effective in providing the humanitarian aid that is so essential a step to rehabilitation of war-torn polities.

Nongovernment organizations (NGOs) played an important role in organizing and making successful the United Nations Women's Convention, held in September, 1995, in Beijing, China. Here we see the platform from which major addresses were made, shown at the time of the speech by the convener of the NGO Forum on Women.

(Kees/Sigma)

International military alliances such as NATO and the Warsaw Pact have been the most profoundly affected agencies of international governance. The latter lost all reason for existence and disappeared; the former has assumed peacekeeping functions of its own, particularly in the former Yugoslavia, and is being urged to bring in new members from east and central Europe, and eventually even Russia and other former Soviet states.[53]

International Nongovernment Organizations

Private international organizations seeking to improve the human condition by attacking particular problems are gathering more international recognition and support; at the same time, they often find the problems on which they focus to be ever more massive and intractable. As Peter J. Spiro says, "Environmentalists, human rights activists, women, children, animal rights advocates, consumers, the disabled, gays, and indigenous peoples have all gone international. . . . These groups have developed distinct agendas at the global level, and in the form of nongovernmental organizations (NGOs) they are working with increasing sophistication to further these interests in international institutions." The "explosion" in the number of such groups—there are now some 14,500 international NGOs—has been made possible by the greater ease of travel and more rapid means of communication (including the fax and the Internet). It has been made necessary by the global nature of the problems we face today, many of which are directly linked to the recent upheavals caused by regime change.[54]

Not all NGOs work by bringing pressure to bear on official international agencies. Sometimes they work alone, sometimes they seek to pressure national governments, sometimes they seek to arouse public opinion—and, of course, the same agency may combine several methods. When the Human Rights Watch issued its report for 1995, it called upon the United Nations to be less committed to neutrality, more prepared to act forcefully when "faced with genocide and mass slaughter." At the same time, the organization made a sharp attack on the governments of the United States, Germany, France, Canada, and Australia for putting "geopolitical designs and commercial motives" ahead of concern for human rights abuses and for "hawking trade and investment deals while relegating human rights to the ineffectual realm of private diplomacy."[55]

In other cases, the relationship is reversed and government aid programs seek out the NGOs, believing that funneling public assistance through such agencies may be a better way of reaching "the poorest." However, observers find little evidence that NGOs are able to reach the neediest any better than well-meaning government bureaucrats (although they may do so more cost effectively) and point out the danger to such groups of being co-opted by officialdom, thereby losing their legitimacy as independent and effective agents of social transformation. Naturally enough, the groups themselves tend to welcome the opportunity to expand their funding and effectiveness.[56]

International Business

In the best of all semantic worlds, we would recognize that transnational corporations are also NGOs, albeit profit-seeking NGOs. However, scholarly usage forbids us to call them that; the acronym of choice is TNC. As you may have noticed, the first qualification for the study of international relations today is an ability to master the acronyms. It isn't fair to change them in midstream, and so we will stick with TNC.[57]

The causal relationship between TNCs and contemporary regime change is clearly reciprocal. International business interests have strongly influenced the decisions of the international funding agencies that are so actively shaping the new economies; the investment opportunities thus produced have in turn revolutionized the international business world. The rush to privatize has opened investment opportunities to businesses as well as to individuals. The readiness of new regimes to welcome foreign owners as well as investors has led to the building of new plants in cities never considered before.[58] At the same time, the liberalization of trade means that it is often not necessary to build such plants in order to be multinational—key steps in the production and distribution of many products are now routinely "outsourced" to entrepreneurs in other lands, where lower wage costs and "less restrictive" labor practices contribute to higher profits.

One of the most interesting developments in the relationship between transnational businesses and regime change is the new link between some TNCs and large-scale international development banks (IDBs). We have often mentioned the two most important banks of this type, the World Bank and the International Monetary Fund; two others with major funding are the International Finance Corporation (affiliated with the World Bank) and the Inter-American Development Bank. The declared mission of such banks, which are put together by the governments of nation-states and financed by taxpayers, is to help less-developed countries (LDCs) out of chronic poverty. Each year they generate about $30 billion in contracts.

Such contracts are more and more likely to go to private entrepreneurs than to the governments concerned. "The Cold War's demise removes the philosophical underpinnings for the earlier support of government intervention," says one former top official of the World Bank. By this he means that it is no longer necessary to make loans directly to governments to keep them from "going communist." In addition, the banks are now beginning to align themselves more openly with private investment funds in the developed nations, serving as advisors and sometimes entering into cofinancing of projects that are likely to bring those private investors profits as high as 25 percent a year.[59] To understand how this process works, read Box 14.3.

The competition for TNC investment monies has also had a profound effect on developed nations, now engaged in sometimes drastic re-creations of themselves. New Zealand is an interesting example. Long ruled by a socialist party, the new New Zealand is now completing a massive privatization program and has little concern for the nationality of the buyers of the formerly state-owned enterprises. As one CEO (chief executive officer)—whose forestry business snapped up the state timber operation during privatization and was then itself acquired by the International Paper Company—says, "We think internationally now." Today, over half of New Zealand's stock market capitalization is foreign money. But attracting foreign investors has meant downsizing the labor force and reducing workers' rights and services "that were once taken for granted." The Employment Contracts Act of 1991 gives employers in New Zealand the right to negotiate directly with employees; since its adoption, "union membership has plunged 38 percent through layoffs."[60]

Richard J. Barnet has written one of the most scathing attacks on the effect TNCs are having on the economy and labor force of the United States. Outraged by such facts as "the world's 358 billionaires have a combined net worth of $760 billion, equal to that of the bottom 45 percent of the world population . . .

BOX 14.3   INTERNATIONAL DEVELOPMENT—OF WHAT, FOR WHOM?

The Inter-American Development Bank is owned by forty-six nations. Its mission is to reduce the chronic poverty of Latin America, and it loans billions of dollars to private businesses in those nations. In the fall of 1995 the bank entered into a "first-of-its-kind" alliance with a private group of investors, including Lloyd M. Bentsen, U.S. secretary of the treasury in 1993 and 1994 and a former governor of the bank, now a private businessman. The alliance will provide a "billion-dollar investment fund banked by giant corporations and pension funds. They hope to realize profits of as much as 25 percent a year by investing in Latin American power projects, telecommunications systems and toll roads." The agreement with the Inter-American Development Bank will include "information sharing and possible co-financing," according to Mr. Bentsen. Many of the managers of the investment group formerly held high positions in this or other international development banks (IDBs), including the World Bank.

Jerome Booth, head of emerging markets research for a private bank, points out that the fund's natural emphasis on profit seeking may distort the kind of development pursued. He believes that banks like the Inter-American Development Bank should just be "in the business of helping development of countries, typically things like water, sanitation, health and education, not toll roads, telecommunications or power stations."

The bank's president, Enrique V. Iglesias, recognizes that the new alliance could pose some problems. He promises that the bank will "prod Mr. Bentsen's fund to follow its lead and invest in the region's neediest countries. But he . . . fears 'money will only flow to the best projects' since Mr. Bentsen's fund's stated intention is to make 80 percent of its investments in the region's six richest countries."

Louis T. Wells, professor of international management at Harvard Business School, says, "It's going to be questioned in the host country where somebody is going to say we could have raised this money a lot cheaper. It's an interesting dilemma."

Donald Strombon, a business consultant in Washington, D.C., isn't worried. He says forming links with the IDBs is good business: "The multilateral development banks do $30 billion a year in contracts awarded by borrowers, and . . . give out another $4–$5 billion in consulting contracts. It's a very sizable market."

Moeen Qureshi, a former top official of the World Bank and identified as the "brains" behind the new alliance, agrees with Strombon and points out the advantages of working through an IDB: "The risk is lower with the presence of a multilateral institution. Governments will think twice about reneging on an obligation where a public institution is involved."

Source: Drawn from Jeff Gerth, "In Post-Cold-War Washington, Development Is a Hot Business," *New York Times*, 25 May 1996, 1, 6.

the average CEO in the United States now brings home about 149 times the average factory worker's pay . . . an estimated 18 percent of American workers with full-time jobs earn poverty-level wages; [and] since 1973, the number of American children living in poverty has increased by 50 percent," Barnet puts the blame squarely on the "stateless corporations" of the world. They are, he says, just "walking away from the enormous public problems their private decisions create for American society." Gone are the good old days when "big companies created tens of millions of well-paid jobs, provided health care and pensions, and brought women and minorities into the work force." Now "a global pool of bargain labor is available to companies making virtually anything" and "about a third of the jobs in the United States are at risk to . . . low-wage workers . . . elsewhere." Strikes don't work anymore—"management now wields the more credible threat: Take it or we leave"—and only 12 percent of the U.S. workforce in private industry is now organized for collective bargaining. U.S. workers in the "superstar" category "bring home a fortune every year," but the median earnings of the professional class and most entertainers are staying flat, and the real wages of low-ranked workers like janitors, bank tellers, and back-office employees in brokerage houses have fallen 15 percent or more. Layoffs and CEO salaries are up, often in tandem (twenty-three of the nation's top "job-slashers" received raises averaging 30 percent in 1993). The corporate share of federal income taxes has fallen from 23 percent in the 1950s to 9.2 percent in 1991, as TNCS have improved their competitiveness by going "stateless" and basing their accounting operations in tax havens abroad.

Barnet does not offer any easy cures. He thinks the dependency of both political parties and their leaders on "the obscenely expensive, never-ending campaign that now defines American politics" means that even in the United States free elections are not enough to guarantee that those chosen will be able to carry out their programs (he cites the failures of Clinton's health care reform and job creation programs, which he ascribes to the "medical-industrial complex" and the bond market, respectively). Furthermore, it is hard to get the message out, says Barnet: "[The] rage and the fury found almost everywhere . . . is directed almost exclusively at government because the mainstream media . . . never target global corporations as major contributors to the nation's socio-economic woes, and because even if they did, the business behemoths would seem beyond reach."[61]

A. G. Kefalas agrees that the TNCS now have amazing power, surpassing that of the nation-state, and describes them as "at the center of the entire world-reshaping scheme." But Kefalas has hopes that Barnet does not seem to share. He outlines three ways of looking at TNCs—pessimistic, optimistic, and melioristic (it can get better)—and tends to take a point of view somewhere between the second and the third positions. International businesses are, Kefalas says, "a potent and potentially valuable force that must be integrated into" the process of building a new world order that brings "a more equitable distribution of material wealth." He is confident the nation-states of the world "share the goals of establishing world security, increasing world productivity, stabilizing the world populations, sustaining economic growth, creating equitable conditions for de-velopment and promoting world monetary stability," and he is sure international business possesses "great potential for facilitating the accomplishment of these goals." Kefalas therefore recommends recognizing such businesses as "full-fledged partners" in the work at hand, and he urges the businesses themselves to "engage in a process of self-assessment in order to bring [their] philosophies, policies, and operating procedures in line with the idea of an interdependent world of diverse but unified societies."[62]

The ideas of Kefalas are reassuring; those of Barnet are tough to take. Both writers agree that we are giving too little attention to the power these giants now wield over our lives. Kefalas's point that TNCs are helping to bring a more equi-table distribution of material wealth may have some rough truth to it, but when your company moves its business to another land, it is hard to be joyous about the fact that a fraction of what was your salary now goes to someone who still lives in poverty. Barnet's point about our growing inability to keep control of our own governments, given the dependency of elected leaders on those who paid for their campaigns, is one I have made in this book (see Chapters 7 and 8) and one with which many others agree. As we have seen throughout this chapter, it is difficult to deepen democracy in the nations that have recently adopted free elections; Barnet reminds us it may be time to take soundings on the profundity of those democracies we take for granted, including our own. Kefalas's recom-mendation to take TNCs in as full partners seems a bit behind the times, inas-much as they appear already to be senior partners, and it is difficult to find realistic grounds for his pious hope they will engage in "self-assessment" and re-form. Both authors agree there are serious problems to resolve.

CONCLUSION

But the human polity never gives up. There must be a way out of the complex and interwoven dilemmas that have followed so swiftly and dishearteningly on the regime changes that initially promised such a brave new world. There must be something the individuals who make up the human polity—like you, like me—can do to insist that change be followed by change, that the problems that have emerged be solved, and to help find the solutions. What must we do? What can we do?

Our first job, it seems to me, is to know what our values are and figure out which of them matter the most. Can you make a list of your values? Can you fig-ure out which comes first, which last? Are you willing to sacrifice one on behalf of another that is higher on your list?

A second, and equally important, job is for us all to develop a new and deeper respect for the truth, as well as we are able to determine what that strange animal may be. "Reason from evidence" is easy to say, not so easy to do. We need to act on our values, of course, but we must not let serving them cause us to deny obvi-ous realities or entertain unreal hopes that all our woes will somehow magically just go away. There is real work to be done.

That being so, the next thing to do is to choose a task and choose a way to work on it. We cannot all do everything, but every one of us can make some kind of contribution. Really working on one small part of one small problem is surely better than *thinking* about working on everything. Maybe you will join others who are trying to do the same thing—that's a good way to learn what works and to maximize the effect of the work you do. But you may be a loner, at least for now, and that's okay. Everyone can find a way to help.

Suppose, however, that the public service work you decide to do just makes the job chosen by that guy who sits on the other side of the classroom harder to do? We don't all have the same values; we do sometimes work at cross-purposes. There is no total cure for this, but there are a couple of partial ones. Keeping respect for the truth (see earlier) means hearing what "that guy" has to say and basing your defense of what you are trying to do on the most solid facts you can find. You two may find you can work together after all.

The other partial cure for the tendency of human beings to cancel each other out is for us all to learn to keep a new thought constantly in mind: *connectedness*. By this I do not mean only that the human polity consists of all the world's peoples, ever more dependent on one another for their well-being (so be nice). I mean something a bit more tangible than that. To see what connectedness means, pick up a copy of today's newspaper, and make a list of all the headlines having to do with national or international news. Then ask yourself what each one has to do with all the others. Anything? Everything? Try it and see. Then think about how the problem you have decided to work on is connected to other problems and other efforts (not all of them benign). If you do this, chances are you will find a way to work on your problem that is less likely to be at cross-purposes with the work of others who share your general hopes for a better and fairer world.

While you are doing all this, you may as well give some thought to what you think the role of international institutions should be and how to get them to play it. Would it be best to follow the Kefalas approach and join efforts that seek to persuade the TNCs of the importance of self-reform? Or is that unreasonable in a world where "noncompetitive" today can mean "nonexistent" tomorrow? Would it be better to work to strengthen international governance institutions whose reach might eventually match that of the TNCs? Or is any form of business regulation simply antithetical to your values?

Whatever you decide and whatever you do, a final thought to keep in mind, or so it seems to me, is the need to work where and when we can. This is a tricky one. Whether they end up working in the schools, the government, or the business world, political scientists have tough work to do that may or may not be related to saving the world. And tough choices must often be made between keeping one's job and serving one's values. Each of us must decide what kinds of recommendations and activities on behalf of our beliefs are reasonable and appropriate in our own line of work. But do not be too quick to say, "In my case, none at all." Because then you must answer this question as well: How will the behaviors of governments or businesses ever improve if living and breathing social scientists, bureaucrats, elected officials, and businessmen and -women take no responsibility beyond that of earning a living wage? Let us hope that you will make a point of taking **connectedness** seriously, in every aspect of your own life as well as in the way you read the headlines.

Who can tell if you will? Not I. But I can hope. And only thus, it seems to me, can any of us hope for the creation of a human polity in which all humanity has a home. This new ethic—this very *old* ethic—must somehow be made to grow and thrive in all our connected worlds. Making this happen is a tremendous challenge. And an absolute necessity.

Selected Readings

Adelman, Sammy, and Abdul Paliwala. *Law and Crisis in the Third World.* London: Hans Zell, 1993. Essays examining the major issues in law and development in light of changes in the world system.

Barnet, Richard J., and John Cavanagh. *Global Dreams: Imperial Corporations in the New World Order.* New York: Simon and Schuster, 1994. The rise of multinational corporations, with a discussion of how transnational business is affecting the standard of living throughout the world.

Cameron, Maxwell A. *Democracy and Authoritarianism in Peru: Political Coalitions and Social Change.* New York: St. Martin's, 1994. A discussion and analysis of the recent political history of Peru.

Dahl, Robert A. *Democracy and Its Critics.* New Haven: Yale University Press, 1989. A detailed overview of the history of democracy from ancient Greece to modern times.

Markoff, John. *Waves of Democracy: Social Movements and Political Change.* Thousand Oaks, Calif.: Pine Forge Press, 1996. An attempt to locate current efforts of democratization within a historical context, giving special emphasis to the role of social movements in this process.

Sorensen, Georg. *Democracy and Democratization: Processes and Prospects in a Changing World.* Boulder, Colo.: Westview Press, 1993. Sorensen reviews the elements of democracy and discusses new systems that may result from the changing world order.

Stokes, Gale. *The Walls Came Tumbling Down: The Collapse of Communism in Eastern Europe.* Oxford: Oxford University Press, 1993. An examination of the decline and fall of communism in eastern Europe, from 1965 to the early 1990s.

Notes

1. Carole Pateman, "Democracy and Democratization," *International Political Science Review* 17, no. 1 (1996): 5–12. As Pateman points out, "Never before has democracy been so popular" (p. 5).

2. Georg Sorensen, *Democracy and Democratization: Processes and Prospects in a Changing World* (Boulder, Colo.: Westview Press, 1993), p. 31.

3. Philippe C. Schmitter and Terry Lynn Karl, "What Democracy Is . . . And Is Not," in *The Global Resurgence of Democracy*, ed. Larry Diamond and Marc F. Plattner (Baltimore: Johns Hopkins University Press, 1993), p. 40.

4. Robert A. Dahl, *Democracy and Its Critics* (New Haven: Yale University Press, 1989), pp. 106–15.

5. Peter H. Merkl, "Which Are Today's Democracies?" *International Social Science Journal* 136 (May 1993): 257–58.

6. George Munda Carew, "Development Theory and the Promise of Democracy: The Future of Postcolonial African States," *Africa Today* 40, no. 4 (1993): 46–50.

7. Sidney Verba, "A Research Perspective" in "Threats to Democracy: Plenary Session IV," National Research Council, Commission on Behavioral and Social Sciences and Education, *The Transition to Democracy: Proceedings of a Workshop* (Washington, D.C.: National Academy Press, 1991), p. 78.

8. Schmitter and Karl, "What Democracy Is," p. 49.

9. Ibid., p. 51; Jane Mansbridge, "Politics," in "What Is a Democracy? Plenary Session I," National Research Council, *The Transition to Democracy*, p. 6.

10. Mansbridge, "Politics," p. 5. Mansbridge bases this statement on unpublished data from the Yale Human Relations Area Files on 186 societies. She notes it requires us to presume that Germany was a monarchy in World War I and a dictatorship in World War II and that Lebanon in 1967 was a military regime. We might add that the statement also requires us to ignore civil wars within democracies and the readiness of other democracies to come to the aid of one side or the other in such internal battles.

11. Sorenson, *Democracy and Democratization*, pp. 29–30.

12. Charles Tilly, "Overview," in "Comment and Synthesis: Plenary Session III," National Research Council, *The Transition to Democracy*, pp. 60–61; see also p. 25.

13. *New York Times*, 21 Nov. 1995, A14.

14. Kenneth Ka-Lok Chan, "Poland at the Crossroads: The 1993 General Election," *Europe-Asia Studies* 47, no. 1 (1995): 125–27.

15. "Nostalgia Wins the Day in Poland," *New Statesman and Society* (1 Oct. 1993): 20–21.

16. Ray Taras, "The End of the Walesa Era in Poland," *Current History* 95, no. 599 (Mar. 1996): 127.

17. "Kwasniewski Wins: Political Lessons Explored," *Current Digest of the Post-Soviet Press* 47, no. 47 (1995): 15–17.

18. *New York Times*, 6 Nov. 1995, A3.

19. "Kwasniewski Wins," pp. 16–17.

20. Kate Hannan, "Reforming China's State Enterprises, 1984–93," special issue on "Enterprise Reform in Post-Socialist Societies," *Journal of Communist Studies and Transition Politics* 11, no. 1 (Mar. 1995): 33–55.

21. David S. G. Goodman, "Collectives and Connectives, Capitalism and Corporatism: Structural Change in China," special issue on "Enterprise Reform in Post-Socialist Societies," pp. 12–32.

22. Shen Tong, "The Next Revolution," *New York Times*, 1 Sept. 1992, A15.

23. Goodman, "Collectives and Connectives," p. 19.

24. Some of these cases are treated in Guillermo O'Donnell, Philippe C. Schmitter, and Laurence Whitehead, eds., *Transitions from Authoritarian Rule: Prospects for Democracy* (Baltimore: Johns Hopkins University Press, 1986).

25. "Democracy, African-Style," *The Economist* (3 Feb. 1996): 17.

26. "Democracy in Africa," *The Economist* (22 Feb. 1992): 17–20.

27. Jeffrey Herbst, "The Dilemmas of Explaining Political Upheaval: Ghana in Comparative Perspective," in *Economic Change and Political Liberalization in Sub-Saharan Africa*, ed. Jennifer A. Widner (Baltimore: Johns Hopkins University Press, 1994), p. 194. Herbst highlights urban populations and military and security forces as the two groups whose interests must be addressed for African leadership to stay in power.

28. Ernest Harsch, "Structural Adjustment and Africa's Democracy Movements," *Africa Today* 40, no. 4 (1993): 8.
29. Ibid., p. 23.
30. Ibid., p. 19.
31. John F. Clark, "Elections, Leadership and Democracy in Congo," *Africa Today* (Third Quarter 1994): 41–60.
32. Brian Loveman, "'Protected Democracies' and Military Guardianship: Political Transitions in Latin America, 1978–1993," *Journal of InterAmerican Studies and World Affairs* 36, no. 2 (Summer 1994): 105–89; quote from p. 105.
33. Ibid., p. 114.
34. Ibid., p. 115; Carlos M. Vilas, "Latin America in the 'New World Order': Prospects for Democracy," *International Journal of Politics, Culture and Society* 8, no. 2 (1994): 275.
35. Frances Hagopian, "After Regime Change: Authoritarian Legacies, Political Representation and the Democratic Future of South America," a review article in *World Politics* 45 (Apr. 1993): 464–500; quote from p. 500.
36. Ibid, p. 467. In general, Hagopian stresses the need to examine each regime separately, particularly when attempting to assess the impact of the period of military rule.
37. Loveman, "'Protected Democracies' and Military Guardianship," pp. 123–25, 157–58.
38. Guillermo O'Donnell, "Introduction to the Latin American Cases," in O'Donnell, Schmitter, and Whitehead, *Transitions from Authoritarian Rule*, pp. 14–15.
39. Ibid., p. 15.
40. Scott Mainwaring is another author who rejects all-encompassing pessimism, assessing democratic reforms in Chile as successful and pointing to some gains in Brazil and Uruguay. Mainwaring appears to accept, however, the truncated version of democracy that other authors cited here repudiate. See his "Democracy in Brazil and the Southern Cone: Achievements and Problems," *Journal of Interamerican Studies and World Affairs* 37, no. 1 (1995): 113–79.
41. Terence Roth, "Gap Widens between Winners and Losers," *Central European Economic Review* 2, no. 2 (Spring 1994): 5–7.
42. Mark M. Nelson, "Russia's Far East Attracts Intrepid Western Investors," *Central European Economic Review* 2, no. 2 (Spring 1994): 14. As the title of the article suggests, the opportunities Polumordvinov and Levin have depend in large part on the presence of foreign investors—and investments.
43. Lee Hockstader, "Spending Russia's New Money: Lavish Mansions Are Sprouting Next to Communist-Era Hovels," *Washington Post*, 23 June 1994, A18. Not all the rich new capitalists are *newly* rich; see John Pomfret, "In E. Europe, Old Comrades Are New Rich," *Washington Post*, 30 Apr. 1994, A1, a news story about the ability of former communist party members to make the shift to the free enterprise system. ("People who made it in the old regime are going to make it in the new one too.")
44. Michael Specter, "Russia's Elite Scientists Turn High School Tutors," *New York Times*, 25 July 1994, A1.
45. Margaret Shapiro, "Moscow's Hard-Luck Flea Markets," *Washington Post*, 15 Feb. 1992, A1, A35.
46. Lynne Haney, "From Proud Worker to Good Mother: Women, the State and Regime Change in Hungary," *Frontiers* 14, no. 3: (1994), 113–50.

47. "The Human Rights Watch Global Report on Women's Human Rights," *Human Rights Watch* (Aug. 1995): 307, 316.
48. Barry Newman, "Women in Poland Find Little Liberation in Shift to Democracy," *Wall Street Journal*, 19 Nov. 1993, 1.
49. Haney, "From Proud Worker," p. 128.
50. Ibid., p. 144; Newman, "Women in Poland," pp. 1, A11. *York Review of Books* July 15, 1993, 17.
51. Jeff Gerth and Elaine Sciolino, "I.M.F. Head: He Speaks, and Money Talks," *New York Times*, 2 April 1996, A1.
52. Nicholas Bayne, "International Economic Relations after the Cold War," *Government and Opposition* 29, no. 1 (Winter 1994): 3–21.
53. *New York Times*, 24 Nov. 1994, A6. For an argument against expanding NATO, see Charles A. Kupchan, "Expand NATO—and Split Europe," *New York Times*, 27 Nov. 1994, 11. For a scholarly analysis of the link between regime change and alliances in general, see Randolph M. Siverson and Harvey Starr, "Regime Change and the Restructuring of Alliances," *American Journal of Political Science* 38 (Feb. 1994): 145–61.
54. Peter J. Spiro, "New Global Communities: Non-governmental Organizations in International Decision-Making Institutions," *Washington Quarterly* 18, no. 1 (1994): 45–56.
55. *New York Times*, 11 Dec. 1994, 10.
56. Michael Edwards and David Hulme, "NGO Performance and Accountability in the Post–Cold War World," *Journal of International Development* 7, no. 6 (1995): 849–56. See also Roger Charlton and Roy May, "NGOs, Politics, Projects and Probity: A Policy Implementation Perspective," *Third World Quarterly* 16, no. 2 (1995): 237–55.
57. This, of course, used to be the MNC, the multinational corporation. Think about the difference between *multi* and *trans*. What does it tell you about the process of globalization that it has seemed necessary to make this change?
58. "Coca-Cola Moves to Broaden Business in the Soviet Union," *Wall Street Journal*, 30 Aug. 1991, A3.
59. Jeff Gerth, "In Post-Cold-War Washington, Development Is a Hot Business," *New York Times*, 25 May 1996, 1, 6.
60. *Wall Street Journal*, 2 Oct. 1995, R16, R22.
61. Richard J. Barnet, "Stateless Corporations: Lords of the Economy," *The Nation* 259, no. 21 (19 Dec. 1994): 754–57. Barnet also points out that the world's 200 largest corporations now control more than a fourth of the world's economic activity. This article is drawn from Richard Barnet and John Cavanagh, *Global Dreams: Imperial Corporations and the New World Order* (New York: Simon and Schuster, 1994).
62. A. G. Kefalas, "The Global Corporation: Its Role in the New World Order," *National Forum* (Fall 1992): 26–30.

GLOSSARY

A teacher I know has an answer for students who complain that he some-times uses words they don't understand: "I'm sorry," he says sympatheti-cally. "I just wish there were a book somewhere that could tell you the meanings of all the words in the English language."

Unlike a dictionary, a glossary is not comprehensive and does not give all possible meanings of the terms listed. But this glossary *will* help you un-derstand each term as it is used in this book. For a fuller definition, please do consult your dictionary.

Ad hoc coalition.   A temporary organization created to allow several political organizations to pool their resources in a joint effort in which all are interested.
Administration.   The offices and personnel responsible for carrying out the functions of gov-ernment; *see* Bureaucracy.
Administrative law.   The rules and decisions of administrative agencies.
Admiralty and maritime law.   Law governing shipping and water-borne commerce.
Aggregation of interests.   Gathering and compromising different points of view on a topic in order to facilitate the making of policy. It is often seen as a prime function of political parties.
Amorphous groups.   Groups of individuals who share an interest and act on its behalf in a way that indirectly affects government policy.
Apartheid.   The South African system of strict racial segregation, maintained by that nation's minority government of white supremacists. Under apartheid, black Africans were required to live in isolated "homelands," and other nonwhite populations were confined to particular neighborhoods within the cities.
Ascription.   A basis for leadership recruitment, specifically, the placing of persons in posi-tions of leadership because their possession of other characteristics (e.g., placement in a lin-eage system) leads one to believe they must have the necessary qualities to rule.
Associational group.   A fully organized group formed specifically to represent the interests of its members.
Authoritarian system.   A political system in which the power of the rules is virtually unlim-ited, although this power is not always exercised in all domains. *See also* totalitarian system.
Authority.   The right to exercise the power and influence of a particular position that comes from having been placed in that position according to regular, known, and widely accepted procedures; a person in such a position.

Balance of power.   The theory that the best way to prevent war is to ensure that the major nations of the world remain roughly "balanced" in the power each has to wage war successfully. *See also* Deterrence.

Behavioral approach.   A way of studying politics that focuses on how an individual acts politically and that seeks explanations for that behavior within that individual.

Belief.   The conviction that a certain thing is true or false. *See also* Opinion.

Bicameral legislature.   A legislature with two houses, usually an upper house and a lower house. *See also* Unicameral legislature.

Bureaucracy.   The administration of government through departments and subdivisions managed by sets of appointed officials following fixed rules of procedure.

Bureaucrat.   A government employee responsible for carrying out some aspects of the administrative work of government according to fixed rules of procedure.

Bureaucratic.   A tendency to follow rules closely, without regard for differences in rank or circumstance of the persons to whom they apply. The term is often used pejoratively to refer to someone who insists on following a routine in a mechanical way, insisting on proper forms and petty rules.

Bureaucratic drift.   A movement away from control by elected representatives of the people they serve.

Cabinet.   A body composed of the heads of the most important subdivisions of a nation's executive branch and led by the nation's chief executive. Its functions are normally to advise the chief executive and to assist in the formulation of legislation to be proposed to the national legislative body. In a presidential system the cabinet is under the control of the president and is responsible to that leader, whereas in parliamentary and presidential-parliamentary systems its ultimate responsibility is to the legislature.

Capitalism.   An economic system in which individuals are free to invest their savings (capital) as they wish, to purchase goods and hire labor in order to develop private enterprise, and to reinvest profits (also capital) in such businesses or in those of other citizens.

Cartels.   Associations of businesses formed in the early twentieth century to establish national or international monopolies over particular raw materials or manufactured goods.

Ceremonial leader.   *See* Chief of state.

Charisma.   Having the gift of leadership and being recognized as having that gift.

Chief executive.   The most powerful leader in a given polity's executive branch—usually the most powerful leader in the state, with the title of prime minister or president.

Chief of state.   The official who performs the ceremonial roles of government leadership, normally a hereditary monarch or an elected but relatively powerless president. In a presidential system, the functions of chief of state and chief executive are combined.

Civic culture.   A culture in which citizens combine a commitment to moderate political participation with a belief in the legitimacy of officialdom and a tendency toward parochialism.

Civil law.   Law governing unfair (but not criminal) behavior that affects only other individuals, not the community. Civil law calls for retribution to the offended party, not punishment on behalf of the public order.

Class.   A kind of group identity, normally based on differences in level of income, level of education, and kind of occupation, sometimes also based on differences in accent, dress, and kinds of material acquisitions desired and purchased.

Codified law.   Laws that have been set down in writing in conjunction with other laws. Edicts, treaties, decrees, legislative enactments, and judicial precedents are among the forms of law that may be codified. *See also* Statutory law.

Colonialism.   The system by which a nation maintains control over a distant territory in order to exploit that territory's resources. *See also* Neocolonialism.

Committee system.   The use of specialized or standing committees by legislative bodies to organize and facilitate their work.

Common law.   Law made by using the rulings of judges in earlier cases as precedents, sometimes referred to as "judge-made law." *See also* Precedent.

Communications media.   A term referring to the technical devices employed in mass communication, typically including newspapers, magazines, radio, and television. Commonly known as the media.

Communism.   A form of socialism emphasizing the absolute abolition of private property, economic equality, rule by the workers (the proletariat), and access to power by armed revolution. Subcategories of communism include Marxism, Leninism, and Maoism.

Comparative government.   The subfield of political science devoted to the study of foreign polities, using the comparative method.

Confederal system.   A system of government in which the units are independent states that have decided to join together in a formal alliance, acting as a single unit for some limited purpose but not for others.

Confederation.   A system of government in which nearly all powers are reserved to the constituent units of the nation—that is, to the states, provinces, or cantons.

Conservatism.   An ideology that stresses conserving what exists; takes a nonegalitarian view of human nature; and holds order, continuity, loyalty, protection of individual freedoms, piety, and nationalism as its highest values.

Constituency.   All the people, especially voters, served by a particular elected official, especially a legislator; the district of such a group of voters.

Constitution.   A set of rules prescribing the institutions and procedures of government and having precedence over all other rules in a given polity.

Constitutional law.   A nation's constitution and the body of judicial rulings about the meaning of the constitution; the subfield of political science devoted to the study of the institutions and procedures of government as these are formally prescribed in constitutions and explicated in judicial rulings.

Co-optation.   Granting prestigious appointments or other benefits to one whose support is sought but not yet certain, as a means of securing that support.

Corporatism.   An economic system in which formal ownership of the means of production remains in private hands, but the state requires that all industries and other productive enterprises be grouped into units according to the function performed. *See also* Neocorporatism.

Council.   *See* Elected board.

Coup d'état.   A French term meaning overthrow of the state, normally by armed force. A coup is different from a revolution in that it usually entails replacement of the top leadership of a regime by another narrow elite and is not based on a mass movement.

Criminal law.   Law governing crimes. Criminal law views an act of crime as an offense against the public order and therefore deserving of punishment by society.

Cultural relativism.   The idea that each society sets its own standards in accordance with its own culture and that what is correct in one society may be repugnant in another.

Cultural values.   Values shared by a group of people.

Culture.   The ideas and customs of a given people in a given period.

Decree.   A rule issued by a leader in a given polity's executive branch and having the force of law.

Democracy.   Rule by the people; a system of government in which all adults not disqualified by criminal behavior or mental incapacity have the right and the means to exercise some form of genuine control over government. The means of ensuring democratic government normally include the protection of individual liberties, free elections, and political equality.

Democratic socialism.   An ideology espousing the principles of socialism but stressing the need to achieve and exercise power democratically.

Deterrence.   The theory that the best way to prevent nuclear war is to build up such a massive and threatening arsenal of nuclear weapons that no other nation will dare to attack. *See also* Balance of power.

Diplomat.   A representative of a government who conducts relations with another government in the interests of his or her own nation.

Division of labor.   The assignment of different tasks to different persons in a community.

Domestic law.   The body of laws that nations apply within their own territories.

Economic and Social Council.   A United Nations organization whose function is to promote international cooperation in economic and social matters.

Economic development.   The transformation of natural resources (the nation's own or those imported from other nations as raw materials) into ever more valuable processed goods, the improvement of services, and the marketing of those goods and services in order to enhance the material well-being of the nation's people.

Economic equality.   The condition that exists when all citizens have approximately the same amount of material wealth.

Economy.   A system of producing, distributing, and consuming wealth.

Elected board (council).   The most common rule-making body of local government.

Electoral system.   The rules and regulations governing how citizens vote in a polity.

Equality.   Having the same fundamental needs as well as the same rights under the law. Such rights may be political, economic, and/or social.

Equity law.   Law designed to supplement the common law by providing relief when the operation of the law will wreak irremediable harm. An example is the injunction.

Ethnic group.   A self-identified group with distinctive racial and/or national characteristics and a shared set of beliefs and values.

Executive veto.   A veto by the person in the highest government position.

Extraconstitutional forces.   Forces outside the formal government by a polity that are nevertheless strong enough to shape public policy.

Extraconstitutional power.   Power exercised by the government when groups external to the government are able to pressure the agents of the government into a situation in which they feel they have no choice but to comply.

Fascism.   A far-right ideology based on the principle that race, nationalism, and absolute obedience to authoritarian leadership are the highest values.

Federal system.   A system of government in which certain powers are reserved to the central government but others are constitutionally reserved to the governments of the nation's constituent parts—that is, to the states, provinces, or cantons.

Feedback.   A term used in political systems analysis to denote the transmission of information, rewards, or punishments from one element of a system to another, as a form of response to input from that element. *See also* Input.

Freedom.   The condition of being able to act without restraint.

Functional regionalism.   A form of regionalism, often temporary, established to deal with a single problem; more limited in scope than structural regionalism. *See also* Regionalism *and* Structural regionalism.

General Assembly.   The organization of the United Nations to which each of the member states sends a representative and which has the power to make recommendations in the name of the United Nations if a two-thirds vote can be obtained. *See also* Security Council.

Government.   The institutions responsible for making and carrying out the laws of a polity and for adjudicating disputes that arise under those laws; the arena in which political choices are made manifest; in political systems analysis, the decision-making apparatus that receives inputs and emits outputs.

Guerrilla warfare.   The attempt to accomplish political change by training and arming a band of revolutionaries who live in hiding, preferably in difficult and well-forested terrain; who attempt to recruit others to their cause; and who make only limited attacks on the forces of the state until the balance of power between them and the state is sufficiently equal to permit open warfare.

Head of state.   In a parliamentary system, the nation's monarch or president.

Ideology.   A comprehensive set of beliefs and attitudes about social and economic institutions and processes.

Inflation.   An increase in the amount of money in circulation, resulting in a relatively sharp and sudden fall in its value and a rise in prices.

Influence.   The ability to affect the behavior of another. *See also* Power.

Initiative.   A provision in a polity's electoral system that permits citizens to vote directly on specific proposals for new legislation, provided a certain number of citizens petition for the opportunity to do so.

Injunction.   A court order issued to prevent an action until the offended party has had time to prepare and present a fuller legal argument that the action should not take place.

Input.   A term used in political systems analysis to denote the support and demands coming to governments from such forces as public opinion, interest groups, and political parties. *See also* Feedback.

Institution.   A structure with established, important functions to perform; with well-specified roles for carrying out those functions; and with a clear set of rules governing the relationship between the people who occupy those roles.

Interest.   A clearly identified personal stake in a decision or the outcome of an event.

Interest group.   An organization whose main purpose is to affect the operation of government by persuading key persons in government to act in accordance with the group's interests.

International Court of Justice.   The judicial branch of the United Nations, with jurisdiction only over cases the members of that body agree to refer to it; sometimes called the World Court.

International law.   The law that applies in relationships between nations or between the citizens of one nation and either the government or the individual citizens of another nation.

International relations.   The relationships between nations; the subfield of political science devoted to the study of relationships between nations.

Judicial independence.   The protection of the judiciary, usually by constitutional guarantees, from interference by the other branches of government in the conduct of its work.

Judicial review.   The power of a judiciary to review legislative and executive enactments in order to decide whether or not they conform with a polity's constitution and to declare such enactments null and void where they are found not in conformance with that constitution.

Judiciary.   The branch of government concerned with adjudicating disputes that arise under the law.

Justice.   Fair treatment under the law. As such, justice is the possible (but not inevitable) result of decisions made by those who have been granted authority to determine what constitutes fair treatment.

Kinship system.   A means of ordering sociopolitical relationships in which each person's right to use a parcel of land and to own cattle or other property is determined by his or her place in the family lineage.

Laissez faire.   A French term meaning "let them do as they will." A laissez-faire economy is one in which government stays out of the world of business as much as possible.

Law.   A regulation established by public authorities and backed by the collective power of the polity to which it applies.

Left.   A term used to describe political ideas comparatively. Those on the political left tend to take a more positive view of human nature and to be convinced that change and progress are necessary and possible to improve the human condition. *See also* Right.

Legislature.   A body of persons given the responsibility and power to make laws for a polity.

Legitimacy.   The condition of being considered correct and proper. *See also* Political legitimacy.

Liberalism.   An ideology that sees the role of government as protecting individual liberties while at the same time ensuring everyone the chance to lead the best possible life and to fulfill his or her individual potential.

Liberty.   The absence of constraint.

Lobbying.   Seeking to influence public officials by direct personal contact; often attempted in the lobbies of public buildings by the paid representatives (lobbyists) of groups or individuals.

Local government.   Subnational government that is under the jurisdiction of provincial and national (and sometimes regional) government and that is within the reach of the citizens it governs.

Material benefits.   Goods and services made available to an interest group's members.

Mercantilism.   A theory urging that the state use its powers openly to provide the best possible conditions for private entrepreneurs to carry on their business, thereby identifying the interest of the state with that of private business.

Minister.   A high officer appointed to head a segment of government.

Minority government.   In a multiparty parliamentary system, a cabinet composed of representatives of parties that have, altogether, only a minority of seats in the legislature.

Mixed economy.   An economy based on a mixture of public and private ownership of the means of production and on considerable public regulation of the private sector.

Model.   An imitation of something that is or that is thought to be or that may someday come to be; a representation of the essence of the subject. *See also* Simulation.

Multinational corporation (MNC).   *See* Transnational corporation.

Multiparty party system.   A party system with more than two parties.

Municipal law.   Collective name for local ordinances.

Nation.   A relatively large group of people who feel they belong together by virtue of sharing one or more traits such as race, language, culture, history, or a set of customs and traditions.

Nationalism.   A collective identity shared by the citizens of a polity; the belief that national interests are more important than international considerations.

Nation-state.   A polity in which all citizens share a sense of common identity (nationhood) and in which subunits, if any, are wholly or partly under the domain of a central government. *See also* State.

Natural law.   Law based on laws that already exist in nature and that have been, according to some philosophers, implanted there by a divine creator. Those who believe in natural law believe it is discoverable by "right reason" and is binding on everyone. *See also* Positive law.

Natural law legal culture.   Basing judicial decisions on the precepts of religious and philosophical thought. Found throughout the Islamic world and often also found in coexistence with more modern legal cultures, especially at the local level, as in many villages in India and in non-Islamic African nations.

Natural resources.   The material wealth that can be drawn from a nation's natural environment.

Neocolonialism.   A system for maintaining the economic dependence of one state on another while permitting it to acquire or maintain its political independence. The usual methods are the establishment of cooperative political leadership in the dependent nation, backed up by the promise of military assistance from the dominant nation, and the creation of trade agreements beneficial to the dominant nation and to the indigenous elite. *See also* Colonialism.

Neocorporatism.   An economic system in which the state gives official recognition to different interests by establishing boards of representatives to advise the government and grants subsidies or enacts supportive legislation favoring those that are cooperative with the state. *See also* Corporatism.

Norms.   The values or standards that an individual, a group, or a social system decide to apply to the facts of a situation.

OPEC.   The Organization of Petroleum Exporting Countries, an international organization formed to promote the interests of the world's major oil-producing states. Its members include Algeria, Ecuador, Gabon, Indonesia, Iran, Iraq, Kuwait, Libya, Nigeria, Qator, Saudi Arabia, the United Arab Emirates, and Venezuela.

Opinion.   The conviction that a certain thing is probably true, often combined with an evaluation. *See also* Belief.

Order.   The condition of peace and serenity, in which everything appears to be functioning properly.

Ordinance.   A ruling made by a local government body; sometimes referred to as municipal law.

Organization.   A body of persons working together in a structured way to achieve a specific purpose.

Outputs.   A term used in political systems analysis to denote the work produced by governments: laws (including ordinances and proclamations), the steps taken to implement laws, and the decisions made to settle disputes that arise under the law.

Pardon.   A chief executive's cancelation of punishments decreed by jurists, including those in military tribunals, by constitutional right.

Parliament.   A national legislative body, normally composed of an upper house and a lower house. *See also* Parliamentary system.

Parliamentary system.   A system of government in which the national legislature (parliament) is linked to the national bureaucracy by the fact that both are ruled by the same body, the cabinet, which is itself responsible to the legislature. *See also* Cabinet *and* Parliament.

Parochialism.   The tendency to withdraw into the private sphere; to be concerned only with matters in one's own immediate area; and to take a narrow, limited, and provincial outlook on life.

Party primary.   An election held to choose the person who will stand as a political party's nominee for an elective post.

Party system.   A political system defined by the number of parties that operate within it.

Phenomenological approach.   An approach to the study of politics that focuses on change and the events (the *phenomena*) that led up to that change. It is an inquiry into the causes of a significant change in a political system.

Planned economy.   An economy guided by the state in accordance with a general plan.

Pluralism.   A condition in which all groups within a polity have an equal right and opportunity to form, put forward their points of view, win adherents, and influence decision makers. Under such circumstances, polity is the result of a pluralistic struggle for power. Pluralist theorists argue that such a condition actually exists in Western democracies and, further, that the net result is the fairest possible form of government.

Political appointment.   An appointment to government office that is made by someone already serving in another government position.

Political behavior.   The subfield of political science devoted to the study of political attitudes and acts.

Political bias.   Partiality on the part of the media, expressed through the media's deliberately shaping the content and presentation of the news to favor certain political interests, actors, practices, and/or ideas over others.

Political consultant.   Political operatives who help candidates deal with all aspects of campaign politics.

Political culture.   A set of political values, beliefs, and attitudes that is widely shared throughout a polity.

Political documents.   Forms of the written word that are studied by political scientists; namely, constitutions, statutary laws, judicial decisions, party statutes and platforms, leaders' speeches and memoirs, records of legislative proceedings, newspaper accounts of political happenings, and the like.

Political economy.   The relationship between economic conditions and the political choices we make; the subfield of political science devoted to the study of the relationship between economic and political factors.

Political equality.   The condition that exists when all citizens have an equal right to participate in the political process and to be treated equally in it.

Political event.   An event that affects the right to allocate scarce resources in a polity.

Political legitimacy.   The condition of being considered correct and proper in the exercise of political power. *See also* Legitimacy.

Political organization.   An organization that is not itself a government agency but whose main purpose is to affect the operation of government; the subfield of political science devoted to the study of nongovernmental organizations that seek to influence government.

Political party.   An organization that seeks to place representatives in government by nominating candidates to stand for election, claiming that power so won will be exercised in the public interest.

Political socialization.   The ongoing processes through which citizens acquire—and amend—their personal views of the political world.

Political system.   A structure with interdependent parts that deals with political matters.

Political systems analysis.   An analytical framework that treats political units (particularly political organizations and nation-states) as systems composed of interdependent parts and explores the relationships among those parts.

Political theory.   The subfield of political science devoted to the study of political philosophy, including the formulation of concepts, categories, and logical explanations of political phenomena.

Politics.   The process that determines who will occupy roles of leadership in government and how the power of government will be exercised; the authoritative allocation of scarce resources throughout a polity.

Polity.   A state, or any society with an organized government; any group of persons who have some form of political relationship with one another. The interdependence of human beings around the globe has created a worldwide polity, the human polity.

Polls.   Studies of the opinions of the public, or of selected portions thereof, normally based on interviews with a random sample of the group in question.

Positive law.   Law made by humans, pragmatically, to meet specific needs. *See also* Natural law.

Power.   The ability to control the behavior of others by threatening and/or carrying out severe sanctions if that behavior is other than compliant. *See also* Influence.

Precedent.   A court case used as an example to be followed in succeeding similar cases. *See also* Common law.

Predictions.   The content of well-founded speculation on the part of political scientists about the feared or hoped-for events of the future.

Presidential-parliamentary system.   A system of government in which the chief executive is elected directly by the people and in turn appoints a prime minister who must be approved by the parliament (the national legislature) before taking responsibility, with his or her cabinet, for carrying out the laws of the land and developing legislative proposals to put before the parliament. In this system, sometimes referred to as a quasi-presidential system, the prime minister is responsible to both the president and the parliament.

Presidential system.   A system of government in which the chief executive is elected directly by the people, is responsible for carrying out the laws of the land, and has only advisory powers with respect to the actual content of those laws, which are made by a separate legislative body whose members are elected independently of the president.

Pressure methods.   The means groups use to exert pressure on government.

Pressure points.   The levels and branches of government that groups seek to influence.

Prime minister.   The chief executive in a parliamentary system and the second in command in a presidential-parliamentary system. A prime minister is chosen by the ceremonial chief of state in the former system and by the president in the latter. He or she must be approved by parliament in both systems and normally leads the party with the most seats in parliament.

Proportional representation (PR).   An electoral system that gives each political party contesting an election a number of seats (usually in a legislature) roughly proportionate to the number of votes its candidates received in combination.

Protectionism.   The policy of sheltering domestic producers—both agricultural and industrial—by adopting government policies that shield them from the competition of the world market. The favored methods of protectionism are the imposition of high tariffs on imported goods, the establishment of price supports for domestic goods, insistence on trade agreements favoring domestic businesses, and the setting of quotas on the amount of certain foreign goods that may be imported.

Public administration.   The subfield of political science devoted to the study of the bureaucratic processes and institutions of government.

Public interest group.   A group that claims to work for a cause that is in the public's interest, not its own. *See also* Special interest group.

Public opinion.   The collective nature of a body of individual opinions.

Public opinion poll.   A study of the opinions held by a representative sample of the entire population.

Purposive benefits.   The satisfaction some members of interest groups get from working on behalf of a value or cause in which they believe.

Quasi-presidential system.   *See* Presidential-parliamentary system.

Recall election.   A special election held when a sufficient number of voters petition to remove an official (usually an elected official) from office.

Recruitment.   The process of finding, persuading, and training candidates to run for electoral office. It is often seen as a major function of political parties.

Referendum.   A provision in a polity's electoral system enabling a group of citizens to "refer" a piece of legislation passed by the government to the voting public, provided a sufficient number of citizens petition for the right to do so.

Regionalism.   A level of intermediate government below the level of the national government and usually (but not always) above the level of the province. *See also* Functional regionalism *and* Structural regionalism.

Right.   A term used to describe political ideas comparatively. Those on the political right place greater stress on the importance of maintaining tradition and order than those on the political left. *See also* Left.

Ruling.   An interpretation, usually by a judicial body, of a regulation, decree, ordinance, or law.

Security Council.   The organization of the United Nations in which the United States, Russia, China, Great Britain and France have permanent membership, each with the right of veto. Intended to be the chief decision-making body of the United Nations, the Security Council has so frequently been prevented from acting by its members' use of their right to veto that power has increasingly shifted to the General Assembly. *See also* General Assembly.

Separation of powers.   The constitutional establishment of three branches of government—legislative, executive, and judicial—each with separate and independent bases of support, terms of office, and powers of office.

Simulation.   A process in which computer technology is used to gather all available information about a subject, form a model of that subject, and then manipulate that model by introducing other factors and examining their impact on it. *See also* Model.

Single-party system.   A political system in which only one political party is allowed.

Social equality.   The condition that exists when every citizen has the right to be treated as a social equal, at least with respect to basic characteristics and needs.

Socialism.   An ideology that holds that human beings readily engage in cooperative social activity and that the state, controlled by the workers, should own or at least control the means of production; an economic system in which the state controls all or most of the means of production.

Solidary benefits.   The benefits provided by an interest group when it gives its members a sense of belonging, a chance to socialize with others, and/or improved social status.

Sovereignty. The power of a polity to make decisions that cannot be overruled by any other body.

Special interest group. A group that works exclusively for the interests of its own members. *See also* Public interest group.

Specialized committee. A legislative committee that is responsible for bills having to do with a specific area of policy, such as agriculture or health. *See also* Standing committee.

Spontaneous groups. Groups of organized individuals who act together politically and deliberately but in an unconventional and often violent fashion.

Standing committee. A legislative committee that is not limited in scope, to which different kinds of bills may be referred. *See also* Specialized committee.

Stare decisis. A Latin phrase meaning "let the decision stand," referring to the practice in common law legal cultures of basing decisions in contemporary cases on those made in earlier similar cases.

State. A structure that has the legal right to make rules that are binding over a given population within a given territory. *See also* Nation-state.

Statutory law. Written law, including legislation, treaties, executive orders, decrees, and codes of law. *See also* Codified law.

Structural-functional approach. A way of studying politics that focuses on the political functions that must be carried out in every political system and that seeks to discover which structures do, in fact, perform these tasks.

Structural regionalism. A form of regionalism in which provincial units are grouped in regions by constitutional fiat and are expected to be permanent additions to the body politic. *See also* Functional regionalism *and* Regionalism.

Structure. A set of patterned role relationships.

Subnational government. Government below the level of the nation, regional, provincial, and local government.

Surrogate. A person who takes the place of another and stands in for that person. In politics, surrogates often stand in for the chief executive in public ceremonies or for political candidates in election rallies.

System. A structure all of whose parts are interrelated, so that a change in one part means a change in all.

Technological development. The use of high-level and up-to-date skills to improve processes of transforming natural resources into useful goods and services.

Totalitarian system. A political system in which the authorities have unlimited power and attempt to exercise it over all domains of life; authoritarianism carried to the ultimate extreme.

Transnational corporation (TNC). A cluster of businesses located in several different nations but commonly owned and managed. An independent network of fiscal, research, productive, and distributive institutions, often with gross annual sales larger than the gross national products of many nations.

Treaty. A document signed by representatives of two or more nations that sets the terms for relations between those nations with regard to particular matters.

Two-party party system. A system in which two parties compete for an absolute majority that is within the reach of either.

Unicameral legislature. A legislature with only one house, as in the state of Nebraska in the United States. *See also* Bicameral legislature.

Unitary system.   A political system in which all the powers of government are reserved to the central government. That government may delegate the exercise of those powers to subunits but can revoke such delegation at any time.

Urban politics and government.   The subfield of political science devoted to the study of politics and government in cities.

U.S. government.   The subfield of political science devoted to the study of the political processes and institutions of the United States.

Value.   A serious and deeply held normative principle with wide applicability.

Veto.   The constitutional right of a ruler to reject bills passed by a legislative body.

Vote of confidence.   A vote taken in a parliamentary or presidential-parliamentary system to demonstrate the legislature's continued confidence—or lack of confidence—in the prime minister and his or her cabinet, usually called for by the prime minister during a period of crisis. If the vote is lost, the government is normally dissolved and new elections are held.

Xenophobia.   The fear or hatred of anything foreign or strange.

INDEX